The later Stuart Church

MANCHESTER
1824

Manchester University Press

Politics, culture and society in early modern Britain

General editors

PROFESSOR ANN HUGHES
PROFESSOR ANTHONY MILTON
PROFESSOR PETER LAKE

This important series publishes monographs that take a fresh and challenging look at the interactions between politics, culture and society in Britain between 1500 and the mid-eighteenth century. It counteracts the fragmentation of current historiography through encouraging a variety of approaches which attempt to redefine the political, social and cultural worlds, and to explore their interconnection in a flexible and creative fashion. All the volumes in the series question and transcend traditional interdisciplinary boundaries, such as those between political history and literary studies, social history and divinity, urban history and anthropology. They thus contribute to a broader understanding of crucial developments in early modern Britain.

Already published in the series

The later Stuart Church, 1660–1714

Edited by
GRANT TAPSELL

Manchester
University Press
Manchester and New York

distributed exclusively in the USA by Palgrave Macmillan

Published by Manchester University Press
Oxford Road, Manchester M13 9NR, UK
and Room 400, 175 Fifth Avenue, New York, NY 10010, USA
www.manchesteruniversitypress.co.uk

Distributed exclusively in the USA by
Palgrave Macmillan, 175 Fifth Avenue, New York, NY 10010, USA

Distributed exclusively in Canada by
UBC Press, University of British Columbia, 2029 West Mall,
Vancouver, BC, Canada V6T 1Z2

British Library Cataloguing-in-Publication Data
A catalogue record for this book is available from the British Library

Library of Congress Cataloging-in-Publication Data applied for

ISBN 978 0 7190 8160 6 *hardback*

First published 2012

The publisher has no responsibility for the persistence or accuracy of URLs for external or any third-party internet websites referred to in this book, and does not guarantee that any content on such websites is, or will remain, accurate or appropriate.

Typeset in Scala with Pastonchi display
by Koinonia, Manchester

Printed in Great Britain
by TJ International Ltd, Padstow

In memory of E.A.O. (Anne) Whiteman (1918–2000)

Contents

List of contributors

Tony Claydon is Professor of History at Bangor University.

Gabriel Glickman is British Academy Postdoctoral Fellow and Junior Research Fellow in History at Hertford College, Oxford.

Jeremy Gregory is Professor of the History of Christianity at the University of Manchester.

Clare Jackson is College Lecturer, Director of Studies in History and Admissions Tutor at Trinity Hall, Cambridge.

Jacqueline Rose is Lecturer in History at the University of St Andrews.

George Southcombe is Departmental Lecturer in Early Modern History at Brasenose College and St John's College, Oxford.

John Spurr is Professor of History at Swansea University.

Grant Tapsell is Fellow and Tutor in History at Lady Margaret Hall, Oxford.

Nicholas Tyacke is Honorary Professor of History at University College, London.

Preface

This volume was inspired by Kenneth Fincham (ed.), *The Early Stuart Church, 1603–1642* (Basingstoke: Macmillan, 1993), in particular its combination of erudition and accessibility. All of the contributors to *The Later Stuart Church, 1660–1714* have endeavoured to present their own detailed research in a similarly direct and useful style. I am extremely grateful to each of them for agreeing so enthusiastically to be involved in the first place, and then for honouring their commitments with great good humour. It has been a pleasure to work with all the team at MUP, as well as the series editors.

Most of the editorial work required to bring this project to fruition was undertaken while I had the great good fortune to be a Lecturer at the University of St Andrews. I learned a great deal from colleagues there in the Reformation Studies Institute, and the Institute of Scottish Historical Research. I gratefully acknowledge financial assistance from St Andrews in the form both of research allowances and sabbatical leave.

The Later Stuart Church, 1660–1714 is dedicated to the memory of one of my formidable predecessors at Lady Margaret Hall. Although I met Anne Whiteman only once, several of the contributors knew her as a teacher, and her meticulous scholarship continues to provide much of the bedrock for ongoing research into the religious, political, and social history of late seventeenth-century England.

GPT
Lady Margaret Hall, Oxford
October 2011

List of abbreviations

AAW	Archives of the Archbishop of Westminster, Kensington
Add. MS	Additional Manuscript
AHR	*American Historical Review*
BL	British Library
Bodl.	Bodleian Library, Oxford
CRS	Catholic Record Society
EHR	*English Historical Review*
HJ	*Historical Journal*
HLQ	*Huntington Library Quarterly*
HMC	Historical Manuscripts Commission
HMPEC	*Historical Magazine of the Protestant Episcopal Church*
HOP 1660–1690	B.D. Henning (ed.), *The House of Commons 1660–1690*, 3 vols (The History of Parliament, 1983)
HOP 1690–1715	D.W. Hayton, Eveline Cruickshanks and Stuart Handley (eds), *The House of Commons 1690–1715*, 5 vols (The History of Parliament, Cambridge, 2002)
IHS	*Irish Historical Studies*
JBS	*Journal of British Studies*
JEH	*Journal of Ecclesiastical History*
LPL	Lambeth Palace Library
ODNB	H.C.G. Matthew, Brian Harrison and Lawrence Goldman (eds.), *Oxford Dictionary of National Biography* (60 vols, Oxford, 2004; and regularly updated online edn)
NEQ	*New England Quarterly*
n.s.	new series
P&P	*Past & Present*
RO	Record Office
SCH	*Studies in Church History*
SHR	*Scottish Historical Review*
SPCK	Society for the Promotion of Christian Knowledge
SPG	Society for the Propagation of the Gospel
SR	*Statutes of the Realm*, 11 vols (1810–28)
TRHS	*Transactions of the Royal Historical Society*
WMQ	*William & Mary Quarterly*
YUB	Yale University Beinecke Library, New Haven

All printed titles were published in London unless otherwise stated. Editorial interventions into quotations are given in square brackets.

Further reading

A 'further reading' section for each chapter may be found online via the editor's webpage on the Lady Margaret Hall, Oxford site: http://www.lmh.ox.ac.uk/Tutors/Fellows/Profiles/Dr-Grant-Tapsell.aspx.

Introduction:
the later Stuart church in context

Grant Tapsell

———◆———

There are since the [Act of] Toleration [1689], many chapells builded. Lord, grant it may be for the good of souls. We all preach the same doctrine, pray for the same things; all the difference consists in garments, gestures and words; and yet that difference breedeth heats, dissensions, divisions, prejudice, jealousies, suspicions, censorious judgings, strangeness and coldness of charity and christian affection amongst friends. I am afraid that this is the effect of such separate meetings, and different modes of worship. Lord, take away all matters of contention ... (Robert Meeke, minister of Slaithwaite, near Huddersfield, 1694)[1]

... I am resolved to keep out Fanatischisme on one hand, & Popery, Symonie & Atheisme on ye other hand. (William Gulston, bishop of Bristol, 1683)[2]

The later Stuart church inherited many of the problems that had been faced by its antecedents at institutional, social, and intellectual levels, but was also rocked by several new and profound challenges.[3] It is important, therefore, to locate the established church within a long-term framework of gradual developments and sharp disjunctures. Some appreciation of the wider geographical world in which it was situated will also help to lay foundations for several of the chapters that follow. But it is important first to offer an account of how clerics and laymen experienced the events of the period between the Restoration of the monarchy in 1660 and the Hanoverian succession of 1714. The nature of the national church was a crucial issue within many of the acrimonious debates that animated public life during these years; a supreme irony, since most contemporaries felt that a uniform religious settlement was vital for the stability of the realm. In the sonorous words of the Act of Uniformity (1662): 'nothing conduceth more to the setling of the Peace of this Nation ... nor to the honour of our Religion and the propagation thereof then an universall agreement in the Publique Worshipp of Almighty God'.[4] Politics and religion under the later Stuarts were powerfully intermingled, rather than sharply differentiated categories. Some clerics exercised considerable secular power, whilst many laymen dictated the terms of the church's position at local and national levels. Indeed it could hardly have been otherwise when religious beliefs were made into a shibboleth for holding public office and clerics expounded political maxims from pulpits across the land.

I

Since they were accustomed to understanding historical events as details within the vast tableau of God's providential plan for the world, it was natural for contemporaries to describe the Restoration of the Stuart monarchy in religious terms.[5] As the prospect of the Restoration became sharply focused in the spring of 1660, Bishop Brian Duppa thought himself 'to be in such a dream as David mentions when God turn'd away the captivity of Sion'.[6] The opposite thought occurred to the fiercely anti-clerical, and vehemently republican, John Milton. For him, the process of Restoration represented an appalling collective act of self-enslavement: he described Englishmen as 'chusing them a captain back for *Egypt*'.[7] But the English were also habituated to comparing their own times with earlier phases of their national history, usually in order to lament the falling away from a previous 'golden age'.[8] According to one grumpy old man in Norfolk in 1667, the present time could be very unfavourably contrasted with 'the glory of our church of England, and the flourishinge state of the kingdome about 40 yeers since (w[hi]ch I well knew)'.[9] Such pessimistic sentiments were the more remarkable coming just five years after the legal re-establishment of a church that had been condemned to oblivion and persecution by the collapse of Charles I's monarchy two decades earlier. Some churchmen appeared to have quickly forgotten the bleak years of the 1650s: at that time, preaching before the exiled royal court at The Hague, William Stamp had lamented 'the present melancholy complexion of our dear Mother, stripped, mangled, and wounded unto death, by the sons of her own bowels'.[10]

The apparent amnesia or ingratitude of many clerics after the legal re-establishment of the church in 1662 was the product of the consequences of the schism that ensued from it. Between 1660 and 1662 Charles II's efforts to implement his deeply held desire for 'a liberty to tender consciences' were frustrated and a narrowly based, intolerant church was established by law.[11] As a direct result of this failure, much of what had existed before 1640 as the Puritan wing *within* the Church of England was forced into internal exile as a divided but numerically significant 'nonconformist' Protestant minority.[12] Various attempts substantially to reframe the church in ways that would have allowed many nonconformists to be 'comprehended', or assimilated, back into it failed in turbulent political circumstances in 1667–73, 1679–81 and 1689.[13] The last of these failures was part of a broader crisis over the post-revolutionary identity of the church, when a further 'nonjuring' schism saw 400 clerics refuse to accept that their old oaths of allegiance to James II could be superseded by new and exclusive ones to William and Mary, and were in consequence legally deprived of their livings.[14] From the early 1690s to the end of our period the established Church of England thus found itself under vigorous polemical assault from eloquent and angry authors appalled that it was not what they believed it should be: either a broadly based Church of England that included Presbyterians and other moderate nonconformists, or an institution sufficiently deeply wedded to its principles of loyalty and obedience that it would not make expedient political compromises with a powerful usurper like William of Orange, 'the troubler of ye world'.[15]

Yet, despite such divisions and criticism, the Church of England retained very important legal privileges and the allegiance of a significant majority of the population.[16] Indeed, according to one controversial scholar, it remained the core of an English *ancien régime* until the massive legal and constitutional changes of 1828–32.[17] Few critics of the pretensions of clerics within this church-state expressed themselves with such brilliant scorn as the author and MP Andrew Marvell. Invoking one of Ben Jonson's celebrated characters on the early Stuart stage, Marvell labelled the more arrogant and meddling clergy of his own day 'the *Politick would-be's* of the Clergy'.

> They are Men of a fiery nature that must always be uppermost, and so they may increase their own Splendor, care not though they set all on flame about them. You would think the same day that they took up Divinity they devested themselves of humanity, & so they may procure & execute a Law against the Nonconformists, that they had forgot the Gospel. They cannot endure that Humility, that Meekness, that Strictness of Manners and Conversation, which is the true way of gaining Reputation and Authority to the Clergy ...

Marvell argued that the experience of deprivation and poverty in the 1640s and 1650s had taken a heavy toll on these men: 'of all Beasts, none are so fierce and cruel as those that have been taught once by hunger to prey upon their own kind'. They had learned nothing from the consequences of the rampant clericalism of the 1630s under Archbishop Laud: 'The former Civil War cannot make them wise, nor his Majesties Happy Return, good natured; but they are still for running things up unto the same extreams.'[18]

Although unusually felicitous in his writing, and complex in his religious views, Marvell here spoke for many MPs and much lay opinion during the 1660s and 1670s.[19] The Church of England was re-established in law after the Restoration, but this did not mean that laymen wished to recreate a powerful clerical caste that might seek to challenge their social and political pre-eminence.[20] As Sir John Holland MP put it during the debates on whether to restore the temporal jurisdiction of the clergy in 1661, 'I think it will be much better for both [church and state] if the bishops would not entangle themselves with secular affairs'.[21] But entangle themselves they did. Gilbert Sheldon, archbishop of Canterbury from 1663–77, displayed considerable flair in promoting the interests of the church via parliament, both by organising like-minded MPs and by managing the voting of the bishops, who had been restored to their seats in the House of Lords.[22] The co-operation between the episcopate and the ministry dominated by Thomas Osborne, earl of Danby

3

in the mid-1670s was sufficiently strong to prompt criticism of the bishops' role.[23] This would only intensify when the bishops played a crucial part in the defeat of parliamentary measures to exclude James, duke of York, from the line of succession as a result of his avowed Roman Catholicism. Pictorial prints duly presented bishops as greedy and monstrous figures, half Anglican, half papist, eagerly hunting for preferment and profit through a covert plan to take the country back to Rome.[24]

Such images would be partially superseded by the events of James II's reign. When Bishop Fell of Oxford addressed the clergy of his diocese during the triennial visitation of 1685, he began by reminding them of the Church of England's difficult strategic position early in the reign of James II, the country's first Catholic monarch since Mary Tudor: 'I need not tell you in what Condition the Church now is assaulted by the furious Malice of Papists on the one hand, & Fanaticks on the other.'[25] As Fell went on to explain, things were even worse than this difficult position initially suggested because the established church was not itself in good enough health to repel threats from outside. The 'licentiousness & sloth' of a third group – 'those who are Indifferent to any or opposite to all' religion – was a crippling internal problem. Facing external opposition, and weakened by its own irresolution, the prospects for the Church of England were poor: 'When these unhappy Numbers are subducted, 'tis lamentable to think how few the remainder are, what scanty gleanings are left to God, amidst the plenteous Harvest which the Devil makes.'[26] Fell completed the gloomy picture by lambasting the clergy for their failure to redouble their efforts in the face of contemporary problems. This was the rhetoric of an ailing and elderly man whose death the following year would allow James II to appoint a more pliant man in his stead.[27] But however bleak things appeared, the acute problems of 1685–88 cumulatively prompted vigorous clerical action, and a degree of popularity for the church hierarchy that was unprecedented in the Restoration age. In the parliament of 1685, the bishops had spoken out against James's efforts to maintain a significant standing army that contained Catholic officers. In London, many of the parochial clergy preached uncompromising anti-Catholic sermons, while working together in a substantial campaign of anti-Catholic publications. And in May/June 1688 seven bishops offered the king their celebrated refusal to read out his reissued Declaration of Indulgence, the publication of which prompted a trial that was a public relations disaster for the king. During the course of the trial, the Presbyterian clergyman Roger Morrice – normally a severe critic of the 'Hierarchists' – noted that on their way into the packed court there were 'much respects shewed to the Bishops ... and many kneeled down to have their blessing, and they laid their hands upon many of them and blessed them'.[28] Huge cheering crowds greeted them across London after their acquittal.

This moment of popularity would be overtaken by the acrimonious aftermath of the Dutch invasion, and the divisions it sowed amongst both clerics and laymen. The predominance of the Church of England was shaken by the Toleration Act (1689), which removed the option of persecuting dissenters for their religious beliefs.[29] Nevertheless, it is important to recognise that many churchmen continued to hope that toleration could be overturned: it appears permanent to us only with the benefit of hindsight. At the time, a noisy campaign was whipped up around the slogan 'the church in danger', with allegations that the Church of England was being undermined by the proliferation of dissenting meeting houses and academies, as well as by the practice of 'occasional conformity', of dissenters receiving communion within the established church just often enough to qualify themselves for office under the terms of the Test Acts (1673, 1678).[30] Efforts to drive legislation through parliament against occasional conformity proved hugely controversial, while clerical debates within convocation in the first decade of the eighteenth century were at least as acrimonious.[31] In essence, those who were increasingly commonly labelled as being of the 'High Church' were seeking to unpick many of the consequences of the Revolution of 1688. Those whose 'Low Church' views led them to place greater value on good relations with Protestant dissenters than rigidly to maintain every privilege of the Church of England were appalled. Again, pictorial prints can help us here, with images of prominent 'High Church' figures caricatured as closet Jacobites scheming for the return of James II or, after 1701, 'James III'; and 'Low Church' leaders ridiculed as disguised republicans longing for the good old days of Oliver Cromwell and the rule of the saints.[32] Such angry terms of debate served to make the decades after the Revolution of 1688 'an anxious age' of lingering uncertainty: in 1703 the Low Church bishop Gilbert Burnet of Salisbury could write to the designated heir to the throne, Sophia Electress of Hanover that "Tis now a full hundred years that we have been fluctuating *from one expedient to another*'.[33] Indeed, the crowning moment of post-revolutionary reaction occurred right at the end of our period when a Tory-dominated parliament passed the Schism Act (1714), which required all schoolteachers to get a license from their bishop; to be communicating Anglicans; and to take the oaths of supremacy and allegiance.[34] The Hanoverian succession, and the gradual entrenchment of Whig ministries consistently supportive of Low Church appointments to the episcopate, would transform the situation once more.

II

If these were the contingent events of the period, what of their broader historical and geographical contexts? Clerics and laymen both interpreted the later Stuart church powerfully in relation to past ages. Jonathan Scott has offered a vigorous argument that much of the political instability that rocked the Restoration period reflected the extent to which politicians remained haunted by memories of the civil wars and Interregnum.[35] Such arguments can be overstated, however useful they were in tearing down the artificial dividing wall that 1660 used to represent in historical scholarship: the period actually witnessed innovation as well as repetition.[36] Yet with regard to the later Stuart church they are extremely valuable, especially if fitted into an even longer-term historical awareness. Church of England clerics were obsessed with the history of their own church, both in the sense of tracing its roots in the scriptures and writings of the early Fathers, and arguing over which features of its post-Reformation development were most important and valuable.[37] This historical scholarship was just one feature of what historians now increasingly commonly describe as 'England's long reformation'; a process that extended in time far beyond traditional understandings of the Elizabethan religious settlement as the culmination of a rapid and inevitable sixteenth-century reformation.[38]

This historical perspective was not simply a matter of rarefied academic discussion. Looking back from the vantage point of 1714, the Devonian clergyman John Walker claimed that when the Church of England was restored in 1662 it was 'so clean swept with the Besom of Destruction, that there was scarce any thing left to shew that the Gospel it self had been once planted in our Island.'[39] Walker's claim was part of a much wider, and highly polemical, project: a published volume to celebrate the 'sufferings' that orthodox clergymen had endured during the civil wars and Interregnum.[40] In particular, he wrote as a counter-blast to the publication in 1702 of Edmund Calamy's abridged version of the autobiography of Richard Baxter, one of the most prolific Puritan authors of the seventeenth century. Calamy's intent had been to emphasise the suffering of the Puritan clergy who had been ejected from the Church of England in 1662 and then endured significant persecution over the next quarter of a century. As Walker furiously argued, 'Why should not the *Church* be as much at liberty to preserve the History of Her *Sufferings*, as the *Separation*, to set forth an Account of Theirs?'[41] Walker's researches involved the circulation of a number of letters of enquiry, via archdeacons, to the families of clergy who had suffered. He received more than a thousand letters in reply.[42] This alone would be suggestive of how memories of the Civil War era were inscribed within family tradition. The last known surviving 'sufferer' amongst the clergy, Robert Rowden, died in 1712 at the age of ninety-six.[43]

The impact of death during the mid-century upheavals was literally carved in stone for all to see throughout the later Stuart era. Although she died in 1652, Bridget Gournay was not commemorated in stone until 1662. As the carved text on her monument in Norwich Cathedral explained:

> King Charles 2nd having been restored
> By whose return not only the sleeping places of the living
>   but also those of the dead
> As well as the sacred shrines themselves are preserved
>   from the violations of fanatics.

What was a cause of anger for Bridget Gournay's descendants could be presented in a much more positive light by those inclined to remember glorious achievement and personal distinction during the mid-century upheavals. When the dean of Norwich, Henry Fairfax, died in 1702 his surviving family erected a monument to his memory in the cathedral that scandalised his successor, Humphrey Prideaux, thanks to its celebration of the role that Fairfax's parliamentarian uncle had played in the crushing victory over Charles I at Naseby in 1645. Prideaux had the monument covered in a cloak until a mason chipped away enough of the words to render what remained anodyne. According to Prideaux,

> no place could be more improper for the putting up of it in than the city of Norwich at this time, for Toryism to the height being now the prevailing humour of the place, should the dean and chapter permit this inscription to stand in our church it would provoke the rabble to break in upon us and tear it down and ... execute other violences upon us; and what would we say for ourselves if they should, as long as such an occasion is given for it?[44]

Whether or not the civil wars should be presented as 'wars of religion', the impact of conflict on the church 'as by law established' was devastating in the short term, and destabilising in the medium term.[45] In the 1690s and 1700s the 'passions of posterity' moved some authors and publishers to produce memoirs and diaries from the mid-century period, whilst a 'cult' of Charles I as king and martyr flourished during the later seventeenth century.[46]

III

However powerful historical memories (and myths) undoubtedly were in shaping contemporary minds during the later Stuart period, so too were geopolitical realities: Englishmen were keenly aware of events beyond their borders, even whilst viewing many foreigners with xenophobic contempt. The Church of England existed within a constellation of Protestant churches throughout the British Isles and continental Europe, as well as having increasing interests further afield in the North American colonies, the islands of the Caribbean, and nascent outposts in Africa and Asia.[47] What was far out of sight could nevertheless trouble the mind of a senior cleric like Bishop Fell, who, four years before his outburst to the parochial clergy of Oxfordshire, opined that in the East Indies 'we had attemted nothing towards the conversion of the natives when not only the papists, but even the Hollanders had labour here'.[48] As these words suggest, distant conflicts were often of greatest concern as reflections of tensions closer to home. Fell pointed to the rival Protestant power of the Dutch Republic, whose public church was Presbyterian in structure, and to the broader threat posed by European Catholic powers – most notably Louis XIV's France – that had, over the course of the seventeenth century, recovered many earlier territorial losses to confessional rivals.[49] How was the Church of England to interact with 'foreign' churches?[50]

Here the answer was significantly complicated by the fact that there was no single unified 'Church of England view'. Opinion necessarily varied between different groups.[51] For those who emphasised the unique character and special development of the Church of England, not least as a result of the magisterial rather than rebellious origins of the English Reformation, doctrinal and ecclesiological suspicions of foreign Protestant churches loomed large.[52] Anxieties were increased by royal marriages to continental Reformed or Lutheran princes, notably Princess Mary to William of Orange in 1677, and Princess Anne to George of Denmark in 1683. Such nascent dynastic entanglements achieved concrete form with William III's rule over both the Stuart kingdoms and the Dutch Republic between 1689 and 1702, and would recur again between 1714 and 1837 with the Hanoverians' continuing close engagement with the politics of the Holy Roman Empire.[53] At a sub-elite level, it is also clear that sudden influxes of Protestant refugees from troubled parts of Europe were not always and everywhere welcomed with open arms by the English populace.[54] Nevertheless, news of Catholic atrocities against Protestants in Europe could arouse considerable English sympathies, and the evident poverty of some migrants prompted a number of charitable briefs organised by the Church of England's hierarchy. Nor were all churchmen convinced that their establishment would not benefit from more substantial ecumenical relations. Hopes for some kind of reunion of churches remained an aspiration for men as prominent as William Wake, bishop of Lincoln from 1705 and archbishop of Canterbury from 1716.[55] However downtrodden churchmen might feel at various points during the later Stuart period, it must have been bracing to be reminded by persecuted foreign Protestants of how comparatively good things were within England. Members of the Fraternal Unity of the Bohemian Confession referred in 1683 to the 'calm Sea of felicity' into which· God's providence had moved the Church of England.[56]

Despite fine theatrical notions of its being a 'sceptred isle' set in a 'silver sea', England was self-evidently not an island.[57] The Church of England not only had to negotiate its place within a continental European world; it also had to engage with established churches elsewhere within the British Isles.[58] North of the border, a very different style of reformation in the sixteenth century produced a very different church polity – Presbyterianism – to that which developed in England.[59] Efforts by James VI and, especially, Charles I to champion episcopacy in Scotland contrived to provoke a massive backlash in the form of Bishops' Wars (1639–40) which were a vital trigger for the fall of the British monarchies.[60] Militant Presbyterianism would continue to prompt anxiety and exasperation for Church of England clergy thereafter. The violently anti-Scottish bishop of Rochester, John Warner, bequeathed £80 *per annum* to Balliol College, Oxford in 1666 to support scholarships for Scots so that, as he acidly noted, 'there may never be wanting in Scotland some who shall support the ecclesiastical establishment of England'.[61] The picture was even more uncertain across the Irish Sea. Although the Protestant and episcopal Church of Ireland represented the church 'as by law established', its actual purchase beyond Dublin and other major towns was weak.[62] A largely unsuccessful sixteenth-century reformation was overtaken by a highly effective late sixteenth- and seventeenth-century counter-reformation which left the Church of Ireland far outstripped in the battle for popular affections by the Roman Catholic Church.[63] Even amongst Irish Protestants, the Church of Ireland faced vigorous competition from dissenting groups, especially in Ulster, where Presbyterians were bound by powerful networks to their co-religionists and kin in the west of Scotland.[64] The combination of episcopal establishments in Scotland and Ireland that failed to establish majority support in the early seventeenth century, long-standing tensions between the three Stuart kingdoms, and the widely felt misrule of Charles I left massive lingering scars on the confessional map of the British Isles. The prominent Scottish Presbyterian, Robert Baillie, feared measures in 1661 that might lead 'bak upon us the Canterburian tyms, the same designs, the same practises', and which would only 'bring on at last the same horribill effects'.[65] Such fears would periodically exercise statesmen in the decades that followed.

IV

Having sketched in the basic framework of relevant events in the later Stuart period, and their historical and geographical contexts, it remains to conclude by drawing them together. Three themes emerge as paramount because of their capacity to ignite contemporary discussion in the light of past experience: the conflicting sources of authority for the Church of England; the relations between clergy and laymen; and the question of how successfully the church exercised its pastoral function.

The king could be described as 'ye Attlas of our Ch[urch]', but in practice he could prove to be more like a sapper laying mines beneath its ramparts.[66] Charles II's efforts to enforce liberty of conscience through exercises of the royal prerogative in 1662 and, especially, 1672 were bitterly resented by many people. Indeed the Declaration of Indulgence of 1672 prompted a furious parliamentary backlash, with the Supreme Governor of the Church of England bluntly told that he did not adequately understand the statutory basis of the church's authority. The king could not set aside whole pieces of legislation he happened to dislike. Here was writ in the language of public controversy the ambiguous origins of the Church of England. Since Henry VIII had used statute law to effect the break with Rome in the 1530s, the Church of England had repeatedly been moulded by legislation. But because the monarch was also the Supreme Governor of the church it was simultaneously a royal church.[67] The problems that this could cause were most striking between 1685 and 1688, when the Supreme Governor was a Roman Catholic. Even after that, William III's Dutch Calvinist sensibilities were regarded with suspicion by many 'High Church' figures. Only Anne appeared comfortably to fit the picture of a pious and orthodox Anglican ruler.[68] A river of tension running through the period was thus the product of the church's reliance on uncertain sources of power: this was why clerics of a certain disposition looked back fondly to the 1630s, when Charles I and Archbishop Laud had worked hand in glove to increase the power and prestige of the church within English society.

The fact that successive monarchs, and many peers and MPs, were very unreliable friends was part of a broader tension between the interests of clerics and the prickly superiority of lay gentlemen and lords. If some churchmen in the 1660s exulted that 'our Church is restored', others focused on the physical despoliation and financial losses that had to be dealt with by 'our wasted Church'.[69] The latter sense of pessimism lingered, not least because of the clergy's awareness that many laymen, even those who had supported the re-establishment of the Church of England, resented adequately funding it.[70] Indeed, Archbishop Sheldon was sufficiently alarmed by the 'evil eye' with which 'some men look upon the possessions of the Church' that in 1670 he solicited information from all cathedrals about their expenditure over the previous decade for publicity purposes.[71] The picture that emerged was, and would remain, extremely mixed. An impressive £2,800 had been spent at Norwich, largely funded through the windfall resources provided by new leases on church lands. Bishop Hacket of Coventry and Lichfield has left ample evidence of tenacious efforts to rebuild his completely ruined cathedral, and his success was widely noted. But the clergy of Rochester Cathedral had to begin a new administrative book to keep track of their chronic debts to local tradesmen throughout the period. At Lincoln Minster, luxury items like cushions were not purchased until 1688, and Margaret Bowker has argued that the real restoration of the church in its vicinity did not occur until c.1680. Nor was the picture one of unilinear improvement over time. Wells Cathedral suffered substantial damage at the hands of the duke of Monmouth's rebel troops in 1685. And even without such specific jolts, Norwich Cathedral's financial woes were so serious by the early eighteenth century that temporary relief came only with a loan of £250 from the dean's mother-in-law.[72] In this sense the cathedrals were emblematic of a broader lay suspicion that the church was still too rich, and that clerical landlords were greedy and unreasonable, though research has tended to emphasise the fragile character of the finances of even many senior figures within the hierarchy.[73]

So far in these concluding reflections, questions of authority and lay/clerical relations have been presented as generally negative in their impact upon the church. It would be tempting to regard as normative the kind of prickly and intolerant mindset exhibited in the quotation from Bishop Gulston's correspondence offered at the head of this introduction. But this was far from the whole story, and it is certainly possible to describe powerful forces of co-operation resulting in significant positive outcomes of the kind that this chapter's first epigraph shows Robert Meeke having prayed for. Although no one could deny the suffering endured by many Protestant dissenters and Catholics in this period, nor ignore the extent to which many individual parish communities were poorly served by lazy or inept Church of England clergy, it is right to end this introduction on a more constructive note. Indeed, literally so, since we are now beginning to realise how significant phases of church building and refurbishment were in the later Stuart period.[74] Cathedrals across the country recovered from their mid-century trauma, thanks in large part to the munificence of lay donors. And at a parish level, it is striking that so much of the acrimony that had characterised debates about increasingly lavish church furnishings in the 1630s were absent or subdued after 1660.[75] This may have been because of the fashionable example set by the numerous new churches designed by Christopher Wren for the City of London in the period of rebuilding after the Fire. These gave considerable prominence to altars as a focus for worship, and by 1700 this was increasingly being copied in the country at large.[76] In the 1630s, it had been widely feared that Laudian clerics were seeking to downgrade the importance of sermons at the same time as increasing the formality of worship. But in the later Stuart period it is clear that sermons retained enormous force, not least as a staple of the print trade in their printed forms.[77] New societies for the reformation of manners flourished in the 1690s and 1700s, and witnessed the close co-operation of laymen and clerics; whilst confessional divides were insufficiently broad to prevent some at least from reaching out in various forms of dialogue and mutual respect.[78] In sum, we need to recognise that this period was less a prologue to an 'age of negligence' than the roots of an 'eighteenth-century Reformation' in England that featured substantial efforts to continue the mission of the church in new and challenging circumstances.[79]

NOTES

I am grateful to George Southcombe and Catherine Wright for their comments on a draft of this introduction. I am also happy to acknowledge the British Academy and the Arts and Humanities Research Council for their support, in the form of a Postdoctoral Fellowship held at Darwin College and the Faculty of History, Cambridge, and an Early Career Fellowship sponsored by the University of St Andrews.

1 H.J. Morehouse (ed.), *Extracts from the diary of the Rev. Robert Meeke* ... (1874), pp. 86–7 (30 Aug. 1694). Meeke's ministry is noted in the chapter by Grant Tapsell in this volume; for charity between Christians, see the essay by George Southcombe.

2 Bodl. MS Tanner 34, fol. 123: Gulston to William Sancroft, archbishop of Canterbury, 29 Aug. 1683.

3 For a consideration of the shifting sands of theological opinion, see Nicholas Tyacke's chapter in this volume.

4 *SR*, V, 364: 14 Car. II, cap. 4.

5 B. Worden, 'Providence and politics in Cromwellian England', *P&P*, 109 (1985), 55–99; J. Spurr, *The Restoration Church of England, 1646–1689* (New Haven and London: Yale University Press, 1991), pp. 29–30.

6 G. Isham (ed.), *The correspondence of Bishop Brian Duppa and Sir Justinian Isham 1650–1660* ... (Northamptonshire Record Society, 17, 1949–51), p. 180: Duppa to Sir Justinian Isham, 27 Mar. 1660. See also, A. Macfarlane (ed.), *The diary of Ralph Josselin 1616–1683* (British Academy Records of Social and Economic History, n.s., 3, 1976), p. 463.

7 John Milton, *The readie and easie way to establish a free commonwealth* (2nd edn, 1–10 Apr. 1660), in R.W. Ayers (ed.), *Complete prose works of John Milton: volume VII 1659–1660* (New Haven and London: Yale University Press, rev. edn, 1980), p. 463.

8 Though notions of a golden age could also be hubristic: see G. Parry, *The golden age restored: the culture of the Stuart court, 1603–42* (Manchester: Manchester University Press, 1981).

9 Bodl. MS Tanner 45, fol. 276: Mr Saltmarsh of Great Ellingham, Norfolk, to William Sancroft, [8 Feb. 1667].

10 Quoted in R.S. Bosher, *The making of the Restoration settlement. The influence of the Laudians 1649–1662* (Dacre Press, 1951), p. 81.

11 S.R. Gardiner (ed.), *The constitutional documents of the Puritan revolution, 1625–1660* (Oxford: Oxford University Press, 3rd edn, 1906), p. 466 (the 'Declaration of Breda', 4 Apr. 1660).

12 See recently J. Spurr, 'Later Stuart Puritanism', in J. Coffey and P. Lim (eds), *The Cambridge companion to Puritanism* (Cambridge: Cambridge University Press, 2008), pp. 89–107; G.S. De Krey, *London and the Restoration, 1659–1683* (Cambridge: Cambridge University Press, 2005); and D. Appleby, *Black Bartholomew's Day. Preaching, polemic and Restoration nonconformity* (Manchester: Manchester University Press, 2007).

13 The best account is now M. Goldie, *Roger Morrice and the Puritan Whigs* (Woodbridge: Boydell, 2007).

14 The best account of the mechanics of deprivation remains J. Findon, 'The nonjurors and the Church of England 1689–1716' (DPhil dissertation, University of Oxford, 1978, i.e. 1979).

15 Bodl. MS Tanner 26, fol. 89: William Lloyd, deprived bishop of Norwich, to William Sancroft, deprived archbishop of Canterbury, 11 Apr. 1691.

16 See the painstaking scholarly reconstruction of the returns to the 'Compton Census' of 1676 in the introduction to A. Whiteman, with the assistance of M. Clapinson (ed.), *The Compton census of 1676: a critical edition* (Oxford: Oxford University Press, 1986).

17 J.C.D. Clark, *English society, 1660–1832: religion, ideology, and politics during the ancien regime* (Cambridge: Cambridge University Press, 2nd edn, 2000), and the exchange with J. Innes in *P&P*, 115 (1987), 165–200; 117 (1987), 195–207.

18 'The Rehearsal Transpros'd' (1672), in A. Patterson *et al.* (eds), *The prose works of Andrew Marvell*, 2 vols (New Haven and London: Yale University Press, 2003), I, 161–2. I am grateful for George Southcombe for pointing me towards this passage.

19 See John Spurr's chapter in this volume for a broader discussion of laymen and the church.

20 For the reluctance of many justices of the peace to prosecute Protestant dissenters except during times of political crisis, see A. Fletcher, 'The enforcement of the Conventicle Acts 1664–1679', *SCH*, 21 (1984), 235–46.

21 *HOP 1660–1690*, II, 557.

22 J. Spurr, 'Gilbert Sheldon', *ODNB*; R.A. Beddard, 'Sheldon and Anglican recovery', *HJ*, 19 (1976), 1005–17; A. Swatland, *The House of Lords in the reign of Charles II* (Cambridge: Cambridge University Press, 1996), via index, *sub* 'bishops'. For the post-revolutionary parliamentary role of bishops, see A.S. Turberville, *The House of Lords in the reign of William III* (Oxford: Oxford University Press, 1913), chapter II; Turberville, *The House of Lords in the XVIIIth century* (Oxford: Oxford University Press, 1927), via index, *sub* 'bishops'; C. Jones and G. Holmes (eds), *The London diaries of William Nicolson, Bishop of Carlisle 1702–1718* (Oxford: Clarendon Press, 1985).

23 M. Goldie, 'Danby, the bishops and the whigs', in T. Harris, P. Seaward, and M. Goldie (eds), *The politics of religion in Restoration England* (Oxford: Blackwell, 1990), pp. 75–105.

24 See, for instance, *A prospect of a popish successor* (1681), discussed in G. Southcombe and G. Tapsell, *Restoration politics, religion and culture: Britain and Ireland, 1660–1714* (Basingstoke: Palgrave Macmillan, 2010), pp. 39–41; and *The time-servers: or, a touch of the times ...* (1681), in J. Miller, *Religion in the popular prints 1600–1832* (Cambridge: Chadwyck-Healey, 1986), pp. 122–3.

25 Bodl. MS Tanner 31, fol. 156: 'B[isho]p Fell's speech at his triennial visitation in the year 1685'. For James II as a Catholic ruler, see J. Miller, *Popery and politics in England, 1660–1688* (Cambridge: Cambridge University Press, 1973), esp. chapters 12–14; and, more recently and controversially, S. Pincus, *1688: the first modern revolution* (New Haven and London: Yale University Press, 2009), esp. chapters 5–7. More broadly, see Gabriel Glickman's chapter in this volume.

26 Bodl. MS Tanner 31, fol. 156.

27 For various episcopal reactions, see Bodl. MS Tanner 30, fols 3, 83, 93.

28 M. Goldie (gen. ed.), *The entering book of Roger Morrice 1679–1691*, 7 vols (Woodbridge: Boydell, 2007–9), IV, 293.

29 *SR*, VI, 74–6: 1 Gul. & Mar., c. 18. Properly titled, 'An act for exempting their Majestyes Protestant subjects dissenting from the Church of England from the penalties of certaine lawes'.

30 G.V. Bennett, *The Tory crisis in church and state, 1688–1730: the career of Francis Atterbury, Bishop of Rochester* (Oxford: Oxford University Press, 1975).

31 G. Holmes, *British politics in the age of Anne* (Macmillan, 1967), via index, *sub* 'Occasional Conformity bills'; G.V. Bennett, 'The Convocation of 1710: an Anglican attempt at counter-revolution', *SCH*, 7 (1971), 311–19.

32 See, for instance, Miller, *Religion in the popular prints*, pp. 138–47

33 Quoted in Julian Hoppit, *A land of liberty? England 1689–1727* (Oxford: Oxford University Press, 2000), p. 2.

34 *SR*, IX, 915–17: 13 Annæ, c. 7; Holmes, *British politics*, pp. 54–5, 103–4. The Schism Act was repealed in 1719.

35 J. Scott, *England's troubles. Seventeenth-century English political instability in European context* (Cambridge: Cambridge University Press, 2000).

36 G. Tapsell, *The personal rule of Charles II, 1681–85* (Woodbridge: Boydell, 2007), pp. 11–13; and, more widely and polemically, A. Houston and S. Pincus (eds), *A nation transformed: England after the Restoration* (Cambridge: Cambridge University Press, 2001).

37 J.-L. Quantin, *The Church of England and Christian antiquity: the construction of a confessional identity in the 17th century* (Oxford: Oxford University Press, 2009); A. Milton, *Laudian and royalist polemic in seventeenth-century England: the career and writings of Peter Heylyn* (Manchester: Manchester University Press, 2007); and the essays by Heal, Spurr, and Starkie in P. Kewes (ed.), *The uses of history in early modern England* (San Marino, CA: Huntington Library, 2006).

38 Compare A.G. Dickens' classic *The English Reformation* (Batsford, 1964; 2nd edn, 1989) and N. Tyacke (ed.), *England's Long Reformation 1500–1800* (University College London Press, 1998).

39 John Walker, *An attempt towards recovering an account of the numbers and sufferings of the clergy of the Church of England ... who were sequester'd, harrass'd, &c. in the late times of the Grand Rebellion* (1714), p. v. (A 'besom' is a broom.)

40 For recent published accounts of Walker and his project, see A. du Toit, 'John Walker', *ODNB*; B. Griggs, 'Remembering the Puritan past: John Walker and Anglican memories of the English civil war', in M.C. McClendon, J.P. Ward, and M. MacDonald (eds), *Protestant identities: religion, society, and self-fashioning in post-Reformation England* (Stanford, CA: Stanford University Press, 1999), pp. 158–91. These have now been largely superseded by Fiona Youngman's unpublished dissertation, '"Our dear mother stripped": the experiences of ejected clergy and their families during the English Revolution', 2 vols (DPhil dissertation, University of Oxford, 2008).

41 Walker, *An attempt*, p. i.

42 Youngman, '"Our dear mother stripped"', I, 17.

43 *Ibid.*, I, 34 n. 20. (Richard Cromwell, briefly Lord Protector after the death of his father, Oliver, in 1658, also died in 1712, aged eighty-five.)

44 J. Firth, 'The monuments', in I. Atherton *et al.* (eds), *Norwich Cathedral: church, city and diocese, 1096–1996* (Hambledon Continuum, 1996), pp. 477–8. For the context, see I. Atherton and V. Morgan, 'Revolution and retrenchment: the cathedral, 1630–1720', in *ibid.*, pp. 567–74.

45 J. Morrill, *The nature of the English Revolution* (Harlow: Longman, 1993), esp. chapter 3; I. Green, '"England's wars of religion?" Religious conflict and the English civil wars',

in J. van den Berg and P.G. Hoftijzer (eds), *Church, change, and revolution* ... (Leiden: Brill, 1991), pp. 100–21; G. Burgess, 'Was the Civil War a war of religion? The evidence of political propaganda', *HLQ*, 61 (2000 for 1998), 173–201; C.W.A. Prior and G. Burgess (eds), *England's Wars of Religion, revisited* (Aldershot: Ashgate, 2011).

46 B. Worden, *Roundhead reputations: the English civil wars and the passions of posterity* (Allen Lane, 2001); A. Lacey, *The cult of King Charles the Martyr* (Woodbridge: Boydell, 2003); R. Beddard, 'Wren's mausoleum for Charles I and the cult of the royal martyr', *Architectural History*, 27 (1984), 36–45.

47 W.R. Ward, 'The eighteenth-century church: a European view', in J. Walsh, C. Haydon and S. Taylor (eds), *The Church of England c.1689–c.1833: from toleration to Tractarianism* (Cambridge: Cambridge University Press, 1993), pp. 285–98; N. Etherington (ed.), *Missions and empire* (The Oxford History of the British Empire Companion Series, Oxford: Oxford University Press, 2005); and Jeremy Gregory's chapter in this volume.

48 Bodl. MS Tanner 36, fol. 57: Fell to William Sancroft, 21 June [1681]. For organised efforts to evangelise Native Americans, see *ibid.*, 32, fols 1–2.

49 S.C.A. Pincus, *Protestantism and patriotism: ideologies and the making of English foreign policy, 1650–1668* (Cambridge: Cambridge University Press, 1996); J. Scott, 'England's troubles 1603–1702', in R.M. Smuts (ed.), *The Stuart court and Europe: essays in politics and political culture* (Cambridge: Cambridge University Press, 1996), pp. 20–38; S. Taylor, 'An English dissenter and the crisis of European Protestantism: Roger Morrice's perception of European politics in the 1680s', in D. Onnekink (ed.), *War and religion after Westphalia, 1648–1713* (Aldershot: Ashgate, 2008), pp. 177–96.

50 For the role of the 'foreign churches' within England in this period, see R. Gwynn, *Huguenot heritage: the history and contribution of the Huguenots in Britain* (Brighton: Sussex Academic Press, 2nd edn, 2001); O.P. Grell, 'From toleration to integration: the decline of the Anglo-Dutch communities in England, 1648–1702', in O.P. Grell, J.I. Israel, and N. Tyacke (eds), *From persecution to toleration: the Glorious Revolution and religion in England* (Oxford: Oxford University Press, 1991), pp. 97–127; C. Wright, 'The consistory and community of Austin Friars in the later seventeenth century', *Proceedings of the Huguenot Society of Great Britain and Ireland*, 28 (2007), 626–39.

51 See Tony Claydon's chapter in this volume.

52 For an earlier period, see A. Milton, *Catholic and Reformed: Roman and Protestant churches in English Protestant thought, 1600–1640* (Cambridge: Cambridge University Press, 1994), and the helpful redaction, 'The Church of England, Rome and the true Church: the demise of a Jacobean consensus', in K. Fincham (ed.), *The early Stuart church, 1603–1642* (Basingstoke: Macmillan, 1993), pp. 187–210.

53 See in particular A.C. Thompson, 'The confessional dimension', in B. Simms and T. Riotte (eds), *The Hanoverian dimension in British history, 1714–1837* (Cambridge: Cambridge University Press, 2007), pp. 161–82; *Britain, Hanover and the Protestant interest, 1688–1756* (Woodbridge: Boydell, 2006); *George II* (New Haven and London: Yale University Press, 2011).

54 M.R. Thorpe, 'The anti-Huguenot undercurrent in late-seventeenth-century England', *Proceedings of the Huguenot Society of London*, 22 (1976), 569–80; H.T. Dickinson, 'The poor Palatines and the parties', *EHR*, 82 (1967), 464–85.

55 N. Sykes, *From Sheldon to Secker: aspects of English church history, 1660–1768* (Cambridge: Cambridge University Press, 1959), chapter IV, is a helpful introduction to his much

larger, *William Wake*, 2 vols (Cambridge: Cambridge University Press, 1957). For an earlier period, see W.B. Patterson, *King James VI and I and the reunion of Christendom* (Cambridge: Cambridge University Press, 1997).

56 Bodl. MS Tanner 34, fol. 69v.

57 Shakespeare, *Richard II*, 2.1.40, 46.

58 F. Heal, *Reformation in Britain and Ireland* (Oxford: Oxford University Press, 2003).

59 A. Ryrie, *The origins of the Scottish Reformation* (Manchester: Manchester University Press, 2006); J.E.A. Dawson, *Scotland re-formed, 1488–1587* (Edinburgh: Edinburgh University Press, 2007), chapters 9–10.

60 D.G. Mullan, *Episcopacy in Scotland: the history of an idea, 1560–1638* (Edinburgh: John Donald, 1986); J. Morrill, 'A British patriarchy? Ecclesiastical imperialism under the early Stuarts', in A. Fletcher and P. Roberts (eds), *Religion, culture and society in early modern Britain: essays in honour of Patrick Collinson* (Cambridge: Cambridge University Press, 1994), pp. 209–37; M.C. Fissel, *The bishops' wars: Charles I's campaigns against Scotland, 1638–1640* (Cambridge: Cambridge University Press, 1994); C.S.R. Russell, *The fall of the British monarchies, 1637–1642* (Oxford: Oxford University Press, 1991).

61 Quoted in E. Lee-Warner, 'John Warner', *DNB*.

62 A. Ford, J. McGuire, and K. Milne (eds), *As by law established: the Church of Ireland since the Reformation* (Dublin: Lilliput Press, 1995), chapters by Ford, MacCafferty, and Murray.

63 H.A. Jefferies, *The Irish church and the Tudor Reformations* (Dublin: Four Courts, 2010); A. Ford, *The Protestant Reformation in Ireland, 1590–1641* (Dublin: Four Courts, 2nd edn, 1997); C. Lennon, 'The Counter-Reformation in Ireland 1542–1641', in C. Brady and R. Gillespie (eds), *Natives and newcomers: essays on the making of Irish colonial society, 1534–1641* (Dublin: Irish Academic Press, 1986), pp. 75–92.

64 P. Kilroy, *Protestant dissent and controversy in Ireland, 1660–1714* (Cork: Cork University Press, 1994); R.L. Greaves, *God's other children: protestant nonconformists and the emergence of denominational churches in Ireland, 1660–1700* (Stanford, CA: Stanford University Press, 1997).

65 O. Airy (ed.), *The Lauderdale Papers*, 3 vols (Camden Soc., n.s., 34, 36, 38, 1884–5), I, 95. This is discussed further in Clare Jackson's contribution to this volume.

66 Bodl. MS Tanner 29, fol. 57v: John Garbrand to William Sancroft, London, 30 Aug. 1687. (It must be admitted that Garbrand was not the most perspicacious reader of Restoration public life: in the early 1680s he had hotly denied that James was a Catholic, viewing talk of it as deliberate public slander: *ibid.*, fol. 57.)

67 See C. Russell, 'Parliament, the royal supremacy and the Church', *Parliamentary History*, 19 (2000), 27–37, and the chapter by Jacqueline Rose in this volume.

68 William had initially been partially shielded from criticism by the Anglican piety of his wife, Mary II, until her early death in 1694. Mary and Anne had both received their Protestant education from Bishop Compton: Andrew M. Coleby, 'Henry Compton', *ODNB*.

69 Bodl. MS Tanner 48, fol. 6: Robert Gayer to William Sancroft, Stoke, 18 Apr. 1662; *ibid.*, MS Tanner 45, fol. 206: Robert Pory to William Sancroft, Much Hadham, 12 Aug. 1667.

70 For pithy examples of clerical gloom on this subject, see Bodl. MS Tanner 48, fols 21, 71.

71 Quoted in P. Mussett, 'The reconstituted chapter, 1660–1820', in N. Yates, with the assistance of P.A. Welsby (ed.), *Faith and fabric: a history of Rochester Cathedral 604–1994* (Woodbridge: Boydell, 1996), p. 77. For the earlier fate of the cathedrals, see Ian Atherton, 'Cathedrals and the British Revolution', in Michael J. Braddick and David L. Smith (eds), *The experience of revolution in Stuart Britain and Ireland: essays for John Morrill* (Cambridge: Cambridge University Press, 2011), pp. 96–116.

72 Atherton *et al.* (eds), *Norwich Cathedral*, pp. 560–1, 674, 569; B. Quintrell, 'John Hacket', *ODNB*; Mussett, 'Reconstituted chapter', p. 78; M. Bowker, 'Historical survey, 1450–1750', in D. Owen (ed.), *A history of Lincoln Minster* (Cambridge: Cambridge University Press, 1994), pp. 197, 199; J.R. Guy, 'From the Reformation to 1800', in L.S. Colchester (ed.), *Wells Cathedral: a history* (Shepton Mallet: Open Books, 1982), pp. 167–8.

73 C. Clay, '"The greed of whig bishops"? Church landlords and their lessees 1660–1760', *P&P*, 87 (1980), 128–57.

74 For a lavishly illustrated recent account, see T. Friedman, *The eighteenth-century church in Britain* (New Haven and London: Yale University Press, 2011).

75 K. Fincham, 'The restoration of altars in the 1630s', *HJ*, 44 (2001), 914–40, and '"According to ancient custom": the return of altars in the Restoration Church of England', *TRHS*, Sixth ser., 13 (2003), 29–54; K. Fincham and N. Tyacke, *Altars restored. The changing face of English religious worship, 1547–c.1700* (Oxford: Oxford University Press, 2007), chapters 4–6, 8.

76 Fincham and Tyacke, *Altars restored*, pp. 305–6, 325–37, 347–55. This is not to say that there was no resistance to the revival of ritualism: see *ibid.*, pp. 337–41.

77 See the chapter by Grant Tapsell in this volume.

78 See the chapters by Jeremy Gregory, Tony Claydon, George Southcombe and Gabriel Glickman in this volume.

79 J. Gregory, 'The eighteenth-century Reformation: the pastoral task of Anglican clergy after 1689', in Walsh, Haydon and Taylor (eds), *Church of England*, pp. 67–85.

Part I

Ideas

Chapter 1

By law established: the Church of England and the royal supremacy

Jacqueline Rose

The Restoration Church of England rested on a paradox. It proudly proclaimed itself the church 'by law established', constitutionally entitled to unique uniformity and ubiquity; the nation – not just the nascent Tory party – at prayer. As the national church, it professed its outstanding allegiance to the monarchy: obedience was 'the main Article that distinguishes ours from all other Communions'.[1] Yet it was simultaneously a holy catholic society, a 'spiritual Corporation, distinct from the Common-wealth, and antecedent to its being embodied in it ... with a jurisdiction distinct from the civil Government',[2] by *divine* law established. Perfectly reformed, with apostolic episcopal government, it had survived the abolition of the monarchy and official outlawing during the Interregnum. Yet the half-century following 1660 perhaps suggested that Interregnum proscription was easier to manage than Restoration prescription. The novelty of the church-state relationship after 1660 was not the powers of the crown but the only patchy commitment of monarchs to the ecclesiastical establishment. The church endured, in turn, a king who undermined as often as he upheld it, an openly Catholic ruler, and a Dutch Calvinist invader. Despite her high-church sympathies, Queen Anne disappointed many by prioritising her freedom from party government above her sympathies. And this period witnessed the death of the church's legal monopoly on English worship, when nonconformity was tolerated by statute. The Revolution of 1688 was inglorious for the church, but even the nonjuring schism did not leave the juring remnant united.

This chapter explores how the church tried to negotiate various pitfalls caused by its monarchs, the church's 'one fatal flaw'.[3] The royal supremacy was not the only problem contributing to its disquiet between 1660 and 1714, but it does provide a window onto the church's relationships with the crown, with other religious groups (dissenting and Catholic), and its internal heterogeneity. Churchmen almost never denied the supremacy, but they constantly tried to tweak it to their individual views of the nature of the church as a society amidst the demands of particular polemical circumstances. To understand the framework in which they worked, however, we need to begin not in the 1660s but one and a half centuries earlier, in the 1530s.

I

The royal supremacy lay at the heart of the English Reformation. Henry VIII had ejected the pope whilst rejecting doctrinal reform, but the Edwardian Reformation welded supremacy to evangelism.[4] While Elizabeth I forestalled the more reforming inclinations of her early episcopate, she had no qualms about reasserting the full panoply of royal ecclesiastical powers after the Marian return to Rome, merely changing her title from Supreme Head to Supreme Governor of the church – an alteration quite literally nominal, and frequently ignored.[5] The ecclesiastical supremacy which proved such a defining feature of Tudor *imperium* was passed intact to the Stuart line, albeit Stuart historians have taken less notice of it.

Every churchman swore the Oath of Supremacy of 1559, but what did it mean? Four powers proved key. Firstly, monarchs could shape English worship by royal proclamation. Although William III was the only later Stuart monarch to issue such 'Injunctions' (in 1696), royal supremacy exercised by proclamation would be used by both Charles II and James II to bypass parliament and declare liberty of conscience. Secondly, the crown could delegate its supremacy to other laity, either a single vicegerent or a collective ecclesiastical commission. This aspect of supremacy would become most prominently debated under James II. Thirdly, the crown's status as 'patron paramount' allowed it to appoint bishops and, perhaps, to deprive them too. This power could be deemed to reduce bishops to merely royal servants; conversely, the asymmetrical ease of appointment and difficulty of deprivation would be exposed by the nonjuring schism. Fourthly, by the Act of Submission of the Clergy (1534), monarchs had power to summon convocation, license its debates, ratify its canons – or to inhibit all of these, indeed, to suppress it. With the lapse of synodical activity under Charles II and James II, debate on convocation declined, but it revived under William and Anne.

These powers were entrenched in law, frequently at the highest possible level – statute. Later Stuart monarchs inherited wide-ranging powers over their church, but these came parcelled with a poisonous legacy of conflicting accounts of the location, extent, and purpose of those powers. Did statutes which *declared* monarchs supreme heads mean that kings could thereafter ignore parliament's wishes on religion? Or did a statutory Reformation mean that parliament could claim a role in church governance? Even the foremost theorist of the Tudor supremacy, Richard Hooker, subversively suggested that supremacy rested not in the monarch alone, but in crown-in-parliament.[6] Did kings have to use their supremacy on behalf of the established church? Or might they abolish bishops, tolerate dissenters, patronise Catholics? Over a century of debate on such questions was both continued and exploited by Restoration writers, for in a society which still seems to have felt itself to be part of the Reformation, such evidence could not be lightly bypassed.

Discussions of church–state relationships were thus unavoidably enmeshed in a legal framework which was overlaid with over a hundred years of polemic. Often, therefore, the story of the church and the supremacy in the later Stuart period is one of battles over how to interpret a particular statute, or a historical disquisition over past precedents. The supremacy was both a topic of and an arena for debate, and professing allegiance to it was the beginning, not the end, of disputes.

II

A churchman's precise position on the supremacy might have been enunciated and refined in response to particular circumstances, but it was a product too of their standpoint on the society of the church. There was a vast difference between Edward Stillingfleet, whose (in)famous *Irenicum* asserted that church government was to be decided by the monarch, and Simon Lowth, who refused to build his church upon the sandy soil of the 'Wills and Passions of Princes'.[7] Importantly, there was no 'typical' stance on this. Historians can note the various prominence and popularity of different accounts, but it is impossible to argue convincingly that any one idea was hegemonic. Whilst the foremost historian of the Restoration church recognises the diversity of stances on ecclesiology, he is overly optimistic about the ability of the church to maintain unity.[8] Before 1689, there was no schism, but nor was there consensus.

Although the broad thrust of *Irenicum* was the legitimacy of imposing uniformity in *adiaphora* (rites left 'indifferent', not specified, by scripture), Stillingfleet focused on civil rather than ecclesiastical decisions about such items, in which he included church government. For him, scripture had set down no form of ecclesiastical hierarchy for all time; and indeed, no one form could suit all times and places. Nor was the governance of the early church much use as a model: the times too different, the records too uncertain.[9] 'The determining of the Form of Government is a matter of liberty in the Church; and … may be determined by lawful authority.' Albeit clergy could offer advice on it, only civil powers could *oblige* worshippers to obey a certain form, for 'he only hath power to oblige who hath power to punish'.[10] Where God was silent, Leviathan spoke.

Stillingfleet could envisage few problems with this theory, since he could see no reason why 'a National society incorporated into one civil Government

23

... should not be called a Church'. Echoing Hooker, Stillingfleet conflated the membership of church and polity and announced that 'the chief authority in a Commonwealth as Christian, belongs to the same to which it doth as a Commonwealth'.[11] Civil supremacy was logical in a national church. But for not a few readers, a church of this nature was one not incorporated, but dissolved, into the state. Whilst Anglicans were eager to argue that the civil magistrate could use their royal supremacy to impose uniformity of worship, many denied that church government was a matter indifferent. Not only Lowth, but also the vicious polemicist Samuel Parker, often thought of as subordinating the church to the state,[12] argued that episcopal church government could not be altered by the magistrate: 'a wild conceit'.[13]

Assumptions about the nature of the church as a society led to different modes of argument: some 'constitutional', based on its establishment in English law, others on its creation by Christ in the New Testament, still more (increasingly popular in this period) using the first three centuries of Christianity as a model. This patristic era was vital to Anglican ideas because it showed a church divided into independent dioceses or provinces, each under its own bishop; joined universally by synods and episcopal correspondence – but not by popes. This picture could be easily incorporated into that of national churches once sovereigns turned Christian. Christ had deliberately proved that His church could survive under persecution before granting it royal 'nursing fathers'[14] in its full maturity.

When discussing questions of church and state (ecclesiology), there were two risks. One was rendering the church a creature of the state, the other was ring-fencing the church's power so securely as to impinge on the supremacy. The first was labelled 'Erastian' or 'Hobbist', the latter constituted the sin of papistry and the crime of *praemunire*.[15] It is revealing that these epithets were flung at each other by the jurors and nonjurors within months of the overthrow of a monarch who could be accused of manipulating Erastianism on behalf of papistry. However, the Restoration church moved towards emphasising its universal catholicity more than its national, territorial, status. This was far from being Romish, but it meant that being too Erastian was now a bigger problem than it had been before. This is symbolised by Stillingfleet's grovelling appendix to the 1662 edition of *Irenicum*, which protested his protection of the spiritual integrity of the church – and by the continuing criticisms of him well into the 1680s, despite this.[16]

Several solutions were offered to this problem, none of which were novel in the later Stuart period, but two of which were especially prominent. The first was that royal supremacy was a jurisdictional but not sacerdotal power: it entailed legislation, patronage, and oversight, not ministering sacraments, ordination, or consecration. This had been the key defence of the church against its Catholic enemies since at least the 1560s and was nowhere better summarised than in the Elizabethan Injunctions of 1559. These explained that supremacy was not to 'chalenge auctoritie and power of ministrie of divine Offices in the Churche' but only 'under God, to have the soveraigntie & rule over all maner persons ... of what estate either ecclesiasticall or temporall so euer they be, so as no other forraine power shal or ought to have any superioritie over them'.[7] Classically, it reposed itself in the concept that kings licensed bishops to exercise jurisdiction, but only other prelates could consecrate them to the episcopate. Thus a monarch could *deprive* a bishop of his temporal powers, but not *degrade* him from his status as of a higher order than a minister. Secondly, obedience to sovereigns was reconciled with moral integrity by a strong doctrine of counsel. If a monarch sinned, they might be privately rebuked – indeed, all good churchmen had a duty to warn them of their vices. The paramount example of this was the punishment of the Emperor Theodosius by Bishop Ambrose in the fourth century, although churchmen often fudged the issue of whether to call this excommunication.

Ideally, a jurisdictional supremacy, wielded to best effect through a king hearing Anglican counsel, was the perfect partnership of magistracy and ministry. Four instances of circumstances in which it was strained to breaking point after 1660 will now be discussed in turn: toleration by royal prerogative, ecclesiastical commissions, deprivation of bishops, and the summoning of convocations. Respectively, these show churchmen's positions on the supremacy when provoked by dissenters, Catholics, schism, and internal rifts.[18] *Pace* Spurr, churchmen before as well as after 1689 'pitted the royal supremacy against episcopal authority'; indeed, Jeffrey Collins rightly discerns a 'hostility' between clergy and crown 'unprecedented since the Reformation'.[19] Albeit the following concentrates on the Anglican side of the argument, it also reveals how useful a tool the supremacy was to opponents of the established communion, and how diverse positions on it within the church were never fully reconciled. The question of the church's establishment by divine or human law was the underlying theme of these discussions.

III

Under Charles II the church experienced swings of royal favour and disfavour. Before the mid 1670s Charles flirted with dissenters and connived with Catholics; afterwards, he submitted to an Anglican–Royalist alliance. But there was a more complex chronology, for royal inclinations could change rapidly. In the early 1660s the king switched from promoting conferences for comprehension[20] (1660–61) to backing uniformity (early 1662) to prerogative indulgence (December 1662), dropping the last within months. In 1667 and 1668 he encouraged comprehension, then signed the vicious Second Conventicles Act (1670), then issued his most famous Declaration of Indulgence (1672).[21] Both

25

churchmen and their opponents could be easily bewildered by, and remained on their guard against, such vicissitudes.[22]

Increasingly, however, some dissenters felt that there was more hope for toleration by royal prerogative than from Cavalier Anglicans in parliament. They not only thanked the king for the provision of such 'indulgence', but pushed him towards it throughout the Restoration. Philip Nye's works exemplify the nature and persistence of this argument. His tract on the supremacy of 1662 was republished with a different title in 1670 and 1686;[23] that of 1672 was posthumously published in 1687 under two different titles.[24] Nye's description of the partnership of clerical and civil authority echoed that of Anglican defenders of the supremacy, some of whom he cited. Yet he subverted this tradition by redefining 'the church' as church*es*, individual congregations. Nye told the king that Independency was 'much more *consistent*' with the royal supremacy than a powerful episcopate. Supremacy gave Charles the power to 'suspend ... yea wholly deprive' a bishop, to '*dispence* with any ... *Canons* or Ecclesiastical Laws' if not breaking divine law, and to grant 'tender consciences a *Forbearance*'.[25]

Nye's argument is representative of a powerful antiprelatical theme within dissent, one which emphasised how bishops had undermined royal authority. It was an argument deployed in the early Reformation by evangelicals against Catholic bishops, but one which by the later Stuart era was put to good use against Anglican prelates by dissenters and anticlericals. Andrew Marvell explored how churchmen had flattered and manipulated emperors out of their power; Shaftesbury how the episcopate exalted royal power over lay subjects whilst seizing ecclesiastical supremacy for itself.[26] In justifying toleration by royal proclamation, dissenters elevated the prerogative and downplayed parliament; civil and religious liberty did not develop in simple tandem.

The most notable opponent of the 1672 Declaration was Francis Fullwood, a former Puritan who turned to defend uniformity throughout the Restoration. Fullwood was faced with a difficult task: to oppose royal policy without explicitly contradicting the king. His solution was twofold. He firstly minimalised what the Declaration offered: exemption from penalties rather than abolition of uniformity. The king had neither abandoned the church nor legalised conventicling. 'Toleration' of nonconformity was still a pejorative term. Secondly, Fullwood maintained that schism remained a heinous sin. Dissenters *could* take out licences; that did not mean they *should*.[27] Fullwood's case rested on an insistence that the king was truly committed to the established church. It was a claim often repeated, albeit one somewhat contrary to the evidence of royal policy – especially in 1672. With a monarch like Charles II, tying the church to human law and royal supremacy was not a very secure defence. Some churchmen therefore retreated to the safer terrain of divine law.

Pre-eminent among such churchmen in the early Restoration was Herbert

Thorndike. His bold defences of the divine society of the church were born of a career of opposing Hobbist incursions against the spiritual society. It is true that some Anglicans found him too strong a sacerdotalist.[28] But he was far from intellectually isolated. Archbishop Sheldon commissioned his responses to the late 1660s comprehension proposals and Thorndike reflected the increasingly clericalist tone of some Restoration churchmen, who venerated the pre-Constantinian church.

Thorndike argued that the route to religious peace was adhering to the catholic faith of the early church, not comprehension. Obligation, not authorisation, would tame dissent. Faced with the prospect of comprehension, Thorndike was less subtle than Fullwood (although perhaps he could afford to be, writing against toleration proposed rather than proclaimed). There was 'no question' about whether the sovereign could indulge nonconformity. 'The civil power cannot make that change in the ecclesiastical laws, which this Comprehension requires, without the authority and against the consent of the church.' Any hint that secular power should 'define' rather than 'fence' religion smelt like *Leviathan* to Thorndike, who could be relied on to denounce the merest whiff of Hobbism as unchristian. 'The Comprehension pretended is the manifest produce of that accursed doctrine, which makes the Church and the whole right of the Church to stand only by the law of the land, and not at all by God's law.'[29] The king had a duty 'not to suffer Sects to persecute' the church.[30] Thorndike did find a role for the royal supremacy, but one which he labelled 'accumulative'. Civil authority made church decisions binding on the people, it did not – could not – arbitrarily decide what religion was. Sovereigns, he specified, had rights over ecclesiastical persons and causes, but not 'ecclesiastical power'. He even suggested that the Oath of Supremacy needed rewriting to clarify that supremacy was not unbounded.[31] Thorndike said little about the Church of England as a national church, defined by Reformation statutes and established by Tudor monarchs. Instead he spoke of the visible society of the church, united by bishops. 'The Unity of the Church is not derived from *Constantine*, but from our Lord and his Apostles.'[32]

The paradox of dissenters elevating the prerogative while Anglicans circumscribed it continued under James II, in particular in 1688 with the widespread refusal to comply with the royal order that the second Declaration of Indulgence be read from all Anglican pulpits. Anglican defiance was defended in the *Letter from a Clergyman in the City*, which posited that to read the Declaration was an act of assent to it, and would 'teach the dispensing Power, which alters, what has been formerly thought, the whole Constitution of this Church and Kingdom: which we dare not do, till we have the Authority of Parliament for it'.[33] This was denounced as sacerdotal arrogance and arrant sedition. 'Can this consist with Ecclesiastical Headship and Obedience?'[34] The Seven Bishops who protested to James against the measure, and who were tried for seditious libel for so doing (their petition having been published, albeit without their knowledge), gained the support of many nonconformists, but some dissenters mockingly professed horror at Anglican disloyalty. Henry Care's insistence on the clergy's obedience was not a generic case for submission to an absolute monarch, but one specifically geared to the royal supremacy: the king as 'Supreme Ordinary of all *England*' who could 'deprive [clergy] for Non-Obedience'.[35]

The *Letter from a Clergyman* was redolent of the multiple strategies which Anglicans deployed against James; weapons wielded by the Seven Bishops. The first was that the dispensing power was unwarranted by English law. The bishops petitioned that dispensing had 'often been declared illegal in parliament'. Counsel for the bishops at their trial read a series of denunciations of the dispensing power and one judge admitted that the petition was not libellous, for it was true that the Declaration was illegal.[36] Archbishop Sancroft's planned speech, which he never had the chance to read, noted how:

> it shook the force of all our laws, and the very foundation of the reformed Church of *England*, and in that the whole Protestant Religion ... it seemed to alter the whole frame of the Government, and introduce a new Constitution.[37]

Second, the bishops declared that their consciences precluded them from reading the Declaration. Since James offered liberty of conscience to dissenters, he could not deny it to his episcopate. Indeed, the bishops went so far as to claim that they had 'most pretence [claim] to it'.[38] Third, they invoked their status as royal counsellors, whose advice it was *necessary* to take before changing religious policy. As subjects, as magistrates, as peers, and especially as prelates, the bishops had a right and duty to protest against an act they thought illegal.[39] James might be supreme head, but he was morally bound to hear episcopal counsel about the church.

Sancroft was horrified at the idea that the church 'as it was the Religion of the State, had no other subsistence but by the King's meer favour'. 'As a Prelate', the archbishop argued, he must oppose anything that 'tended to [the Church's] ruine, and struck at her safety'; 'as a Peer of the Realm' he was under 'very great obligations ... not to betray the laws'.[40] Defending the church against James thus highlighted its dual establishment: by human *and* by divine law. By the first, James's supremacy was legally restrained; by the second, the bishops were authorised – obliged – to tell him so.

IV

The dispensing power was the constructive element of James's Catholicising policy. The complementary weapon used to deconstruct Anglican hegemony was the Ecclesiastical Commission. As with dispensing, most people were neither satisfied with the legality of the policy nor unambiguously certain of its illegitimacy. The Commission typified how difficult it could be to define the powers of the supremacy by the late seventeenth century, for three statutes pointed in contradictory directions. The Elizabethan Act of Supremacy (1559) empowered the queen 'by vertue of this Acte' to appoint commissioners 'by *lettere*s Patentes' to judge ecclesiastical 'Erroures ... Abuses Offences Contemptes and Enormitees'. In 1641, parliament repealed this clause of the Act of Supremacy, decreeing that no court with 'like Power, Jurisdiction, or Authority' to the High Commission should be erected. In 1661, a third Act ambiguously sought to reassert the legality of 'ordinary' spiritual jurisdiction in the church courts but not to allow 'extraordinary' commissions. It repealed the 1641 statute 'excepting what concerns the High Commission-Court, or the Erection of some such like Court by Commission'. But then it also contained a proviso that the statute should not 'abridge or diminish' the royal supremacy.[41] If the power to set up a commission was part of the royal prerogative, rather than a new grant from parliament in 1559, then in effect a new commission could not be prevented.

The Commission dealt with a wide range of cases, yet its reputation undoubtedly stemmed from the most prominent of these: those against Bishop Compton of London, the University of Cambridge, and Magdalen College Oxford.[42] Compton, Cambridge, and Magdalen all challenged the jurisdiction of the Commission when cited but the Commissioners refused to be drawn into debate on their powers. Instead defences were mounted in printed tracts, most notably by the dissenter Henry Care and the Anglican royalist Nathaniel Johnston. Both argued that the greatness of royal ecclesiastical prerogative was able to override any statutory limitation (which they also denied existed). 'The *Power of the* KING, in Matters Ecclesiastical, is too ample to be *limited by an Act of Parliament.*'[43] Both added that James might have used such supreme authority to greater effect: to make the church subscribe to liberty of conscience or to Catholicism. The church had not suffered persecution but enjoyed 'great Clemency'.[44] Both writers offered an exalted view of royal supremacy: their kings held papal power,[45] able to make canons and invest and deprive bishops independently of parliament. Much of Johnston's tract consisted of a historical demonstration that such powers had been wielded by kings before the Reformation. Sixteenth-century statutes *declared*, not created, royal supremacy, not making a new power, but rendering an old one more conspicuous than before.[46]

A survey of four attacks on the Commission (the printed works by Edward Stillingfleet, Robert Washington, and the anonymous 'Philonomus Anglicus', plus the advice given by the lawyer Roger North to Archbishop Sancroft) exposes a tendency towards an 'ancient constitutionalist' argument.[47] Frequently these authors used a dual method of invoking history to demonstrate that royal supremacy was bounded by law in general, and specific Acts to suggest that the power to erect ecclesiastical commissions was introduced by statute. Philonomus applied the generic case (kings 'bound by the Laws of the Realm in the exercise of their Jurisdiction') to their headship of the church. Although Tudor monarchs were not made heads of the church by statute, they were so by common law, historical enquiry into which revealed supremacy to be no pure royal absolutism. Norman bishops who appealed to the king were heard in parliament; monarchs made canons in conjunction with their Great Council. 'Our Kings Antient Ecclesiastical Jurisdiction was not a Personal Supremacy, separate and distinct from the States of the Realm [but ...] in the King encompassed with Peerage and Cominalty.' North pointed out that common law gave supremacy to the king, but 'secundum Leges, & Consuetudines'.[48] Both Stillingfleet and Washington offered disquisitions on Anglo-Saxon and medieval history to prove that 'the *Ancient Ecclesiastical Supremacy* of the Kings of this Realm, was no *personal Prerogative*' but exercised in conjunction with parliament.[49] 'The whole Fabrick of the *English Saxon Church* was built upon Acts of Parliament.'[50]

Furthermore, ancient royal jurisdiction did not include the power to erect ecclesiastical commissions and delegate supremacy to them. *That* power was newly created by statute in 1559, removed in 1641, and not re-granted in 1661. Whereas Care argued that there was an ancient prerogative, which statute could not remove, to create commissions, Philonomus had no compunction about arguing that, had such a power existed, the statute of 1641 abolished it.[51] Stillingfleet noted that ecclesiastical commissions were not part of supremacy from time immemorial, but a grant by statute.[52] He and North argued that the clause saving the royal supremacy in the 1661 statute could not be intended to overthrow its main body, which banned erecting any court with 'like power' to High Commission.[53] Such precision about exactly what powers were (or were not) included in ancient royal supremacy was reiterated by Stillingfleet and Washington, revealing an increasing sense that the Reformation had done more than recover ancient prerogatives. Washington offered the most careful account of exactly how a long-established, and legitimate, legally bounded supremacy had become mistakenly inflated into an absolute and purely royal prerogative 'without any warrant from *Antiquity, Law,* or *History*'. As papal power grew during the Middle Ages, pure ancient supremacy was lost. At the Reformation, in an effort to re-secure due royal authority, novel powers had been added. While Washington was careful to assert that Reformation parliaments had retained control over religion, creating and granting powers to kings, a mistaken supposition that monarchs simply took over papal authority had grown up. Despite a venerable tradition of court cases which had used this argument to elucidate judgments, it is striking that both lawyers writing under James – Washington and North – vehemently denied that royal supremacy involved papal power: 'a vulgar Notion'.[54]

The condemnation of the Commission during the Revolution backfired on the new monarch in autumn 1689. When William set up a commission of clergymen to draft comprehension proposals, some questioned its authority. The future Archbishop Tenison was left weakly asserting that the Williamite commission was of 'a very differing Nature, and has differing Ends' to James's.[55]

V

Even the most intransigent opponents of comprehension and/or toleration in 1689 had already made the momentous decision to accept William. Those who refused to swear allegiance to William, the nonjurors, included Archbishop Sancroft, eight bishops (including five of the Seven Bishops), and circa four hundred clergy, and they were deprived by parliamentary statute.[56] To the question of the legality of the Revolution government was now added the legitimacy of the Williamite church, for how could a civil authority deprive God's ministers?

There are few modern studies of the nonjurors, and their juring opponents have received even less attention.[57] Here the crucial nonjuring writers will be seen to be Henry Dodwell, John Kettlewell, and Nathaniel Bisbie; of the jurors, Edward Stillingfleet was the most prominent and Edward Welchman the most penetrating polemicist.[58] When discussing deprivations of bishops they turned in particular to three past examples: Solomon's removal of the high priest Abiathar, the deprivation of the church Father John Chrysostom, and the purges of Tudor bishops in the 1540s and 1550s. Each of these was significant because occurring in periods deemed exemplary for the church. Solomon's actions, for example, were important because the second canon of 1604 decreed that English kings' powers were modelled on those of ancient Israel.

Nonjurors protested that the meaning of the text that Solomon had 'thrust out Abiathar from being a priest before the Lord' (1 Kings 2:27) was opaque. Abiathar had not been deprived, merely removed from the exercise of his offices, banished. His successor, Zadok, was already his equal or superior, and had not received power from Solomon: the monarch had simply fulfilled a prophecy of the restoration of the priesthood to the true line of succession. Nonjurors occasionally drew a distinction between Abiathar's crime of rebellion and that of the nonjuring schism or, more radically, rejected the idea that Old Testament ecclesiology was the model for a Christian church-state.[59] But the jurors refuted these caveats, finding the example a powerful weapon. The deprivation of Abiathar by the magistrate for a temporal crime was cited by Stillingfleet in 1691, Humphrey Hody in 1693, and an anonymous author in 1698. 'Where was the Act of the Church, in the Deposition of *Abiathar*?' 'Are our Bishops Ecclesiasticks? So was *Abiathar*. Is our King a Lay Man? So was *Solomon*.'[60]

Secondly, the deprivations of bishops in the age of the Fathers were dissected. Here the jurors were less successful than on Abiathar, for nonjuring scholarship comprehensively demonstrated that early Christian emperors had used (albeit manipulated) synods to remove bishops, whose replacements were rarely accepted.[61] But the nonjurors had a harder task explaining away the deprivations of Catholic bishops by Elizabeth I in 1559. Whilst the Reformation could not be ignored, the nonjurors desperately tried to pick and choose their Tudor precedents, overriding particular English examples with the 'Doctrine and Practice of the Church in all Ages'.[62]

Was the deprivation of bishops by an Act of parliament in 1689 intolerable Erastianism or English law?[63] Underlying the division between the jurors and the nonjurors were two views of the church–state relationship: one of incorporation, the other of independence. Both sides admitted that both situations were possible, but they diverged in their emphases and preferences. The doctrine of the church as a society, capable of self-government, lay at the heart of the nonjuring concept of episcopal authority untouchable by secular hands. As a society, the church (or rather its founder, Christ) appointed its own governors.[64] Bishops 'never did, nor could receive [spiritual powers] from the Civil State, on which [Christ] never conferr'd it, but which they hold independantly of *Christ*'. A lay state could not consecrate, so could not deprive, bishops.[65]

The nonjurors were more explicit – though not always more extreme – than their Restoration forebears about the church's ability to exist independently of the state. Dodwell's claim that the priesthood was 'the *cement* of a *Spiritual Society*'[66] highlights his sense of the church. Adhering to the principle of an independent collegial (not papal or conciliar) church governed by bishops in their dioceses, nonjurors focused on the way in which a bishop linked a particular congregation with the universal catholic church. The case for the collegiality of the catholic church, maintained by letters communicatory between bishops, was an idea proposed by high churchmen before the Revolution. Nevertheless, nonjuring language was more explicitly subversive of the supremacy. Kettlewell spoke of the necessity of one bishop, one *head*, in each church, Dodwell of bishops as 'the *Supreme Governours* of the *Church*', its only visible heads.[67] Such ideas neatly refuted the juring insistence that kings could deprive bishops of their particular sees but not degrade them from their episcopal order (leaving them 'bishops at large'). Hody, Stillingfleet, Welchman, and Williams all stated that deprivation of the exercise of jurisdiction was not loss of 'Episcopal Character'.[68] The jurors' case was consistent with that of prior reformers, and some nonjurors had to go to new lengths to deny it. For Dodwell and Milles, 'the Exercise of a Spiritual Power within a particular District' was 'certainly' a spiritual authority inviolable by the state.[69] Only a synod held the requisite ecclesiastical authority to deprive such powerful figures, as North confirmed in legal advice to the nonjurors.[70]

Whilst North was giving such counsel, his former ally against the Ecclesiastical Commission, Stillingfleet, was defending William's right to replace the nonjurors. The juring argument emphasised the incorporation of church and state, both governed by the royal supremacy. Stillingfleet declared that to deprive bishops of an incorporated church for 'an offence against the State' had 'just reason', especially when those bishops 'wholly disown' royal authority. Behind this was the juring assumption that the church '*must* be Incorporated into the State'.[71]

Welchman offered the most detailed explanation of how the church, able to subsist independently when necessary under an infidel state, was nevertheless incorporated if the state was Christian. Whilst the nonjurors turned to Cyprian, Welchman utilised Hooker:

> How should the Church and State make two distinct Societies, where both Church and State consist of the very same Persons? ... 'Tis true indeed, to be a State is one thing, and to be a Church is another; but yet both the one thing and the other are Accidents, and such as may well consist in the same Subject. For is not the same Man a Member of both? Do not the very same Persons bear Authority in both? Nay is not the King supreme Head and Governor in both?[72]

Although churches were designed with the *ability* to subsist independently, their *primary* design was for unity with the state – and unity could be had without the two being wholly confounded.[73]

Nonjurors admitted that church and state could conjoin, but they saw this alliance as fragile, and readily emphasised its disadvantages. Dodwell arrogantly asserted that the benefits of incorporation all accrued to the magistrate, who thus had to submit humbly to whatever terms the church offered. Such a 'coalition' left spiritual power intact and untouchable. Collier's church was 'perfectly *sui juris*' before incorporation, and not to be 'dissolve[d] ... into the State' afterwards.[74] When the two societies quarrelled, the nonjurors were quick to facilitate their divorce. After all, wrote Dodwell, 'Gods establishing it otherwise at *first* shewed plainly that it was *better* for the *Church* to be *independent* on the *State*, whensoever there should be any *difference* between it and the *secular Magistrate*'.[75]

Ironically, these arguments were quite proximate to Welchman's declaration that royal apostasy dissolved royal headship over the church: should a king 'turn Infidel, he falls from his Supremacy in Church Affairs; he ceaseth to be Head'.[76] Whilst perforce the jurors could not call William an infidel, by the end of the 1690s some had very real doubts about his commitment to the church and, in particular, to convocation.

VI

By the late 1690s rifts were opening up within the Williamite church over how to deal with the threats of nonconformity and irreligion. For the controversialist Francis Atterbury, a convocation was the 'true and only proper means' of defending the church. Atterbury admitted that a royal writ was needed to summon convocation, but insisted that William was obliged to issue one, because he was constitutionally bound to call convocation every time parliament sat.[77] Atterbury and his most famous opponent, William Wake, pursued a protracted battle over the nature of convocation, its relationship to parliament, and the powers of the Supreme Governor over it.[78] Perforce this meant attending to the circumstances of the Submission of the Clergy to Henry VIII. Although the Convocation Controversy overlapped with the nonjuring debate, the two need to be kept distinct.[79] They referred to different elements of the supremacy: deprivation of bishops versus summoning of synods. The nonjurors emphasised the independence of the church from the state; high-church Atterburians desired to weld the two together. Concerned as they were to resist Erastianism, high-church jurors' emphasis on parliament and contract would have been anathema to the nonjurors.

Much could be said about the role of historical scholarship in the Convocation Controversy, not least because it highlights the ecclesiastical dimension to ancient constitutionalism, which historians have tended to read in secular terms.[80] Both Atterbury and Wake believed that clergy had attended the king's great councils (the supposed precursors to parliament) in Anglo-Saxon times, and had been forced to assemble by medieval kings in order to grant subsidies. These state assemblies and ecclesiastical synods had become muddled in their business.[81] For Atterbury, this was sufficient to imply that a convocation was an ecclesiastical body, but one modelled on parliament and part thereof.[82] For Wake, a convocation and a synod were distinct entities. Furthermore, a 'provincial convocation' was different to the clergy meeting as part of parliament. The latter derived from royal writs to every bishop, with representatives of the lesser clergy being summoned by the (now practically defunct) *praemunientes* clause. Convocation was, however, summoned by each archbishop in his own province issuing writs to the bishops and clergy. Wake denied that these two provincial assemblies were called by the *praemunientes* clause; they were no part of parliament.[83] Furthermore, since the Act of Submission, the archbishop could only arrange convocation in response to a royal request, an order which Canterbury could not deny.[84] Albeit Atterbury was right that it had become customary since the 1530s to summon the clergy at the same time as parliament, this was not a sufficiently established custom to be binding on the king.[85]

The debate about the summoning of convocation was distinct from that over when it was permitted to act – necessarily so, for it became a favoured royal tactic to summon and immediately adjourn convocation without any debates being held. Atterbury insisted on the 'great Parliamentary Priviledge' of the clergy to free debate, not needing royal permission.[86] Wake retorted with the Act of Submission's prohibition on clerical legislation without royal licence, which stated that the clergy

> wyll never frome hensforthe presume to attempte, allege, clayme, or putt in ure, or enacte, promulge or execute any newe canons, constitucions, ordynaunce provynciall or other, or by what soo ever other name they shall be called in the convocacion, onles the Kynges most royall assente and licence may to theyme be had to make, promulge and execute the same.[87]

A pedantic debate ensued over these words. Atterbury asserted that the word 'attempt' referred to pre-Reformation canons, and the statute only banned the 'enacting' of new ones. To debate and draft was not to 'make' a canon. No later licences to convocation recited the 'attempt' clause.[88] Wake dismissed such claims as nonsense. Through an exhaustive account of the legislation, he proved that the clergy needed permission to debate as well as to enact canons.[89] With the Submission 'Restraining them from *Attempting*, as well as from *Enacting* ... From *Alledging* and *Claiming*, as well as from *Putting in ure*', they 'need a *License* in every Step that they take'.[90] Wake sealed his case by noting that, in the 1530s, neither king nor parliament was likely to favour independent clerical power.

Wake emphasised the royal supremacy's constraints on convocation, albeit adding the caveat that in dire necessity (a persecuting monarch) the church could act on its own authority. Since his opponents were quick to denounce his 'Erastian' ideas, he repeatedly (and rightly) asserted his ideas to have been the constant sense of the church since the Reformation, publishing a whole book of citations from Anglican writers to prove it.[91] Such ecclesiastical authority, Wake insisted, was part of the original power of all sovereigns. If no particular English law could be shown to limit it, William's power over the church was as absolute and free as any Roman emperor's.[92]

No writer would overtly deny the supremacy. But Atterbury refused to condone an unbounded one. Royal ecclesiastical authority was 'accumulative' not 'privative' of the church's rights – Thorndike's formula. By comparison, Wake described kings in councils acting 'rather like a *Patriarch*, than a *Prince*'. Where Wake's supporters likened an English convocation to the Council of Nicea, Atterbury computed William's supremacy not as 'Heir to the Imperial Authority of *Constantine* ... but ... by the Laws of *England*'.[93] In England, surely king-in-parliament was more powerful 'in Church-matters, and over Church-Synods than the *King Alone*?':

> *out of Parliament* it is manifest, that he is not so Absolute in Ecclesiastical Matters as [the Roman] Emperors were ... [The English Church is] under the Government both of the *Absolute*, and *Limited Sovereign*.[94]

35

Whatever the consensus about England being a mixed monarchy in civils after the Revolution, this equivalent account of an ecclesiastical supremacy of crown-in-parliament was denounced by some as *praemunire*.[95] Conversely, if Whiggish churchmen disliked a limited monarchy which could not prevent convocation, high-flying divines could use Whig ideas to good effect. Samuel Hill – who had defended William's church against the nonjurors – argued that only an original contract created royal supremacy. It was impossible to prove royal rights from a generic account of sovereignty; the only feasible description was of the specifics of the English ecclesiastical polity. Contract, not Constantine, gave William his supremacy.[96]

Hill's tracts, barely mentioned by historians of the controversy, are more revealing than those of Atterbury and Wake on the nature of the church as a society. Hill reminded his readers that the church had existed for three centuries before Christian emperors. By neglecting this period, Wake implied that the church only existed incorporated with the state. But before Constantine the church governed itself by synods summoned on its own authority, and these councils were key bonds of unity for a federal church of independent episcopal dioceses. An imperial authority which subsequently overlaid this pre-existing self-governing church could only be intended to protect, not devour, it.[97] If Hill did not use the formula of cumulative, not privative, royal authority, he certainly shared the sentiment, and was rebuked for it by Humphrey Hody: 'where all profess the same Religion, they should all be subject to the same *Common Head*'.[98]

Anne was frequently feted as a nursing mother to the church and the realm, lauded as Deborah for warfare on behalf of European Protestantism.[99] If Old Testament models were applied to her ecclesiastical supremacy in a less detailed manner than before, that did not prevent her from tetchily defending her prerogative. When the lower house of convocation insisted on pursuing the complaint of 'the church in danger' in defiance of episcopal resolutions of the church's safety, Anne wrote to Archbishop Tenison declaring her resolution 'to maintain our supremacy and the due subordination of presbyters to bishops' as 'fundamental parts' of the Anglican constitution.[100] A year later the lower house questioned the royal writ proroguing convocation, stating that the writ was illegal, since between 1532 and 1705 convocation had never been prorogued while parliament was sitting. The Upper House sent this to the Queen, who replied angrily that it amounted to 'a plain invasion of our royal supremacy which is reposed in us by the law and the constitution of the Church of England'. She threatened to use all legal punishments against 'so dangerous an attempt' – an implicit threat of *praemunire*.[101] She could be just as fiercely defensive of her prerogative against her lay ministers. Although she wished to promote clergy who had 'shown a due zeal for her Supremacy' – ruling out those high churchmen whose religiosity she partly shared – she refused to bow to pressure from the Whig Junto to renege on her promises of sees to Tories in the 'bishoprics crisis' of 1707.[102]

Augustan debates on supremacy were perpetuated by arguments on the nonjurors and convocation, dissecting the ecclesiastical prerogative and Israelite, early Christian, and Reformation models for it. At the start of the reign, Charles Leslie's *Case of the Regale* condemned the juring substitutes for the nonjurors along with the perfidious Erastianism of the English church.[103] He reasserted earlier denials that Solomon had deprived Abiathar ('the Greatest *Refuge* of the *Regale*'), claims which astonished Edward Welchman: 'if *thrusting* one out from being Priest, and *putting* another in his room, be not a proper *Deprivation*, I know not what is'. Where Leslie warned that a bad king could abolish all good bishops by his supremacy, Welchman retorted that this would be illegitimate. Welchman's claim that bad nominees should not be consecrated was trumped by Leslie's reminder that this was *praemunire* under Henrician statutes.[104] This specific debate widened into a general one about what supremacy Israelite kings had held. Leslie interpreted Isaiah as implying that kings served the church and he asserted that Israelite monarchs were given extraordinary authority over religion. Alternatively, he suggested, their authority was no more than civil power over ecclesiastical persons and the right of all kings to use the civil sword to uphold religious truth. For him, interpreting supremacy as involving ecclesiastical powers destroyed the spiritual independence of the church.[105] He accused those who denied the church's *iure divino* spiritual independence of betraying the trust which Christ had given them – denouncing even Atterbury for arguing from custom rather than divine law. This divine right of self-government did not simply lapse to the church when a bad king threatened her safety; it was a permanent state of spiritual independence.[106] Leslie snidely compared the establishment of supremacy to the request of the Israelites for a king – a rejection of God's sovereignty – attributed the early use of supremacy to the heretical emperor Constantius, and linked its rise to popery: 'both *Enlarging* their *Powers* upon the *Ruins* of *Episcopacy*'.[107] Yet both he and Welchman laid claim to Reformation authorities, both citing the Thirty-nine Articles, Welchman the 1604 canons, and Leslie the Elizabethan Injunctions.[108] In all these echoes of earlier rhetoric a handful of changes can be observed. One was an especial concern with supremacy's relationship to synods, arising from post-Revolution worries. The other was the willingness of both Leslie and Welchman to speak of sovereign supremacy 'be it in *One* or *Many*'.[109]

One of Leslie's reasons for denouncing Anglican '*Heterogeneous Erastianism*' was that it was exploited by the '*Priest-Craft-men*'.[110] A priestcraft-man *par excellence* was Matthew Tindal, who complained that 'no Clergyman since the Restoration ... does not maintain an Empire within an Empire' by upholding independent church power. Even *Irenicum* was no use, given Stillingfleet's appendix of 1662. Churchmen swore the Oath of Supremacy and prayed for the king, but preached it away in their sermons.[111] If Leslie detested Tindal, the feeling was mutual: associating high church jurors with nonjurors and both with Jacobites, Tindal denounced Leslie and Hill.[112] He noted that motions to call convocation without royal assent were *praemunire*, and snidely remarked that clerical councils had damaged the church. The only useful council would be an exclusively lay one, for pure Reformation needed lay agents. For Tindal, this had occurred to an extent in England, where the church was 'a perfect Creature of the Civil Power'.[113] He defended monarchical powers to appoint, oversee, and remove clergy – Christian kings 'every where' deprived bishops.[114] He praised Anne for her letter to Tenison declaring her intent to maintain her supremacy. But he also argued that she could do no otherwise, for she 'has no power in Ecclesiasticals except by the Laws of the Land, and can't divest her self of any part of it without Consent of Parliament'.[115] In an account infused with Lockean language of fiduciary power, Tindal insisted that parliament 'trusted' authority over the church to kings. Although administered by the king, episcopal appointments and deprivations ultimately stemmed from parliament. Parliament could enact and annul canons; it might judge heresy. Anglo-Saxon parliaments governed civil and religious matters together, and the Reformation 'reviv'd' 'the Parliament's Right in making Ecclesiastical Laws' – here Tindal cited Washington.[116] Indeed, he ultimately argued for popular, not parliamentary, ecclesiastical sovereignty by insisting that the people could appoint and deprive bishops. This stemmed from his sense of the church as a voluntary society which, echoing Locke, he called a club.[117] In his concern about the dangers of clerical independence manifested in excommunication of the magistrate, he sounded like 'the Great *Erastus*' in 'his excellent Treatise', endorsing Erastianism in its fuller form when criticising any notion of an independent church government. Importantly, though, he could manipulate Reformation laws on the supremacy to argue that such independent church government was 'inconsistent with the Constitution of the Establish'd Church' – citing the 1604 canons.[118] Tindal was misrepresenting the intent of Reformation laws, but his ability to do so brought him ironically close to Leslie. Both read supremacy as an exalted power, however different their reactions to it were.

Although supremacy remained a live issue under Anne, it featured only marginally in the *cause célèbre* of Augustan clerical politics: Sacheverell's impeachment for attacking the notion of resistance in the Revolution of 1688 and toleration of dissenters.[119] The Whig managers for the impeachment insisted that Sacheverell's assertion that spiritual censures could not be reversed by any earthly authority impugned the supremacy. The defence replied that the spiritual power of pastors did not derive from the civil magistrate, although of course judicial processes of excommunication in church courts were subject to common law.[120] The prosecution noted Sacheverell as an example of those who 'cancel the Queen's Supremacy ... and erect a Church Independent on the Civil Government'; one even suggested that toleration of dissenters was less dangerous for royal power than the 'late Notion of a Hierarchy [is] to the Supremacy of the Queen's Majesty'.[121] But a slippage from royal to civil supremacy was noticeable in Nicholas Lechmere's speech which denounced Sacheverell for striking at 'the Legal Supremacy of the Government, in Matters Ecclesiastical' which subjected the ecclesiastical to the 'Civil Power'. Lechmere defined the royal supremacy as 'the Legal Supremacy of the Crown and Legislature'. And he portrayed the Henrician Reformation as asserting popular as well as royal rights. In declaring the freedom of the *realm* from the pope, Henrician statutes acted as 'Declarations, and Ratifications, of the Original Contract'.[122]

Supremacy over all ecclesiastical persons and causes was no mere titular or nominal royal authority, but one which could be crucial in determining the shape of English worship. Between 1660 and 1688 in particular, it was courted by dissenters and exploited by Catholics. The church bowed to its power and swore to uphold royal prerogatives, yet insisted on the kingly duty to uphold the episcopal establishment. This was not a world of creeping secularisation or the onward march of pluralism, but of fierce ecclesiological warfare. Much of the story of the later Stuart church is illuminated by the clash between coercive jurisdiction, held by monarchs, and moral authority, wielded by the church. The church was by law established, but by what law – divine or human? Churchmen's perpetual proclivity to answer 'both' had undoubted advantages, but also threw up problems which would not – perhaps because they could not – be solved.

NOTES

I am grateful to Mark Goldie and John Morrill for commenting on a draft of this chapter, the themes of which are further explored in my book *Godly kingship in Restoration England* (Cambridge: Cambridge University Press, 2011).

1 Samuel Parker, *A reproof to the Rehearsal Transprosed* (1673), p. 305.

2 Samuel Parker, *The case of the Church of England* (1681), p. 37.

3 G.V. Bennett, *The Tory crisis in church and state, 1688–1730: the career of Francis Atterbury, Bishop of Rochester* (Oxford: Oxford University Press, 1975), p. 8.

4 See esp. J. Guy, 'The Henrician age', in J.G.A. Pocock (ed.), *The varieties of British political thought, 1500–1800* (Cambridge: Cambridge University Press, 1993), pp. 13–46; G.D. Nicholson, 'The nature and function of historical argument in the Henrician Reformation' (PhD dissertation, University of Cambridge, 1977).

5 C. Cross, *The royal supremacy in the Elizabethan Church* (Allen & Unwin, 1969), although she overemphasises the change of title.

6 Richard Hooker, *Of the laws of ecclesiastical polity*, VIII.6.11.

7 Simon Lowth, *Of the subject of church-power* (1685), p. 169.

8 J. Spurr, *The Restoration Church of England, 1646–1689* (New Haven and London: Yale University Press, 1991), chapter 3 and p. 104.

9 Edward Stillingfleet, *Irenicum* (1660), pp. 180–1, [294] (mispag. 286).

10 *Ibid.*, pp. 416, 48.

11 *Ibid.*, pp. 156, 127; repeated in Edward Stillingfleet, *The mischief of separation* (1680), pp. 18–19.

12 G.J. Schochet, 'Between Lambeth and Leviathan: Samuel Parker on the Church of England and political order', in N. Phillipson and Q. Skinner (eds), *Political discourse in early modern Britain* (Cambridge: Cambridge University Press, 1993), pp. 189–208. Cf. J. Rose, 'The ecclesiastical polity of Samuel Parker', *The Seventeenth Century*, 25 (2010), 350–75.

13 Parker, *Case*, p. 246 (announcing his opponents, he silently [p. 136] quotes *Irenicum*); Lowth, *Church-power*; see also his *Letter to Edw. Stillingfleet* (1687).

14 Isaiah 49: 23.

15 *Praemunire*: the crime and associated writ of elevating foreign over royal authority; originally levelled against the pope, it could be deployed against English clerical pretensions.

16 Spurr, *Restoration Church*, pp. 155–6; Rose, 'Ecclesiastical polity'.

17 'An admonition to simple men, deceyued by malicious', in *Iniunctions geuen by the Quenes Maiestie* (1559), sigs D2v–[D3]r.

18 This is far from an exhaustive list: ecclesiastical patronage and the controversies over limiting the supremacy in the later 1670s, Sacheverell, and the prosecution of Whiston might be others.

19 Spurr, *Restoration Church*, pp. 132, 164, 107, 399; J.R. Collins, 'The Restoration bishops and the royal supremacy', *Church History*, 68 (1999), 549–80, at p. 549.

20 Where 'toleration' (liberty outside the Church) was granted by royal prerogative, historians tend to use 'indulgence'; contemporaries confused the two, but kept them distinct from 'comprehension' (broadening the Church to include dissenters). See R. Thomas, 'Comprehension and indulgence', in G.F. Nuttall and O. Chadwick (eds), *From uniformity to unity, 1662–1962* (SPCK, 1962), pp. 189–253.

21 On the Cabal debates see: G.S. De Krey, 'The first Restoration crisis: conscience and coercion in London, 1667–73', *Albion*, 25 (1993), 565–80; G.S. De Krey, 'Rethinking the Restoration: dissenting cases for conscience, 1667–1672', *HJ*, 38 (1995), 53–83; J. Rose, 'Royal ecclesiastical supremacy and the Restoration church', *Historical Research*, 80 (2007), 324–45; M. Goldie, 'Toleration and the godly prince in Restoration England', in J. Morrow and J. Scott (eds), *Liberty, authority, formality: political ideas and culture, 1600–1900: essays in honour of Colin Davis* (Exeter: Imprint Academic, 2008), pp. 45–66.

22 On declarations of indulgence the most important literature is: G.R. Abernathy Jr, 'The English Presbyterians and the Stuart Restoration, 1648–1663', *Transactions of the American Philosophical Society*, 55:2 (1965), 5–101; G.R. Abernathy Jr, 'Clarendon and the declaration of indulgence', *JEH*, 11 (1960), 55–73; F. Bate, *The declaration of indulgence, 1672* (Constable, 1908); R.E. Boyer, *English Declarations of Indulgence, 1687 and 1688* (The Hague: Mouton, 1968); J. Spurr, 'The Church of England, comprehension and the toleration act of 1689', *EHR*, 104 (1989), 927–46.

23 Philip Nye, *The lawfulness of the oath of supremacy* (1662); repr. as *The best fence against popery* (1670, 1686).

24 Philip Nye, *The kings authority in dispensing with ecclesiastical laws* (1687) and *A discourse of ecclesiastical lawes and supremacy of the kings of England* (1687). The latter lacks the dedicatory epistle to James II by Nye's son Henry.

25 Nye, *Lawfulness*, chapter 5, pp. 122, 162, 164, 166.

26 Andrew Marvell, 'A short historical essay concerning councils', in *Mr Smirke* (1676), p. 67; [Anthony Ashley Cooper, earl of Shaftesbury?], *A letter from a person of quality* (1675), p. [34] (mispag. 32). For a sixteenth-century example see Edward Foxe, *The true differe[n]s betwen [th]e regall power and the ecclesiasticall power*, trans. Henry Lord Stafford (1548), fols 41r–42r. See M. Goldie, 'Priestcraft and the birth of whiggism', in Phillipson and Skinner (eds), *Political discourse*, pp. 209–31.

27 Francis Fullwood, *Toleration not to be abused* (1672), pp. 14–15, 5. Richard Baxter took up this question in *Sacrilegious desertion of the ministry rebuked* (1672).

28 See his *Discourse of the right of the church in a Christian state* (1649) and *Two discourses* (Cambridge, 1650). Edward Hyde thought his writings 'greatest scandal': Collins, 'Restoration bishops', 576; William Falkner attacked his critique of supremacy: *Christian loyalty* (2nd edn, 1684), pp. 66, 70.

29 Herbert Thorndike, *Theological works*, 6 vols (Oxford, 1844–56), V, 319, 329, 361, 364–5.

30 Herbert Thorndike, *A discourse of the forbearance or the penalties which a due reformation requires* (1670), p. 165.

31 Thorndike, *Discourse of the forbearance*, p. 45 and chapter 21; Herbert Thorndike, *Just weights and measures* (1662), pp. 135, 131–3.

32 Thorndike, *Just weights*, sig. A2v.

33 Anon., *A letter from a clergy-man in the city* (1688), p. 6.

34 Andrew Poulton, *An answer to a letter from a clergyman in the city* (1688), p. 6; anon., *The clergy's late carriage to the king* (1688), p. 2.

35 Henry Care, *An answer to a paper importing a petition* (1688), p. 20. Ordinary: ecclesiastic exercising jurisdiction permanently attached to their office.

36 John Gutch, *Collectanea curiosa*, 2 vols (Oxford, 1781), I.337; *State Trials*, XII, columns 371–97, 427.

37 Gutch, *Collectanea*, I, 365.

38 Gutch, *Collectanea*, I, 368, see also p. 339 and M. Goldie, 'The political thought of the Anglican revolution', in R. Beddard (ed.), *The revolutions of 1688* (Oxford: Clarendon Press, 1991), pp. 102–36.

39 Gutch, *Collectanea*, I, 364, 369.

40 *Ibid.*, I, 363–4.

41 1 Eliz. I c. 1; 16 Car. I c. 11; 13 Chas. II c. 12.

42 Cf. J.P. Kenyon, 'The commission for ecclesiastical causes, 1686–1688: a reconsideration', *HJ*, 34 (1991), 727–36, at p. 735.

43 Henry Care, *A vindication of the proceedings of his majesties ecclesiastical commissioners* (1688), p. 41, see also p. 38.

44 Henry Care, *The legality of the court held by his majesties ecclesiastical commissioners defended* (1688), pp. 23–4, 35; Care, *Vindication*, pp. 3, 75–6; Nathaniel Johnston, *The king's visitatorial power asserted* (1688), p. 11 (qu.).

45 Johnston, *Visitatorial power*, p. 145.

46 *Ibid.*, pp. 146, 148, 155, 104–5, 328; Care, *Legality*, pp. 18, 8–9.

47 For this rhetoric, see J.G.A. Pocock, *The ancient constitution and the feudal law* (Cambridge: Cambridge University Press, 1957; reissued, 1987).

48 Philonomus Anglicus, *A letter to the author of the vindication of the proceedings of the ecclesiastical commissioners* ('Eleutheropolis' [Oxford], 1688), pp. 8, 10–11, 15; Bodl. MS Tanner 460, fol. 26v.

49 Edward Stillingfleet, *A discourse concerning the illegality of the late ecclesiastical commission* (1689), e.g. pp. 11, 18; Robert Washington, *Some observations upon the ecclesiastical jurisdiction of the kings of England with an appendix in answer to a late book intituled, the king's visitatorial power asserted* (1689), p. 8 and *passim*.

50 Washington, *Observations*, p. 20.

51 Philonomus, *Letter*, pp. 3, 12, 16–17; cf. Care, *Legality*, p. 11.

52 Stillingfleet, *Discourse*, pp. 8–9; Washington, *Observations*, p. 101.

53 Stillingfleet, *Discourse*, p. 55; Bodl. MS Tanner 460, fol. 25r.

54 Washington, *Observations*, pp. 285 (qu.), 39, 41, 109, 127, 156–7; Bodl. MS Tanner 460, fol. 26r (qu.).

55 Thomas Tenison, *A discourse concerning the ecclesiastical commission* (1689), p. 1. See Edward Carpenter, *Thomas Tenison* (SPCK, 1948), pp. 98–102.

56 1 G. & M. c. 8.

57 The best work on the non-jurors is M. Goldie, 'The nonjurors, episcopacy, and the origins of the convocation controversy', in E. Cruickshanks (ed.), *Ideology and conspiracy: aspects of Jacobitism, 1689–1759* (Edinburgh: Edinburgh University Press, 1982), pp. 15–35; on the jurors, G.V. Bennett, 'King William III and the episcopate', in G.V. Bennett and J.D. Walsh (eds), *Essays in modern English church history in memory of Norman Sykes* (Adam & Charles Black, 1966), pp. 104–31.

58 None of these men was united: the tone of Dodwell's writings was very different from Kettlewell's.

59 Nathaniel Bisbie, *Unity of priesthood necessary to the unity of communion in a church* (1692), pp. 32–4; Henry Dodwell, *A defence of the vindication of the deprived bishops* (1695, dated by Goldie to 1697), pp. 49–54; Henry Dodwell, *The doctrine of the Church of England, concerning the independency of the clergy on the lay-power* (1697, dated by Goldie to 1696), pp. 54–7; Samuel Hill, *Solomon and Abiathar* (1692), pp. 22–3; Samuel Grascome, *Two letters written to the author of a pamphlet entituled, Solomon and Abiathar* (1692), pp. 36–7; John Kettlewell, *Of Christian communion* (1693), part II, pp. 30–2.

60 John Williams, *A vindication of a discourse concerning the unreasonableness of a new separation* (1691), p. 12 (qu.); Edward Welchman, *A defence of the Church of England* ([1692]), p. 12 (qu.); Edward Stillingfleet, *A vindication of their majesties authority to fill the sees of the deprived bishops* (1691), p. 23; Humphrey Hody, *The case of sees vacant* (1693), pp. 17–24; anon., *Reflexions on ... remarks on the occasional paper* (1698), p. 9; Edward Welchman, *A second defence of the Church of England* (1698), pp. 18–22.

61 Goldie, 'Nonjurors', pp. 21–3.

62 Nathaniel Bisbie, *An answer to a treatise out of ecclesiastical history* (1691), sig. A4r.

63 Bisbie, *Answer to a treatise*, sig. A2v; Welchman, *Second defence*, p. 17.

64 Dodwell, *Defence*, p. 76.

65 Kettlewell, *Christian communion*, part II, pp. 3–4 (qu.); Jeremy Collier, *A brief essay concerning the independency of church power* (1692), p. 3.

66 Dodwell, *Defence*, p. 76.

67 Kettlewell, *Christian communion*, part III, pp. 3–8, esp. p. 6; Dodwell, *Defence*, pp. 94 (qu.), 19.

68 Humphrey Hody, *A letter ... to a friend* (Oxford, 1692), p. 27; Stillingfleet, *Vindication*, p. 16 (qu.); Welchman, *Defence*, p. 10; Williams, *Vindication*, p. 11.

69 Dodwell, *Defence*, pp. 81–2; Thomas Milles, *Remarks upon the occasional paper* (1697), p. 4.

70 BL Add. MS 32523, fols 78r–81r.

71 Stillingfleet, *Vindication*, pp. 20–1 (1st pag.; my emphasis).

72 Welchman, *Defence*, pp. 7–9; compare Hooker, *Laws*, VIII.i.5.

73 Welchman, *Second defence*, pp. 12–13.

74 Dodwell, *Defence*, pp. 82–94; Collier, *Essay*, pp. 5–6.

75 Dodwell, *Defence*, pp. 100–1.

76 Welchman, *Defence*, p. 16.

77 Francis Atterbury, *A letter to a convocation man* (1697), pp. 13, 30; Francis Atterbury, *The rights, powers, and privileges of an English convocation* (2nd edn, 1701), p. 28.

78 On the controversy see Norman Sykes, *William Wake*, 2 vols (Cambridge: Cambridge University Press, 1957), I, chapter 2; Norman Sykes, *From Sheldon to Secker. Aspects of English church history 1660–1768* (Cambridge: Cambridge University Press, 1959), chapter 2; Bennett, *Tory crisis*, chapter 3; G.V. Bennett, *White Kennett, 1660–1728, Bishop of Peterborough. A study in the political and ecclesiastical history of the early eighteenth century* (SPCK, 1957), chapter 2; Carpenter, *Tenison*, chapter 11; Goldie, 'Nonjurors'; M. Greig, 'Heresy hunt: Gilbert Burnet and the convocation controversy of 1701', *HJ*, 37 (1994), 569–92.

79 *Pace* Goldie, 'Nonjurors', p. 17; Spurr, *Restoration Church*, pp. 380–1.

80 M. Goldie, *Roger Morrice and the Puritan Whigs* (Woodbridge: Boydell, 2007), pp. 183–4.

81 Atterbury, *Rights*, chapter 2 and pp. 226–37.

82 Atterbury, *Letter*, p. 29; Atterbury, *Rights*, pp. 49–58, chapter 7.

83 William Wake, *The state of the Church and clergy of England* (1703), chapters 1–2. *Praemunientes*: clause in parliamentary writs summoning bishops ordering them to bring representatives of the lesser clergy.

84 Wake, *State of the Church*, p. 12.

85 William Wake, *The authority of Christian princes over their ecclesiastical synods* (1697), pp. 140–1, 229; see also his description of the Act of Submission as 'but one *Alteration* added to many that had gone before': Wake, *State of the Church*, p. 122.

86 Atterbury, *Letter*, pp. 40–1; Atterbury, *Rights*, p. 76 (qu.), chapter 8.

87 25 Hen. VIII c. 19. In ure: into use.

88 Atterbury, *Letter*, pp. 55–6; Atterbury, *Rights*, chapter 3, esp. pp. 99, 100, 103–5, 114.

89 Wake, *State of the Church*, chapter 10, esp. pp. 536–64; see similarly William Wright, *A letter to a member of parliament* (1697), pp. 34–43.

90 Wake, *State of the Church*, pp. 552, 539.

91 William Wake, *An appeal to all the true members of the Church of England, in behalf of the king's ecclesiastical supremacy* (1698), pp. xxii–xxiii; Wake, *State of the Church*, p. xii; Wright, *Letter*, pp. 20–4. See also anon., *Some observations on a late book, call'd Municipium Ecclesiasticum* (1699), p. 29. On Erastianism: Atterbury, *Rights*, p. 174; Samuel Hill, *Municipium Ecclesiasticum* (1697), p. 5.

92 Wake, *Authority of Christian princes*, pp. v, 95–8.

93 *Ibid.*, p. 66; anon., *Observations*, p. 21; Atterbury, *Rights*, pp. 175, 211–12.

94 Atterbury, *Rights*, pp. 213–15.

95 HMC, *Portland*, IV, 127; Wright, *Letter*, p. 18; anon., *Observations*, pp. 34–5.

96 Hill, *Municipium Ecclesiasticum*, pp. 136, 165–6.

97 *Ibid.*, chapters 4–7, esp. pp. 3, 44–5, 95, 22, 118–19; Samuel Hill, *The rites of the Christian Church* (1698), p. 27.

98 Humphrey Hody, *Some thoughts on a convocation and the notion of its divine right* (1699), p. 33.

99 John Spademan, *Deborah's triumph over the mighty* (1706), p. 3; John Sharp, *A sermon preach'd at the coronation of Queen Anne* (1702), on Isaiah 49: 23.

100 G. Bray (ed.), *Records of convocation, vol. IX, 1701–8* (Woodbridge: Boydell, 2006), p. 365.

101 Bray, *Convocation, vol. IX*, pp. 377, 379, 382–3; see also HMC, *Portland*, IV, 399–400.

102 G.V. Bennett, 'Robert Harley, the Godolphin ministry, and the bishoprics crisis of 1707', *EHR*, 82 (1967), 726–46, qu. p. 731; Edward Gregg, *Queen Anne* (Routledge & Kegan Paul, 1980), chapter 9.

103 Charles Leslie, *The case of the regale and of the pontificat* (2nd edn, 1702), pp. xxi–xxii, xxxi, 21, 25.

104 [Edward Welchman], *The regal supremacy in ecclesiastical affairs asserted* (1701), pp. 39–51 (qu. 45), 58. Cambridge University Library's copy of this (shelfmark Bb*.10.48) is annotated as being by 'Edward Welshman', the approving reference at p. 28 to Welchman's *Second defence* suggests this is a mistake for Welchman. Leslie, *Regale*, pp. 41–58; supplement (in response to Welchman) pp. 60, 39 (qu.).

105 Leslie, *Regale*, pp. 31–9, 64, supplement pp. 29–30, 2–4, 15–12 (irreg. pag.); cf. Welchman, *Regal supremacy*, p. 26.

106 Leslie, *Regale*, pp. vii–xvi, 13–14.

107 Leslie, *Regale*, pp. xix, 74 (2nd pag.), 103–4 (qu.), 161.

108 Welchman, *Regal supremacy*, pp. 89–93; Leslie, *Regale*, pp. 228, 65–6.

109 Welchman, *Regal supremacy*, sig. [A5]v; Leslie, *Regale*, supplement, p. 2.

110 Leslie, *Regale*, pp. 147, xxiii.

111 Matthew Tindal, *The rights of the Christian Church* (1706), pp. 226–7, liv–lv (qu.); like Shaftesbury, he argued that divine right monarchy was a bargain for clerical independence: p. 59.

112 *Ibid.*, pp. lxxv, 145–7.

113 *Ibid.*, pp. 203–4, 210–11, iv (qu.); p. 196 quotes Marvell's 'Essay concerning councils'.

114 Tindal, *Rights*, p. 367.

115 *Ibid.*, pp. lxxix–lxxxi.

116 *Ibid.*, pp. xvii (qu.), xxvi, xxix–xxxi, viii–xi.

117 *Ibid.*, pp. 387, 236–7, 356–7, 362–3, 23–4, xxx; see John Locke, *A letter concerning toleration*, trans. William Popple (1689), p. 51. Tindal defended Lockean toleration in *An essay concerning the power of the magistrate and the rights of mankind in matters of religion* (1697).

118 Tindal, *Rights*, chapter 1, pp. 38–9, 45, 107 (qu.), v (qu.), 44, 35. The second canon of 1604 excommunicated those denying supremacy.

119 On Sacheverell, see Grant Tapsell's chapter in this volume, along with G.S. Holmes, *The trial of Doctor Sacheverell* (Methuen, 1973); M. Goldie, 'Tory political thought, 1689–1714' (PhD dissertation, University of Cambridge, 1978), chapter 13.

120 *The tryal of Dr Henry Sacheverell* (1710), pp. 4, 89–90, 206.

121 *Ibid.*, pp. 121, 305, see also p. 313.

122 *Ibid.*, pp. 23, 25; citing the Act for the exoneration of exactions paid to the see of Rome (25 Hen. VIII c. 21); the defence merely replied that Henry would not have endorsed resistance theory: *ibid.*, p. 140.

Chapter 2

From Laudians to Latitudinarians:
a shifting balance of theological forces

Nicholas Tyacke

Ever since its emergence in the course of the sixteenth century, the Church of England has represented a coalition of more or less disparate interests. Heterogeneity indeed is arguably of the 'Anglican' essence. Over time these diverse elements have undergone change and, in the process, acquired a variety of labels. The different groups involved have also tended to vie with one another for dominance. Certainly that was the experience in the first half of the seventeenth century, with the rise of the Laudians and their characteristic Arminian theology – at the expense of Calvinism.[1] Closely identified with the cause of Charles I, the Laudians had gone down with him in defeat during the English Civil War, and there followed the destruction of bishops and prayer-book at the hands of the victorious Puritans. Theologically speaking, the beneficiaries of this catastrophe were the Calvinists, who remained in the ascendant until the restoration of the monarchy in 1660. As regards the subsequent fate of the established church, too much had happened in the interim for it to be possible simply to turn back the clock, not least because Puritan nonconformity had now become much more entrenched. By the end of 1662 bishops and a revised prayer-book were once more in place, while some two thousand Puritan clergy had been driven out – taking many of their followers with them. Meanwhile the doctrinal standard of the English church again became the Elizabethan Thirty-nine Articles, the ambiguous phrasing of which had in the past allowed Calvinists and Arminians to draw rival conclusions concerning the theology of grace.[2]

The exodus of Puritan clergy, who with few exceptions were committed Calvinists, in the early 1660s undoubtedly strengthened the hand of the Laudian faction. The latter had also held together rather more successfully than their episcopal rivals, in the Interregnum period, because of a marked unwillingness to compromise. In addition they proved themselves highly adept at propaganda. One feature of this was the rehabilitation of Archbishop

Laud, who had been executed for treason in 1645, a process well under way by the time of the Restoration. Thus, for example, Laud features as the hero of William Dugdale's *History of St Paul's* (1658), his wealthy nephew John Robinson paying for four of the engraved plates and the archbishop being described as the 'pre-eminent restorer' of the cathedral. The hagiographical life of Laud by Peter Heylyn was to be dedicated to Robinson in 1668.[3] Prior to this, in the year 1660 itself, there appeared Heylyn's *Historia quinqu-articularis: or a declaration of the judgement of the Western Churches, and more particularly of the Church of England, in the five controverted points, reproched in these last times by the name of Arminianism.* By his own account the author had been set to work on this task by 'some very able and discerning men'. In the event, the only direct challenge to this 'historicall narration' was to come in 1673 from Henry Hickman, an ejected minister. De facto, therefore, Heylyn filled the role on this issue of spokesman for the establishment. Like his other works published around this time, the *Historia quinqu-articularis* argues that the Church of England was 'Arminian' in doctrine from its foundation, albeit temporarily subverted by Calvinists, and as such in accord with orthodox Christian teaching. According to this view 'predestination to life', or election, has reference to believers who 'lay hold' on Christ, as opposed to being a matter of God's arbitrary decree. Its converse, reprobation, describes the fate of those who reject the offer of salvation. A crucial element of free choice, therefore, is involved, something which the Calvinists deny.[4]

The highly polemical nature of Heylyn's *Historia quinqu-articularis* is, however, evident from the opening sentence, which charges Calvinists with 'blasphemy'. 'Of all the heresies which exercised the Church in the times foregoing, there never was any more destructive of humane society, more contrary to the rule of faith and manners, or more repugnant to the divine justice and goodness of Almighty God, then that which makes God to be the author of sin.' This same damning allegation had been made by Catholics against the teachings of Luther and Calvin from the early days of the Reformation, meeting then as now with vigorous denials, by those so accused, that this was a logical consequence of the doctrine of absolute or unconditional reprobation.[5] But because Heylyn failed to gain promotion in the Restoration church, dying in May 1662, his views have sometimes been portrayed as untypical of the new clerical leadership. Nevertheless, the fact remains that all three archbishops of Canterbury between 1660 and 1691 were men in the Laudian mould. William Juxon had shadowed Laud ever since their days together at Oxford, succeeding him as president of St John's College, then as bishop of London, and finally as archbishop of Canterbury. During the 1630s especially, Juxon and Laud had worked closely together as a team. Gilbert Sheldon, who was appointed to Canterbury on the death of Juxon in 1663, personally licensed for publication a volume of Laud's private devotions and recruited William Sancroft to oversee the editing of further writings by the late archbishop. Sancroft, who in turn succeeded Sheldon at Canterbury in 1677, was himself a devotee of the ultra-Laudian John Cosin.[6]

Until recently the role of Sheldon in the promotion of Arminianism has largely gone unremarked. Yet, as a literary executor of the leading English Arminian theologian Thomas Jackson, he made available for publication manuscripts which earlier had proved too hot to handle for Laud. These were first published in the 1650s and again in 1673, latterly as part of a grand, three-volume collected edition of Jackson's works – the entire set dedicated to Sheldon by the editor Barnabas Oley. Jackson argued at length that election and reprobation are a consequence of how individuals lead their lives.[7] Arguably even more striking, however, is the involvement of Sheldon in the publication of two highly controversial books by George Bull – also during the 1670s. Thus in his *Harmonia apostolica* of 1670 Bull launched an attack on the traditional Protestant teaching of justification by faith alone, claiming on the basis of the epistle of James in the New Testament that works had a role to play. Defending himself, in a further book of 1676, Bull made explicit here the connection between justification and predestination, in that both were conditional on behaviour. Each of these works of Bull included an *imprimatur*, i.e. license to print, granted by chaplains of Sheldon from Lambeth Palace.[8]

Yet at least as important as what was actually published is the role played by university teaching, particularly since religious censorship of the press was now largely inoperative. In the 1650s Calvinism passed for orthodoxy at both Oxford and Cambridge, as it had up to the 1620s. Nevertheless there were some long-standing religious differences between the two seats of learning, Cambridge tending to be more polarised between extremes than Oxford – with the former producing under Elizabeth the Presbyterian Thomas Cartwright as well as the Arminian *avant la lettre* Peter Baro. Even during the chancellorship of Archbishop Laud in the 1630s a greater degree of outward consensus prevailed at Oxford than it did at Cambridge, where rival groups openly battled for supremacy. This helps to explain why in Restoration Cambridge Arminianism largely swept the board in the course of the long incumbency of Joseph Beaumont as regius professor of divinity, while at Oxford there was something of a stalemate between the Calvinist Thomas Barlow and the Arminian Richard Allestree, divinity professors both, and this despite their very different theological views. Moreover Cambridge continued to provide a livelier theological environment than Oxford, proving among other things more receptive to the scientific ideas of Isaac Newton.[9]

Beaumont had been a Cambridge protégée of Matthew Wren and John Cosin at Peterhouse during the 1630s. Subsequently driven out, he returned in the early 1660s first as master of Jesus and then of Peterhouse. In 1674 he also became regius professor. His predecessor in the chair Peter Gunning had already inaugurated an Arminian tradition at Cambridge, whereby the Calvinist theology of grace in its various aspects was regularly refuted. Although the evidence for Gunning is fragmentary, many of the lectures Beaumont gave and the divinity theses which he moderated survive in manuscript. Collectively, these reveal a remarkable picture and one without precedent. Even during the heady 1630s such blatant partisanship would have been regarded in the main as unacceptably provocative. Absolute predestination and the concomitant doctrine of guaranteed perseverance were now repeatedly denied, while the traditional Pauline proof texts were interpreted in an anti-Calvinist sense. As well as endorsing this stance in his capacity of regius professor, Beaumont introduced the same themes into his sermons, attacking, for example, the 'new reprobating doctors' who 'sett limits' to salvation . On the contrary, 'Christ declares that he excludes none who will beleve, and whosoever hath a true lively faith, working by love and crowned by perseverance, hath the condicion he requires and thereupon may be assured of his salvacion'. Indeed by the 1690s overt Calvinist opposition in Cambridge would seem to have been reduced to the lone voice of John Edwards, a former college fellow living in semi-retirement.[10]

During these same decades, however, from the Restoration onwards, Beaumont and his allies were becoming increasingly aware of a very different and growing religious challenge in the form of what contemporaries called Latitudinarianism, a movement perhaps best understood as the liberal theology of its day.[11] Beaumont himself had delivered an early warning in 1665 against 'the Latitudinarians' and their propensity to interpret creedal statements 'figuratively' instead of 'properly', but by 1675 the situation appeared considerably more threatening. In September of the latter year, a Peterhouse colleague of Beaumont, John Standish, devoted part of a court sermon preached in the presence of Charles II to sounding the alarm more generally as regards certain 'false apostles and deceitful workers' – comprising an enemy within 'that would supplant Christian religion with natural theologie and turn the grace of God into a wanton notion of morality'. They make 'reason, reason, reason their only trinity and sole standard, whereby to measure both the principles and conclusions of faith'. But this is 'at best beginning at the wrong end and making superstructures without a foundation, for the Jew cannot be saved by the law of Moses, much less the Gentile by all the works of the law of nature'. Judging by his choice of phraseology, Standish seems to have been alluding in particular to a recently published book from the pen of the late Bishop John Wilkins entitled *Of the principles and duties of natural religion*. He was also probably emboldened to speak out by the political eclipse at this time of Wilkins's former patron the Duke of Buckingham and the concomitant rise to power of the Earl of Danby.[12]

'A mighty rising man, as being a Latitudinarian', and 'Buckingham his great friend', was how Samuel Pepys described Wilkins in 1669, the year after his elevation to the bishopric of Chester. During the late 1660s Wilkins had been closely involved in negotiations with Protestant dissenters, as Puritan nonconformists were now rechristened, aimed at measures of both comprehension and indulgence – i.e. expanding the boundaries of the 1662 religious settlement, on the one hand, and extending toleration, on the other, to those who nevertheless still felt unable to conform. Not only did this render him religiously suspect with many of his episcopal colleagues but also, as the brother-in-law of Oliver Cromwell, his political loyalties remained open to question.[13] With the death of Wilkins in 1672 it fell to his son-in-law John Tillotson to prepare the manuscript of his *Natural religion* for publication, only the first part of the book having been left in a finished state. The aim of the author, as summarised by the editor, was threefold: (i) 'to establish the great principles of religion, the being of God and a future state, by shewing how firm and solid a foundation they have in the nature and reason of mankind', (ii) 'to convince men of the natural and indispensable obligation of moral duties', and (iii) 'to perswade men to the practice of religion and the vertues of a good life', as conducing to their 'happiness and prosperity' in 'this present life' and to a 'future blessedness in another world'. By thus appealing to the inherent religious capacity of humans, Wilkins was concerned to counter both Calvinism and infidelity. Only in his very last chapter, however, did Christianity feature as such, its 'excellency' and 'the advantages of it ... above the meer light of nature' being spelt out; for mankind is indeed now sunk into a 'dark and degenerate state'. Yet even here the possibility was raised that heathens could be saved by observing the 'law of nature'.[14]

Some idea of how startling Wilkins's *Natural religion* is likely to have seemed to some readers can be illustrated by comparing it with a similarly titled book published the previous year – *Natural theology*, by the dissenting minister Matthew Barker. In the course of his own exposition, while treating of 'the principles that are owned by the light of nature', Barker repeatedly underscores the supremacy of scriptural revelation and includes a long section on the 'deficiency of natural theology'. The 'blind heathen', deprived of 'scripture-light', live 'under the dominion of nature's moonlight and are but in the night, feeling after God as men in the dark'.[15] Presumably it was the failure of Wilkins and his editor, Tillotson, sufficiently to police natural religion or theology in this way that made their joint effort a particular target. But another author of whom Standish may also have been thinking, apropos the elevation of reason in matters of religion to what he deemed unacceptable heights, was Joseph Glanvill, especially a visitation sermon by him first published in 1670 as *Logou threskeia: or a seasonable recommendation and defence of reason in the affairs of religion; against infidelity, scepticism and fanaticisms of all sorts*. The multiple meanings of the term *logos* provided Glanvill with his theme. 'Reason is, in a sense, the word of God ... whereby he hath spoken to all mankind.' It is the 'candle of the lord' and 'that light whereby Christ hath enlightened every one that cometh into the world'. Glanvill went on to argue that 'when any thing is offered us for an article of faith that seems to contradict reason we ought to see that there be good cause to believe that this is divinely revealed and in the sense propounded', because 'if the contradiction be real this can be no article of revelation'.[16]

One contemporary in little doubt concerning the identity of those styled 'false apostles' by Standish was Simon Patrick. In an anonymous reply of 1676 Patrick challenged him to supply names, at the same time suggesting that the sermon was aimed at certain clerical 'brethren' based in London. 'Why', he asked Standish, 'do you scorn reason so much?' But the fact that the sermon, according to the title page, was 'published by his majestie's command' would indicate that the author had friends in high places. Moreover another fellow of Peterhouse, Miles Barne, preaching at court the month after Standish, in October 1675, had similarly warned against undermining revelation by the employment of 'humane reason' and of 'atheism creeping in by insensible degrees, from indulging too great a latitude in matters of religion'. He had also ventured to criticise 'the several projects of comprehension [and] toleration'.[17]

Granted that Standish and Barne were minor figures, this was not the case as regards Benjamin Laney, successively bishop of Lincoln and of Ely, whose 'last' court sermon was licensed posthumously for the press, in May 1675, by a chaplain of Archbishop Sheldon. Laney had been master of Pembroke College, Cambridge, during the 1630s, and was a prominent member of the Laudian old guard. As early as 1665 he can be found preaching at court against the 'man of moderate opinions', described as a hybrid who is 'part church-man and part schismatick', and 'our new philosophical divines' who advocate 'liberty of conscience' because 'without a free market they cannot vent their ... bold speculations'. His last sermon has the running title 'Of comprehension' and it largely consists of an attack on this policy, which he links with the principle of 'latitude'. Thus 'our Christians of the latitude ... believe in Christ without a creed, they obey him without doing his will; they worship him no man knows how, but every man as he likes'. Moreover 'what shall we think of a religion that in design is made up of all sects and divisions?' This so-called 'comprehensive church' is 'a drag-net that will fetch in all kinds of fish, good or bad, great or small'. Yet 'how shall the church be drawn out to such a bredth and latitude?' Laney claimed that in reality a Puritan plot was involved. 'It is not toleration but mastery they aim at.'[18]

Laney died in 1674 and the remainder of the reign of Charles II was marked by renewed persecution of Protestant dissenters, save for a brief respite around the time of the parliamentary agitation to exclude the Catholic James, duke of York, from the succession. Nevertheless the advocates of comprehension did not abandon hope, the mantle of Bishop Wilkins now being inherited by John Tillotson – dean of Canterbury since 1672. Not only did Tillotson continue to discuss proposals along such lines with leading dissenters but he also gave concrete expression to their shared ideals. Thus, in the mid 1670s he and a group of fellow churchmen including Edward Fowler, Simon Patrick, Edward Stillingfleet, and Benjamin Whichcote joined with the dissenters William Bates, Richard Baxter, and Thomas Gouge, among others, in forming the Welsh Trust, a body dedicated to the evangelisation of Wales. Gouge was the guiding light in this enterprise, the Puritan ancestry of which stretched back via the Interregnum committee for the propagation of the gospel in Wales to the Elizabethan John Penry.[19] Preaching in December 1678, Tillotson also dared to express the hope that 'the governours of our church ... would be content ... not to insist upon little things, but yield them up ... to those who differ from us'. When Gouge died in November 1681, Tillotson preached the funeral sermon at St Anne's Blackfriars, describing him as 'our deceased brother' and 'friend'. Rehearsing the charitable activities of this 'pattern of well-doing' and touching lightly on his nonconformity, he concluded with the words of Christ: 'well done [thou] good and faithful servant'.[20]

The parish of St Anne's Blackfriars had a long Puritan tradition dating from the sixteenth century, represented by Stephen Egerton and William Gouge (father of Thomas) the latter ministering there for forty-six years. Moreover, religious divisions continued to run deep, the parish in 1663 said to be split three ways, between 'covenanters', 'Church of England' and 'moderate' men. Moderate was in fact the term that Latitudinarians preferred to use of themselves, and it would seem to bear this meaning in the Blackfriars context, since the incumbent at the time was Benjamin Whichcote, himself a seminal influence on the movement. As well as his sermon preached at the funeral of Thomas Gouge, in 1682 Tillotson published a collection of sermons by the late Bishop Wilkins, declaring in the preface that 'I am still of the old opinion that moderation is a virtue', and this despite its now being 'declaimed against with so much zeal'. Moderation is the requisite 'temper' if 'ever we seriously intend the firm establishment' of the English church.[21]

The following year Thomas Tenison, currently rector of St Martin-in-the-Fields, can be found arguing along similar lines to Tillotson as regards comprehension. Existing liturgical arrangements are 'capable of improvement by the change of obsolete words, phrases and customs, by the addition of forms upon new occasions', and 'by adjusting discreetly some circumstantials of external order'. On the other hand, Miles Barne of Peterhouse, in the dedication of a sermon preached at the Hertfordshire assizes in July 1684, was happy to accept the 'abusive' allegations of both 'intemperate zeal' and 'popery' as levelled by the 'men of moderation'. Hence he acknowledged his 'constant, hearty, and unreserved affection for the king and government', and 'steadfast unfeigned adhesion to the Church of England in all her height and under the greatest discouragements'. In the body of the sermon Barne also claimed that, had the comprehension Bill, as introduced into the parliaments of 1680 and 1681, reached the statute book it 'would certainly have failed', for 'our scrupulous brethren would not have rested content even after resigning [the] cross in baptism, kneeling at communion, surplice etc.'.[22]

Barne's thinking at this date clearly chimed much more closely with official policy than did that of Tillotson and Tenison. Thus Bishop Francis Turner of Ely, preaching before Charles II in November 1684, identified with the cause of Archbishop Laud against those who claimed that the late primate 'liv'd and dy'd in the design of introducing popery', and 'that the governing part of the present clergy have made what advances they could, treading in his footsteps', and were now 'marching ... fast to Rome'. These false accusers, he said, were also the same sort of people who condoned the execution of Charles I, and backed the perpetrators of the recent Rye House Plot in their attempt to murder the king and his brother. In other court sermons Bishop Turner also spoke of an alleged plan by the plotters to 'introduce a chaos or deform'd mass of all religions' in the name of Protestantism, while castigating dissenters more generally for setting up 'fanatic schools' and 'country academies' in order 'to breed up their children so as to make them rebels'. Turner, it has been suggested, was at this juncture being groomed as the likely successor of Archbishop Sancroft at Canterbury.[23]

Charles II died in February 1685 and during the first two years or so of his successor, James II, persecution continued much as before. This period saw the trial of Richard Baxter at the hands of Judge Jefferies, for what the prosecution claimed was seditious libel contained in his *Paraphrase on the New Testament*. Witnesses for the defence included two future bishops, John Moore and John Sharp, although they were not permitted to speak.[24] From the 1660s onwards Baxter had participated with first Wilkins and then Tillotson in a series of discussions concerning comprehension, but now, with what a contemporary dubbed 'Laudean principles' (*sic*) so much in the ascendant, the future looked bleak indeed for any such aspirations.[25] What, however, transformed the situation was the attempt by King James to improve the position of his fellow Roman Catholics. Having failed to persuade parliament to repeal the penal laws in 1685, he resorted instead to achieving the same ends by means of the royal prerogative. Faced with this novel challenge to their hegemony, Protestant collaboration against the common enemy now increasingly recommended itself to the leaders of the established church. An initial product of this altered outlook was a growing body of anti-Catholic literature, the authors being drawn from across the Church of England spectrum. As a means of broadening the basis of support for his Catholicising policies

James also sought to entice Protestant dissenters with the offer of toleration. Responding to this threat, Sancroft was prevailed upon to promise them a new deal vis-à-vis the Church of England, although it remains a moot point what this undertaking actually involved and how sincere were the intentions of the archbishop and others of the same ecclesiological stripe.[26]

These religious negotiations were, of course, part of a deepening political crisis which culminated with the invasion of William of Orange and the ensuing flight of James II in 1688. In the event, Archbishop Sancroft, along with a number of fellow bishops and lesser clergy, felt unable to swear allegiance to the successor regime. While the fate of these non-jurors was still unresolved, the desire of the new rulers to accommodate dissenters resulted in two government bills being introduced into parliament, one for comprehension and the other for toleration. Only the latter became law, the former being referred instead to consideration by the clergy in convocation. In advance of this, however, an ecclesiastical commission was set up in order to draft proposals for comprehension. The members appear to have been carefully chosen with an eye to providing a cross-section of views, although many of the 'High Churchmen', as the more intransigent clergy were coming to be known, effectively boycotted the proceedings. Conversely a Latitudinarian 'pressure group' has been identified, among its members Patrick, Stilling-fleet, Tenison, and Tillotson, which proceeded to undertake a major review of the existing Prayer Book. A very important role was also played by Gilbert Burnet, who had served as a chaplain to William and Mary in the Netherlands and was currently advising them on religious affairs. But what killed the comprehension scheme was a rebellion in the lower house of convocation in November 1689, when Tillotson was defeated in the election for prolocutor or chairman. His successful rival was William Jane, the Oxford regius professor of divinity, who was resolutely opposed to any concessions to dissenters and had already crossed swords in print with Tenison over the proceedings of the commission.[27]

Toleration of Protestant dissenters was now, however, on the statute book and the non-juring impasse was resolved by depriving the clergy concerned. Six bishops, including Sancroft, lost their posts as a result, and a further eleven deaths brought the total number of episcopal vacancies during the years 1689–92 to seventeen.[28] While it would be an exaggeration to describe all the new bishops as Latitudinarian, a definite bias in this direction is none the less detectable. Among the influences at work here was that of Burnet, a Scottish Presbyterian by origin but who had moved in Latitudinarian circles since the 1660s and in his memoirs was to provide an illuminating account of the origins and development of the movement. Born in the Cambridge of the 1650s, its exponents, according to Burnet, had 'declared against superstition on the one hand and enthusiasm on the other' – coded references for

Laudianism and Puritanism respectively. 'They loved the constitution of the church, and the liturgy, and could well live under them; but they did not think it unlawful to live under another form.' At the Restoration 'they wished things might have been carried with more moderation; and they continued to keep a good correspondence with those who differed from them in opinion, and allowed a great freedom both in philosophy and divinity: from whence they were called men of latitude. And upon this men of narrower thoughts and fiercer tempers fastened upon them the name of Latitudinarians.'[29]

Of the seventeen new bishops consecrated between 1689 and 1692 eleven have some claim to be regarded as Latitudinarians. Eight of them have already been encountered, namely Burnet, Fowler, Moore, Patrick, Sharp, Stillingfleet, Tenison, and Tillotson. Of the remaining three, Richard Cumberland was a philosopher closely identified with natural theology, while Robert Grove had emerged by 1688 as an enthusiast for comprehension, and Richard Kidder, who his predecessor as bishop of Bath and Wells described as a 'Latitudinarian traditour', was an admirer of the Dutch Arminian Philip van Limborch as well as being an active member of the 1689 liturgical reform commission.[30] Even more to the point, however, churchmen of this type had been notable for their absence from the episcopal bench in 1688, the only two possible candidates at that date being Herbert Croft of Hereford and William Lloyd of St Asaph.[31] The religious change thereafter in the composition of the episcopal bench goes far to explain the clashes between the lower and upper houses of convocation which came especially to mark the reign of Queen Anne.[32]

Exemplifying this shift in the balance of theological forces is the replacement of Sancroft by Tillotson as archbishop of Canterbury in 1691. Like other Latitudinarians, Tillotson remained committed to countering, partly by philosophical means, what he regarded as the pernicious influence of Thomas Hobbes – the apostle of infidelity. Preaching at court in March 1689 on the theme of loving your enemies, he maintained that 'so far is it from being true which Mr Hobbs asserts as the fundamental principle of his politicks that men are naturally in a state of war and enmity with one another, that the contrary principle, laid down by a much deeper and wiser man, I mean Aristotle, is most certainly true, that men are naturally akin and friendly to each other'. He similarly cited Cicero to the effect that 'the two great foundations of love are relation and likeness'. In another court sermon of the following month, Tillotson had also turned his attention to what he deemed the misplaced zeal of heresy hunters and their obsession with 'little speculative opinions in religion, which they always call fundamental articles of faith'. But 'God will sooner forgive a man a hundred defects of his understanding than one fault in his will', for 'the greatest heresy in the world is a wicked life'. Putting such preaching into practice Tillotson had collaborated with the philanthropist and anti-Trinitarian Thomas Firmin, notably as regards the Welsh Trust.[33]

Hence it is not so very surprising that Tillotson, in 1692, accepted the dedication by van Limborch of his *Historia Inquisitionis*. This book comprised an edition of the early fourteenth-century proceedings of the Toulouse Inquisition against the Albigensians, with a long historical introduction. John Locke had acted as the intermediary between the two men and, in presenting his labours to the archbishop van Limborch, described the work as a record of 'papal tyranny' in action. 'It is not lawful for any men to give a law to consciences, or prescribe the rules of believing, because this is in reality to ascend the tribunal of Christ himself.' The only legitimate weapons in doctrinal disputes are 'the force of reason and the plain testimony of scripture'. Van Limborch went on in his history to ascribe the origins of persecution by Christians to the reign of the Emperor Constantine, a development, he claimed, which completely subverted the teachings of Jesus. The 'nature of Christ's kingdom' is quite distinct from the 'kingdoms of this world'. Compulsion has no place in the former because it 'is opposite to the genius of Christianity to persecute the erroneous'. Archbishop Tillotson, with his 'charity and benevolence to all', is held up as an exemplar of this ideal.[34]

Bishops Burnet and Kidder, along with Tillotson, were sent presentation copies of the *Historia Inquisitionis*, but just how unconventional were the views of van Limborch on the subject of persecution is evident from the furore caused a quarter of a century later, in 1717, when Benjamin Hoadly advanced essentially the same case in a sermon which served to launch the Bangorian controversy.[35] Nevertheless during the 1690s High Churchmen tended to direct their fire at another work by van Limborch – his *Theologia Christiana*, first published in 1686. Both this book and its author came under attack in *A preservative against Socinianism*, by Jonathan Edwards, principal of Jesus College Oxford. Published at Oxford, the first two parts each bear an *imprimatur* by Henry Aldrich, dean of Christ Church and vice-chancellor, who, along with William Jane, had helped to sink the cause of comprehension in the convocation of 1689. The index of *A preservative* lists 'Limborch Heterodox', while in the text Edwards describes the *Theologia Christiana* as 'one of the corruptest systems of divinity that hath bin published of late years' and laments that the book is 'put into the hands of many young students ... by whom it is perused with approbation and applause'. Van Limborch was allegedly unsound on the doctrine of the Trinity and generally ascribed far too much to the powers of reason, as opposed to revelation, in matters of religion.[36]

A very different publishing enterprise, however, with which Tillotson was also associated, to the extent that his *imprimatur* appears on the title page, is the first volume of the collected works of Archbishop Laud. As already noted, this venture had had the enthusiastic backing of archbishops Sheldon and Sancroft, and it finally came to fruition thanks to Henry Wharton – a chaplain of the latter. The public involvement of Tillotson, by contrast, probably reflects a desire on his part to prevent Laud's oeuvre becoming a focus for disaffected churchmen. Published in 1695, this first volume mainly comprised an autobiographical account by Laud of his 'Troubles and tryal' at the hands of the Long Parliament, which was designed to rebut the charge that he had sought to 'introduce popery and arbitrary government'. On the assumption that Laud was indeed innocent of this alleged design, he might justifiably be deemed a 'blessed martyr', the term used by Wharton on the title page of the volume and in his preface. But it seems unlikely that Tillotson also gave his seal of approval to the frontispiece, which portrays Laud with a martyr's crown and is captioned *'qui pro Christi Ecclesia martyrium passus est'*. Suffering for English church and king was one thing, for Christianity quite another. Sensitivity over this issue may explain why the second volume of the works of Laud, published in 1700, omits any reference to him as a martyr. By this time both Tillotson and Wharton were dead. Yet, indicative of a continuing wish to damp down the fires of faction was the decision by Tenison, who had succeeded Tillotson as archbishop of Canterbury, to attend the Westminster Abbey funeral of Wharton in 1695.[37]

Laud nevertheless remained a divisive figure, and not only in the eyes of dissenters, Bishop Burnet, for example, commenting adversely on the posthumously published 'Troubles and tryal' that 'his defence of himself ... is a very mean performance'. Burnet was especially critical both of the reluctance of Laud to take responsibility for his actions and of his unapologetic tone. Thus 'he does not, in any one part of that great work, acknowledge his own errors'. At the same time Burnet claimed that the execution of Laud had had the paradoxical result of 'setting him up as a pattern, and the establishing all his notions as standards by which judgements are to be made of men, whether they are true to the church or not'.[38]

On the face of it, less contentious were the lectures founded in 1692 under the terms of the will of Robert Boyle 'for proving the Christian religion against notorious infidels, *viz.* atheists, theists, pagans, Jews, and Mahometans'. Boyle had gone on to specify that the lecturers on his foundation should not handle 'any controversies that are among Christians themselves'. The names of the four original trustees, however, can hardly have reassured High Churchmen. The sole cleric was Tenison, who had been appointed archdeacon of London in 1689. Of the three laymen, John Evelyn was in turn a great admirer of Tenison, characterising him as 'absolutely one of the most profitable preachers in the Church of England'. Back in 1668, Evelyn had also described the newly consecrated Bishop Wilkins as 'this incomparable man' and 'most universaly beloved of all that knew him'. The other two laymen, Sir Henry Ashurst, a London merchant, and Sir John Rotherham, a lawyer, were both of them Presbyterian sympathisers and closely associated with Richard Baxter.[39] Moreover, by the 1730s the Boyle lectures had acquired the collective designation as *A defence of natural and revealed religion.* Tenison, in the event, outlived his three fellow trustees, only replacing them shortly before his own death in 1715. The new team comprised Richard Boyle, earl of Burlington, representing the founder's family, and four clergy: Samuel Bradford, Edmund Gibson, White Kennett, and Charles Trimnell, all of them on the Latitudinarian wing. Trimnell was already a bishop and the other three were to join him on the episcopal bench soon after the accession of George I.[40]

Of the seventeen Boyle lecturers appointed between 1692 and 1714, only three were obviously of High Church persuasion: Francis Gastrell (1697), Offspring Blackall (1700), and George Stanhope (1701–2). Two of the others, Samuel Clarke (1704–5) and William Whiston (1707), were subsequently to wreck their careers over the doctrine of the Trinity.[41] Although such latent religious tensions were successfully contained by the Boyle trustees, they famously erupted in both convocation and parliament at the turn of the century. After the impasse over comprehension in 1689 convocation had remained in abeyance until 1701. By then, however, the resurgent Tories had exacted as part of their price for supporting the government an agreement that convocation should again be allowed to function. This was also against the background of a fierce pamphlet controversy launched by Francis Atterbury, in his *Letter to a convocation man* of 1697. The claims advanced by Atterbury and his allies, as regards the powers of convocation, were indeed so far reaching as to smack of desperation. Analogies were drawn with parliament, and the lower house of convocation was likened to the Commons – the specific issue being the right of the clergy to conduct their own business independently of either crown or bishops. At the same time, readers of Atterbury could have been left in little doubt as to the probable consequences of proceeding along this path. The 'Catholick faith' of the Church of England was threatened, so he claimed in 1697, by a welter of 'Deists, Socinians, Latitudinarians, deniers of mysteries and pretended explainers of them'.[42]

Thus, when convocation met in 1701, heresy proved high on the agenda of the lower house and one of the publications it proceeded against was *An exposition of the Thirty-nine Articles of the Church of England* (1699) by Bishop Burnet. According to the 'representation' made by it to the bishops, 'the said book tends to introduce such a latitude and diversity of opinions as the Articles were framed to avoid', as well as offering interpretations 'which appear to us to be contrary to the true meaning of them'. What seems to have rankled especially was that the historical approach adopted by Burnet served to introduce a degree of relativism. Given the frequent disagreements in the past among leading theologians, many present-day certainties would appear, from this point of view, to be at best provisional. An obvious example here was the dispute about predestination between Calvinists and Arminians, its antecedents traceable to the break made by St Augustine with the teaching of the Greek fathers. Furthermore 'this is a controversy that arises out of natural religion', says Burnet, 'for if it is believed that God governs the world and that the wills of men are free then it is natural to enquire which of these is subject to the other, or how they can both be maintained'. Wisely, the Church of England 'has not been peremptory' in this matter but 'a latitude has been left to different opinions'. Indeed, rather than seeking a compromise formula, mutual respect for divergent views is often 'the only possible way of a sound and lasting reconciliation'.[43]

The harrying of Burnet by the lower house of convocation continued as late as 1705, its efforts repeatedly rebuffed by Tenison and the bishops. A much more serious High Church challenge, however, had by then emerged via parliament in the form of a campaign to outlaw occasional conformity – the practice of dissenters receiving Holy Communion according to the rites of the established church so as to qualify for civic office. Opponents of occasional conformity regarded it as a cynical manoeuvre to circumvent the Corporation and Test Acts. On the other hand, advocates of comprehension looked on the practice in a much more favourable light, as a way of keeping the door open for dissenters to return to the fold. Three bills against occasional conformity passed the House of Commons during the years 1702–4, only to be defeated in the Lords, where Burnet played a major role in their rejection. In the course of a speech on the subject in 1703, he treated the listeners to a history lesson, claiming that Queen Elizabeth had 'encouraged the occasional conformity of papists' as a way of wooing them to Protestantism. The dissenters, by comparison, presented much less of a threat and, since the passing of the Toleration Act in 1689, so Burnet claimed, their numbers had diminished by 'at least a fourth part'. Turning to the self-styled High Churchmen who favoured the Bill, he commented that 'I know no high church but the Church of Rome'. As for himself, 'I began the world on a principle of moderation which I have carried down through my whole life and in which I hope I shall continue to my life's end'. Writing up the episode in his *History*, Burnet further recorded that 'I have long looked on liberty of conscience as one of the rights of human nature, antecedent to society, which no man could give up because it was not in his own power', and 'our Saviour's rule, of doing as we would be done by' is 'a very express decision to all men who would lay the matter home to their own conscience and judge as they would willingly be judged by others'.[44]

The record of voting by the Lords in 1703 on the Occasional Conformity Bill reveals that nine bishops were in favour and fourteen against, the core of the second group being composed of Latitudinarians or 'Low Churchmen' – a term which was emerging as a synonym around this time. The only obvious defector was Sharp, now archbishop of York, of whom Tenison is recorded as saying that 'he had been formerly a profest Latitudinarian'. Meanwhile the failure of occasional conformity legislation contributed to the 'church in danger' agitation, which peaked in 1705, with votes in both Lords and Commons on this subject.[45] Undoubtedly an important new element in the situation was the accession three years earlier of Queen Anne and the boost this had given to the Tories, along with their High Church clerical allies. During the parliamentary election of 1702 'no moderation' had featured as a slogan, and by 1705 this had escalated into 'no fanatic, no occasional conformity'. The workings of this politico-religious alliance can be seen particularly clearly in the case of Oxford University, where one of the two local MPs, William Bromley, played a leading role in promoting the occasional conformity bills. It was Oxford also that spawned the firebrand Henry Sacheverell, fellow of Magdalen College, and a group of his aptly named 'lieutenants', who gave increasingly stentorian voice to High Church aspirations. Thus, while preaching before the assembled university in May 1702, Sacheverell had mounted an attack on 'treacherous Latitudinarians' who sought to debauch the English church both in doctrine and in practice. Occasional conformity, he claimed, was part and parcel of the problem.[46]

The same year, 1702, Sacheverell published an anonymous parliamentary election pamphlet entitled *The character of a Low-Church-man*. Written on behalf of Sir John Pakington, a particular target was Bishop William Lloyd, who had by now been translated from St Asaph to Worcester. But the pamphlet clearly had much wider application. According to Sacheverell, a Low Churchman is characterised by 'an universal latitude, comprehension and indifference to every sect and party', and moreover he 'believes very little or no revelation, and had rather lay his faith upon the substantial evidences of his own reason than the precarious authority of divine testimony'. An 'ambidexter' in doctrine, 'the scholastick jargon of the Trinity will ill suit with one of so polite a genius'. Apropos worship, a Low Churchman, 'rather than offend religious ears', 'will silence the unhallow'd sound of an organ' and 'in nothing [more] shews his obstinacy against superstition than in standing still at the name of Jesus'. By contrast, a High-Churchman, like Pakington, observes 'the traditionall customs as well as the written laws of the Church' in bowing 'very low towards the altar and at the name of Jesus'. Meanwhile referring back to the censuring of Bishop Burnet by the lower house of convocation, Sacheverell linked his 'misrepresenting, distorting and corrupting, the true and genuine scope and sense of the Articles of our Church' with 'that noble design', as he ironically described it, 'of Archbishop Tillotson ... to have fetch'd in all dissenters upon the same bottom with that of the Church of England'. They were merely different aspects of the same attempt at comprehension, and over the next seven years Sacheverell was to continue harping on such themes, as well as the evils of dissenter academies, culminating with his notorious sermon of 5 November 1709, which appeared to cast doubt on the legitimacy of the Williamite revolution. On this latter occasion he also proclaimed that 'whosoever presumes ... to explain the great credenda of our faith in new-fangl'd terms of modern philosophy must publish a new gospel, un-God his Saviour and destroy his revelation'.[47]

A similar High Church message was propagated by other Oxonians, preaching to university audiences and further afield – notably in the form of assize sermons. Their names include Charles Jones, John Mather, William Tilly, and John Willett.[48] Cambridge contributed as well, including two sermons by Thomas Sherwill, a fellow of Christ's College, published in 1704.[49] Especially remarkable, however, is a sermon by Tilly, fellow of Corpus Christi College, preached at Oxford in May 1710 and in the aftermath of the impeachment by parliament of Sacheverell for his sermon of the previous November. The title of Tilly's sermon is *A return to our former good old principles and practice, the only way to restore and preserve our peace*. As published, this is prefaced by a letter of support to Sacheverell. Calling in his sermon for a return to the 'old paths', Tilly complained of 'novel expositions of the Articles of our Church and holy faith', by 'the gentlemen of reason'. He went on to exclaim 'take but the Church of England as it stood from the first days of Queen Elizabeth till about the death of Charles the martyr and how unlike herself she now appears'. Since then, 'primitive truths' have been 'blasted' and some have 'run into downright heresy', while others 'have entertained such a latitude of opinions' and 'separating notions' as to render themselves 'odious and offensive to all the world'. In what is admittedly a somewhat ambiguous passage, Tilly appears to lay the blame for these developments at least partly at the door of Bishop Wilkins and his book on *Natural religion*.[50]

Sacheverell was likened in 1709, by one of his critics, to Don Quixote – as going about 'in quest of imaginary giants and monsters'. But was he, along with Tilly and company, simply tilting at windmills? For hard on the heels of the Sacheverell affair came the successive causes célèbres of William Whiston and Samuel Clarke, former Boyle lecturers both, whose views on the Trinity clearly broke the bounds of orthodoxy, while also owing a debt to Newton. In 1709, Whiston, Lucasian professor of mathematics at Cambridge, had published his *Sermons and essays*, where he stated unequivocally that Christ was 'subordinate' to God the Father, who is 'the only true God in the highest sense of that word'. This statement is contained in an essay entitled 'Reason and philosophy no enemies to faith'. Tried and condemned for heresy by the university authorities, Whiston then had the temerity to present a statement of his views to convocation in 1711.[51] Subsequent attempts, however, to discipline him further ran into jurisdictional difficulties and were overtaken by the publication in 1712 of *The scripture-doctrine of the Trinity* by Samuel Clarke, recently appointed rector of St James Westminster. Like Whiston, Clarke argued that Christ was 'subordinate' to God the Father, and his case was in turn pursued by convocation, in 1714. But a compromise form of words, agreed with Clarke by the bishops, was rejected by the lower house of convocation and proceedings thereafter stalled.[52]

Yet matters did not rest here because some of the supporters of Whiston and Clarke decided, in effect, to appeal over the heads of convocation, emboldened to do so by the accession of the Hanoverian dynasty in 1714. The key player turned out to be Benjamin Hoadly, consecrated bishop of Bangor in 1716. Far from the famous sermon on *The nature of the kingdom or church of Christ*, which he was to preach in March 1717, coming out of the blue, Hoadly had in fact been thinking along such lines for at least fifteen years previously. Hence two surviving sermons preached by him in 1703 were almost certainly triggered by the fate of Thomas Emlyn, a Presbyterian minister fined a thousand pounds and imprisoned for two years on account of his anti-Trinitarian views. Similarly, four other sermons preached by Hoadly in 1712–13 need to be understood against the background of proceedings against Whiston and Clarke. These sermon series are described respectively, by Hoadly, as concerning 'the divisions and cruelties, of which the Christian religion hath been made the occasion', and an 'impartial enquiry into religion, and the two extremes of implicit subjection and infidelity'. Hoadly himself was a great admirer of Burnet and Tenison, conversely regarding Laud as the lodestar of High Churchmen, and the solution which he and his allies now appear to have come up with was a relaxation of the terms under which clergy currently held their posts – specifically as regards subscription to the Thirty-nine Articles (which included teaching on the Trinity), for Christ has left 'no interpreters upon whom his subjects are absolutely to depend'. Certainly we know that a petition to parliament along these lines was planned. This original goal, however, was largely lost sight of in the ensuing Bangorian controversy, as it is known, about relations between church and state.[53]

Hoadly and Sacheverell clearly belonged to the more radical wings of their rival religious groups, the latter ending his days as rector of St Andrew, Holborn, where he provided further evidence of Laudian sympathies by commissioning a magnificent east window, with panels depicting the Last Supper and the Ascension, and choosing to be buried under the altar. Hoadly, by contrast, was to finish his career enthroned as bishop of Winchester, and Latitudinarians or Low Churchmen more generally were to exercise a powerful influence in the upper echelons of the Hanoverian establishment. Furthermore, after 1717 convocation (and its lower house, which had become something of a High Church platform), was to be silenced for well over a hundred years. Meanwhile the eighteenth century was to prove the great age of English natural theology, although the subject never entirely lost a reputation for heterodoxy. By 1734, Wilkins's *Natural religion* had reached a ninth edition, and Burnet's *Exposition of the Thirty-nine Articles* was still being published as late as 1837. The counterattack, when at last it came, emanated first from Evangelicals and then from

Tractarians, the term 'liberalism' being used to sum up all that was considered wrong with the previous dispensation.[54]

Between 1660 and 1714, Laudians and Latitudinarians had vied for supremacy, with Calvinism increasingly becoming the preserve of Protestant dissenters. Much hinged on the religious predilections of successive monarchs, yet all were constrained to some extent by circumstances. During these same years the dream faded of a restored Church of England embracing all manner of Protestants, as the balance of forces shifted in one direction and then another. Crucial in retrospect was the self-inflicted wound of those High Churchmen who refused to acknowledge the change of regime after 1688, thus allowing their Latitudinarian opponents to gain the initiative and opening the way for toleration of dissenters. As regards the English church itself, the new centre of gravity was most obviously represented by Archbishop Tillotson, whose legacy lived on via his own voluminous published sermons and those of numerous imitators – serving to inculcate what has been called the 'doctrine of divine benevolence'.[55]

NOTES

A number of fellow scholars have helped to guide my researches for this chapter. Especially to be thanked are Rosemary Dixon, Anthony Fletcher, Marilyn Lewis, Stephen Hampton, Anthony Milton, Isobel Rivers, Benet Salway, and David Wykes.

1 N. Tyacke, *Anti-Calvinists. The rise of English Arminianism, c. 1590–1640* (Oxford: Clarendon Press, 1987; pbk edn 1990); Tyacke, *Aspects of English Protestantism, c. 1530–1700* (Manchester: Manchester University Press, 2001), pp. 160–221. Purists prefer the term 'Reformed' to Calvinist, on the grounds that Calvin was only one among a variety of sources. On the other hand 'Calvinist' does have contemporary warrant, used as a piece of shorthand. Moreover 'Reformed' is itself ambiguous, since this was sometimes employed as a synonym for Protestant.

2 For Laudianism, especially in its more ceremonial aspects, see K. Fincham and N. Tyacke, *Altars restored. The changing face of English religious worship, 1547– c.1700* (Oxford: Oxford University Press, 2007), index references and *passim*.

3 William Dugdale, *The history of St Pauls Cathedral in London* (1658), pp. 162–5; Peter Heylyn, *Cyprianus Anglicus* (1668), sigs.A2r–v.

4 Peter Heylyn, *Historia quinqu-articularis* (1660), part ii, 6–7, 33–68; Henry Hickman, *Historia quinqu-articularis exarticulata* (1673). See also Heylyn's *Ecclesia restaurata* (1661) and *Cyprianus Anglicus* (1668).

5 Heylyn, *Historia quinqu-articularis*, part i, 1–2; Martin Luther, *The bondage of the will*, trans. J.I. Packer and O.R. Johnstone (Cambridge: James Clarke & Co, 1957), pp. 97–102, 201–9; John Calvin, *Concerning the eternal predestination of God*, trans. J.K.S. Reid (James Clarke & Co, 1961), pp. 19, 120–6, 168–70, 176–82.

6 A. Milton, *Laudian and royalist polemic in seventeenth-century England. The career and writings of Peter Heylyn* (Manchester: Manchester University Press, 2007), pp. 190–7; T.A. Mason, *Serving God and Mammon. William Juxon, 1582–1663, bishop of London, Lord*

High Treasurer, and archbishop of Canterbury (Toronto: University of Delaware Press, 1985); W. Scott and J. Bliss (eds), *The works of William Laud* 7 vols (Oxford, 1847–60), III, 120–7; William Sancroft, *A sermon preached in St Peter's Westminster* (1660), dedication.

7   Tyacke, *Anti-Calvinists*, pp. xiii–xiv; Tyacke, *Aspects*, pp. 22–3.

8   George Bull, *Harmonia Apostolica* (1670) and *Examen censurae* (1676); Tyacke, *Aspects*, pp. 297–9.

9   H.C. Porter, *Reformation and reaction in Tudor Cambridge* (Cambridge: Cambridge University Press, 1958), pp. 174–8, 376–90; Tyacke, *Aspects*, pp. 292–7; J. Gascoigne, *Cambridge in the age of the Enlightenment. Science, religion and politics from the Restoration to the French Revolution* (Cambridge: Cambridge University Press, 1989), pp. 142–84.

10 Tyacke, *Aspects*, pp. 324–5, 330–2; Peterhouse, Cambridge, MS 448, pp. 17–18. The situation in the Church of England more generally has now been reassessed by Stephen Hampton in his important book *Anti-Arminians. The Anglican Reformed tradition from Charles II to George I* (Oxford: Oxford University Press, 2008).

11 For the modern debate about Latitudinarianism see, on the one hand, J. Spurr, '"Latitudinarianism" and the Restoration Church', *HJ*, 31 (1988), 61–82 and, on the other, I. Rivers, *Reason, grace and sentiment: a study of the language of religion and ethics in England 1660–1780*, 2 vols (1991–2000), I, chapter 2. Having begun in the ranks of the sceptics, my own view now is that this concept provides a valuable tool of analysis, especially as regards longer-term developments.

12 Joseph Beaumont, *Some observations upon the apologie of Dr Henry Moore* (Cambridge, 1665), p. 31; John Standish, *A sermon preached before the King ... September 26, 1675* (1676), pp. 24–5; A. Browning, *Thomas Osborne earl of Danby and duke of Leeds*, 3 vols (Glasgow: Jackson, 1944–51), I, 146–84.

13 R. Latham and W. Matthews (eds), *The diary of Samuel Pepys*, 11 vols (Bell & Hyman, 1970–83), IX, 485; B. Shapiro, *John Wilkins 1614–1672. An intellectual biography* (Berkeley: University of California Press, 1969), pp. 169–77.

14 John Wilkins, *Of the principles and duties of natural religion* (1675), sigs. A2–5v, pp. 394–410. For the evolving attitude of Latitudinarians to Calvinism see Tyacke, *Aspects*, pp. 3–4, 325–6, 334–6.

15 Matthew Barker, *Natural theology or the knowledge of God, from the works of creation, accommodated and improved to the service of Christianity* (1674), sig. A2v, pp. 111–28.

16 Joseph Glanvill, *Logou threskeia* (1670), pp. 24–6; J.I. Cope, *Joseph Glanvill, Anglican apologist* (St Louis, WA: Washington University Studies, 1956), pp. 31–2.

17 [Simon Patrick], *An earnest request to Mr John Standish* (1676), pp. 2, 5, 10–11; A. Taylor (ed.), *The works of Simon Patrick*, 9 vols (Cambridge, 1858), IX, 446–7; Miles Barne, *A sermon preached before the King ... October 17, 1675* (1675), pp. 20–2, 38–9, 41.

18 Benjamin Laney, *Five sermons* (1669), pp. 22–4; Laney, *A sermon preached before the King* (1675), pp. 13, 25–6, 29.

19 Matthew Sylvester (ed.), *Reliquiae Baxterianae* (1696), part iii, 156–7, 179; M.G. Jones, 'Two accounts of the Welsh Trust, 1675 and 1678 (?)', *Bulletin of the Board of Celtic Studies*, 9 (1937–39), 71–80; 'Charles Edwards', *Dictionary of Welsh Biography*, ed. J.E. Lloyd *et al.* (1959), p. 184; Tyacke, *Aspects*, pp. 122–3.

20 John Tillotson, *A sermon preached at the ... meeting of the gentlemen ... born wthin the county of York* (1679), p. 28; Tillotson, *A sermon preached at the funeral of ... Thomas Gouge*

(1682), pp. 58–9, 64, 82, 95–7. Earlier, in October 1677, at the funeral of the leading Presbyterian Thomas Manton, it is recorded that the conformist and nonconformist clergy present 'walked in pairs': J. Hunter (ed.), *The diary of Ralph Thoresby*, 2 vols (1830), I, 7.

21 Tyacke, *Aspects*, p. 116; B. Burch, 'The parish of St Anne's Blackfriars, London, to 1665', *Guildhall Miscellany*, III (1969–71), 44, 50–1; John Wilkins, *Sermons ... never before published* (1682), sigs A2v–3.

22 [Thomas Tenison], *An argument for union* (1683), pp. 37, 41–2; Miles Barne, *A sermon preach'd at the asizes at Hertford ... July 10, 1684* (Cambridge, 1684), sigs A2–A4, 20–1; H. Horwitz, 'Protestant reconciliation in the exclusion crisis', *JEH*, 15 (1964), 201–17.

23 Francis Turner, *A sermon preached before the King ... November 5, 1684* (1685), pp. 18–19, 22–6; Turner, *A sermon preach'd before the King ... September 9, 1683* (1683), p. 23; Turner, *A sermon preached before the King ... January 30, 1684/5* (1685), pp. 22–3; P. Hopkins, 'Francis Turner', *ODNB*.

24 T.B. Howell *et al.* (eds), *A complete collection of state trials*, 33 vols (1816–28), XI, 494–502; M. Goldie (gen. ed.), *The entering book of Roger Morrice 1679–1691*, 7 vols (Woodbridge: Boydell, 2007–9), III, 12. In retrospect Tillotson was to describe this trial as Baxter's finest hour – 'never more great then [than] then': N.H. Keeble and G.F. Nuttall (eds), *Calendar of the correspondence of Richard Baxter*, 2 vols (Oxford: Clarendon Press, 1991), II, 330.

25 Sylvester (ed.), *Reliquiae Baxterianae*, part iii, 23–4, 156–7, 179; Daniel Neal, *The history of the Puritans*, 4 vols (1822), IV, 458; William Cobbett, *Cobbett's parliamentary history, 1066–1803*, 36 vols (1806–20), IV, 1240.

26 T. Jones, *A catalogue of ... tracts for and against popery ... in the reign of James II*, 2 vols (Chetham Soc., 48, 64, 1859–65); T.J. Fawcett, *The liturgy of comprehension 1689* (Southend-on-Sea: Mayhew-McCrimmon, Alcuin Club, 1973), pp. 10–23.

27 Tyacke, *Aspects*, pp. 76–7; Fawcett, *Liturgy of comprehension 1689*, pp. 24–46.

28 This represents a turnover of two-thirds. The statistics are derived from J. Le Neve (ed.), *Fasti ecclesiae Anglicanae 1541–1859* (Oxford, 1854), revised by J. Horn *et al.* (1969–2007).

29 O. Airy (ed.), *Burnet's history of my own time*, 2 vols (Oxford: Oxford University Press, 1897), I, 334. Burnet also makes the point that Wilkins and his fellow Latitudinarians were reacting in part against the teachings of Thomas Hobbes: *ibid.*, 333–4.

30 J. Parkin, *Science, religion and politics in Restoration England: Richard Cumberland's De legibus naturae* (Royal Historical Society, 1999), pp. 168–78; Fawcett, *Liturgy of comprehension 1689*, pp. 27–8, 30; E.H. Plumptre, *The life of Thomas Ken*, 2 vols (1888), II, 133–4, 138–9; E.S. de Beer (ed.), *The correspondence of John Locke*, 8 vols (Oxford: Oxford University Press, 1976–89), IV, 525–6.

31 W. Marshall, 'Herbert Croft', *ODNB*; M. Mullett, 'William Lloyd', *ODNB*.

32 Cf. G.V. Bennett, 'King William III and the episcopate', in G.V. Bennett and J.D. Walsh (eds), *Essays in modern church history in memory of Norman Sykes* (Adam & Charles Black, 1966), pp. 104–31.

33 John Tillotson, *A sermon preach'd before the Queen ... March 8, 1688–9* (1689), p. 8; Tillotson, *A sermon preach'd before the King and Queen ... April 14, 1689* (1689), p. 16; Jones, 'Welsh Trust', 72, 76, 78.

34 De Beer (ed.), *Correspondence of John Locke*, IV, 463–4, 589–90; Philip van Limborch,

Historia Inquisitionis (Amsterdam, 1692); van Limborch, *The history of the Inquisition*, (trans.) Samuel Chandler (1731), pp. i–vii, [part ii], 1–7.

35 De Beer (ed.), *Correspondence of John Locke*, IV, 525–6. Chandler, in his own introduction to the translation of van Limborch, explicitly makes the connection with Hoadly: *The history of the Inquistion*, [part i], 89–90.

36 Philip van Limborch, *Theologia Christiana* (Amsterdam, 1686); Fawcet, *Liturgy of comprehension 1689*, p. 45; Jonathan Edwards, *A preservative against Socinianism* (Oxford, 1694–1703), part ii, 66–7 and index.

37 Scott and Bliss (eds), *Works of William Laud*, III, 112–27; Henry Wharton (ed.), *The history of the troubles and trial of ... the blessed martyr William Laud*, 2 vols (1695–1700), I, frontispiece; W.M. Jacob, 'Charles Trimnell', *ODNB*.

38 Airy (ed.), *Burnet's history of my own time*, I, 85–6.

39 T. Birch (ed.), *The works of Robert Boyle*, 5 vols (1744), I, 105–6; E.S. de Beer (ed.), *The diary of John Evelyn*, 6 vols (Oxford: Oxford University Press, 1955), III, 517–18; IV, 307–8; V, 89; G.S. De Krey, 'Sir Henry Ashurst', *ODNB*; S. Handley, 'Sir John Rotherham', *ODNB*.

40 S. Letsome and J. Nicholl (eds), *A defence of natural and revealed religion* [Boyle lectures], 3 vols (1739); R.L. Warner, 'Samuel Bradford', *ODNB*; S. Taylor, 'Edmund Gibson', *ODNB*; L. Okie, 'White Kennett', *ODNB*; W.M. Jacob, 'Charles Trimnell', *ODNB*. The names and dates of the new trustees are derived from the dedications to the lectures as published.

41 S.W. Baskerville, 'Francis Gastrell', *ODNB*; A. Starkie, 'Ofspring Blackall', *ODNB*; R.L. Warner, 'George Stanhope', *ODNB*.

42 G.V. Bennett, *The Tory crisis in church and state 1688–1730: the career of Francis Atterbury, bishop of Rochester* (Oxford: Oxford University Press, 1975), pp. 44–62; Francis Atterbury, *A letter to a convocation man concerning the rights, powers and priviledges of that body* (1697), p. 6.

43 M. Grieg, 'Heresy hunt: Gilbert Burnet and the convocation controversy of 1701', *HJ*, 37 (1994), 569–92; Gilbert Burnet, *An exposition of the Thirty-nine Articles of the Church of England* (1699), pp. v–vii, 145–70.

44 E. Cardwell, *Synodalia*, 2 vols (Oxford, 1842), II, 718–19; Cobbett, *Parliamentary history*, VI, 157–65; M.J. Routh (ed.), *Burnet's history of his own time*, 6 vols (Oxford: Oxford University Press, 1833), V, 108–9.

45 Cobbet, *Parliamentary history*, VI, 170–1, 359–67, 479–510; Gascoigne, *Cambridge in the age of enlightenment*, p. 76.

46 Gascoigne, *Cambridge in the age of enlightenment*, pp. 96–7; L.S. Sutherland and L.G. Mitchell (eds), *The history of the university of Oxford. Volume V. The eighteenth century* (Oxford: Clarendon Press, 1986), pp. 62–3, 68–9, 72–5.

47 Henry Sacheverell, *The character of a Low-Churchman* (1702), pp. 8–9, 12–13, 16, 26; Sacheverell, *The nature and mischief of prejudice and partiality* (Oxford, 1704), p. 54; Sacheverell, *The perils of false bretheren* (1709), p. 7.

48 Charles Jones, *Against hypocrasie* (1705), pp. 21–8; John Mather, *A sermon preached before the University of Oxford ... May 29, 1705* (Oxford, 1705), pp. 15, 22–3; William Tilly, *A sermon preach'd before the University of Oxford ... January 31, 1703/4* (Oxford, 1706), pp. 17–22; John Willett, *The nature and mischief of hypocrasie* (Oxford, 1708), pp. 8–10, 14–15.

49 Thomas Sherwill, *Church-conformity asserted* (Cambridge, 1704), pp. 9–10, 19, 21–3; Sherwill, *The degeneracy of the present age* (Cambridge, 1704), pp. 18–19, 23–6.

50 William Tilly, *A return to our former good old principles* (Oxford, 1710), pp. 10–13, 16–17.

51 G. Holmes, *The trial of Doctor Sacheverell* (Methuen, 1973), p. 48; M. Wiles, *Archetypal heresy. Arianism through the centuries* (Oxford: Clarendon Press, 1996, repr. 2004), pp. 77–134; L. Stewart, 'Clarke, Newtonianism and the factions of post-revolutionary England', *Journal of the History of Ideas*, 42 (1981), 53–72; William Whiston, *Sermons and essays* (1709), pp. 213–16; E. Duffy, '"Whiston's affair": the trials of a primitive Christian', *JEH*, 27 (1976), 129–50.

52 Samuel Clarke, *The scripture-doctrine of the Trinity* (1712), pp. 144–96; J.P. Ferguson, *An eighteenth century heretic. Dr Samuel Clarke* (Kineton: Roundwood Press, 1976), pp. 83–97.

53 Benjamin Hoadly, *Several tracts* (1715), pp. 67–97, 453–511; [Hoadly], *An account of the state of the Roman-Catholick religion* (1715), pp. xi–xv, xl, lxix–lxxi, lxxvi; Hoadly, *The nature of the kingdom or church of Christ* (1717), 11; William Whiston, *Historical memoirs of the life of Dr Samuel Clarke* (1730), pp. 101–7; A. Starkie, *The Church of England and the Bangorian controversy, 1716–1721* (Woodbridge: Boydell, 2007), pp. 117–18 and *passim*.

54 Holmes, *Trial of Doctor Sacheverell*, pp. 266–7; C. Barron, *The parish of St Andrew Holborn* (1979), pp. 65–6; Gascoigne, *Cambridge in the age of enlightenment*, pp. 129–34, 237–69; M.G. Brock and M.C. Curthoys (eds), *The history of the university of Oxford. Volume VI. Nineteenth-century Oxford, Part I* (Oxford: Clarendon Press, 1997), pp. 72–6, 210–11, 221–2, 599; J.H. Newman, *Apologia pro vita sua*, ed. M.J. Svaglic (Oxford: Oxford University Press, 1967), pp. 256–62.

55 N. Sykes, *From Sheldon to Secker. Aspects of English church history 1660–1768* (Cambridge: Cambridge University Press, 1959), pp. 151, 176–87.

Part II

People

Chapter 3

Pastors, preachers and politicians:
the clergy of the later Stuart church

Grant Tapsell

In 1713, Edmund Gibson, archdeacon of Surrey, published his two-volume *Codex Juris Ecclesiastici Anglicani*, a vast edited collection of documents organised by theme to illustrate the structures and legal authorities of the Church of England. For Gibson, it was self-evident that '*England* is governed by two distinct Administrations: one *Spiritual*, for matters of a Spiritual nature; and the other *Temporal*, for matters of a Temporal nature.'' Gibson was a rising man within the Church of England, thanks to his position as chaplain to the archbishop of Canterbury, Thomas Tenison, and his great work would continue to be regarded as a crucial resource for the study of church government by clerics until at least the 1940s.[2] Dedicating the massive volumes to Tenison, Gibson claimed to have been inspired to provide such a comprehensive text by the archbishop's frustration at various examples of clerical neglect, often born of ignorance of the correct rules within which clergymen should operate: 'How often have I heard you declare, that nothing but a *strict* Regard and *uniform* Adherence to those *Rules*, both by *Bishops* and *Clergy*, can preserve the Church in a peaceable, orderly and flourishing State!'[3]

Gibson's ventriloquising of the archbishop's sentiments is a fair reflection of many senior clerics' zeal to improve the efficiency of the Church of England as an institution in the later Stuart period, one of many themes that connected them with their predecessors and successors. But their efforts met with mixed success, locally and nationally, which encouraged some clergy to lament the declining respect in which they felt they were held within English society. A year before he was ordained priest in 1698, the antiquary Abraham de la Pryme committed a memorable rant to the pages of his diary after a pessimistic conversation about current affairs with a nearby cleric:

> The House of Commons are commonly a company of irreligious wretches who cares not what they do, nor what becomes of the church and religious things, if they can but get their hawkes, hounds, and whores, and the sacred possessions of the

church. It is plainly visible that the nation would be happier if there was no House of Commons ... for we commonly see that whatever mischief has been wrought in the nation has been carryd on and back'd by ... [MPs] who vallue ... the weal politic above the ecclesiastic, and their own worldly ends above their salvation.[4]

If Gibson described a theory of separate but harmonious administrations, clerical and lay, de la Pryme reminds us that in practice the clerical sphere was repeatedly invaded by lay interests. He gave voice to a long-running unease that the reform of the church during the sixteenth century had gone too far in denuding it of the material resources, social cachet, and political clout necessary to pursue its work effectively, with its resources co-opted and then tenaciously retained by grasping laymen.[5] De la Pryme was not alone in thinking that clerical efforts to reclaim alienated resources from the laity were rarely effective for long, and that the Laudian reforms of the 1630s represented a lost golden age of clerical prestige.

Such gloomy thoughts suggest that by the later Stuart period, the Church of England had suffered irremediable financial, social, and political decline. Was Gibson's *magnum opus* of 1713 in fact an irrelevant folly of rococo scholarship that merely chronicled the archaic structures of an obsolete institution entering into an 'age of negligence'?[6] Whilst consistently noting the scale of the challenges that the clergy faced in this period, this chapter will depict a far more robust and significant clerical establishment than a superficial reading of de la Pryme would suggest. For it is one of the ironies of the later Stuart era that fears of religious indifference and ecclesiastical sclerosis were so pervasive when clergymen were amongst the most prominent and active public figures of the day. Gilbert Sheldon, archbishop of Canterbury, was a crucial player at court and in parliament during the 1660s and 1670s;[7] his successor, William Sancroft, worked phenomenally hard throughout the 1680s to improve the pastoral efficiency of the church; and the post-revolutionary world of the 1690s, 1700s, and 1710s abounded in vociferous clerical polemicists of very varying hues, notably Gilbert Burnet, William Sherlock, Henry Sacheverell, and Francis Atterbury. Small wonder, then, that a major theme of later Stuart political discourse was 'priestcraft': the power the clergy enjoyed or abused on the basis of their continuing position in society, both individually within parish communities and collectively as a wealthy and legally privileged body.[8]

Examining conflicting perceptions of decline and vigour requires us to recognise that the clergy undertook several roles in this period. They were God's priests first and foremost, and supposed to act as pastors to the people, but they were also significant political actors. As a result of their vocation, temperament, and circumstances, clergy were often vigorous contributors to a burgeoning public culture of debate, one that was increasingly bitterly divided along partisan lines, and consequentially prone to fears of misrepresentation and deceit.[9] For analytical purposes, in this chapter a more clear-cut division will be made between clerics' core religious function and their 'extra-curricular' political activities than was the case in reality, with each taken in turn alongside a consideration of their verbal and written contributions to public life and controversy. All of this will then be drawn together with an extended concluding case study of warring clerics that illuminates how the conflicts of a cathedral close both encapsulated and aggravated the tensions of the Augustan age.

I

Autumnal rain deterred the attendance of some less dedicated clerics, but enough came together in the small Hertfordshire town of Braughing on 25 September 1679 to permit a substantial conference. Called at the behest of their diligent diocesan, Henry Compton, bishop of London from 1675 to 1713, this body of rural clergymen solemnly discussed how best to serve their flocks. Mixing elements of a self-help group, a team-building exercise, and an academic debate, clerical conferences such as this one had been known in England for some time. But they had often been viewed with suspicion by senior clerics, notably those in the Elizabethan period who had fretted that 'prophesyings' formed but one part of a broader and insidious threat from Puritans keen to subvert the Church of England from within.[10] Clearly such worries did not unduly trouble Compton, 'the Protestant bishop', whose surviving papers reveal that he prompted a number of such conferences both within and beyond the metropolitan parts of his uniquely populous diocese.[11] The report he received on the Braughing conference revealed a striking range of opinion about how clergymen could most effectively engage with laymen.[12] Some of those present 'very earnestly recommended plain & practical preaching, as that which was sure to have most authority upon the consciences of men'. Others, however, hankered after a little more drama. According to these speakers, 'wee should ... make use of as much action in o[u]r preaching as would consist with gravity, because by such things the generality of people were taken'. In other aspects of clerical life, it was thought best to demonstrate 'Gravity of conversation, as opposed to jesting, drolling or talkativeness'. Clerics should frequently visit the sick. It 'was thought absolutely necessary, for the interest & reputation of the whole body', that individual clergymen should not gossip about their brethren. Indeed clergy should behave towards each other with 'publique respect' in order 'to teach the rude multitude better manners'. The clergy should act diligently in catechising their flocks, not just to instruct the laity in the tenets of the Christian faith but as an act of self-interested prudence: it 'would lay a foundation for better times to come'.

Any historian reading this letter cannot but be struck by what it reveals – often unconsciously – about clerical life in the early modern period. Some of the bruited courses of action are so obvious that their very banality suggests the uphill struggle that many clerics faced in their day-to-day working lives. The fact that the people could be described as a 'rude multitude', in need either of theatrics or very blunt words from the pulpit, is a stark reminder of many clerics' adversarial or strained relations with their parishioners.[13] 'Better times to come' has a rather self-pitying air as a phrase, and can easily be slotted into a generally pessimistic clerical mindset, not least because so many clergy were acutely aware of lay hostility towards their activities. If some nobles and gentry confined their most sardonic criticisms of the clergy's greed to private manuscripts and banter with their chaplains, the Whig versifier John Tutchin's furious 1691 depiction of the clergy as 'pious vermin' who were a 'plague' on the nation was painfully public.[14] In the face of such problems, clergymen needed to present a united front; they were, after all, a separate part of society, a 'whole body' whose 'interest & reputation' had to be maintained.

Yet the account of proceedings sent to Compton offers two further key insights reflective of events specific to, or at least more pronounced in, the later Stuart period. The first was that besides behaving courteously to one another, clergy should also aim 'to maintaine uniformity that is the same tenor and practice of conformity, to avoid partialities and odious comparisons'. In other words, different clergy worked out their vocations in subtly or substantially different ways, risking debate, division, and dissension. The seventeenth century had seen, and would continue to see, clerics bitterly criticising one another, with a frequent recourse to a language of schism and destructive disharmony.[15] The second insight, and one offered with startling candour, was that all of the measures discussed by this particular subset of the Anglican clergy in September 1679 were 'the ways that either papists or phanatics have gained proselytes by', and which the clergy of the established church should consider 'how farr they were imitable ... or (if to be avoided yet) might warne us where o[u]r danger entered'. Like warriors learning from the tactics of their enemies, Anglican clergymen had to absorb the lessons which their denominational rivals served up on a regular basis.

How successfully did the clergy of the later Stuart church discharge their core function as spiritual pastors to the people? Until relatively recently, most historical scholarship in the field focused on the administrative structures, career patterns, and financial sinews of the church, especially its higher clergy. This was hardly surprising when some of the central archives for any historical enquiry into the later Stuart church are littered with examples of clergy whose most pressing concern seems to have been self-promotion and place seeking.[16] When, in 1683, the archbishop of Canterbury, William Sancroft, was deluged with requests for a vacant East Anglian archdeaconry, he replied to one applicant with heavy sarcasm: 'I perceive if all ye 4 Archdeaconries in Norwich-Diocese were actually void, we might find worthy persons ready to accept of them.'[17] Particularly because many of the most successful place seekers held multiple livings and appointments at the same time, even the finest modern historians have spiced their accounts of widespread pluralism and economic self-interest with ironical or judgemental language. Geoffrey Holmes, for instance, evocatively described a rich living being 'disgorged' by a wealthy cleric after he had received an even greater prize.[18] Certainly the cocky self-regard of a tirelessly place-hunting cleric like Laurence Womock in the 1660s, 1670s, and 1680s is hard to admire, and his ultimate 'reward', the exceptionally poor and remote diocese of St Davids in Wales, provides strong supporting evidence that Archbishop Sancroft had a sense of humour.[19]

Casting the net more widely, it is easy to draw a pessimistic set of images from the evidence left by clerical diaries, court records, and reports on diocesan affairs. At the level of individual clergymen, even the most dedicated and highly motivated figures could feel that they were thanklessly rowing against a tide of lay indifference or hostility. In Yorkshire, an extremely poor rural minister, the appropriately named Robert Meeke, recorded his desire 'to shine as a burning light, and to walk in such ways that others may safely follow'.[20] Meeke served as the minister of the chapelry of Slaithwaite, near Huddersfield, from 1685 to 1724, rejecting more lucrative alternative livings whilst retaining a sense of his limited pastoral success. He was, for instance, deeply touched by a gift of potatoes from an elderly parishioner in 1691, but punctiliously noted that it was one of only two such kindnesses he had received, and otherwise 'Nothing is given but the customed dues'.[21] Many clergy expressed frustration that their main source of funding, tithes from their parishioners, could be the source of deep resentment, despite being lawfully granted.[22] The Sussex clergyman Giles Moore angrily recorded that he had wasted more than £7 'foolishly' on lawyers' fees in the early 1660s trying to recover tithes long disrupted by political and legal upheavals. By 1676, one of his parishioners was so vexed over the question of tithes that he repeatedly calling Moore 'knavish priest' – the sub-Chaucerian dialogue a reminder of the timeless quality of lay/clerical tensions in England.[23]

Traditionally, many of these disputes had played themselves out in the ecclesiastical courts. These were regarded by the clergy as a means not just of protecting their own rights and privileges, but also of policing the morals and spiritual activities of the Christian commonwealth that was the English nation.[24] Yet this essentially benevolent and reformatory ideal concealed a complex structure of mixed utility and popularity. Aspects of the old order of pre-Civil War days were too tainted by association with Laudian clericalism to be revived by parliament after 1660: despite occasional clerical hopes, the Court of High Commission did not return as the keystone in the arch of the church's legal machinery.[25] Without such a supreme authority, the remnants of the edifice have often been depicted as mere rubble, a system that was 'complicated if not confused'.[26] There is much to be said for this. Although the church was primarily administered by bishops within dioceses, more than three hundred 'peculiar' jurisdictions existed outside of immediate episcopal supervision, eighty-two of them within the control of the dean of Salisbury alone.[27] The officials of the diocesan courts, especially chancellors, were often appointed for life, making their effective supervision difficult – even a clerical personage as exalted as the archbishop of Canterbury could express resentment that a key subordinate was too independent.[28] Overall, despite initial significant efforts to recreate the pre-Civil War world, the ecclesiastical courts saw a significant decline in business across our period, not least as a result of the passage of the Toleration Act (1689) – more properly 'An Act for Exempting their Majestyes Protestant Subjects dissenting from the Church of England from the Penalties of certaine Lawes'.[29] In London, the burgeoning metropolis of the nation, the church courts 'never regained their position' at all.[30] Elsewhere, the reimposition of ecclesiastical discipline via the courts during the 1660s could be heavily compromised by the vigorous resistance of men old enough to have resisted the Laudians during their former heyday in the 1630s and 1640s, and who proved more than willing to reignite anticlerical sentiments with accusations of court officials' 'offences against his majesty's laws', and the oppression of the king's subjects.[31] Bishops in many parts of the province of Canterbury were also frequently reduced to impotent fury by those censured in their courts successfully appealing for relief to the central Court of Arches.[32]

Nor is an image of clerical activity necessarily improved by looking beyond clerics' diaries, and the records of the church courts, to examine life more generally in the dioceses that formed the core unit of ecclesiastical administration. Abundant evidence survives to illustrate the degree to which clergy succumbed to backbiting and fratricidal feuds.[33] Some clerics clearly were lazy, venal, or given to flagrant immorality. Few were as egregious as Thomas Wood, dean and subsequently bishop of Lichfield and Coventry. Variously described by his superiors as 'an affliction sent by God', 'our wretched Dean', 'absurd', 'the bad man', 'phrentique', 'most untractable and filthy natur'd', 'scandalous & incorrigible', and 'a monster of unworthiness', Wood was precisely the kind of non-resident, fortune-hunting, malicious idler of which anticlerical authors' dreams were made.[34] But a clergyman did not have to be lazy or deliberately obstructive to damage the church's affairs. The correspondence of successive archbishops of Canterbury displays a virtual textbook of illnesses, ailments, and general symptoms of old age and decrepitude amongst the episcopate – whose job it was to enforce clerical standards and to lead by example – ranging from declining vision and hearing, bloody urine, injuries sustained in the overturning of a coach, through botched surgery on a foot, to 'skirvy & dropsy' and 'singing in my head'.[35] Admittedly, such claims were most commonly offered as excuses in the course of efforts to avoid attendance at parliament, but some bishops went so far as to secure doctors' notes testifying to their unfitness for business.[36] If even a proportion of such afflictions had a basis in fact, the later Stuart episcopate cannot have offered uniformly active and diligent supervision over the lesser clergy.

II

So far, so bad. But a more balanced assessment of the clergy suggests a significantly more positive picture. Here it is necessary both to read much of the negative evidence 'against the grain', or at least carefully in context, and to acknowledge broader, but less eye-catching, evidence of spiritual activity and leadership. Returning to an earlier example, Robert Meeke's diary presents at one level a bleak picture of lay indifference, as well as feelings of personal inadequacy: one of the reasons Meeke refused preferment was terror at the prospect of being expected to deliver learned sermons to congregations of more highly educated men and women than he was used to addressing in Slaithwaite. But the evidence he has left suggests to any eye less perfectionist than his own a minister of high standards and great devotion to his duties.[37] He records taking walks to refresh himself after long periods of study; his tolerance towards local nonconformists; and financial charity to some of his parishioners, despite his own very straightened circumstances.[38]

Nor should bitter disputes over tithes be taken as a universal feature of the English parish landscape. Indeed, arguably more striking than the recorded instances of conflict between ministers and parishioners is the fact that such a huge proportion of tithe payments has left no trace of discord, or else signs of bargaining around the edges of widely acknowledged obligations.[39] The broader picture of business within the church courts is also more mixed than has so far been suggested.[40] Undue weight should probably not be placed on the striking survival of stern penalties meted out by the abnormally active courts on the Isle of Man, where as late as 1715 a female prostitute was sentenced 'to be dragged from a boat on such a day as the vicar will appoint'.[41] But a theme of broader significance can be drawn from this obscure example: the force of active individual clergy – in this case the long-serving bishop of Sodor and Man, Thomas Wilson – could animate legal and administrative structures to a high pitch of activity.[42] With regard to courts, if efficient redress could regularly be found by litigants, business could still proliferate in certain areas, notably women anxious to protect their honour in the face of perceived defamation.[43]

Force of personality held good in other clerical spheres too. William Lloyd, bishop of Worcester, has left us evidence of some of the problem cases he faced amongst his lesser clergy. He blasted those who petitioned him to remove the suspension of John Goodwin, rector of Moreton Bagot, in 1701 for their temerity. Goodwin, he noted, was guilty of numerous 'senseless things' in his clerical life, and was 'fitter to be a day labourer than a minister'. Lloyd was no less harsh on Edward Vernon, rector of Redmile in Leicestershire in 1704. Writing directly to the hapless Vernon, Lloyd referred to his 'supine negligence, minding nothing but yo[u]r humor and yo[u]r Lusts', before concluding that 'I pity yo[u]r poor wife and children, but much more yo[u]rself, to whom God has given good gifts for better purposes than you apply them to.'[44] How should such examples best be interpreted? At one level, of course, they illustrate the continuing extent to which the undeserving and negligent could gain clerical orders, despite decades of efforts by senior churchmen to improve the rigour of ordination examinations.[45] But they also reveal the on-going zeal of many members of the ecclesiastical hierarchy to weed out the small numbers of seriously inept ministers in order to save the clerical order from popular ridicule and the better to honour God.[46] Once again returning to an earlier example, the abundant evidence of Thomas Wood's negligence survives precisely because of the lengths to which Sheldon and Sancroft successively went in order to encourage him to mend his ways, before the latter finally suspended him from 1684 to 1687.[47] The scandal that such cases inevitably prompted needs to be tempered with the warning message that was consciously being sent to other potential malefactors.[48] Bishop Compton of London has left us amongst the most chilling evidence of clerical severity during the period. When informed that one of his clergy, John Thomas, was a persistent drunk, he told Sancroft that 'If your Grace can do nothing w[i]th him I will have his Orders taken from him, his ragged habit taken off his back, & him whipt from constable to Constable, till he comes to his last abode'.[49]

As well as re-examining prominent cases of clerical negligence and censure, we may also turn to more quotidian instances of clerical zeal and activity. In the conference at Braughing with which the previous section began, the clergy were reported as being in support of a renewed emphasis on catechising the young. This was clearly not mere pious rhetoric. Ian Green's exhaustive account of early modern English catechising suggests that the peak period for printing explanations of the catechism lasted from the 1680s through to the 1710s, fully reflecting Archbishop John Tillotson's published claim that 'catechizing and the history of the martyrs have been the two great pillars of the Protestant religion'.[50] The religious education of children was described by Bishop Lloyd of Worcester to the clergy of his diocese as 'a Principal Part of your Duty', and the culmination of this phase of life – confirmation – was undertaken with massive industry by a number of diocesans.[51] During the reign of the Catholic James II, the confirmation tours of bishops in their dioceses served as morale-boosting propaganda to support the contention that few were turning apostate to Rome: more than seven thousand were confirmed by Bishop William

Lloyd of Norwich during Lent 1686, a figure that a contemporary well-wisher thought was three times greater than normal.[52] But the senior clergy's zeal to confirm met with enthusiastic lay demand long after James II's fall. In 1712, for instance, William Wake, bishop of Lincoln, confirmed 11,207 individuals across his massive diocese.[53]

Catechistical endeavours and confirmation tours are just two parts of the broader vibrant health of the clerical body evident in our period. We have already noted the existence of clerical conferences sanctioned by Bishop Compton of London to discuss topics of mutual interest and to promote what might now be called 'life-long learning'. Other diocesans promoted comparable events in their dioceses, or more generally worked hard to maintain an intimate knowledge of the lesser clergy's activity, notably the two William Lloyds – bishops successively of St Asaph, Lichfield and Coventry, and Worcester; and of Peterborough then Norwich, respectively – Gilbert Burnet of Salisbury, and John Sharp, archbishop of York.[54] Sharp was one of a number of senior clerics who sought to ensure that close supervision of the lesser clergy extended beyond his own episcopate by laying down detailed written surveys of his diocese for the benefit of his successors, often including parish-by-parish accounts of clergy and laity.[55] Although such records can easily be perceived as dry-as-dust administrative exercises, when viewed as evidence of bishops' sustained engagement with local clerical standards, they impart a sense of dynamism at odds with the traditional stereotype of an institution stagnating into Georgian slumber.[56] Archbishop Sharp's twenty-two-year stint at York, up to his death in 1714, is also emblematic of a broader drive by senior clergy to ensure a high pitch of clerical activity as a means of advertising the health of the established church in difficult times. Hard-working, authoritarian, and intolerant of low standards, Sharp in the 1690s and 1700s may be compared with William Sancroft in the 1680s: both were archbishops who believed uniformity and adherence to the rubrics of the church to be vital for the nation as a whole.[57] This could set them apart from Low Church clerics, imbued with a sense of the need to reach out the right hand of charity to Protestant nonconformists, but the basic sense of hard labour and persistent effort emphasises what united clerics at a day-to-day level, even when specific issues and political strains pulled them apart.

In no sphere was this sense of zealous activity across the church more obvious than in harnessing the power of print. Religious literature of all kinds dominated the presses throughout the early modern era, and the later Stuart period was no exception. Indeed it seems likely that these years witnessed the culmination of publishing trends that had developed over the seventeenth century as a whole, notably a greater diversity of styles and formats of texts, and a greater social depth of consumers.[58] Nor would the 'market share' of religious works decline between the Revolution of 1688–89 and the end of our period.

Of all new printed titles in 1668–69, 29.5 per cent may be labelled under the broad penumbra 'divinity', and this had risen to 50.5 per cent in 1700–4, with an average of 41.8 per cent across the period 1668–1709. By way of perspective, the next largest comparable category of works was 'history' with just 7.6 per cent of new titles.[59] The raw numbers of texts that were produced are, if anything, even more striking. In excess of 140,000 catechisms and primers, psalters and psalms were produced in 1663, and this rose to over 180,000 in 1703; while a best-selling devotional work, Richard Allestree's *Whole Duty of Man* (1657), was printed so many times and in such volume that there may well have been enough to supply one in ten English households with a copy by the end of Queen Anne's reign.[60]

Recent work has sharpened our awareness of the fact that religious works would continue to dominate the English publishing market throughout the eighteenth century.[61] By no means all these works were produced by clerics, though vast numbers certainly were: the cathedral clergy in particular were an exceptionally productive subset of authors.[62] Individual clerics advertised their pride in their writings. Humphrey Prideaux, prebendary (1681–1702) and later dean (1702–24) of Norwich, emphasised how much time he spent combating Catholic authors in print during the reign of James II, while ambitious men like Laurence Womock and Thomas Comber pursued promotion in part on the back of their publishing efforts.[63] Some clerics became such prolifically published figures that their prominence produced very mixed results: Gilbert Burnet's *History of the Reformation of the Church of England* (2 volumes, 1679–81) gained him the thanks of both houses of parliament and a Doctorate of Divinity from Oxford, but he was also vigorously satirised in a number of popular pamphlets for his excessively garrulous and self-confident character.[64] Such thrusting and ambitious clerical authors could naturally slide into fratricidal slanging matches. Comber published a second part to his *History of Tithes* partly as a response to what he regarded as Burnet's spiteful reflections: 'his parts & popularity enable him to do great mischief'.[65]

Clerical vanity was most obvious in an extremely important section of religious publishing: sermons. Robert Meeke was highly unusual in refusing to publish his sermons, explicitly on the basis that he feared the sin of pride.[66] It was far more common for the dedications and epistles to the reader which preceded the text of printed sermons to emphasise how the author had reluctantly been dragged into print by the importunities of friends or patrons. Whatever the precise motivation, huge numbers of clerics certainly chose to publish their sermon texts.[67] It has been estimated that around 24,000 sermons were printed between 1660 and 1783.[68] Inexpensive and widely available, sermons were so lucrative that some printers were able to specialise in their production, a commercial fact that has been used to emphasise the frailties of arguments concerning the growing 'secularisation' of later Stuart cultural and political norms.[69] Indeed, the 'ubiquity' and 'pivotal place' of sermons in seventeenth- and eighteenth-century discourse is now widely recognised.[70] Nearly 2,500 sermons were published in 1710 alone.[71] Some were runaway best sellers, notably William Beveridge's *A Sermon Concerning the Excellency and Usefulness of the Common Prayer*, which went through twenty-two editions between 1681 and 1714, including a Dublin edition (1698) in which the bookseller, Jacob Milner, mixed piety with self-interest when he urged the archbishop of Dublin 'to recommend to his Clergy, the buying some Dozens of them, to be distributed amongst their poor Parishioners'.[72] With a developing statistical understanding of the print world it is difficult simply to deride clerics who claimed great value and significance for their preaching efforts, even if those claims do display considerable self-regard. John Hacket, bishop of Lichfield and Coventry, for instance, reported claims that his 1665 visitation sermon in Wem was so persuasive that it had reduced the number of Presbyterians in the town by one hundred, while a Northamptonshire vicar's 'constant preaching & pious conversation' in the early 1680s was said to have 'brought allmost ye whole parish to a conformity'.[73] Although John Lake, bishop of Chichester, might inveigh against dissenters' 'old loud music of the pulpit' in the difficult circumstances of 1687, a number of his peers were more than prepared to devote significant time to their own preaching endeavours.[74] William Lloyd of Worcester preached eight times in twelve days during a visitation in 1700, and even a clergyman like Sancroft, who was chary of printing his sermons, has left substantial manuscript notebooks to indicate how seriously he took this aspect of his clerical vocation.[75] John Tillotson, who would succeed Sancroft at Canterbury from 1691, embraced the press more wholeheartedly, indeed he was one of the preaching celebrities of the age. Fifty-four of his sermons had appeared in print by the time of his death in 1694, and another two hundred were subsequently edited by his chaplain for publication in fourteen volumes between 1695 and 1704.[76] It would be foolhardy to claim that all later Stuart clerics were eager, still less prolific, preachers – Ralph Josselin, for instance, declined an invitation from the town's corporation to preach in Colchester, and confided to his diary that he did not wish to be a paid lecturer there, 'as not fitt to deale with their wrangling spirits'.[77] Nevertheless, preaching was clearly taken very seriously indeed by a huge number of later Stuart clergy who continued and developed, rather than fell away from, the activity of their late Elizabethan and early Stuart forbears.[78]

III

Sermons provide a convenient connection between later Stuart clerics' day-to-day religious duties and their more controversial activity as political actors. The marquis of Halifax did not mince his words when he wrote against pluralists and argued that 'your sermons are but a very indifferent barter for your tithes'.[79] Halifax, and other lay critics of outspoken clergy, regularly urged preachers to stick to expounding scripture and to avoid engaging with current affairs.[80] Overtly political sermons only ever constituted a small minority of those preached across the country as a whole.[81] Nevertheless, because they tended to be delivered in particularly prominent places – particularly at court and before parliament – and on notable public occasions, they often excited significant wider commentary.[82] Thus the vicar of Rodbourne-Cheney in Wiltshire chose to publish a sermon that he had originally delivered during an episcopal visitation in 1682 only after the accession of James II in 1685. The original sermon, he noted, had led to his being scorned and abused in front of his congregation because he had chosen to criticise the House of Commons for passing Bills of Exclusion against James as duke of York. He was unrepentant, and emphasised what he saw as the inextricable links between divine and royal authority:

> surely it is the bounden Duty of every Minister, in an especial manner to defend his Religion, and the Prerogatives Royal. We that are Christ's Ambassadors, may not suffer the Royalties of his Vineyard to be torn from him, without betraying our Trust to our God and our King too.[83]

Others were not so sure, especially when James II's promotion of Roman Catholicism threatened the Church of England's privileged status.[84] One of the king's most prominent clerical supporters, Thomas Cartwright, bishop of Chester, admonished a preacher in his cathedral for 'reflecting so imprudently as he did upon the King's religion'.[85] The London clergy were even more outspoken, and Bishop Compton's refusal to clamp down on their aggressive anti-Catholic preaching led James to secure his suspension.[86] A conflict for control of the pulpits was thus at the very heart of James's troubled reign: when preachers abruptly shifted away from a quarter of a century of preaching up the necessity of obedience to God's anointed, God's anointed was clearly in very serious political trouble.[87]

Politicised preaching only increased in fervour and prominence after the Revolution of 1688–89.[88] This was inevitable, thanks to the widespread tensions prompted by regime change, and more particularly the fact that the clergy were peculiarly affected by the trauma of James's fall at the hands of a Williamite invasion. Although strikingly few clerics had preached against the invasion as it occurred, subsequently more than four hundred clerics, including some of the most dynamic bishops of the previous decade, could not reconcile taking oaths of loyalty to William and Mary with their pre-existing oaths to James and became 'non-jurors', losing their livings as a result.[89] Such clerics were especially antagonised by the rise to favour of those eager to trumpet the providential and positive aspects of William's intervention, in particular Gilbert Burnet, whose indefatigable preaching and publishing on behalf of 'Revolution principles' made him appear a tame propagandist for the new court.[90] And between the extremes of non-jurors and Low Church clergy, High-Churchmen who remained a part of the Church of England also played a prominent role in influencing the nation from the pulpit. To take one prominent example from many, the splendidly named Ofspring Blackall, Tory bishop of Exeter from 1708, preached a mammoth series of eighty-seven sermons that were published as *Discourses on the Sermon on the Mount*, yet attracted very little attention. But when, on the seventh anniversary of Anne's accession, he preached before her in St James's Chapel on the theme of *The Divine Institution of Magistracy*, he triggered a major controversy with the Deist John Toland about the right of resistance in the state and the origins of episcopal authority.[91] All of this paled into insignificance, compared to the furore surrounding a sermon preached in 1709 by the High Church zealot Henry Sacheverell, to which we will return shortly.

Clerics did not just intervene in political affairs through the texts of their sermons. In our period they were also enfranchised as voters for the first time, as well as continuing to exert influence through the bishops' role in the House of Lords and as local grandees. More fitfully, clergy of several degrees of status achieved prominence through their representative assembly, convocation.

Clerical voting was inaugurated in a bizarrely haphazard way. As a result of an oral agreement in 1664 between the Lord Chancellor, Edward Hyde, and the archbishop of Canterbury, Gilbert Sheldon, the clergy surrendered their right to be taxed separately from the laity through convocation in return for the right to vote in parliamentary elections on the basis of the property attached to their ecclesiastical benefices.[92] This had the immediate consequence of ensuring that convocation did not sit to debate matters of substance until 1689: it no longer fulfilled a sufficiently clear fiscal purpose for the crown to guarantee its survival. But in the long term it brought clergy into the heart of parliamentary electioneering with significant results: by 1714 a Whig politician in Wiltshire could write with a certain sense of weariness that 'a good or bad clergyman for a neighbour is capable of giving much ease or much trouble to a gentleman who concerns himself in public elections'.[93] In Leicestershire the clergy were described as 'generally bewitch't with State Politicks', and the archdeacon of Bedford, Thomas Frank, urged the need 'to keep the clergy quiet, that during the election they may not run into any extravagant heats, and that when it is over we may meet together as friends and unanimously pursue the great ends of our holy calling'.[94]

Frank was clearly whistling to keep his spirits up. In reality, a significant proportion of the clergy were deeply engaged with contemporary electoral politics, either from personal interest, or from a concern to secure parliamentary returns that would safeguard their vision of the church's best interest, or both.[95] Even before the creation of a substantial clerical electorate after 1664, twelve clergy were sworn in as freemen of the town by the mayor of Rochester in an effort to block the election of the Presbyterian Royalist Sir William Batten in 1661.[96] This was an early indication of the perceived influence of solid voting blocs of cathedral clergy in their home towns, both in terms of their own numbers in relatively small electorates and as a socially significant force to influence other voters.[97] A particularly blatant example of clerical activity occurred in Durham in 1708, when the bishop and chapter invited a local schoolmaster to preach in the cathedral and market-place church on the same day in order to harangue the city's mayor and aldermen. 'By hard straining', the preacher 'perverted' the text I Samuel 12:3 'into the management of elections, on which his whole discourse ran, lashing all those who opposed Mr [Thomas] Conyers, concluding that damnation would be their future lot if they did not repent of such a heinous sin, as the very attempting to reject so true and trusty a member of the Church'.[98] Other cathedral towns saw clergy involved in even more fractious divisions. Nowhere was this more fevered than in Norwich, where a written death-threat was left for Bishop Sparrow on his stall in the cathedral in 1678. Signed 'S. Blood', this bluntly stated: 'I will kill you ... it seems you are grown a viper not fit to live; you limb of Satan.'[99]

Sparrow was both a vigorous persecutor of nonconformity and a highly active local political leader in terms of mobilising the lesser clergy at election time.[100] He was one of a number of bishops in the period who issued circular letters to his clergy in an attempt to direct their vote. At a by-election in 1675, for instance, the bishop of Bristol, Guy Carleton, informed the clerical electors of Dorset that 'I cannot in discharge of my duty to God' allow a candidate backed by the earl of Shaftesbury, a leading opponent of the court, to be elected without opposition:

> and therefore humbly desire you will not only vote yourselves for ye L[or]d Digby a person of great honor and known loyalty, but ingage what freeholders you can to vote with you. For at this time it is both your duty and Interest ... as wee honor ye King and love ye peace of ye Church and state.[101]

Although in this case he contributed to a successful election campaign, Carleton would enjoy only mixed results once translated to Chichester, a dissenting stronghold. He was keen to boast of his success in the Sussex shire elections in 1685: 'there had certainly been a great opposition had not my intrest in this my Diocess with the clergy, and theirs upon my account w[i]th ye freeholders of their parishes made my number soe great, that the Whigg party did lay downe their resolutions'.[102] But within Chichester itself his provocative actions as an increasingly irascible and sickly old man were rewarded with the vigorous and bitter opposition of local dissenters and their conforming Whig allies.[103]

After the Revolution a number of senior clerics took their efforts to act as local political power-brokers to an even higher level.[104] For some, this represented an effort to bolster the Revolution settlement, and the new regime it was ushering in. Thus Bishop Compton, who had secretly contributed to the 'Invitation' to William to invade in 1688, proved a formidable organiser of the clergy within his diocese.[105] And even before he was raised to the episcopate, William Nicolson did not hesitate to lecture the clergy within the archdeaconry of Carlisle in May 1689: 'The short of our case is, the late King was pleased unexpectedly to leave us; and their present Majesties have stepped into the throne as the next lawful successors. And where is the mischief of all this?'[106] Others needed to shore up their personal political positions after *not* visibly supporting the Revolution. Sir Jonathan Trelawny, successively bishop of Bristol, Exeter, and Winchester, voted against the offer of the crown to William and Mary in the Convention, but thereafter worked hard to build up his family's West Country networks of patronage into a formidable electoral machine. It has been sardonically noted that by 1713 Trelawny 'made it a point of canonical obedience in the clergy to solicit' for a Tory candidate.[107] When one Exeter clergyman failed to toe the episcopal pro-Tory line in 1705, Trelawny worked to destroy his career, saying he had acted 'in a violent contradiction to the measures which I was taking in this diocese for her Majesty's service'.[108] But in his ardent pro-Tory electioneering Trelawny was an increasingly unusual relic of the 1680s, when the Sancroftian church had provided vigorous support for the right of James, duke of York to succeed to the throne. The sea-change in episcopal appointments that had occurred over the course of the 1690s resulted in a bench that was often strikingly at political odds with the lesser clergy, dominated as the latter were by Tories.[109] Despite the fact that the bishop of Norwich in 1703 was the prominent Low Churchman John Moore, a Tory brewer in the town triumphed in a by-election, partly on the back of clerical support: the dean censoriously noted that several minor canons of the cathedral had 'disgraced themselves ... by running after Mr Palgrave's chair and hallowing and flinging up their hats among the mob'.[110] Across the border in Suffolk things went even further awry from a Low Church perspective: eighty clergy polled en masse for the Tory candidates in the county election at Ipswich as a mob shouted 'no '48, no Presbyterian rebellion, save the Queen's white neck'.[111]

Such historically inflected religious rhetoric was a core part of the electoral process in the later part of our period, particularly as a result of a long-running clerical institutional conflict and an individual cause célèbre. Fault-lines within the clergy were exposed by a developing High Church campaign to secure the recall of convocation (after a temporary and contentious return in 1689) as a counter-balance to what many clerics increasingly saw as the kow-towing of Whig state ministers to nonconformists and their Low Church allies.[112] This was finally achieved in 1701, with consequences every bit as divisive as William III had feared. Francis Atterbury, who would rise to the bishopric of Rochester in 1713, was at the heart of agitation developing around a language of 'the church in danger'; in danger, that is, from the twin threats of Erastian laymen outside the clerical body and craven bishops (especially Burnet) within it who were willing to sacrifice the rights of the church on the altar of maintaining good relations with nonconformists.[113] Repeated stand-offs between vehement High Churchmen in the lower house of convocation and the bishops in the upper, exacerbated the ill-feeling many clerics felt for the role that the bishops played in supporting Whig ministries in the House of Lords.[114]

The hostility that many of the lesser clergy felt towards many of the bishops came to fruition in the Sacheverell crisis of 1709–10.[115] On 5 November 1709 the ultra-High Church preacher Henry Sacheverell delivered a sermon on I Corinthians 11 – St Paul's warning about being 'in peril among False Brethren' – in St Paul's Cathedral before the Whiggish governing elite of the City.[116] He could not have spoken more intemperately, railing against nonconformists as 'monsters and vipours in our bosom', those 'clamorous, insatiable and Church-devouring malignants', 'miscreants begot in rebellion, born in sedition, and nurs'd up in faction'.[117] And he urged sound Churchmen 'to confront the false brethren by presenting "an army of banners to our enemies", by putting on "the whole armour of God", and by wrestling "not only against flesh and blood, but against principalities, against powers, against the rulers of the darkness of this world, against spiritual wickedness in high places"'.[118] The printed version of the sermon became a sensation, with more than 100,000 copies printed, suggesting a likely readership of between 250,000 and 500,000 in a world of communal reading and shared texts.[119] The excitement generated by the sermon transformed Sacheverell into one of the most prominent public figures of the day. This may in part be measured by the number of prints that were produced disseminating his portrait, and a wider range of satirical prints for and against him as a High Church champion.[120] But it was even more obvious in the Whig government's unwise decision to prosecute him for seditious libel via impeachment proceedings in parliament.[121] This became a public relations disaster. Sacheverell was escorted by more than one hundred clerical supporters to his trial, while the pulpits resounded to High Church sermons of support in January and February 1710.[122] Much of the London populace was whipped up to a frenzy by the fighting talk that followed Sacheverell's own violent rhetoric.[123] Massive riots ensued in London on the night of 1–2 March in which High Church-supporting mobs deliberately targeted dissenters' meeting houses, the private homes of leading Whig politicians and Low Church clerics, as well as the Bank of England as a symbol of the new 'monied interest' whose profits Tories believed to be the key factor maintaining the long and otherwise debilitating war with France.[124]

The political temperature would be maintained long after the riots had been quelled. Sacheverell embarked on a tour of England, lauded by huge crowds as a champion of the church against its subtle and semi-concealed opponents.[125] The Sacheverell affair provided a fevered backdrop to the general election of 1710, which resulted in a thumping Tory victory at the polls. Predictably, many clergy were at the heart of events. In the Shropshire election fifty clergy voted as a body for the Tory candidates: ''twas a very fine sight'.[126] In York, the dean of the minster rode at the head of 'a great body of clergy' whilst schoolboys paraded with a flag featuring an image of Sacheverell.[127] In Pembrokeshire, the feeling was so strong that the usual Whig power broker, Sir Arthur Owen, was swept away by an electoral tsunami after comparing current clerical pretensions with those of the Laudian era: fifty clergy voted against him.[128] In the Essex county election 125 of 143 clerical voters voted solely for Tory candidates; around 300 did the same in Lincolnshire, compared to only 15 or 16 for Whig candidates.[129] In Northampton, clergy were said to be busy 'brow-beating and discouraging the electors', whilst in Kent those clergy brave enough to espouse Whig opinions were derided as 'chaplains to the Calves-head Club', a scandalous reference to meetings of republicans and Deist free-thinkers.[130] Cathedral clergy were prominent, including at Carlisle and Bristol, while John Harvey, the Tory candidate for Bedfordshire, boasted that he was standing 'at the request of the whole body of the clergy' in the county.[131] The last four years of Anne's reign thus featured a substantial Tory majority in parliament that owed a tremendous amount to the politics of religion in general, and the electioneering activity of clerics in particular. It would take time for Sacheverell's popularity to decline to the extent that a canny entrepreneur spotted a gap in the market and made a killing by manufacturing chamber-pots with the controversial clergyman's image depicted at the bottom.[132] A face once deemed to excite women so much that they were pictured in hostile prints as kissing his arse thus ultimately attracted a very different form of devotion.[133]

Yet any account of the clergy's political role should end with a sense of balance. Although they were undoubtedly influential figures in local communities, and were seen as formidable groups when organised into mass voting blocs at election time, the clergy did not command automatic obedience from the laity, nor does the evidence suggest that they always got their way. Two significant caveats need to be noted, then, to the general picture of clerical electioneering influence. The first is that a really well-organised lay politician, deeply enmeshed in local society, and careful to mobilise all his ties of patronage and influence, was not at the mercy of clerical opposition. A particularly striking example is that of the bitter conflict in Worcestershire during the 1700s between the local Tory grandee, Sir John Packington, and the Whig bishop, William Lloyd. Despite persistent efforts to mobilise his clergy against Packington, and to influence lay electors via the bailiffs of several manors in the county, Lloyd proved unable to prevent Packington's repeated electoral success. For his part, Packington reacted to the bishop's accusations of personal immorality and Jacobite tendencies by complaining to the House of Commons in 1702. The House voted the bishop and his son guilty of 'malicious, unchristian, and arbitrary proceedings' and successfully called on the queen to remove Lloyd from his position as lord almoner within the Chapel Royal.[34] Such a lack of clerical political success may also be generalised. To give just one example: although Thomas Lewis, the Tory candidate to be knight of the shire for Hampshire in 1705, was thought likely to win in part because 'He is secure of the clergy', in fact he lost by a substantial margin.[35]

The second caveat is that, as several of the examples previously cited have already shown, the clergy did not represent a homogeneous political body. Although stress is usually laid on the conflicts between a predominantly Whig episcopate, by the latter part of our period, and a predominantly Tory parish clergy, this should not obscure the divisions within both the upper and lower ranks of the clerical order. Tory bishops like Sir Jonathan Trelawny and Nathaniel, Lord Crewe remained forces to be reckoned with, while most areas retained a minority of Whig clergymen: forty clerics voted for John Harvey's Whig opponent in Bedfordshire even at the Sacheverell-inspired Tory zenith of the 1710 elections.[36] Although we have seen that Sir Arthur Owen was defeated in Pembrokeshire in the same election, partly due to fifty clerical opponents, a Tory noted bitterly that there was nevertheless 'a Judas among the Apostles; 7 of them polled for Sir Arthur'.[37] The electorate was too volatile in this period, and the issues at stake both locally and nationally too varied, for clergy automatically to dominate events, even before we take into account the anticlericalism that clearly influenced some lay voters. Circumstances in Oxford were peculiarly influenced by the close proximity of so many clergymen in the university's colleges, leading to notoriously poor town–gown relations, but when a mob shouted at the 1681 election for the city's representatives 'No universities, no scholars, no clergy, no bishops!' it was giving voice to critical sentiments that in more reserved form may have influenced many.[38] Such qualifications always need to be kept in mind when considering what, it has been argued, were the very significant and prominent political roles played by clergymen throughout the later Stuart period.

IV

The core themes of this chapter may be pulled together through a concluding case study that is, on one level, merely sordidly unpleasant. Thomas Naish was a native of Wiltshire, born in 1669 to parents who were 'highly zealous for the Church of England established by law'.[39] After entering the priesthood, Naish proved extremely ambitious for promotion, his hunger for better livings and higher status apparently only fuelled further by an extremely advantageous marriage to a woman whose dowry lands in Devon he sold in 1694 for the very substantial sum of £1,000.[40] The same year saw Naish made sub-dean of Salisbury Cathedral through the patronage of the local bishop, Gilbert Burnet. In time, however, Burnet came to realise that he had clasped a snake to the episcopal bosom: Naish's strident Tory politics and High Church beliefs were strikingly at odds with the bishop's position as an outspoken champion of Whig interests. The decline in their relationship makes for gruesomely absorbing reading in the pages of Naish's diary. In 1696 Naish referred to Burnet as 'my noble freind and patron', and the bishop assured Naish's father that his son would benefit from episcopal love and 'be a considerable man in the Church'.[41] But steel entered Naish's soul when Burnet persistently passed him over for further offices, notably a prebend in Salisbury Cathedral, between 1697 and 1701.[42] So frustrated was he by May 1701 that he agreed to co-operate with a legal assault on Burnet, masterminded by the Tory dean of Exeter, by testifying to the bishop's allegedly simoniacal practices. Naish was chillingly frank within the pages of his diary when explaining his motivation in biting the hand that had fed him: 'I consented to my Lord Altham because I think the Bishop of Sarum [i.e. Salisbury] has wronged me in keeping a prebend from me so long.'[43]

Much more was to follow. Seven months after engaging in the partisan legal action, Naish voted for the Tory candidates for knights of the shire in Wiltshire even though he knew that Burnet was strongly backing their Whig opponents.[44] By early 1702 the bishop was sufficiently angry that he called Naish and his father 'two pert and sawcy persons', and successfully ensured that Naish lost one of his offices.[45] Naish's response was to seek influential Tory supporters to maintain his stalled career and future prospects. Sir Jonathan Trelawny, bishop of Exeter, and Laurence Hyde, earl of Rochester, took him under their wings, while at a local level Sir Richard Howe began to provide him with money explicitly to sustain his partisan struggle against Burnet and influenced a powerful local peer, Lord Weymouth, to make Naish his chaplain in 1708.[46] By 1705 the vendetta was so absorbing Naish that he wrote out an account of his dealings with Burnet in a separate book from his diary.[47] The bishop appeared to have reached match-point with his difficult underling when, at this time, he put Naish under a three-year suspension for being inducted into a second clerical living without an episcopal dispensation. But Naish was far from cowed. In July 1706 Burnet sought to rally local loyalist sentiments to the crown by circulating an address to Queen Anne congratulating her on the military successes of her armies in Europe, notably the recent Battle of Ramillies. Unfortunately, the Whig Low Churchman could not resist a swipe at his opponents, including in the address the incendiary words: 'None but the confederates of our enemys, and those who are deluded by them can imagine our Church to be in danger.'[48] Clerical carnage ensued.

Naish recorded that many local clergy were 'shocked' at these words, and in consequence of them refused to sign the address. Sensing a rich opportunity to embarrass his diocesan, Naish promptly drew up an alternative address and indefatigably criss-crossed the diocese until he had gained no fewer than eighty-nine clerical signatures. Riding up to London, Naish succeeded in getting the address brought before the queen, who ordered the (Tory) Secretary of State, Sir Charles Hedges – a man with strong Wiltshire connections – to ensure that the address was noted in the *London Gazette* for wider attention.[49] Nevertheless, Naish's triumph was short lived. In 1707 he suffered the mortification of having an invitation to preach in London at the annual feast for the sons of the clergy withdrawn in the face of the (Whig) archbishop of Canterbury's determination to avoid having 'a party man' hold forth at an event he was expected to attend.[50] Although Naish believed that he had managed to turn the ensuing controversy 'much to my credit' – to the tune of a gift of plate worth £9, and a partisan toast at the feast – his good fortune did not last. Nemesis finally came as a result of Naish's determined support for Sacheverell's cause in 1710, against Burnet's equally determined hostility. When Naish's brother, William, ill-advisedly accused the bishop of preaching 'lies', Burnet successfully pursued him under the writ of *scandalum magnatum*, ultimately being awarded £100 after a trial in February 1711.[51]

This whole sordid tale may be taken as a darker version of the plot of an Anthony Trollope novel, with petty-minded clerics scratching each other's eyes out in pursuit of their own low ambitions. Yet a careful reading of the Naish/ Burnet feud yields a more nuanced picture. It is noteworthy that the two men initially formed an amicable bond because of a shared passion for preaching. Burnet saw in his young protégé someone with a zeal to expound the Word that approached his own: Naish recorded how tired he was in late December 1695 after preaching seven times in eight days.[52] Indeed, he believed that the 'good opinion' his parish had of his preaching attracted envy from other local clergy. As early as 1694 he recorded that he was mocked by the chanter of Salisbury Cathedral, the prominent Low Churchman Daniel Whitby: 'Here is a young cock begins to crow too soon, I must cut his comb for him.'[53]

Naish's preaching vigour was the most obvious manifestation of a strong sense of his clerical vocation. When he was admitted deacon in 1690 he was under the canonical age of twenty-three, but offered a passionate sense in his diary of what the event meant for him:

> O Lord who hast called me to this holy office in thy Church, enable me faithfully to discharge the same; let my life and conversation be such as becomes thy gospell, that I may be an honour to thy Religion. Grant that I may ever remember that day when I dedicated my self to thy service, that I may conscientiously performe all my vows, and so faithfully serve thee in thy Church tryumphant and be numbred with thy saints in everlasting glory.[54]

Nor can such sentiments be dismissed merely as the views of a young man before the canker of careerism disfigured his life. A similar keen sense of vocation pervades his record of being ordained priest in 1691; references to his 'high calling' appear in 1694; and he entered into his twenty-seventh year in June 1695 with 'A Holy Resolution' to abjure all sins.[55] Furthermore, he was charitable with his considerable wealth. In 1699, for instance, after observing how fervently he said his prayers in church, Naish paid for a pious boy from a poor local family to go to school, and continued to assist him at university, and then as a clerical schoolmaster from 1709.[56] Naish also couched his political actions in terms closely connected to his clerical function. When he voted for prospective Tory MPs against Burnet's Whig candidates in 1701 he recorded that 'I have acted according to my conscience in doing what I thought best for the good of the Church', sentiments that would pervade his evident horror at the contrast between the favour shown to the ultra-Low Church Benjamin Hoadly and the legal assault on Henry Sacheverell in 1710.[57] Naish's vendetta with Burnet evidently did not ruin his pastoral reputation: he proudly recorded in 1708 the significant number of his parishioners who had continued to pay him tithes during his three-year suspension.[58] As late as November 1727, Naish was still a vigorous preacher, offering an upbeat account of the similarities between preaching and harmonious sounds to Salisbury's Society of Lovers of Music: preaching 'is sometimes attended with such manner of Expression, such a Happiness of Voice, and Variety of Tone, according to the true Importance of the Words, and, after all, with such true and proper Cadence, that it has come little short of a Musical Performance, and has sometimes wrought Wonders in the Conversion of many'.[59] There is no reason to doubt the sincerity of his belief in the usefulness of preaching, or of his broader clerical vocation.

We do not know whether Naish ultimately felt the frustration bordering on despair that often seems to have afflicted Burnet in the face of the limited efficacy of his actions. In 1710 the latter recorded that he was probably 'doing little good with all this agitation' to increase clerical standards and pastoral efficiency within his diocese.[160] For all their differences in politics and church- manship, Naish and Burnet were united by a shared zeal to expound God's Word and to minister to their flocks. Many clerical diaries include pessi- mistic statements about the poor understanding of Christianity manifested by many laymen, or else about their own poverty and marginal status. Yet no one writing an account of the later Stuart church should be so seduced by such accounts as to lose sight of the fact that thousands of clergymen were less preoccupied with matters of pluralism, political influence, and polemical writing than with the day-to-day exercise of their ministry within parishes and dioceses that remained powerful organising structures in daily life throughout the period and far beyond.

NOTES

I am very grateful to George Southcombe and Catherine Wright for commenting on a draft version of this chapter. I am also happy to acknowledge the British Academy and the Arts and Humanities Research Council for their support, in the form of a Postdoctoral Fellowship held at Darwin College and the Faculty of History, Cambridge, and an Early Career Fellowship sponsored by the University of St Andrews.

1 *Codex juris ecclesiastici Anglicani: or, the statutes, constitutions, canons, rubricks and articles of the Church of England* ... 2 vols (1713), I, xxix.

2 S. Taylor, 'Edmund Gibson', *ODNB*.

3 *Codex juris ecclesiastici Anglicani*, I, sig. A2.

4 C. Jackson (ed.), *The diary of Abraham de la Pryme* ... (Publications of the Surtees Society, 54, 1869), p. 150.

5 For this theme, see J.E.C. Hill, *Economic problems of the church: from Archbishop Whitgift to the Long Parliament* (Oxford: Oxford University Press, 1956); F. Heal, *Of prelates and princes. A study of the economic and social position of the Tudor episcopate* (Cambridge: Cambridge University Press, 1980).

6 To appropriate the title of P. Virgin, *The church in an age of negligence. Ecclesiastical structure and problems of church reform 1700–1840* (Cambridge: James Clarke & Co., 1989).

7 J. Spurr, 'Gilbert Sheldon', *ODNB*.

8 M. Goldie, 'Priestcraft and the birth of Whiggism', in N.T. Phillipson and Q. Skinner (eds), *Political discourse in early modern Britain* (Cambridge: Cambridge University Press, 1993), pp. 209–31; J.A.I. Champion, *The pillars of priestcraft shaken: the Church of England and its enemies, 1660–1730* (Cambridge: Cambridge University Press, 1992).

9 See in particular M. Knights, *Representation and misrepresentation in later Stuart Britain: partisanship and political culture* (Oxford: Oxford University Press, 2004), which focuses on the 1690s and 1700s.

10 P. Collinson, *The Elizabethan Puritan movement* (Jonathan Cape, 1967), part 4, 'Moderate courses'.

11 E. Carpenter, *The Protestant bishop. Being the life of Henry Compton, 1632–1713, Bishop of London* (Longmans, 1956), pp. 208–16.

12 Bodl. MS Rawlinson C 983, fols 38–9: Jo[hn] Goodman to Henry Compton, bishop of London, [?Great] Hadham, 26 Sept. 1679. (Partially noted in Carpenter, *Protestant bishop*, pp. 212–13, where the venue is given as 'Brangham', an accurate transcription of the letter, but not a real place.)

13 Though for more nuanced local perspectives, see C. Holmes, *Seventeenth-century Lincolnshire* (Lincoln: History of Lincolnshire Committee for the Society for Lincolnshire History and Archaeology, 1980); D.A. Spaeth, *The church in an age of danger. Parsons and parishioners, 1660–1740* (Cambridge: Cambridge University Press, 2000), esp. chapters 4–6.

14 M.N. Brown (ed.), *The works of George Savile Marquis of Halifax*, 3 vols (Oxford: Oxford University Press, 1989), III, 441; John Tutchin, 'The tribe of Levi', in W.J. Cameron (ed.), *Poems on affairs of state. Augustan satirical verse, 1660–1714*, volume 5: 1688–1697 (New Haven and London: Yale University Press, 1971), pp. 295, 284.

15   J. Spurr, 'Schism and the restoration church', *JEH*, 41 (1990), 408–24.

16   D.R. Hirschberg, 'The government and Church patronage in England, 1660–1670', *JBS*, 20 (1980–81), 109–39; J.H. Pruett, 'Career patterns among the clergy of Lincoln Cathedral, 1660–1750', *Church History*, 44 (1975), 204–16; V. Barrie-Curien, 'Clerical recruitment and career patterns in the Church of England during the eighteenth century', in W.M. Jacob and N. Yates (eds), *Crown and mitre: religion and society in northern Europe since the Reformation* (Woodbridge: Boydell, 1993), pp. 93–104.

17   Bodl. MS Tanner 34, fol. 144: William Sancroft to William Battie, Lambeth House, 22 Sept. 1683.

18   G. Holmes, *Augustan England: professions, state and society, 1680–1730* (HarperCollins, 1982), p. 99.

19   See, for instance, Bodl. MSS Tanner 38, fols 1, 14, 82; 37, fol. 255; 36, fols 88, 95; 35, fols 71, 138; 34, fols 93, 121, 136, 199, 240; 32, fols 85, 89, 110, and, more generally, J. Spurr, 'Laurence Womock', *ODNB*.

20   H.J. Morehouse (ed.), *Extracts from the diary of the Rev. Robert Meeke ...* (1874), p. 36. (See John 5: 35; 2 Pet. 1: 19.)

21   Morehouse (ed.), *Extracts from the Diary of the Rev. Robert Meeke*, pp. 44–5.

22   On the theme of tithes as a source of dispute, see W.J. Sheils, '"The right of the Church": the clergy, tithe and the courts at York 1540–1640', *SCH*, 24 (1987), 231–55.

23   R.W. Blencowe (ed.), *Extracts from the journal and account book of the Rev. Giles Moore ... 1655 to 1679* (Sussex Archaeological Collections, I, 1848), pp. 90, 121–2.

24   Martin Ingram's work is fundamental here, especially his *Church courts, sex and marriage in England, 1570–1640* (Cambridge: Cambridge University Press, 1987).

25   W.N. Darrell (ed.), *The correspondence of Isaac Basire, D.D., Archdeacon of Northumberland and Prebendary of Durham ...* (1831), p. 224; R.S. Bosher, *The making of the Restoration settlement. The influence of the Laudians 1649–1662* (Dacre Press, 1951), pp. 255–6.

26   B. Till, *The church courts 1660–1720: the revival of procedure* (Borthwick Paper no. 109, York, 2006), p. 12.

27   *Ibid.*, p. 8.

28   *Ibid.*, p. 8; Bodl. MSS Tanner 34, fols 35v, 75, 89 (all of which refer to controversy over the bishop of Bristol's courts in the 1680s); 30, fol. 68; 38, fol. 97 (for the archbishop of Canterbury's reported frustrations).

29   Spaeth, *Church in an age of danger*, chapter 3; W. Marshall, *Church life in Hereford and Oxford 1660–1760. A study of two sees* (Lancaster: Carnegie Publishing, 2009), chapter 3.

30   This is a key finding of an extremely important unpublished thesis: F.N. Dabhoiwala, 'Prostitution and police in London, c.1660–c.1760' (DPhil dissertation, University of Oxford, 1995), p. 94 and chapters 3–4 more widely. (I am grateful to Dr Dabhoiwala for permission to quote from his work.)

31   To quote Colonel Edward King in reference to the courts in the diocese of Lincoln: Holmes, *Seventeenth-century Lincolnshire*, pp. 225–6.

32   E.g., Bodl. MSS Tanner 45, fol. 265; 42, fol. 119; 37, fols 73, 82; 36, fol. 251; 35, fol. 130; 27, fol. 24. For wider information, see T.E. James, 'The Court of Arches during the 18th century: its matrimonial jurisdiction', *American Journal of Legal History*, 5 (1961), 55–66; M.D. Slatter, 'The records of the Court of Arches', *JEH*, 4 (1953), 139–53.

33 For an extended case study of a particularly vicious episode, see the concluding section of this essay.

34 Bodl. MSS Tanner 45, fols 278, 295; 44, fols 15, 22, 66, 69, 128v, 151; and, generally, B.S. Benedikz, 'Thomas Wood', *ODNB*.

35 Here the evidence is so abundant that it is tempting to suggest to medical historians the possibilities of more detailed study concerning episcopal ill-health: Bodl. MSS Tanner 48, fol. 69; 44, fol. 149; 43, fols 68, 74; 42, fol. 142; 40, fols 34, 74 ('skirvy & dropsy'); 39, fols 74, 131, 146; 38, fol. 22; 37, fols 151, 261, 265; 36, fols 84, 180, 196, 228; 35, fol. 162; 34, fols 20, 75, 175, 240, 251; 32, fols 23, 85; 31, fols 4, 23, 25, 27, 28, 59, 123, 209, 232; 30, fol. 170 ('singing in my head'); 27, fol. 7.

36 Bodl. MSS Tanner 38, fol. 23; 37, fol. 181; 31, fol. 26.

37 For a much more extensive clerical 'misery memoir' that nevertheless indicates considerable exertion and devotion to duty, see A. Macfarlane (ed.), *The diary of Ralph Josselin 1616–1683* (British Academy Records of Social and Economic History, n.s., 3, 1976).

38 Morehouse (ed.), *Extracts from the diary of the Rev. Robert Meeke*, pp. 42, 19, 60–1.

39 J. Gregory, *Restoration, reformation and reform, 1660–1828: archbishops of Canterbury and their diocese* (Oxford: Clarendon Press, 2000), pp. 147–60.

40 For the sense of strong regional variation in the courts' health, see J. Walsh and S. Taylor, 'Introduction: the Church and Anglicanism in the "long" eighteenth century', in J. Walsh, C. Haydon and S. Taylor (eds), *The Church of England c.1689–c.1833: from toleration to Tractarianism* (Cambridge: Cambridge University Press, 1993), pp. 5–6.

41 M. Kinnear, 'The correction court in the diocese of Carlisle, 1704–1756', *Church History*, 59 (1990), 205; A. Ashley, 'The spiritual courts in the Isle of Man, especially in the seventeenth and eighteenth centuries', *EHR*, 72 (1957), 55.

42 For the general argument from personal initiative, see J. Gregory and J.S. Chamberlain, 'Introduction', in J. Gregory and J.S. Chamberlain (eds), *The national church in local perspective: the Church of England and the regions, 1660–1800* (Woodbridge: Boydell, 2003), p. 18.

43 Spaeth, *Church in an age of danger*, pp. 72–3. The picture in regard to the prosecution of sexual offences is mixed, with evidence of considerably high levels of business in some regions, balanced by the fundamental shift in London to the secular sessions: Marshall, *Church life in Hereford and Oxford*, pp. 68–71; Dabhoiwala, 'Prostitution and police', esp. pp. 95, 139–40.

44 D. Robertson (ed.), *Diary of Francis Evans, secretary to Bishop Lloyd, 1699–1706* (Worcestershire Historical Society, 15, 1903), pp. 60–2, 97–8.

45 For episcopal concern with standards at ordination, see *ibid.*, pp. 21, 37, 53, 68, 71, 80, 101, 123–4, 131; R. Trappes-Lomax (ed.), *The diary of the Rev. Thomas Brockbank 1671–1709* (Chetham Society, n.s., 89, 1930), p. 74; Jackson (ed.), *Diary of Abraham de la Pryme*, p. 187; Morehouse (ed.), *Extracts from the diary of the Rev. Robert Meeke*, pp. 10–11; Bodl. MSS Tanner 45, fol. 64; 42, fol. 167; 39, fol. 93; 38, fol. 96; 36, fol. 84; 34, fol. 31.

46 See e.g. Robertson (ed.), *Diary of Francis Evans*, p. 60.

47 Benedikz, 'Thomas Wood', *ODNB*.

48 For other cases, see J. Spurr, 'Thomas Barlow', *ODNB*; S. Handley, 'Thomas Watson', *ODNB*.

49 Bodl. MS Tanner 34, fol. 118: Compton to Sancroft, Fulham, 22 Aug. 1683.

50 I. Green, *The Christian's ABC. Catechisms and catechizing in England c. 1530–1740* (Oxford: Clarendon Press, 1996), pp. 88, 1.

51 Robertson (ed.), *Diary of Francis Evans*, p. 16.

52 I. Atherton and V. Morgan, 'Revolution and retrenchment: the cathedral, 1630–1720', in Atherton *et al.* (eds), *Norwich Cathedral: church, city and diocese, 1096–1996* (Hambledon Continuum, 1996), p. 566; S. Wilton Rix (ed.), *The diary and autobiography of Edmund Bohun Esq ...* (Beccles, 1853), pp. 74–5.

53 R.W. Ambler, *Churches, chapels and the parish communities of Lincolnshire 1660–1900* (Lincoln: History of Lincolnshire Committee, 2000), pp. 13–14. (Ambler is scrupulous enough to note that this may not solely have been the result of theologically informed zeal: many contemporaries felt that a bishop's touch brought medical relief.)

54 Besides the *ODNB* entries for these figures, see also T.E.S. Clarke and H.C. Foxcroft, *A life of Gilbert Burnet, bishop of Salisbury* (Cambridge: Cambridge University Press, 1907); A.T. Hart, *William Lloyd 1627–1717: bishop, politician, author and prophet* (SPCK, 1952); A.T. Hart, *The life and times of John Sharp, Archbishop of York* (SPCK, 1949).

55 B. Till, 'James Sharp', *ODNB*; M. Clapinson (ed.), *Bishop Fell and nonconformity: visitation documents from the Oxford diocese, 1682–83* (Oxfordshire Records Society, 52, 1980); Bodl. MS Sancroft 99.

56 See also, A. Whiteman, with the assistance of M. Clapinson (ed.), *The Compton census of 1676: a critical edition* (British Academy Records of Social and Economic History, n.s., 10, 1986), esp. Whiteman's masterly introduction.

57 For efforts to promote weekly communion in cathedrals as a model for individual dioceses, see G. Tapsell, *The personal rule of Charles II, 1681–85* (Woodbridge: Boydell, 2007), p. 126 and the sources listed there in n. 16; and, more widely, R.A.P.J. Beddard, 'William Sancroft', *ODNB*.

58 I. Green and K. Peters, 'Religious publishing in England 1640–1695', in J. Barnard and D.F. McKenzie, with the assistance of M. Bell (eds), *The Cambridge history of the book in Britain Volume IV. 1557–1695* (Cambridge: Cambridge University Press, 2002), pp. 79–82.

59 These figures are culled from *ibid.*, p. 788, table 4, and are derived from analysis of the term catalogues of the Stationers' Company, in which new titles had to be registered.

60 J. Raven, *The business of books. Bestsellers and the English book trade 1450–1850* (New Haven and London: Yale University Press, 2007), p. 93, fig. 4.1; I. Green, *Print and Protestantism in early modern England* (Oxford: Oxford University Press, 2000), p. 353; J. Spurr, 'Richard Allestree', *ODNB*.

61 I. Rivers, 'Religious publishing', in M.F. Suarez, SJ, and M.L. Turner (eds), *The Cambridge history of the book in Britain Volume V. 1695–1830* (Cambridge: Cambridge University Press, 2009), p. 579.

62 S.E. Lehmberg, *Cathedrals under siege: cathedrals in English society, 1600–1700* (Exeter: University of Exeter Press, 1996), pp. 112–13.

63 G. Southcombe and G. Tapsell, *Restoration politics, religion and culture: Britain and Ireland, 1660–1714* (Basingstoke: Palgrave Macmillan, 2010), p. 88; Bodl. MSS Tanner 38, fols 1, 14, 82; 37, fol. 255; 36, fols 88, 95; 35, fols 71, 138; 34, fols 93, 121 (for Womock); 36, fol. 70; 32, fols 47, 49 (for Comber).

64 M. Greig, 'Gilbert Burnet', *ODNB*; Brown (ed.), *Works of George Savile*, II, 425. (A third volume of Burnet's *History of the Reformation* would appear in 1714.)

65 Bodl. MS Tanner 32, fols 47, 49: Comber to Sancroft, York, 5 May 1684, and no date (but after the first letter).

66 Morehouse (ed.), *Extracts from the diary of the Rev. Robert Meeke*, pp. 60–1 (19 Mar. 1693).

67 These printed texts could be significantly different from the original spoken version: A. Hunt, *The art of hearing. English preachers and their audiences, 1590–1640* (Cambridge: Cambridge University Press, 2010).

68 F. Deconinck-Brossard, 'Eighteenth-century sermons and the age', in Jacob and Yates (eds), *Crown and mitre*, pp. 106, 108, fig. 2.

69 T. Claydon, 'The sermon, the "public sphere" and the political culture of late seventeenth-century England', in L.A. Ferrell and P. McCullough (eds), *The English sermon revised. Religion, literature and history 1600–1750* (Manchester: Manchester University Press, 2000), pp. 208–34, esp. pp. 213–14, 225.

70 I.M. Green, *Continuity and change in Protestant preaching in early modern England* (Friends of Dr Williams's Library Sixtieth Lecture, 2009), p. 5; Hunt, *Art of hearing*, p. 392.

71 Deconinck-Brossard, 'Eighteenth-century sermons', p. 108, fig. 2.

72 William Beveridge, *A sermon concerning the excellency and usefulness of the Common Prayer* (12th edn, Dublin, 1698), 'the bookseller to the reader'.

73 Bodl. MSS Tanner 45, fol. 13; 34, fol. 39: William Lloyd, bishop of Peterborough, to Sancroft, Peterborough, 26 May 1683.

74 Bodl. MS Tanner 29, fol. 9: Lake to Sancroft, Chichester, 18 Apr. 1687.

75 Robertson (ed.), *Diary of Francis Evans*, p. 18 (and see also p. 113); Bodl. MSS Sancroft 22, 30, 40–3. Though see Sancroft's *Lex ignea: or the school of righteousness ... a sermon preach'd before the King, Oct. 10. 1666. At the solemn-fast appointed for the late fire of London* (1666).

76 Rivers, 'Religious publishing', p. 593. So lucrative was the publishing of Tillotson's sermons that his widow, Elizabeth, was able to sell the copyright for the massive sum of £2,500.

77 Macfarlane (ed.), *Diary of Ralph Josselin*, p. 494 (18 Dec. 1662).

78 P. Collinson, *The religion of Protestants: the Church in English society, 1559–1625* (Oxford: Oxford University Press, 1983), chapter 3.

79 Brown (ed.), *Works of George Savile*, II, 260. At least, he claimed, they provided the opportunity for gentlemen to nap on Sundays: *ibid.*, II, 418.

80 *Ibid.*, II, 428–9 n. 5. For other criticisms of clergy 'interfering' in temporal affairs during their sermons, see *HOP 1660–1690*, II, 486, 609.

81 One analysis of titles suggests that only around 13 per cent of sermons published between 1688 and 1753 may be categorised as 'political' (Deconinck-Brossard, 'Eighteenth-century sermons', p. 110, fig. 3).

82 M. Jenkinson, *Culture and politics at the court of Charles II, 1660–1685* (Woodbridge: Boydell, 2010), chapter 3; T. Claydon, *William III and the godly revolution* (Cambridge: Cambridge University Press, 1996), esp. chapter 3; J. Caudle, 'Preaching in parliament: patronage, publicity and politics in Britain, 1701–60', in L.A. Ferrell and P. McCullough (eds), *The English sermon revised. Religion, literature and history 1600–1750* (Manchester: Manchester University Press, 2000), pp. 235–63.

83 N. Adee, *A plot for a crown, in a visitation-sermon, at Cricklade, May the fifteenth, 1682* ... (1685), sigs B2r–v, p. 16.

84 For a restatement of the centrality of this theme within James's broader political demise, see Southcombe and Tapsell, *Restoration politics, religion and culture*, chapter 5.

85 J. Hunter (ed.), *The diary of Dr Thomas Cartwright, Bishop of Chester ...* (Camden Society, 22, 1843), p. 30 (31 Jan. 1687).

86 Coleby, 'Henry Compton'.

87 Claydon, 'The sermon', p. 222.

88 For a dual case study, see J. Farooq, 'The politicising influence of print: the responses of hearers and readers to the sermons of Gilbert Burnet and Henry Sacheverell', in G. Baker and A. McGruer (eds), *Readers, audiences and coteries in early modern England* (Newcastle: Cambridge Scholars Publishing, 2006), pp. 28–46.

89 The non-jurors have not attracted a great deal of specialist scholarship in recent years: see C.D.A. Leighton, 'The non-jurors and their history', *Journal of Religious History*, 29 (2005), 241–57; R. Sharp, '*Our Church': nonjurors High Churchmen and the Church of England* (Royal Stuart Society Papers, 57, 2000). The classic accounts are J. Findon, 'The nonjurors and the Church of England 1689–1716' (DPhil dissertation, University of Oxford, 1978, i.e. 1979) – see p. 38 for two rare sermons against the invasion – and J.H. Overton, *The nonjurors: their lives, principles, and writings* (Smith, Elder & Co., 1902).

90 Farooq, 'Politicising influence of print'; Claydon, *William III and the godly revolution*, esp. pp. 28–51, and via index, *sub* 'Burnet'.

91 For his controversial career, see A. Starkie, 'Ofspring Blackall', *ODNB*.

92 N. Sykes, *From Sheldon to Secker. Aspects of English church history 1660–1768* (Cambridge: Cambridge University Press, 1959), pp. 41–4; D. Hayton, 'Introduction', *HOP 1690–1715*, I, 36. (For the long and considered views of Bishop Hacket on the prospective surrender of separate clerical taxation, see Bodl. MS Tanner 47, fols 201r–v.)

93 Edward Ashe, quoted in *HOP 1690–1715*, I, 203.

94 J.H. Pruett, *The parish clergy under the later Stuarts. The Leicestershire experience* (Urbana and Chicago: University of Illinois Press, 1978), p. 163.

95 To give just one regional example, 66 per cent of the parish clergy of Cheshire voted in the highly charged election of 1705: *HOP 1690–1715*, I, 36; II, 62. The clergy also 'voted consistently at election after election': W.A. Speck, *Tory and Whig. The struggle in the constituencies 1701–1715* (Macmillan, 1970), pp. 24–5.

96 *HOP 1660–1690*, I, 281.

97 *HOP 1660–1690*, I, 329, 490; *HOP 1690–1715*, I, 93–4, 204; II, 120, 142, 176, 604, 720.

98 Quoted in *HOP 1690–1715*, I, 203. (For Conyers, see *ibid.*, III, 697–8.) See also G. Holmes and W.A. Speck, *The divided society: party conflict in England 1694–1716* (Edward Arnold, 1967), pp. 51, 57; Speck, *Tory and Whig*, pp. 88–9.

99 Quoted in Atherton and Morgan, 'Revolution and retrenchment', p. 565.

100 R.J. Ginn and S. Kelsey, 'Anthony Sparrow', *ODNB*; Bodl. MSS Tanner 39, fols 174, 179, 200; 38, fol. 121; 36, fol. 230.

101 Bodl. MS Tanner 42, fol. 176: bishop of Bristol to 'Gentlemen of ye Clergy'. For the context see, *HOP 1660–1690*, I, 211; III, 495–7.

102 Bodl. MS Tanner 41, fol. 4: bishop of Chichester to archbishop of Canterbury, Chichester, 30 Mar. 1685.

103 *HOP 1660–1690*, I, 420–1.

104 *HOP 1690–1715*, I, 67.

105 Coleby, 'Henry Compton'. For Compton's place as one of those who invited William to invade, see G. Tapsell, 'The Immortal Seven', *ODNB* (group entry online); and for his careful management of elections in 1685–90: Cambridge University Library, Add. MS 5, fols 328–34.

106 J. Nichols (ed.), *Letters on various subjects ... to and from William Nicolson ...*, 2 vols (1809), I, 9. For Compton's similar zeal to 'sell' the Revolution to the clergy, see Carpenter, *Protestant bishop*, pp. 148–9.

107 *HOP 1690–1715*, II, 137.

108 *HOP 1690–1715*, II, 143. For more on Trelawny as a political animal, see *ibid.*, II, 68; A.M. Coleby, 'Sir Jonathan Trelawny', *ODNB*; M.G. Smith, *'Fighting Joshua': a study of the career of Sir Jonathan Trelawny, bart., 1650–1721, Bishop of Bristol, Exeter, and Winchester* (Redruth: Dyllansow Truran, 1985).

109 G.V. Bennett, 'William III and the episcopate', in G.V. Bennett and J.D. Walsh (eds), *Essays in modern English church history in memory of Norman Sykes* (Adam & Charles Black, 1966), pp. 104–31; Speck, *Tory and Whig*, p. 24; J.S. Chamberlain, *Accommodating High Churchmen. The clergy of Sussex, 1700–1745* (Urbana and Chicago: University of Illinois Press, 1997), pp. 51–4; Pruett, *Parish clergy under the later Stuarts*, p. 166.

110 *HOP 1690–1715*, II, 420.

111 *Ibid.*, II, 544.

112 The failure of parliamentary bills to outlaw the practice of 'occasional conformity' by nonconformists in order to hold public office roused particular ire: Speck, *Tory & Whig*, pp. 51–2, and chapter 7; G. Holmes, *British politics in the reign of Anne* (Macmillan, 1967), very extensively, via index, *sub* 'Occasional Conformity bills'.

113 G.V. Bennett, *The Tory crisis in church and state, 1688–1730: the career of Francis Atterbury, Bishop of Rochester* (Oxford: Oxford University Press, 1975), esp. chapters III–IV; G. Every, *The High Church party, 1688–1718* (SPCK, 1956), chapters 5–6; M. Greig, 'Bishop Gilbert Burnet and latitudinarian episcopal opposition to the Occasional Conformity Bills, 1702–1704', *Canadian Journal of History*, 41 (2006), 247–62; Holmes, *British politics*, pp. 99–103.

114 Holmes, *British politics*, esp. pp. 398–400, 408–9.

115 For the classic study, see G. Holmes, *The trial of Doctor Sacheverell* (Methuen Publishing, 1973). See also W.A. Speck, 'Henry Sacheverell', *ODNB*.

116 Holmes, *Trial of Doctor Sacheverell*, chapter III; Farooq, 'Politicising influence of print', pp. 30, 34–5, 41–4.

117 Quoted in G. Holmes, 'The Sacheverell riots: the crowd and the church in early eighteenth-century London', *P&P*, 72 (1976), 63.

118 *Ibid.*, 61.

119 *Ibid.*, 61 n. 29; F. Madan, *A bibliography of Dr Henry Sacheverell* (Oxford: Oxford University Press, 1884).

120 A number of these prints are helpfully reproduced in M. Knights, *The devil in disguise. Deception, delusion and fanaticism in the early English Enlightenment* (Oxford: Oxford University Press, 2011), chapter 5.

121 Holmes, *Trial of Doctor Sacheverell*, chapters IV–VI. For the articles of impeachment, see *ibid.*, pp. 99–100.

122 Holmes, 'Sacheverell riots', 69–70.

123 For contemporary awareness of the irony of a preacher espousing ideals of non-resistance in such a way that it incited violence, see Speck, *Tory and Whig*, pp. 93–4.

124 Holmes, 'Sacheverell riots', 58–9, 64–6; Holmes, *Trial of Doctor Sacheverell*, chapter VII.

125 Holmes, *Trial of Doctor Sacheverell*, chapter X.

126 Quoted in *HOP 1690–1715*, II, 496.

127 *Ibid.*, II, 720.

128 *Ibid.*, II, 813; III, 138.

129 *Ibid.*, II, 184, 356

130 *Ibid.*, II, 442, 309.

131 *Ibid.*, II, 120, 214, 7. (Harvey overstated his case: forty clerics voted for the Whigs, though the dean of Gloucester – a local resident – led more than twenty clergy in his support.)

132 Speck, *Tory and Whig*, p. 42.

133 See 'The Modern Idol, or Kiss my A-se is no Swearing' (1710), in J. Miller, *Religion in the popular prints 1600–1832* (Cambridge: Chadwyck-Healey, 1986), p. 151.

134 Robertson (ed.), *Diary of Francis Evans*, p. 57; *HOP 1690–1715*, II, 701–3; V, 62–73 (esp. 66–7); Speck, *Tory and Whig*, pp. 89–90; Hart, *William Lloyd*, pp. 152–3, 157–66, 187; M. Mullett, 'William Lloyd', *ODNB*.

135 *HOP 1690–1715*, II, 228.

136 *HOP 1690–1715*, II, 7.

137 *Ibid.*, II, 813.

138 *HOP 1660–1690*, I, 360.

139 D. Slatter (ed.), *The diary of Thomas Naish* (Wiltshire Archaeological and Natural History Society Records, 20, 1964), p. 22.

140 *Ibid.*, p. 28.

141 *Ibid.*, pp. 37–8.

142 *Ibid.*, pp. 39–44.

143 *Ibid.*, p. 44.

144 *Ibid.*, p. 46. (For this election, see *HOP 1690–1715*, II, 649.)

145 Slatter (ed.), *Diary of Thomas Naish*, pp. 47–8.

146 *Ibid.*, pp. 48–50, 54, 57, 61, 62.

147 *Ibid.*, p. 54.

148 *Ibid.*, p. 55.

149 *Ibid.*, pp. 55–7.

150 *Ibid.*, p. 59.

151 *Ibid.*, pp. 67–71.

152 *Ibid.*, p. 33. See also M. Greig, 'Gilbert Burnet', *ODNB*.

153 Slatter (ed.), *Diary of Thomas Naish*, p. 38. For Whitby's controversial career, see J.-L. Quantin, 'Daniel Whitby', *ODNB*.

154 Slatter (ed.), *Diary of Thomas Naish*, p. 25.

155 *Ibid.*, pp. 26–8, 31–2.

156 *Ibid.*, pp. 41, 54, 66.

157 *Ibid.*, pp. 46, 67.

158 *Ibid.*, p. 62.

159 Thomas Naish, *A sermon preached at the cathedral church of Sarum, November the 30th, 1727. Being the anniversary day appointed for the meeting of the Society of Lovers of Musick* (1727), p. 13. For Naish's efforts to protect singing in church in the following decade, see Spaeth, *Church in an age of danger*, pp. 238, 249.

160 Greig, 'Gilbert Burnet'.

Chapter 4

The lay Church of England

John Spurr

Twenty years ago I published a history of the Restoration Church of England that was intended to provide a comprehensive picture of the established church in the reigns of Charles II and James II, one that took account of preaching, piety, and theology as well as politics and preferment, and one that did not rely on the categories of the Augustan era or the Oxford Movement.[1] That book was prompted by a simple thought: why did generations of clergymen promote and defend a single national church and the concomitant proscription of other denominations and churches? If scholars had overlooked such an obvious question, it was perhaps because they had either regarded the established church as a fact of life in the seventeenth century (just as it was in their own time) or saw it as an anachronistic impediment to the inevitable triumph of modern values. *Bien pensant* assumptions ran deep. For many it was axiomatic that religious toleration was a self-evident good even in the seventeenth century, that nonconformists and anti-clericals were the progressive victims whose day would come, and that intellectual and political progress was linked to religious liberty; it followed that opponents of these principles could only be self-interested, bigoted, and reactionary. Yet, on reflection it seemed – and it still seems – implausible that so many clergymen could have been quite so dim and reactionary as to devote their time and energy to what was, on this showing, a morally and intellectually bankrupt project. The truth, of course, is that it was nothing of the sort. The Restoration Church of England pursued a distinct mission – admittedly one that might have won little favour in the late twentieth century – based on Christian principles and aspirations.

Efforts have been made to understand the Church of England's case. The Anglican 'theory of intolerance', a theological argument drawn from St Augustine, has been expertly excavated by Mark Goldie as part of his inquiries into the context of Locke's thought.[2] But such investigations centre upon the churchmen's instrumental case – how they argued – not why. 'Why' requires closer attention to the religious experience offered by the clergy of the Church of England; and this was what I – under the influence of a remarkable group of scholars of Elizabethan and early Stuart religion – attempted to supply.[3] *The Restoration Church of England* argued that the roots of that religious offering lay in the 1640s and 1650s, when beleaguered clergymen had been forced to think hard about their understanding of the doctrine of the church, their pastoral priorities, and the spiritual sustenance of their community, and it treated these decades as an integral part of the story. During the Interregnum the clergy developed an ecclesiology that was based on the office of the bishop and the autonomous authority of a national church while conceding nothing of the royal supremacy. This provided a retort to both Roman Catholic and non-episcopalian Protestant critics. Perturbed by Puritan perversion of the theology of salvation, the clergy of the English church promoted a rigorous Protestant doctrine that fostered human efforts and virtues without any pretence that these could earn or merit salvation. This teaching was promoted within a spiritual life sustained by clandestine Prayer Book worship, private devotional practices, and a deep sense of God's providential care of the world. The Interregnum's legacy was exploited and adapted over the following decades: the Restoration church was always a work in progress. Although the 1662 Act of Uniformity defined the church legally, it was the amplification of that definition in practice – in sermons and in liturgical practice, in compromises over clerical conformity and lay performance, in the political initiatives for comprehension or toleration, in claims for the episcopal office, royal supremacy, and power of prayer, and in the deep trust in a superintending divine providence – that invested the church with an identity which I called 'Anglicanism', a conscious anachronism, to characterise the broad consensus around which the clergy of the Church of England could organise and cohere in the decades between 1646 and 1689.

As a collective clerical enterprise, the Restoration Church of England was always a potential prey to fraternal tensions.[4] Nevertheless, in the face of external threats and internal animosities, the church maintained a generous vision across several generations – accommodating those who had compromised with the regimes of the 1640s and 1650s, those who entered the ministry in the 1660s, or the later generations who came to maturity in the 1680s – and allowed a latitude of clerical practice and opinion. Although my account eschewed party labels for the most part – they had been well studied and, at times, over-compartmentalised – it recognised the evasions which allowed clergymen of different outlooks to rub along with each other and the way in which different religious 'cultures', for example, of the former 'godly' and the self-proclaimed 'moderates' or the preachers and the ceremonialists, overlapped with each other.[5]

The last two decades have seen this picture enriched by other scholars. Maltby, Taylor and Fincham have brought more depth and detail to the sketch of Interregnum conformity.[6] Lacey has explored the cult of Charles the Martyr, while the royal supremacy, the 'anti-Calvinist' tradition, and the reputation of Richard Hooker have been the subject of penetrating studies.[7] Tyacke and Fincham have extended their work on the early Stuart church and advanced a 'Laudian' reading of Restoration altar policy.[8] The Anglican campaign for 'holy living' has become a commonplace in current accounts of the period and its piety.[9] Further light has been shed on the church by those working on anti-clericalism, Whiggery, and the early English Enlightenment, and by scholars of nonconformity whose sensitive studies have shown just how grey the area was between Presbyterianism and moderate conformity.[10] While local and diocesan studies have placed the Restoration church in a longer perspective, some remarkable dissertations have taken the story of the Restoration church far beyond the confines of England and, perhaps most notably, have begun to reconstruct the way in which the Church of England regrouped after 1689.[11]

There was, however, one glaring omission from all of this work. In these accounts the Restoration Church of England is overwhelmingly a clerical construction: lay people play little part. They have walk-on roles as the eager parliamentary proponents of the Uniformity Act or the Clarendon Code, as the JPs, mayors and aldermen who persecuted dissenters, or the constables and informers who harried sectaries. But this is to underestimate the laity's collaboration in the project of the Restoration Church. As this chapter will show, some lay people saw a national parochially based inclusive church as a crucial building block of a hierarchical community, albeit one in tension with other allegiances, and for many the 'church party' had an historically rooted claim on their loyalty and emotions. The laity 'received' the church's religious message through print, preaching, and public and private worship. Consideration of each of these will reveal the complex nature of the evidence and the lessons that we can draw from it: we will pass back and forth between print and manuscript sources, from quasi-official mass publications to the individual's 'reception' of a particular book, from communal activity to private devotion; and in doing so, we will make a start on restoring a missing lay perspective to the history of the Restoration Church of England.

I

Lay collaboration is easily invoked, but difficult to define. Historically and socially, the separation of 'clergy' and 'laity' in seventeenth-century Protestant England is suspect. Those who drew a sharp distinction between the two were making a point, and often hoping to drive a wedge between the clergy and their flock – as when Andrew Marvell made play with the clergy's claim to be the 'mouth' of the church: 'I know not why the Mouth of the Church should pretend to be the Brain of the Church, and Understand and Will for the whole Laity.'[12] For all the fashionably anti-clerical talk of 'black-coats', 'priests of Baal', 'priestcraft', and other supposed marks of 'the tribe of Levi', the clerical profession and lay society were tightly interwoven, not least by the simple facts of marriage, kinship, and economic interest.

It is also clear that the 'laity' is simply too capacious a category to be meaningful on most occasions in the later seventeenth century. If it refers to all of the population that were not in holy orders, then it must include those who had formally opted out of the Church of England by joining another denomination. It would also apply to those who had informally dissociated themselves by attending church irregularly or not at all, preferring the alehouse or the open air to a hard pew. This, perhaps, was the position in the parish of Bassingbourne (Ely), which was reported in 1685 as having 'noe Dissenters many Sluggards'.[13] The majority of parishioners are undoubtedly to be located somewhere along a spectrum between the 'sluggards' and the enthusiastic, for the mass of the population did go to their parish church each week and participate in its services, and presumably they subscribed to its principles and practices after their own fashion. Once we assume that these conforming members of the national church constitute the 'lay Church of England', we immediately confront major obstacles to the study of this group in any depth. After all, these are the very people whose activities left none of the usual records: they are the undemonstrative conformists, the anonymous weekly churchgoers, whose piety was neither so intense that they were noticed nor so lax that they were prosecuted.[14] Most were illiterate or semi-literate and left little account of themselves: these are not the Nehemiah Wallingtons or Agnes Beaumonts whose vivid testimonies of life among the godly leap out of their own laborious writings. Even when conformists did have the means and leisure to record something of their spiritual lives, the results ranged from ardent Anglicanism to something far more tepid or even downright disappointing: 'I often hear good sermons, but seldom or never think of them after,' confessed William Coe.[15]

The suggestion that the 'lay church' ran from the lukewarm conformist to the fervent Anglican thwarts any attempt to identify 'popular' and 'official' religion. Some individuals fulfilled or exceeded the prescriptions of the church, while others – the majority no doubt – could not manage to receive the sacrament three times a year as the church stipulated nor to attend its fasts and festivals. There is no sign of the wide penumbra of para-liturgical or 'folk' practices that we would associate with 'popular religion' in contemporary Catholic Europe. Lay commitment to the Church of England is no easier to stratify into 'popular' and 'elite' forms of religion. Although much of the richest evidence comes, as we will shortly see, from gentle families and the middling sort, the materials upon which their religious practice drew – the Prayer Book, sermons, printed devotional works and the like – were not socially exclusive. In their language and format these were accessible to the lower orders and there were clear attempts to tailor the church's message to those of more limited resources and capabilities: *The Whole Duty of Man* was pointedly described on its title page as for the use of 'the meanest reader'. This is not to say, of course, that the highest ideals propounded by the church for lay private and public devotion were attainable by ploughboys and milkmaids. The sheer time and privacy required for some of the pious exercises, such as self-examination before receiving the sacrament or daily meditations, were a practical challenge, but in principle the same spiritual goals were within the reach of humble folk: 'thy time is as truly sanctified by a trade, and devout, though shorter prayers, as by the longer offices of those whose time is not filled up with labour and useful businesse', advised Jeremy Taylor.[16]

Our image of religious practice has been built from diverse sources, the direct testimony of memoirs, diaries, and correspondence, the indirect evidence of complaints and the prosecutions of those who failed to live up to expectations, and the implications of the large numbers of religious works printed and purchased.[17] The religious behaviour of lay conformists has been uncovered by the meticulous work of Judith Maltby and Christopher Haigh on the pre-1650 period, Donald Spaeth on the late Stuart diocese of Salisbury, and William Jacob on the eighteenth century.[18] Further distinctions are yet to be drawn between urban and rural experiences, provincial and metropolitan practices, and perhaps between the behaviour of men and women, but these will only add to what is already a picture of fluidity: 'parishioners conformed and yet did not conform', writes Spaeth of the Wiltshire countryside. 'They remained committed to the Church, and to the community which it represented, without accepting every aspect of the Anglican liturgy.'[19] A process of adaptation was at work, or some might even see it as negotiation, between the church and its flock: in some places ministers willingly acceded to the ceremonial preferences of their parishioners, reporting that 'I did not sign with the cross because it gave offence', in others the laity pushed for their own forms of religious expression, whether that was singing psalms as a congregation or, as in the early eighteenth century, forming lay parish choirs and bands.[20]

All of this means that an inquiry – even one as preliminary as this chapter – into the laity's engagement with the later Stuart Church of England needs to choose its ground carefully. Here I am concerned not with the level of lay support for the Church of England (which may well have been limited), but with the quality of the commitment of those who did identify with the church.[21] What did it mean to stand up for the Church of England? How did it feel to be an active participant in Prayer Book worship? Such questions can only be answered satisfactorily from individual experiences, with all that that implies about how representative such cases may be of the wider population; on the other hand, the growing number of case studies is steadily enhancing our understanding of seventeenth-century lay religion.[22] The chronology of this inquiry is also carefully limited, since the terms upon which the laity engaged with the national church were changed fundamentally by the Toleration Act (1689), and thereafter by party-political developments: this chapter will look mainly to the reigns of Charles II and James II.

II

The lay Church of England was at its most obvious as the local community at worship in the parish church. Arranged in their pews and benches according to social rank and, in some churches, separated into male and female, the lay members of the national church were obliged to attend twice each Sunday and on other fasts and festivals. We know that some looked on rapt as the Prayer Book services were performed or listened attentively to the sermon, while others were day-dreaming, napping, ogling the attractive members of the congregation or glaring at their enemies. The rites of passage, baptisms, weddings, and funerals, might also bring the community to church. The laity turned up each Sunday out of habit, under the weight of convention and their superiors' expectations, and to please God. Anglican gentlemen, still in shock from the Puritan revolution, saw Common Prayer as inculcating 'principles of sobriety' in 'the people'.[23] It seemed 'unintelligible' to Lady Sarah Cowper that 'the Christian Religion should subsist without an Established Form of Publick Worship, wherby ye Ignorant (which are the most) must be the best instructed'.[24] Gentry or civic leaders self-consciously set an example of regular weekly attendance and many took pride in turning out for special occasions: 'I w[i]th ye best part of my family did appeare at ye church' on Good Friday 1671, wrote one squire.[25] They expected the same of their peers. A gentleman might feel obliged to mention to a neighbour over dinner the 'ill example' that he set by missing the sacrament or turning up after Morning Prayer just to hear the sermon.[26] Authority reinforced example. The resident Anglican squire and JP could be a powerful force for local conformity. On 4 May 1671 the curate of Gilston (Hertfordshire) presented Sir Humphrey Gore with the names of those who absented themselves from the parish church on the previous Sunday 'and yt same day I dispatched a warrant to ye Constable to warne them to appeare before me to answear theire default'. Two days later, Sir Humphrey issued warrants to the churchwardens to impose a twelve pence fine on two men who had neither explained their non-attendance at church nor promised to attend in the future.[27] The work was unending: for example, on 8 November 1674, 'after evening service o[u]r church being very empty, He [Hollynworth the curate] and ye Churchwarden gave a vissitt to ye Alehouse, where was found a house full, whose names they presented me upon their returne': three days later these errant parishioners were summoned to see Sir Humphrey. And the work involved representatives of the whole community. Conformity could not be policed without the help of lay constables and churchwardens, the men who informed on their neighbours and delivered the warrants. At St Thomas, Salisbury, the sidesmen – a baker, tailor, innkeeper, and wire-drawer – were pressed into service to assist the churchwardens to identify those who were absent from church, especially on the Lord's Day.[28]

Within the confines of the social hierarchy, the lay elite often enjoyed close relations with the clergy. Sir Daniel Fleming of Rydal (Westmorland) was on good terms with several dignitaries of the Restoration church, thanks in part to the alumni network of Queen's College, Oxford, and the shared experience of the dark days of the Puritan rebellion. He congratulated Guy Carleton on his consecration as bishop of Bristol: 'I am glad to hear that his Majesty is so kind to one that hath so frankly ventured Life & Limb in his service: & I hope that an old Cavalier may ere long be translated to [an] old Bishopprick; tho' at present there may be some necessity for a stout Prelate to be in a see where there are (I feare too many) Fanatickes.'[29] Staunch service of the church's interests won Fleming recognition too. Bishop Lamplugh of Exeter praised him as one of the 'good Patriotts, & true Sons of ye Church as you have shown your self to be, in suppressing those disorderly & fanatique humours, w[hi]ch we have found to be so pernicious to both church & state'.[30] Fleming and many other conformist gentlemen entrusted family and personal business – the education of their children, the arrangement of marriages, and even marriage guidance – to their friends among the senior clergy.[31] Parish ministers were treated with due respect, and often welcome at the gentleman's dinner table, but there was no pretence that they were social equals. Clergymen were often valued family dependents, serving as chaplains or even spiritual guides: Fleming paid John Braithwaite for visiting his wife's sickbed and preaching at her funeral.[32] It behoved a gentleman to have regard for the position of those in holy orders wherever they were encountered: the two shillings that Fleming gave to 'Mr Curwen, a Poor Preacher' at Ambleside chapel was not untypical generosity.[33] Yet relations between Anglican laymen and clergy could also be prickly. Sir Henry Yelverton was outraged by the 'very lofty style' of a letter from Bishop Henshaw writing 'not as if he had been the Bishop of Peterborough and might want the assistance of gentlemen, but as if he had been the Pope himself, taxing us in effect for fools that we meddled'.[34] In turn, the clergy were acutely sensitive to the condescension and slights they might encounter in their dealings with laymen, even with those who were good sons of the church, and there were frequent instances of offended ministers and curates and a whole genre of popular literature about the 'contempt' faced by the clergy on account of their poverty and lack of status.[35]

Property was a minefield for lay–clerical relations, as were clerical appoint-ments. The two were confused, since lay ownership of advowsons, impropri-ated tithes, and other rights meant that a gentleman could often nominate a parish's minister. Sir Daniel Fleming, that ardent churchman, presented his second son, Henry, to the living of Grasmere in 1684 after his hurried (and possibly irregular) ordination had been facilitated by his old friend Bishop Smith of Carlisle.[36] Given the opportunities for preferment, running from family chaplaincies and parish livings to civic lectureships, cathedral chapters, and other dignities, and the number of patrons, including the Crown, bishops, deans and chapters, corporations, Oxford and Cambridge colleges, and chari-table trustees, it is no wonder that the clergy at all levels were constantly jockeying to catch the eye of potential patrons. But lay patrons also had to respect the needs of those served by these ministers. When Sir William Boothby nominated Thomas Truelove, his domestic chaplain of fourteen years, to the living of Cooling (Kent), he wrote to the leaders of the parish:

> I hope you, and ye rest are well pleased with ye Minister I sent to you, I know him to be an honest and good man, and that you will be happy in him, for I desire to put none upon you but such as you may approve of; and who shall reside and performe his office and Duty amongst you himselfe; as this person shall do so soone as he can settle his affaires heer, and fitt himselfe and family for his remove, w[hi]ch can hardly be Expected now till spring.[37]

Elsewhere parishioners, or perhaps the vestry, might have a greater say in the choice of the curate or minister: there are several examples of clergymen preaching before the parish to see if they were suitable before the parish leaders wrote to the patron to recommend him; and not a few instances of the church's suspicion of the process.[38]

Lay members of the Church of England knew what they wanted from their ministers. The ideal clergyman should be a graduate, of exemplary personal conduct, resident in the parish, providing weekly sermons, sacraments three times a year, morning and evening prayer on a Sunday, and baptism, funeral and wedding services as needed, catechising the young, visiting the sick and counselling the dying, reconciling enemies, and judicious in his demands for tithes and other dues. When a minister conspicuously failed to measure up, the laity took action: Thomas Latimer, vicar of Colerne (Wiltshire), was presented by his parishioners for not conforming to the liturgy, neglect of his pastoral duties, and as 'a Drunkard, a notorious lyar & comon swearer, a Quarreller & Striker, & Railer & defamer of his neighbours'.[39] Money, especially tithe disputes, proved to be the most common root of lay–clerical disagreement in later Stuart Wiltshire. And when a minister proved himself peevish or his parishioners turned out refractory, quarrels could soon escalate into the kind of 'petty war' that raged between the incumbent of Hilperton and his flock for more than twenty years.[40]

The assertive laity of Restoration England is no secret. Emboldened by the individualism of Protestant doctrine or disenchanted by the extremes and hypocrisy of the Puritan revolution, lay people would not now be cowed by the clergy – but then one might question whether they ever had been. Working with the clergy and the ecclesiastical authorities in governing their own communities had long undermined the notion of separate spheres: the lay churchwardens, for example, were charged with secular responsibilities, including the administration of the poor rate, and with reporting religious and moral offenders, including clergymen, to the church courts; vestries, made up of the incumbent, the two annually elected churchwardens, and either all the male householders or, as was becoming more common in this period, a dozen or two of the 'elders' or 'masters and governors', governed each parish.[41] Boroughs were ruled by corporations which comprised of a mayor, aldermen, and burgesses, who were all required by the Corporation and Test Acts to be conformists. While a civic corporation was a chartered secular body that regularly processed in all its finery to reserved seats in the parish church to hear sermons on civic or state occasions, a vestry was an ecclesiastical institution that had been invested by statute with considerable secular duties. The interdependence of the lay and the ecclesiastical was a fact of life in seventeenth-century communities.

It was not, of course, always a comfortable fact of life for lay conformists who had other pressing interests – earning a living, getting on in their community, or exerting their political rights and ambitions – that could conflict with the interests of the church and clergy. The justifiable pride to be taken in being a churchwarden or a mayor was easily tarnished when bumptious clerics quarrelled over a matter of precedence or jurisdiction: many minor storms disturbed the tranquillity of provincial life, such as the spats over the height and location of the mayoral seat in English cathedrals – at York in 1663 and 1684–85, St Paul's in 1663–64, Gloucester in 1671, and Exeter in 1684.[42] A layman's standing in the community counted for a great deal, as did the obligations that it entailed. So nonconformists served as churchwardens and vestrymen: when one affronted Oxfordshire minister rejected a Baptist candidate for churchwarden, 'the ring-leading Dissenter came to me and insolently asked me what my reason was to oppose the parish'.[43] Other ministers took the opposite line. Edward Fowler, vicar of St Giles Cripplegate (London), allowed a number of the parish's partial conformists and dissidents to join the vestry 'to the very ill government of the affairs of the church and the great grief and discouragement of the loyal men of the same ward'. In 1684 Fowler was brought to heel, these 'factious' vestrymen were dismissed, and the conformists of the parish rejoiced; but this was at the height of the Tory Reaction, when 'loyal' was a synonym for Tory and the identity of the Church of England was a party-political battleground.[44] Local politicians, such as Sir John Knight of

Bristol, wrapped themselves in the banner of the church as they bore down on their rivals and drove them out of office. What had been inclusive corporations of Anglicans and nonconformists in the 1660s and 1670s succumbed to 'a party-political transformation' as the 'church party' or Tories came to power, often with the help of a new charter, in the mid-1680s.[45] In the polarised world of post-1689 party politics, lay membership of the Church of England was to become even more deeply politicised.

A different assertion of lay self-confidence sprang from religious initiatives. The formation of parochial youth groups had 'been the practice of serious young men in all ages, and among all the various denominations of Christians', according to one clerical enthusiast.[46] Restoration groups took their lead from the church. In 1681 the 'devout young men' of St Martin-in-the-Fields (London) created an association that was restricted to those who attended the church and received the sacrament. They met every third Sunday of the month, read 'some prayer as shall be useful for our purpose' and a chapter from the Bible, repeated the heads of a sermon, and took a collection for the poor.[47] As such groups proliferated in the capital in the 1680s and 1690s and then spread further afield, they outgrew their parish roots, but remained Anglican in character. In contrast, the moral 'reformation societies' that emerged in the 1690s were self-help initiatives designed to tackle immorality and irreligion in a specific community, but they saw laymen of different denominations co-operating in a field that had been the preserve of the church and its courts.[48]

III

The lay Church of England was manifest at a national as well as local level. In theory this 'confessional state' limited access to the nation's educational, legal, and political institutions to those who were prepared to swear loyalty oaths and, after the Test Acts of 1673 and 1678, to furnish certificates that they had received the sacrament according to the rites of the established church. But, just as in vestries and town councils, semi-conformists, occasional conformists, and men of little or no religion managed to sit in both houses of parliament.[49] So, politically, the lay Church of England was made up of a subset of the parliamentary and political class, men like Fleming, 'good patriots and true sons of the church'. The defence of 'the church' was a powerful rallying cry at Westminster and in the constituencies: writing in the name of 'all ye true Church of England party' to the mayor of Derby about the 1689 general election, Sir William Boothby implored, 'pray you and others honest free men of our church stirre in Derby to secure what votes you can for us'.[50] Yet the 'church party' was a nebulous political grouping: attracting several other labels – the 'cavalier party', the 'court party', and later the 'tory party' – this fluctuating collection of politicians were largely reactive and inarticulate. They could be shepherded towards punitive anti-dissenting legislation by skilful parliamentarians working under the direction of bishops in the House of Lords, but they would often put self-interest before the ideological needs of the Church of England.[51] How they operated at court and in parliament is little studied: some clearly managed to be 'a great defender of the Church of England' in parliament while furthering their careers as courtiers or lawyers.[52] There were undoubtedly opportunists among their ranks, men whose hatred of nonconformity or love of monarchy was deeper than their affection for the church and the Prayer Book, but we have few measures of the authenticity of piety. For the most part, we can judge only by outward professions. These were the 'monarchicall and Church of England men' who assembled for James II's 1685 parliament and declared themselves satisfied with his promises to protect 'the reformed religion of the Church of England as by lawe established, which was dearer and nearer to them then their lives'.[53]

The character of this attachment to the church was as varied as the individuals, but its roots lay in the Bible and experience. Although a royalist Anglican creed was elaborated in historical and philosophical tracts (several of them the work of Anglican divines), the Anglican laity took their principles directly and viscerally from scripture and recent history. They heard St Paul: 'let every soul be subject unto the higher powers. For there is no power but of God: the powers that be are ordained of God ... they that resist shall receive to themselves damnation' (Romans 13: 1–2). They read of Adam, the first father and the first king, and saw that role reprised by Noah; they studied the history of exiled King David and dwelt upon the alliance of Moses and Aaron; and they were persuaded that patriarchalism was the natural order of things. What gave this conviction further emotional purchase was the regicide, the 'parricide' of the Lord's anointed: 'woe unto us that we have sinned, lett every soule girde itselfe with saccloth, and lament the displeasure of God which has smitten our head, and wounded the defence of this our English church, our Solomon', wailed a devout churchwoman; without 'this stately ceader, who was the chiefe supportt of the church of God', she continued, his admirable book, *Eikon Basilike*, would have to speak for him.[54] The sacralised image of Charles the Martyr was created and maintained by that potent volume, but it was inflated to a cult by a stream of hagiographies, the annual commemoration of the martyrdom in services and sermons each 30 January, and such ostentatious gestures as hanging a painting of Charles 'kneeling, with a crown of thorns in his hand, his crown and sceptre lying by' in St Paul's Covent Garden.[55]

The result was a profound belief in the absolute sovereignty of a hereditary monarch with a divine right and a corresponding duty of non-resistance on the part of his subjects. Sir William Boothby embraced passive obedience 'as the true Characteristicall distinguishing Doctrine of our church'.[56] Prayers and tears were the only weapon against a rightful monarch, but subjects had the right to refuse unlawful commands. They should trust in divine providence that alone could restore the rightful order. This deep providentialism came to the fore in Anglican thinking at moments of crisis, whether 'natural' as in the plague or the Great Fire, or man-made: visiting London in March 1672, Sir Humphrey Gore

> mett with most persons much disspirited and sadded w[i]th the kings Declaration newly publisht for a generall indulgence and toleration of all religions[.] I must say I had no small share of griefe in so unwellcome a passage: but God is above all and I shall rest my hopes on him for the maintenance of his owne Religion and Church; and yt in his goode time it may appeare amongst use w[i]th more lustre and zeale.

The nation's troubles and discontent were only heightened by the new war with the Dutch, but 'the success of this and all other affayres we must w[i]th all faithfull devotion recomend to ye all wise disposing providence of the Allmighty'.[57]

Sir William Boothby's reaction to the unfolding crisis of 1688–89 is especially revealing of a certain lay Anglican mindset, one formed by close relations with and dependence upon the clergy, but also saturated in the mythology of the persecuted church of the 1650s and convinced of the redemptive power of suffering. As the summer of 1688 progressed, Boothby was deeply anxious about the resolution of the clergy – would they read the King's Declaration of Indulgence? He lamented the recent death of several eminent divines: 'God strengthen them that remaine.' He spent a day in prayer for the bishops and declared himself ready to embrace suffering for the glorious end of religion; 'that wee may see our teachers, & sitt under their minestry, w[hi]ch is the greatest blessing of this life'.[58] Meanwhile he ordered an engraving of the Seven Bishops 'in a Good Ebony frame, and a good diamond Glasse'.[59] In October he welcomed the bishops' paper – 'I hope the B[isho]ps wise manedgement of this great concerne will lay a good foundation to support our hopes heerein, & to prevent what we feare'.[60] Boothby was no political innocent, although it was difficult for anyone to maintain a consistent line in such a fast-changing situation. In July 1688 he praised 'the London clergy's meeting the Dissenters to create an union & right understanding' as 'a good worke', but a year later, he took a different view of negotiations between the Church of England and dissenters: 'I must confesse I am afraid of such proceedings, for their principles will never make them true friends (but rather secrett Enimies) to our Church'.[61]

Boothby was steadfast in his own religious and political principles. Even as disorder broke out in December 1688 and 'many great men' took sides, 'my Allegiance and Religion According to ye Principles of the Church of England keeps me from Joyning with them: I pray God of his Infinite mercy bringe all at Last to a good End, to the happiness & Lasting Establishment of his

Religion amongst us; & our Antient Governm[en]t according to our Excellent Lawes'.[62] Later that month he told his daughter: 'things look dreadfully, and all good Christian[s] are Called to their prayers and tears the only lawfull Armes against such as God hath set over us'.[63] In January 1689 he wrote that 'I pray dayly to God for Direction, and that all in their places (Especially the B[isho]ps and Cleargy) may not be wanting to declare their principles and Act Accordingly'.[64] On 15 February 1689, still avid for political news and full of plans to elect 'such persons as we know to be hearty and true to ye Church of England and ... to preserve this Excellent Church from being broken and Ecclipsed by her many and great Enemies', Boothby was also voicing the old sentiments of resignation and acceptance: 'all these Late Changes are still Governed by the Ruling providence of God, w[hi]ch ought to be a great support to us, his wisdome is infinite, and his wayes all Just: God give us all grace to Carry our selves according to our Duty and obligation'.[65] By 31 March, Boothby was in full Interregnum mode: the Church of England 'will be able still to Continue a Glorious Church (though under persecution)'.[66] He felt abandoned by the clergy, who, divided among themselves, could offer no guidance to the laity on the oaths.[67] 'My soule will mourne in secret under such a Judgement as it must needs be to have so many Excellent B[isho]ps laid aside.'[68] This one over-heated example powerfully illustrates how deeply the political stance of lay Anglicans was rooted in their piety.

IV

Lay Anglican piety was a set of values and practices fabricated from materials supplied by the church but reworked by lay people according to their own needs and circumstances. The process is visible in different contexts. It was, for example, part of the transmission and consumption of print: there was a hunger in this period, especially in the provinces, for all the latest publications; and the Anglican appetite for devotional works was particularly sharp: Laud's *Summarie of Devotions*, Allestree's *The Causes of the Decay of Christian Piety*, and *The Countess of Morton's Daily Exercise* are among the many purchases recorded in Fleming's accounts.[69] Laymen invested in weighty works of ecclesiastical history and religious controversy. Many book collectors were omnivorous, ordering the pious alongside the profane, heedless of what later generations might expect in terms of genres and priorities. Boothby might have the second parts of *Pilgrims Progress* and *The Whole Duty of Man* sent to Derbyshire alongside Joseph Moxon's *Mechanic Exercises*, or John Oldham's poems, John Evelyn's translation of Lucretius, and John Kettlewell's discourse on the sacrament of the Holy Communion.[70] 'Pray send me Shakespeares workes ye Last Edition and Mr Wakes preparation for death,' he instructed the bookseller Richard Bentley in September 1688.[71]

The personal libraries that were created by these and other means were understandably heterogeneous. The sermons of Lancelot Andrewes nestled alongside the poems of Abraham Cowley; geographies, herbals, and histories were shelved with Augustine, à Kempis, and Taylor's 'life' of Christ, *The Great Exemplar*. Elizabeth Freke listed the evergreen manuals of devotion, Lewis Bayly's *Practice of Piety*, Simon Patrick's *Parable of the Pilgrim*, and *The Whole Duty of Man*, beside the scabrous series of *Poems on Affairs of State*.[72] The old were to be found alongside the new: the healthy trade in reprints and new editions of older works and in second-hand books and the acquisitive habits of book collectors meant that most personal libraries included authors – such as Bayly or Andrewes – first published much earlier in the century.

Book buying is one thing; reading is quite another. In general, Anglican tastes were broad. In Hertfordshire 'the long evening howres were shortned w[i]th the varietys of ye history of China', or Tacitus or Guicciardini or a work of edifying Anglican instruction: one Sunday in November, 'Doctor Taylors Excellent booke of ye life and death of ye Holy Jesus entertaind us this long Evening.'[73] When it came to religion, Anne Sadleir claimed 'those that I now read, besides the Bible, are first the late Kings Booke, Hookers Ecclesiasticall Policie, Reverend Bish Andrews sermons with his other devine meditations, Dr Jer Taylers works, and Dr Tho. Jacksone upon the Creed'.[74] William Coe read Jeremy Taylor's *Great Exemplar*, *Holy Living*, and *Holy Dying*, Matthew Hale's *Meditations*, and Samuel Cradock's *Knowledge and Piety* (1659).[75] 'I read over Mr Hornecks book of consideration,' recorded Boothby, 'tis an excellent good & pious Booke I intend much to read and meaditate in that & claustrum Animae.' The latter, Luke Beaulieu's *Claustrum Animae: The Reformed Monastery; Or, The Love of Jesus. A Sure and Short, pleasant and easie way to Heaven. In Meditations, Directions and Resolutions to Love and Obey Jesus unto Death* (1677), made a huge impression upon Boothby: 'my soule was never rased so heavenward by the reading of any Booke pen'd by mere man. I will keepe it & use it as a jewel & often read & meditate in it & I will do what I can to find out the author and get more help fro[m] him.'[76] Like Mrs Sadleir, Boothby, however, still gave pride of place to the Bible. On his nineteenth wedding anniversary he finished reading the Bible over and stated his delight in this above all other books: 'I find and feale in my soule when I read it that I am not able to express ... oh how do I rejoyce when I am come into my closett & take the blessed scriptures into my hands, I not onely kiss it but I lay up its words in my heart: come you who never yet tasted true spirituall joy; & know not what tis; Read & meditate much in this Blessed Booke.'[77]

Devotional reading pays little heed to denominational boundaries: readers pick up what is available, useful and affecting. Yet among popular Anglican devotional there were some clear front-runners: the works of Jeremy Taylor, especially his life of Christ and his manuals on a holy life and death, had a wide appeal, as did the writings of George Herbert, Simon Patrick, and later the printed sermons of John Tillotson. The single work that made the greatest impact was Richard Allestree's *The Whole Duty of Man* (1658). This short, clear *vade mecum* was bought, read, treasured, quoted, given as a gift, or recommended to others, on an astonishing scale. It seemed to complement the official teaching and worship of the Church of England. Boothby had a copy bound with the catechism. When there was no evening prayer at church, Sir Humphrey Gore 'became Chaplaine in my house in reading some part of ye appoynted service and a peece of ye Whole Duty of man being most plaine and sutable to ye capacities of my Auditors'.[78] The devotional content supplied lay people with prayers that they could use in the solitude of their chambers or 'closets'. The *Whole Duty* provided a scriptural slogan for an age: in the 'very uncertaine' times of November 1688, Sir Daniel Fleming told his children 'to be sure to fear God & to keep his Commandments; w[hi]ch I think is ye whole Duty to man'.[79]

The Prayer Book, too, played its part in private and domestic worship. Devout Anglicans maintained household prayers. As well as attending church twice on a Sunday, Gore concluded the day with a scripture reading and prayers.[80] In the week, his household was summoned to daily prayers at 11.00 a.m. by a bell, unless a clergyman was available, when prayer was 'dayly performd noon and night by him'. It was 'a comfort & joy' to Boothby 'to have the prayers read constantly' in his chapel, as it no doubt was to the earl of Shaftesbury. Lay Anglicans would frequently step into the minister's shoes: 'in the afternoon we were left unsupplyed and upon ye score I was obliged to be chaplaine in my house', recalled Gore; on other occasions he 'read to my family some part of ye service of ye day', and read scripture with them.[81] Boothby was used to pray and catechise in his own household, 'and that with great inlargedness & affection'.[82]

The clergy's devotional publications encouraged the extension of the church's public worship into the private devotion of individuals and vice versa. 'Enter into thy closet' was the exhortation of the church in tract after tract on private prayer, domestic devotion, and preparation for a worthy reception of the Lord's Supper. The Common Prayer Book was the 'best companion in the house and closet', but these devotional manuals also provided their own models of private prayer, 'ejaculations' of praise or petition on rising in the morning or retiring to bed, directions on 'how to raise the soul into holy flames before, at, and after receiving the blessed sacrament', longer forms of confession and contrition keyed into a regime of self-examination, and meditative or inspirational texts.[83] In diaries, commonplace books, and simple notebooks we find lay Anglicans copying out these texts, adapting and personalising them to their own circumstances, and then taking the natural next step of composing their own devotions out of the common store of scriptural, patristic, and medieval materials, liturgical texts and the rich tradition of the Anglican devotional writers.[84] John Evelyn, whose archive is probably the richest collection of such material, instructed his daughter to read 'a part of some Meditation or Office of the Day' (meaning the Prayer Book) and then to offer up a prayer 'conceived sometimes by your selfe, as you find your Spirit tender & disposed, or else out of some devout Book'.[85] The ageing duke of Ormond composed prayers that dwelt upon his misspent life and implored God for grace and protection; he humbled himself before God on the death of his son Ossory; he measured himself against the Ten Commandments and confessed his sins; and he composed or transcribed prayers for use before and after receiving the Holy Sacrament.[86] Sir William Trumbull used Sunday for self-examination and 'in these Retirem[en]ts, ye severall Occurences of my Life furnisht me with occasions enought for ye different parts of Devotion, such as are Confession & Sorrow for my great and hainous Offences; Acknowledgem[en]t of my vileness & unworthiness; Imploring Pardon & Grace; Thanksgiving for infinite Signall & Distinguishing mercies & Deliverances'.[87] There was nothing easy about such a regime. 'My God shou'dst thou now cut me off in the mid'st of my sins, a creature made after thy own image, and a soul for which my saviour's bloud was shed wou'd perish,' prayed the youthful Elizabeth Delaval: 'O spare me then a lettle, a lettle while, before I go hence, and be no more seen.'[88]

These prayers were intended as part of the daily round, but they were also related to the special days set aside for spiritual introspection. Like their Puritan predecessors and neighbours, God-fearing Anglicans made a habit of keeping anniversaries, perhaps of their birth, their baptism, or simply at the New Year, for spiritual stocktaking and the solemn renewal of their baptismal covenant.[89] 'The first and most early thoughts of this morning being the day of my Nativitie were sent up to Heaven to acknowledge the mercy and goodness of my Creator in making me in his image, giving me a reasonable soul and understanding, and that now for the space of forty and six yeares he hath guided me and preserved me through infinite dangers,' recorded Sir Humphrey Gore.[90] Gore also kept 3 February – the anniversary of a dental disaster – to acknowledge his sins and ask for God's providential protection from accidents and provoking sins: 'Lord I beseech thee sanctify this affliction to me.'[91] Very occasionally, Anglican diarists recorded the effect of this regime: 'at evening p[rivate?] devotions my poore soule was much inlarged even to Ravishment';[92] 'How sweet & comfortable do I finde these houres w[hi]ch I spend with God in my morning devotions – I am not able to expresse Gods goodness to me the greatest of sinners – Oh that I could spend my life thus.'[93]

Just as closet and household devotion brought the worship of the church into the home, so the devout Anglican took a prepared heart and mind to the public services of the church: Boothby proposed 'by Gods grace to rise early on Sunday mornings & to performe my private solemne devotions &

publicke prayer in family before we goe to church'.[94] Church-going comprised the weekly services and sermon, the great fasts and festivals of the church, and the sacrament of the Lord's Supper. As ever, it is the routine activity that is least well documented. Sunday services may have been lacklustre affairs, with the congregation mumbling the responses from memory or raggedly following the parish clerk's lead. Comments on the effect of this worship are scarce, although the disappointment that some diarists expressed about their own coldness and inattention at church is evidence of their high expectations, and on occasion individuals were raised out of themselves: 'at ye singing of ye psalms I found my heart much lifted up in ye high praises of God whilest I was joining w[i]th ye great congregatio[n] in celebrating his praises'.[95]

Restoration Anglicans were as preoccupied with preaching as their neighbours. Printed sermons were consumed in huge numbers: in 1683 Boothby sent eleven parcels of single sermons to be bound in as many volumes.[96] If Prayer Book services were perhaps too mundane to elicit many observations, the uniqueness of every sermon and the confidence of the laity in judging both the style and substance of preaching guaranteed a flood of commentary. The Countess of Warwick found Stillingfleet's preaching 'admirable', Morley's 'very searching', Burnet's 'heavenly', and Kidder's left her 'much affected and moved'.[97] 'A very pretty, neat, sober, honest sermon' by Nathaniel Crew delighted Pepys; 'the manner of his delivery I do like exceedingly'.[98] But he found another 'the most flat, dead sermon, both for matter and manner of delivery, that ever I heard; and very long beyond his hour, which made it worse'.[99] In the view of lay Anglicans, preaching should be plain, affecting, and useful. A sermon should move and instruct the congregation: they should be able to use it to deepen their understanding of scripture and doctrine, to hone their spirituality, and to live a holy life. Once preached, a good sermon lived on in the memory and the notes of those who had heard it: they discussed sermons, transcribed them, and meditated over them; sitting by her husband's sickbed, the Countess of Warwick 'had time to call ye sermon to mind, & with great earnestness did I pray it over, begging God to make me set my affections more upon heavenly things'.[100]

For obvious reasons, Anglican preaching is more visible in the historical record than is the sacrament of the Lord's Supper.[101] Yet the sacrament was the climax of the Anglican devotional regime. Celebrated at Easter, Whitsun and Christmas, and more frequently in some cathedral cities, the sacrament was promoted by the church as the acme of individual piety. The minister 'warned' the congregation that a sacrament was to be celebrated and often preached a 'preparation sermon' a week or more before the event. Devout lay people prepared themselves carefully: they took up their copies of Patrick or Comber, their Bibles and Prayer Books, and set to the work of self-examination. Saturday 22 April 1671 'being very hott oblig'd' Sir Humphrey Gore 'to ye coole retirem[en]ts of my owne home where I might entertain meditations suitable to ye day preceeding Easter Sunday ye blessed Sacr[a]m[en]t of ye Lords body being then / God willing / to be received by me'. The Easter season of 1674 began well with a preparation sermon on 5 April, which Gore described as 'ye applause of a good sermon'; he then gave up Good Friday (17 April) to preparing himself, 'Being a day of mortification was in part employd in services proper for it as reading and prayers', only to endure 'a great disapoyntm[en]t' when illness prevented him from receiving the sacrament.[102] On notice given of a sacrament, Sir William Boothby and his wife postponed a planned trip, 'all business shall be laid aside & this as is most excellent preferred above all', especially since Sir William, fearing for his health, did not know whether he would live to see another opportunity to receive the 'blessed sacrament'. In due course, 'I went with Earnest longings & holy Breathings after the sa[c] rament w[hi]ch I rec[eived.] Oh the joy & comfort of my soul ... Jesus Christ hath visited me here in this ordinance in a wonderful and inexpressible man[ner]. This is a Blessed day indeed but tis so by this blessed ordinance.' How, asked Boothby, could anyone neglect the opportunity to receive the sacrament 'above all things in the world when once he hath experienced what I poore creature and many ... soules hath tasted of in this Blessed Sacra-ment'.[103] 'Oh Lord I bless thee for this sweet day in w[hi]ch at ye Blessed Sacra-ment I did enjoy most sweet com[m]union w[i]th thee,' sang the Countess of Warwick.[104] Others were less fortunate. Elizabeth Delaval found herself 'far, far short of those raptures of love' which she expected at Easter, while Lady Sarah Cowper did not experience what others do at the sacrament: 'I feel more fear than joys, more tremblings, than transports.'[105] Some church-goers recorded their reception of the sacrament with less extravagance: William Coe, who usually received three times a year, followed a prosaic but revealing formula: 'I received the blessed sacrament of Christ's body and blood, and renewed my covenant with Almighty God (in my Saviour's blood) which I have so often and grievously broken; I beseech God to enable me to keep it better for the future. Lord be mercifull to me a sinner.'[106]

V

Study of the lay contribution to the Restoration Church of England is in its infancy. The available evidence is fragmentary and socially skewed, the possible mechanisms by which lay attitudes shaped the ideals promoted by the clergy were subtle and intangible, and even when we surmise that lay conformists were in some matters a step or two ahead of the official church and in others a few steps behind, we are left with the problem that the clergy of the Church of England did not themselves keep in step, and so, to that extent, the church did not present a single orthodoxy. It is in these gaps, however, that we can begin to explore both what it meant to be a lay member of the Church of England and, even more importantly, how the laity and clergy together moulded the aesthetic and doctrinal substance of the established church.

NOTES

1 J. Spurr, *The Restoration Church of England 1646–1689* (New Haven and London: Yale University Press, 1991). Earlier studies include R.S. Bosher, *The making of the Restoration settlement: the influence of the Laudians 1649–1662* (Dacre Press, 1951); I. Green, *The re-establishment of the Church of England, 1660–1663* (Oxford: Oxford University Press, 1978), and the many learned articles by the most expert scholar of the institutional church, Robert Beddard.

2 M. Goldie, 'The theory of religious intolerance in Restoration England', in O.P. Grell, J.I. Israel and N. Tyacke (eds), *From persecution to toleration: the Glorious Revolution and religion in England* (Oxford: Oxford University Press, 1991), pp. 331–68.

3 Among these are Eamon Duffy, Christopher Haigh, Nicholas Tyacke, Peter Lake, Alex Walsham, Ken Fincham, and Anthony Milton. I read and re-read P. Collinson's *The religion of Protestants* (Oxford: Oxford University Press, 1982), a subtle, many-angled account of the Church of England between 1559 and 1625, while composing my own book.

4 See the chapter by Grant Tapsell in this volume.

5 J. Spurr, '"Latitudinarianism" and the Restoration Church,' *HJ*, 31 (1988), 61–82.

6 K. Fincham and S. Taylor, 'Episcopalian conformity and nonconformity, 1646–60', in J. McElligott and D.L. Smith (eds), *Royalists and royalism in the interregnum* (Manchester: Manchester University Press, 2010); J. Maltby, '"The Good Old Way": Prayer Book Protestantism in the 1640s and 1650s', *SCH*, 38 (2003), 233–56; J. Maltby, 'Suffering and surviving: the Civil Wars, the Commonwealth, and the formation of "Anglicanism", 1642–60', in C. Durston and J. Maltby (eds), *Religion and society in revolutionary England* (Manchester: Manchester University Press, 2006), pp. 158–80.

7 A. Lacey, *The cult of King Charles the Martyr* (Woodbridge: Boydell, 2003); Stephen Hampton, *Anti-Arminians: the Anglican Reformed tradition from Charles II to George I* (Oxford: Oxford University Press, 2008); M. Brydon, *The evolving reputation of Richard Hooker: an examination of responses 1600–1714* (Oxford: Oxford University Press, 2006); A. Milton, *Laudian and royalist polemic in seventeenth-century England: the career and writings of Peter Heylyn* (Manchester: Manchester University Press, 2007).

8 K. Fincham and N. Tyacke, *Altars restored: the changing face of English religious worship, 1547–c.1700* (Oxford: Oxford University Press, 2007).

9 See A. Kugler, *Errant plagiary: the life and writing of Lady Sarah Cowper* (Stanford: Stanford University Press, 2002); B.S. Sirota, 'The Christian monitors: church, society, and the voluntary sector in Britain 1660–1720' (PhD dissertation, University of Chicago, 2007), chapter 1; F. Harris, *Transformations of love: the friendship of John Evelyn and Margaret Godolphin* (Oxford: Oxford University Press, 2002).

10 J. Champion, *The pillars of priestcraft shaken: the Church of England and its enemies, 1660–1730* (Cambridge: Cambridge University Press, 1992); J.D. Ramsbottom, 'Presbyterians and "partial conformity" in the Restoration Church of England', *JEH*, 43 (1992), 249–70.

11 J. Gregory and J.S. Chamberlain (eds), *The national church in local perspective: the Church of England and the regions, 1660–1800* (Woodbridge: Boydell, 2003); J. Gregory, *Restoration, reformation and reform, 1660–1828: archbishops of Canterbury and their diocese* (Oxford: Clarendon Press, 2000); Sirota, 'Christian monitors'; W.J. Bulman, 'Constantine's enlightenment: culture and religious politics in the early British Empire, c.1648–1710' (PhD dissertation, Princeton University, 2009); J. Rose, 'Concepts of royal ecclesiastical supremacy in Restoration England' (PhD dissertation, University of Cambridge, 2007); J. Rose, 'Royal ecclesiastical supremacy and the Restoration Church', *Historical Research*, 80 (2007), 324–45.

12 Andrew Marvell, *Mr Smirke* (1676), in A. Patterson *et al.* (eds), *The prose works of Andrew Marvell*, 2 vols (New Haven and London: Yale University Press, 2003), II, 108.

13 BL Egerton MS 2655, fol. 14v.

14 See M. Spufford, 'Can we count the "godly" and the "conformable" in the seventeenth century?' *JEH*, 36 (1985), 428–38.

15 J. Spurr, '"A sublime and noble service": John Evelyn and the Church of England', in F. Harris and M. Hunter (eds), *John Evelyn and his milieu* (The British Library, 2003); M. Storey (ed.), *Two East Anglian diaries 1641–1729: Isaac Archer and William Coe* (Suffolk Records Society, 36, Woodbridge: Boydell, 1994), p. 204.

16 Quoted in M.-L. Coolahan, 'Redeeming parcels of time: aesthetics and practice of occasional meditation', *The Seventeenth Century*, 22 (2007), 127.

17 M. Spufford, *Small books and pleasant histories: popular fiction and its readership in seventeenth-century England* (Cambridge: Cambridge University Press, 1981); I. Green, *Print and Protestantism in early modern England* (Oxford: Oxford University Press, 2000).

18 J. Maltby, *Prayer Book and people in Elizabethan and early Stuart England* (Cambridge: Cambridge University Press, 1998); C. Haigh, *The plain man's pathways to heaven: kinds of Christianity in post-Reformation England* (Oxford: Oxford University Press, 2007); D.A. Spaeth, *The church in an age of danger: parsons and parishioners, 1660–1740* (Cambridge: Cambridge University Press, 2000); W.M. Jacob, *Lay people and religion in the early eighteenth century* (Cambridge: Cambridge University Press, 1996).

19 Spaeth, *Church in an age of danger*, p. 193.

20 *Two East Anglian diaries*, p. 89.

21 Spurr, *Restoration Church*, p. 37.

22 See, for example, V. Larminie, *Wealth, kinship and culture: the seventeenth-century Newdigates of Arbury and their world* (Royal Historical Society Studies in History, 1995); S.E. Whyman, *Sociability and power in late-Stuart England: the cultural worlds of the Verneys 1660–1720* (Oxford: Oxford University Press, 1999); G. Tapsell, 'Laurence Hyde and the politics of religion in later Stuart England', *EHR*, 125 (2010), 1414–48; S.J.G. Burton, 'Reading the Psalms with Athanasius and Seneca: stoicism and providence in the earl of Clarendon's *Contemplations*', *Renaissance Studies*, 25 (2011), 298–317; A. Hunt, 'The books, manuscripts and literary patronage of Mrs Anne Sadleir (1585–1670)', in V.E. Burke and J. Gibson (eds), *Early modern women's manuscript writings: selected papers from the Trinity-Trent Colloquium* (Aldershot: Ashgate, 2004); Spurr, '"Sublime and noble service"'.

23 Bodl. MS Eng. Letters C 210, fol. 62.

24 Hertfordshire RO MS D/EP F 29, p. 91.

25 Sir Humphrey Gore (1626–95) wrote a diary for 1671–76, now YUB MS Osborn fb 222: the diary is not paginated, so references are made by date of entry; this quotation is under 21 Apr. 1676.

26 BL Add. MS 71689, fol. 26, Sir William Boothby's letterbook. Peter Beal, 'Sir William Boothby, first baronet (*bap.* 1637, *d.* 1707)', *ODNB*, concentrates on Boothby the bibliophile.

27 YUB MS Osborn fb 222: also see entries for 7 Aug., 26 Aug. and 5 Sept. 1671.

28 H.J.F. Swayne (ed.), *Churchwardens accounts of S. Edward and S. Thomas, Sarum 1443–1702* (Wiltshire Record Society, Salisbury, 1896), p. 339.

29 J.R. McGrath (ed.), *The Flemings in Oxford*, 2 vols (Oxford: Oxford Historical Society, 44, 1903; 62, 1913), II, 190.

30 *Flemings in Oxford*, II, 212: see also A. Fletcher, 'The enforcement of the Conventicle Acts 1664–1679', *SCH*, 21 (1984), 235–46.

31 See *Flemings in Oxford*, II, 372; BL Add MS 71691, fols 20–1.

32 *Flemings in Oxford*, I, 474; also see *ibid.*, I, 484; II, 306.

33 *Ibid.*, II, 341.

34 Bodl. MS Add. C 302, fol. 218r.

35 See Spaeth, *Church in an age of danger*, pp. 45–6. The 'contempt of the clergy' debate was, in part, a reflection of 'Hobbist' and other heterodox ideas; see Spurr, *Restoration Church*, pp. 219–29.

36 See *Flemings in Oxford*, II, v–vi, 349–51, 358, 380, 381; I, 200, 214, 237.

37 BL Add. MS 71692, fol. 26r. Truelove was rector of Cooling 1688–1706; see Clergy of the Church of England Database: http://www.theclergydatabase.org.uk/

38 A. Cambers (ed.), *The Life of John Raistrick 1650–1727* (Camden Society, Fifth series, 36, 2010), pp. 3, 82, 85, 102–3, 104; S.S. Thomas, 'Religious community in revolutionary Halifax', *Northern History*, 40 (2003), 89–111; Spurr, *Restoration Church*, p. 203.

39 Spaeth, *Church in an age of danger*, pp. 129–30.

40 *Ibid.*, pp. 19–22.

41 See P. Seaward, 'Gilbert Sheldon, the London vestries and the defence of the church', in T. Harris, P. Seaward and M. Goldie (eds), *The politics of religion in Restoration England* (Oxford: Wiley-Blackwell, 1990), pp. 49–73.

42 R.A. Beddard, 'The privileges of Christchurch, Canterbury: Archbishop Sheldon's enquiries of 1671', *Archaeologia Cantiana*, 87 (1972), 81–100; R.A. Beddard, 'Church and state in Old St Paul's: Dean Barwick's assertion of the church's rights against the City', *Guildhall Miscellany*, 4 (1972), 161–74.

43 M. Clapinson (ed.), *Bishop Fell and nonconformity* (Oxfordshire Record Society, 52, 1980), pp. 2–3.

44 M. Goldie and J. Spurr, 'Politics and the Restoration parish: Edward Fowler and the struggle for St Giles Cripplegate', *EHR*, 109 (1994), 572–96. Other disputes are discussed by Thomas, 'Religious community in revolutionary Halifax'; N. Key and J. Ward, 'Divided into parties: exclusion crisis origins in Monmouth', *EHR*, 115 (2000), 1159–83.

45 M.A. Mullett, 'Conflict, politics and elections in Lancaster, 1660–1688', *Northern History*, 19 (1983), 61–86; D.C. Beaver, *Parish communities and religious conflict in the Vale*

of *Gloucester 1590–1690* (Cambridge, MA: Harvard University Press, 1998); G. Tapsell, *The personal rule of Charles II, 1681–1685* (Woodbridge: Boydell, 2007); J. Miller, *After the civil wars: English politics and government in the reign of Charles II* (Harlow: Longman, 2000); J. Miller, *Cities divided: politics and religion in English provincial towns 1660–1722* (Oxford: Oxford University Press, 2007).

46 Josiah Woodward, *An account of the rise and progress of the religious societies* (2nd edn, 1698), p. 30.

47 BL Add. MS 38693, fol. 137; J. Spurr, 'The church, the societies and the moral revolution of 1688', in J. Walsh, C. Haydon and S. Taylor (eds), *The Church of England c.1689–c.1833: from toleration to Tractarianism* (Cambridge: Cambridge University Press, 1993), pp. 127–42.

48 See the chapter by George Southcombe in this volume.

49 Two examples are Andrew Marvell, MP for Hull and the earl of Shaftesbury, on whom see respectively J. Spurr, 'The poet's religion', in S. Zwicker and D. Hirst (eds), *The Cambridge companion to Andrew Marvell* (Cambridge: Cambridge University Press, 2011), pp. 158–73, and J. Spurr, 'Shaftesbury and the politics of religion', in J. Spurr (ed.), *Anthony Ashley Cooper, first earl of Shaftesbury 1621–1683* (Farnham: Ashgate, 2011), pp. 127–51.

50 BL Add. MS 71692, fols 69r–v; also see Miller, *After the civil wars*, pp. 228–32, on the 'church party' in Norfolk in the mid 1670s.

51 P. Seaward, *The Cavalier Parliament and the reconstruction of the old regime, 1661–1667* (Cambridge: Cambridge University Press, 1989), offers the most detailed account.

52 Examples include Sir Job Charlton and Thomas Chicheley (see R.C. Latham and W. Matthews (eds), *The Diary of Samuel Pepys*, 11 vols [Bell & Hyman, 1970–83], IX, 112).

53 A. Browning (ed.), *The memoirs of Sir John Reresby* (revised by M.K. Geiter and W.A. Speck, Royal Historical Society, 1991), pp. 367, 369.

54 C. Jackson (ed.), *The autobiography of Mrs Alice Thornton* (Surtees Society, 62, 1873), p. 56 (the reference is to Jeremiah 4:20).

55 See Lacey, *Cult of King Charles*; Spurr, *Restoration Church*, pp. 48, 69; and K. Sharpe, *Rebranding rule* (forthcoming, Yale University Press)

56 BL Add. MS 71692, fol. 112r.

57 YUB MS Osborn fb 222, 20 Mar. 1671/2.

58 BL Add. MS 71692, fols 8v, 9v, 11r.

59 *Ibid.*, fol. 27v.

60 *Ibid.*, fol. 48v.

61 *Ibid.*, fols 13v, 112r.

62 *Ibid.*, fol. 57r.

63 *Ibid.*, fol. 57r.

64 *Ibid.*, fol. 68v.

65 *Ibid.*, fol. 82r.

66 *Ibid.*, fol. 93v.

67 *Ibid.*, fols 97, 99v.

68 *Ibid.*, fol. 105v.

69 *Flemings in Oxford*, I, 402, 406, 434, 440, 445.

70 BL Add. MS 71690, fols 34r, 45r. Not always indiscriminate; Boothby returned unwanted items to his bookseller, 'this last parcell is most popish peeces: onely the Continuation of the present State of the Controversy, is much to my satisfaction' (fol. 26v).

71 BL Add. MS 71692, fol. 26v.

72 R. Anselment (ed.), *The remembrances of Elizabeth Freke* (Camden Society, Fifth series, 18, 2002), pp. 173–6.

73 YUB MS Osborn fb 222, 28 Oct. 1672, 26 Nov. 1671.

74 Hunt, 'Books, manuscripts and literary patronage of Mrs Anne Sadleir', p. 216.

75 *Two East Anglian diaries*, pp. 203, 229, 241, 253.

76 BL Add. MS 71689, fols 50v, 24v. Anthony Horneck, *The great law of consideration* (1677). Horneck was a close friend of Boothby, but I have not found any evidence that Boothby was in contact with Beaulieu (1645–1723).

77 BL Add. MS 71689, fols 68–9.

78 *Ibid.*, fol. 73v; YUB MS Osborn fb 222, 1 June 1673.

79 *Flemings in Oxford*, II, 241. Also see Spurr, *Restoration Church*, pp. 281–4.

80 YUB, MS Osborn fb 222, 1 Sept. 1672.

81 YUB MS Osborn fb 222, 17 Jan., 29 Sept., 3 Nov., 15 Dec. 1672; BL Add. MS 71689, fol. 32; Spurr, 'Shaftesbury and religion', p. 127.

82 BL Add. MS 71689, fols 29v–30.

83 The quotations are from the title pages of Edward Wetenhall, *Enter into thy closet* (1666); Thomas Comber, *A companion to the temple* (1684); and Anthony Horneck, *The fire of the altar* (1683). See Spurr, *Restoration Church*, pp. 341–53.

84 *Two East Anglian diaries*, pp. 264–5: 'A prayer for any time of the day when a person has leisure to retire, taken out of a book called Dr Patrick's *Devotions*'.

85 BL Add. MS 78440, item 5, 'point 13', fol. 6r.

86 BL Add. MS 11498.

87 YUB MS Osborn shelves b 177, p. 8.

88 Bodl. MS Rawlinson D 78, fol. 72; also see HRO, MS D/EP F 40.

89 BL MS Add. 71689, fols 39–41.

90 YUB MS Osborn fb 222, 29 Feb. 1672.

91 *Ibid.*, 3 Feb. 1673: Gore's jaw had been broken in several places when he had a tooth drawn.

92 BL MS Add 71689, fol. 94v, also see fol. 117v.

93 *Ibid.*, fol. 38.

94 *Ibid.*, fol. 87.

95 BL Add. MS 27358, fol. 85; also see BL Add. MS 71689, fol. 43.

96 BL Add. MS 71690, fol. 64r. (For more on preaching, see Grant Tapsell's chapter in this volume.)

97 BL Add. MS 27358, fols 17v, 22v, 27v, 56r.

98 *Diary of Samuel Pepys*, VIII, 145.

99 *Ibid.*, III, 99; IV, 36–7.

100 BL Add. MS 27358, fol. 38. I plan to write elsewhere on the laity's 'use' of sermons.

101 Pepys' reception of the sacrament is puzzling: he makes little of it, but external evidence suggests that he was a regular communicant, see *Diary of Samuel Pepys*, III, 54 and note; III, 292; VII, 99.

102 YUB MS Osborn fb 222, 5, 17, 19 Apr. 1674: other practitioners of preparation include Lord Yarmouth, John Evelyn, and John Verney.

103 BL Add. MS 71689, fols 17–18, 25.

104 BL Add. MS 27358, fol. 89r, also see fols 91v–92r, 96v, 99r

105 Bodl. MS Rawlinson D 78, fol. 189; HRO, MS D/EP F 29, p. 182.

106 *Two East Anglian diaries*, p. 211.

Part III

◆

Places

Chapter 5

The later Stuart church as 'national church' in Scotland and Ireland

Clare Jackson

On 5 November 1711, the Chancellor of Christ Church Cathedral in Dublin, John Travers, preached a sermon in the cathedral before the Irish Lord Lieutenant, James Butler, second duke of Ormond. It being the anniversary of the Gunpowder Plot, Travers reminded his congregation that, just over a century ago, the 'Powder was actually plac'd in a Cellar under the Parliament House ... and the Train was laid for setting Fire to it.' The danger at Westminster in 1605 had, however, been only one of a series of threats posed by the Catholic Church since the Reformation that belied 'one of Machiavel's prejudices to Christianity' – that its precepts of meekness, mercy and charity rendered men weak and impotent – since, according to Travers, 'Tyranny, and Cruelty, and Blood-thirstiness, are as Essential to Popery, as Superstition and Idolatry.' On this particular anniversary, Travers combined his chilling catalogue of Catholic conspiracies with grateful commemoration of William III's landing at Torbay in 1688, which had secured 'the deliverance of our Church and Nations'. In a striking allusion to the additional threat posed by Protestant dissent, Travers also paid tribute to the recent enactment by Queen Anne's ministry of legislation to support the church by building fifty new parish churches 'in the great Metropolis' of London.[1]

Preaching in the heartland of Ireland's 'Protestant ascendancy', in an island whose population was overwhelmingly Catholic, Travers explicitly identified and applauded a single, Protestant and Episcopal 'Church' that served plural 'nations'. Between 1660 and 1685, his view would have been plausible, since Charles II's return had been accompanied by the re-establishment of Episcopalian churches in England, Scotland and Ireland, sustained by a consensus that secure and stable government required religious conformity throughout the three kingdoms. By 1711, however, Episcopacy had been abolished in Scotland and Presbyterianism re-established; Protestant dissenters in England had been granted religious toleration in 1689; and, in Ireland, the rapid growth of Protestant nonconformist congregations continually threatened to outnumber members of the established church. All three kingdoms had, meanwhile, suffered the trauma of the proselytising ambitions of the last Catholic monarch, James VII and II. By 1711, therefore, Travers's vision of one Episcopal Church serving three kingdoms was distinctly precarious.

Presented broadly chronologically, this chapter examines the fluctuating fortunes of the later Stuart churches in Scotland and Ireland. In doing so, it outlines the legislative framework that determined ecclesiastical policy, whilst also illustrating the extent to which the period was alternately characterised by periods of intense sectarianism and brutal suppression of nonconformists, alongside rival impulses towards comprehension and toleration. It first examines the desire for religious uniformity that underpinned Charles II's restoration and the degrees of state coercion this decision entailed, whilst the second section considers the impact for the established churches of James VII and II's Catholicising policies, together with the outcome of the Williamite revolution. The ensuing section evaluates the impact, in both Scotland and Ireland, of the enactment of religious toleration for all Protestants in England and of Presbyterianism's re-establishment in Scotland, before concluding with a consideration of events in Queen Anne's reign.

Primarily considering the politics of religion, this chapter focuses more on the relationship between statesmen and prelates in pulpits than on dissenters and narratives of persecution and unjustified tyranny. In Scotland, the imposition of an Episcopal church structure on a predominantly Presbyterian population in 1662, before Presbyterianism's re-establishment in 1690, provoked retrospective denunciations of brutal attempts by Charles II's government to enforce conformity as 'the Killing Times'. This chapter eschews, however, the tenacious tendency to study the later Stuart church in Scotland through sectarian lenses which has been historiographically dominant since the publication of Robert Wodrow's *History of the sufferings of the Church of Scotland* in 1722. It likewise aims to resist subsuming its treatment of the later Stuart church in Ireland within broader nationalist or unionist frameworks that have traditionally served to render historiography of the established church 'a creature of polemic, of a church desperately seeking to create an ideological justification of its peculiar position in Ireland'.[2] Nevertheless, the existence of large numbers of Scottish and Irish subjects who were not members of the established church – more often than not, a majority of the population – inevitably generated different dynamics for the later Stuart church than those prevailing in England. As this chapter shows, recurrent interactions between the established churches and nonconformists from 1660 onwards, whether antagonistic or conciliatory, served to sharpen each denomination's self-understanding, enabling rival traditions to articulate – and sometimes to cement – their religious differences with greater precision by 1714.

I

In his Declaration of Breda, issued from the Netherlands in April 1660, Charles II explicitly connected political stability with religious conformity by committing himself to granting 'a liberty to tender consciences' to those whose convictions 'do not disturb the peace of the kingdom'. The English parliament, however, subsequently adopted a narrower view of potential threats to civil peace and, by the Act of Uniformity (1662), reimposed the Book of Common Prayer and an episcopally ordained clergy as the necessary conditions for legal worship, whilst the colloquially termed 'Clarendon Code' was entrenched in further legislation, such as the Conventicle Act (1664) and the Five Mile Act (1665). A similar premise underpinned the expeditious rehabilitation of the Church of Ireland, whose ecclesiastical structure had remained unchanged during the years of civil war. Following a meeting between Charles II and representatives of the Dublin Convention at Whitehall in June 1660, all but one of sixteen vacant bishoprics were filled within weeks, enabling a mass consecration of two new archbishops and ten new bishops at St Patrick's Cathedral in January 1661 to create a full bench of twenty-one Church of Ireland bishops, nine of whom had been born in England, four in Scotland, two in Wales, and six in Ireland. With the Restoration Irish bench characterised by 'conspicuous loyalty to the Anglican cause during the Interregnum',[3] prospects for church policy initially appeared auspicious, deriving from the cordial working relationship between the church's leading primate, Archbishop John Bramhall of Armagh, and James Butler, first duke of Ormond, appointed Lord Lieutenant in 1662, but which ended prematurely with Bramhall's death the following year. In Scotland, by contrast, Episcopalianism had been formally abolished during the civil wars and thus depended on a preference for ecclesiastical conformity and the reassertion of monarchical prerogative for its re-establishment at the Restoration. As the relevant legislation enacted by the Scots parliament in 1662 confirmed, prescribing 'the externall government and policie of the church' was 'ane inherent right of the croun, by vertew of his royall prerogative and supremacie in causes ecclesiasticall'.[4] Given the Presbyterian dominance that had prevailed since victory over Charles I in the 'Bishops' Wars', however, experienced observers, such as Robert Baillie, doubted the wisdom of bringing 'bak upon us the Canterburian tyms, the same designs, the same practises', predicting in 1661 that it would only 'bring on at last the same horribll effects'.[5] Baillie's fears duly proved prescient when around 270 ministers, or one quarter of all parish incumbents across Scotland, were deprived of their cures for refusing to accept episcopal collation as required by the Act for Presentation and Collation (1662).

For its part, the Church of Ireland served a minority population, vastly outnumbered by Catholics and increasingly threatened by the post-

Cromwellian fragmentation of the 'Protestant interest' into English Presbyterian, Scots Presbyterian, Independent, and Quaker denominations. Of particular concern to the established church was the sizeable number of Scots Presbyterians, largely concentrated in north-east Ulster, who remained implacably opposed to 'prelatical' church government and the use of a prescribed liturgy. Although the only part of the 'Clarendon Code' enacted in Ireland was the Act of Uniformity passed by the Irish parliament in 1666, it brought the Church of Ireland into closer legal conformity with its Anglican counterpart, but sharpened differences with moderate nonconformists by confirming the need for Episcopal ordination and assent to the Book of Common Prayer and the Thirty-nine Articles. Whitehall thus retained a watchful eye over the potential for non-adherence to the national church to foster political instability, giving credence to Archbishop James Ussher of Armagh's warnings in the 1630s about the prospect of having 'a canon obtained in the church, like Poynings' Act ... in the state, giving the Church of England such superintendence over us, that nothing should be made law here that was not first allowed there'.[6]

In both Restoration Scotland and Ireland, the national church was nevertheless obliged to rely on the civil government for support. In Scotland, the bishops found themselves doubly compromised: attacked by Presbyterian opponents as pawns of an arbitrary and ungodly monarchy, whilst undermined by a pervasive anticlericalism amongst Charles II's civil governors. Members of the restored Scottish bench generally avoided producing *iure divino* arguments for Episcopacy, averring instead that specific forms of church government were 'matters indifferent' to salvation and best left to civil magistrates to determine. There was also no prescribed liturgy; as one of the church's most vocal internal critics, Gilbert Burnet, bemoaned in 1666, the Restoration church was 'the only one in the world which hath no rule for worship',[7] whilst another colleague, James Gordon, wished that Scotland's governors would resolve on a uniformity in worship and doctrine to redress a situation whereby 'our National Church should resemble America in its first discovery'.[8] As Presbyterian nonconformity escalated, however, committed support from the lay governing elite was unforthcoming. Writing to Archbishop Gilbert Sheldon of Canterbury in 1664, Archbishop Alexander Burnet of Glasgow admitted that members of the Scottish political establishment were 'jealous of our tottering standing'; indeed, five years later, Burnet issued a remonstrance formally regretting that, despite the re-erection of an Episcopalian edifice to contain dissent, there had been 'so litle done in prosecution of these laws, ffor building on these foundations'.[9] Such criticism was, however, ill-received by Charles II's administration and Burnet was summarily dismissed, whilst the Scottish parliament's enactment of an Assertory Act later in 1669 confirmed that control of ecclesiastical policy lay with the crown. As Archbishop James

Sharp of St Andrews appreciated, 'all King Henry the 8^{ths} ten years work' in England 'was now to be done in 3 dayes in Scotland'.[10]

As in England, government attempts to enforce religious conformity in Scotland and Ireland were predicated on identification of an intrinsic link between religious dissent and political disloyalty. Policy remained largely directed from Whitehall via instructions issued to successive Lord Lieutenants Ormond (1662–69), Robartes (1669–70), Berkeley (1670–72), Essex (1672–77), and Ormond again, which generally endorsed a pragmatic toleration of peaceable dissent. Complete suppression of Protestant nonconformity was deemed to be not only unachievable, since Scots Presbyterians comprised nearly half the population in areas such as counties Antrim, Derry, and Down, but also undesirable, since sizeable Protestant congregations constituted a crucial bulwark against the Catholic majority, particularly when fears of possible French invasion surfaced, as during the Second Dutch War (1665–67). Specific benefits towards dissenters included a pension of £600, known as the *regium donum*, which was paid in 1672 by Charles II to moderate Presbyterian ministers in Ulster to relieve their financial dependence on the laity, who tended to support more radical itinerant preachers from Scotland. A similar rationale underpinned the Scottish government's decision to issue a series of prerogative indulgences to nonconforming clergy in 1669, 1672, and 1679, which succeeded in reinstating around 130 moderate ministers to their parishes. For those who remained obdurate, however, more distinctly draconian legislation was enacted than in Ireland, including the Act against Conventicles (1670), which levied heavy fines on those attending unlicensed religious meetings and made preaching at outdoor conventicles a capital offence. Further bonds imposed in 1674 and 1677 also made individual landlords responsible for ensuring their tenants' compliance with ecclesiastical legislation.

Members of the established church inevitably resented initiatives directed towards de facto religious accommodation and toleration, despite the ostensible design of promoting civil peace and security. As the zealous, English-born Church of Ireland bishop of Down and Connor, Jeremy Taylor, warned in 1662, 'That's no good Religion that disturbs Government, or shakes a foundation of publick peace.'[11] Observing that 'when greedy and voracious flames seize on both ends of a ship, the middle part is like to perish', the dean of Clogher, Richard Tenison, subsequently warned the Church of Ireland's clergy about the twin dangers of popery and Protestant dissent during a visitation to Drogheda in 1679 by Archbishop Michael Boyle of Armagh. Recognising that 'where men differ in Ecclesiasticks, they usually differ in Politicks', Tenison urged the church to 'watch the motions of the Kirk', lamenting that 'our disloyal Separatists in Scotland have run again into Rebellion'.[12] During another visitation, by Archbishop Francis Marsh of Dublin four years later, Samuel Foley likewise insisted that 'Experience shows, that no good success

131

is to be expected from yielding ... to unreasonable people'. Under Presbyterian pretence of reform during the civil wars, 'Episcopacy and the Lyturgie were totally abandoned, and the most sad and miserable distractions introduc'd, that ever these churches laboured under'.[13] Moreover, the civil government's perceived reluctance to enforce conformity was also blamed for an apparent revival of the Catholic Church, since, in contrast to Whitehall's refusal to permit the Church of Ireland's convocation to meet after 1662, a general synod of Catholic bishops was held in Dublin in June 1670 at a time when the numbers of priests throughout the country had reached levels last achieved in the 1630s. Catholic prospects had also been enhanced by Charles II's suspension, albeit short lived, in March 1672 of the penal laws against English dissenters and Catholics, following his subscription to the secret Treaty of Dover two years previously. As one Protestant magistrate complained of the Catholics in 1672, '[i]f the king would stand neuter, he doubted not but we were able to beat them into the sea'.[14]

Hence a recurrent feature of the Restoration was an endemic fear concerning the potentially contagious contamination of one kingdom's affairs during times of unrest and, accordingly, the need to dovetail policies towards noncon-formists where appropriate. As one of the three Lords Justices responsible for governing Ireland before Ormond's appointment as Lord Lieutenant, Roger Boyle, earl of Orrey wrote to Ormond in April 1662 acknowledging that '[i]f England and Scotland fall roundly upon the Papists and nonconformists, and we do not, Ireland will be the sink to receive them all', whilst also recognising that if 'they are fallen upon equally in the three kingdoms, may not they all unite to disturb the peace?'[15] The previous year, all Irish towns had been ordered by the Dublin parliament to stage public burnings of the Solemn League and Covenant,[16] previously agreed by Scottish Presbyterians and English parlia-mentarians in 1643, whilst Bishop Robert Mossom of Derry also complained to Ormond, in the wake of the Covenanters' Pentland Rising in 1666, about 'the factious preachers which run out of Scotland (like wild boars hunted out of a forest and throw their foam of seditious doctrine among the people)'.[17] A decade later, in 1678, a lay supporter of the Church of Ireland in Ulster, Sir George Rawdon, warned that if radical Covenanting Presbyterians rebelled in Scotland, Ireland's 'dance will be after their pipe'.[18] Despite the brutal murder in May 1679 of the head of the established church in Scotland, Archbishop James Sharp of St Andrews, followed by an armed rising of around 8,000 Covenanters at Bothwell Bridge later that month, Irish dissenters neverthe-less remained largely peaceable. When copies of radical manifestos issued by Scots extremists were discovered in Ireland, however, the Dublin government reprinted the 'Sanquhar Declaration' – which advocated regicide as appro-priate punishment for Charles II's betrayal of the National Covenant of 1638 and Solemn League and Covenant – to confirm the seditious threat facing both Ireland and Scotland.[19] Meanwhile, Sharp was replaced as primate by the previously dismissed archbishop of Glasgow, Alexander Burnet, who optimistically reported to Archbishop William Sancroft of Canterbury in January 1680 that 'all things are in a quiet condition' in Scotland and were likely to remain so 'if we be not infected with factious emissaries from England and Ireland'.[20]

The Stuart kings were, however, equally capable of exploiting the politics of multiple monarchy for themselves, as Scotland supplied a potentially convenient laboratory for alternative solutions to English crises. Between 1679 and 1682, Charles II sent his younger brother and heir, James, duke of York, to Edinburgh as parliamentary High Commissioner to remove him from the volatile political atmosphere generated by the 'Exclusion crisis', when Whig politicians unsuccessfully attempted to prevent York succeeding to the English throne on account of his Roman Catholicism. Under York's management, the Scottish parliament of 1681 passed a Succession Act, confirming the hereditary basis of royal succession, together with a Test Act, requiring office holders to pledge commitment to the established church and swear allegiance to Charles II's lawful successors. York having supported the established church in return for its endorsement of his hereditary claim, his departure was lamented by the Scottish bishops. As Alexander Burnet admitted to Sancroft in July 1682, Charles's Catholic brother had looked 'very kindly and favourably upon us while he was here, which obliged many (who before lookd asquint upon us) to treat us with more civility and respect'.[21]

II

The precarious character of the 'national church' in the Stuart kingdoms was quickly exposed after James VII and II's accession in February 1685. Initial prospects nevertheless appeared propitious, particularly following the decisive defeat of the Monmouth and Argyll rebellions in England and Scotland. As Bishop John Paterson of Edinburgh indicated to Sancroft, since the political threat had been vanquished 'for our soveraigne and these kingdoms', he heartily hoped that 'the nationall Church could now be so happie as to have devout forms of worship setled therein', given that the established church in Scotland was apparently assured 'so far a prospect of halcyon-days and tranquillitie' during the forthcoming reign.[22]

Instead, however, James quickly promoted several individuals to senior positions in Scotland, deploying his prerogative powers to dispense such individuals from the provisions of the 1681 Test Act. Following the defeat of Argyll's rebellion in June 1685, the Catholic George Douglas, earl of Dumbarton, was appointed overall military commander in Scotland, whilst the opening of a parliament in Edinburgh in April 1686 saw another suspected 'papist', Alexander Stewart, earl of Moray, appointed as High Commissioner.

Requesting parliament to enact legislation removing the penal sanctions imposed on his Catholic co-religionists – who numbered around 2 per cent of the country's population – James added an incentive in suggesting that he would seek to remove existing trade restrictions between Scotland and England. The previous month, Archbishop Arthur Ross of St Andrews and Bishop Paterson of Edinburgh had, somewhat lamely, sanctioned James's proposal, claiming that 'it seemeth to us, who are not lawyers, equitable and reasonable to be done, considering that the execution of these sanguinarie lawes is fallen into ane absolute desuetude for many years past'.[23] Archbishop Alexander Cairncross of Glasgow and eleven of the fourteen other bishops, however, joined the majority of parliamentary commissioners in opposing removal of the penal laws and remaining recalcitrant to royal pressure, which obliged James to issue a prerogative Declaration of Indulgence in February 1687 which extended toleration not only to Catholics, but also to Quakers and moderate Presbyterians. When the latter refused to accept its benefit, on the grounds that it was primarily designed to assist Catholics, James issued a second Indulgence in June, confirming his decision to suspend the penal laws against nonconformists, thereby allowing Presbyterians to meet freely for worship, whilst retaining the prohibition against field conventicles. For failing to punish anti-Catholic sermons preached within his diocese, in January 1687 Cairncross also became the second Archbishop of Glasgow to be removed from the see in under two decades, later finding refuge in the Church of Ireland as bishop of Raphoe in 1693.

In Ireland, James initially replaced the ageing Ormond as Lord Lieutenant with his Anglican brother-in-law, Henry Hyde, earl of Clarendon, before recalling the latter in favour of Richard Talbot (later earl of Tyrconnel), who, in January 1687, became the first Catholic viceroy since the Reformation. Unconstrained by any Irish equivalent of the English or Scottish Test Acts, James was able swiftly to remodel the civil and military establishments, with the result that 90 per cent of the Irish army was Catholic by the autumn of 1688, whereas all of its officer corps, and the large majority of its rank-and-file, had been Protestant three years earlier.[24] Although the Church of Ireland was prevented from holding its own convocation, a week-long convention of Catholic clergy was held in Dublin in May 1686. Moreover, when the dean of Derry, Peter Manby, announced his conversion to Catholicism in 1687, a royal dispensation was issued allowing him to continue as dean, whilst Manby's publication of a defence of his actions provoked concerns within the Church of Ireland that, if other clerics were encouraged to follow Manby's example and allowed to retain their benefices and remuneration, the Church of Ireland's assets and privileges could eventually be transferred piecemeal to the Catholic Church. As Chancellor of St Patrick's, Dublin, William King published a stridently anti-Erastian *Answer* to Manby's tract, denying that Manby should rely on arbitrary royal favour to remain in post, since the Church of Ireland's episcopate had already determined that he should be deprived of his deanship. As King insisted, 'not only We but every National Church hath the same power of altering all Rites and Ceremonies, of abrogating and making all Ecclesiastical Constitutions ... which the Supream Civil Power hath of altering the Civil Constitutions'. As King reflected, '[i]f National Churches were left to be govern'd by themselves ... contentions must soon come to an end'.[25]

There was no defender of the Scottish Episcopal Church's *raison d'être* of King's calibre. Rather, its bishops watched in dismay at the widespread withdrawals of Presbyterian laity prompted by James's second Indulgence. Whilst calls for a national synod of the established church had been denied throughout the Restoration, monthly meetings of Presbyterians were now held and new meeting-houses constructed. In December 1688, Archbishop Arthur Ross of St Andrews, Archbishop John Paterson of Glasgow and two senior bishops wrote to Sancroft, confirming the Church of England to be 'a great refuge to which wee fly'.[26] In other letters that month, Ross regretted that the Assertory Act of 1669 'leaves us so precarious as to be turned out at pleasure', whilst Paterson pointed out to Sancroft that, whilst Anglican offices and benefices were secured by legal freehold, in Scotland, by contrast, 'if the Court chances to frowne on us, it is farr otherwise', which evidently explained why 'our Bishops here ly open to farr greater tentations to yeeld to the importunities of Court than yours doe'.[27] Certainly, the Scottish bishops made no direct protest against James's use of the royal prerogative to promote Catholicism, as the 'Seven Bishops' did in England; indeed, as seen, some members of the bench had explicitly sanctioned removal of the penal laws. The established church's apparent pusillanimity thus provoked the lawyer John Lauder of Fountainhall to despair that 'when we are struggling against Popery, our bischops comply to let it in, and the English bischops keep ther ground firme to hold it out'.[28]

The unpopularity of the Scottish Episcopate was dramatically confirmed following James's flight to France in 1688, when numerous conformist clergy were forcibly ejected, or 'rabbled', from their parishes. As Tristram Clarke has acknowledged, the 'rhetorical arithmetic' regarding actual numbers cited in rival Presbyterian and Episcopalian pamphlets was often inflated, but around 160 established clergy evidently either were rabbled, demitted their charges, or simply deserted between 1688 and 1690.[29] According to the Claim of Right, produced by the Convention Parliament in April 1689, 'prelacy and the superiority of any office in the church above presbyters is, and hath been, a great and insupportable greivance [sic] and trouble to this nation, and contrary to the inclinationes of the generality of the people ever since the reformatione ... and therefor ought to be abolished'.[30] Significant numbers of ejected clergy thereafter left Scotland for London, where a vigorous publishing campaign sought to impress upon 'the most charitable Church of England ... how to quench those Flames in a Neighbours House, which so visibly threaten destruction to their own', insisting that harassed Episcopalians in Scotland required the Anglican Church's prayers and charity as much, if not more, as persecuted 'Protestants in Piedmont, France or Ireland'.[31]

The formation of a Scottish ecclesiastical settlement during the Williamite Revolution remained, however, predicated on the model of a national church, as were subsequent attempts to comprehend dissenters within that church. For his part, the new monarch was essentially a Latitudinarian who believed that forms of church government were indifferent, but that religious uniformity was desirable.[32] Meanwhile, those members of the established church who had insisted, throughout the Restoration, that church government was a matter for the royal prerogative and inherently an indifferent matter should, in theory, have been willing to accept that a new monarch might entail the disestablishment of episcopacy. The re-establishment of Presbyterianism, enacted on 7 June 1690, conformed to legislation enacted by James VI in 1592 and provided for government by general assemblies, synods, presbyteries and kirk sessions, whilst lay patronage – whereby ministers were appointed to parishes as a proprietary right, on the Anglican model – was separately abolished. The settlement did not, however, concede the crucial claim of Presbyterianism's divine warrant, alleged by its most committed supporters. The parliamentary Act restoring Presbyterian Church government simply described it as 'agreeable to the word of God', whilst a subsequent attempt to pass an Act confirming Presbyterianism's divine right in the General Assembly which convened in October 1690, also failed.[33]

The established church in Ireland faced a different dilemma. On the one hand, events since 1685 had confirmed a real likelihood that the church could be annihilated by the ruling administration, particularly if pro-Catholic statutes enacted by the Dublin parliament of 1689 had taken effect. On the other hand, by the spring of that year, members of the established church feared that a Williamite victory during the 'Jacobite wars' of 1689–91 might entail – as in Scotland – summary disestablishment and Presbyterian replacement. Abandoned by the sudden departure of his senior clerical colleagues for London, William King sought to strengthen the Church of Ireland's position in a manuscript entitled 'Principles of church government', subsequently described as one of the most 'astonishingly outspoken pieces of what must be called Anglo-Catholicism' provoked by the Revolution.[34] Pursuing anti-Erastian themes raised in his earlier attack on Manby, King insisted that his church enjoyed rights and privileges 'distinct from the rights and privileges of civil society'. Churchmen were, by implication, thus entitled to oppose monarchs, such as James, who refused to nominate bishops to vacant sees, forbade clergy from preaching the true religion and suspended bishops who opposed royal policy. Following the Williamite victory at the Boyne on 1 July 1690, and Dublin's liberation a week later, Bishop Anthony Dopping of Meath headed a delegation of Church of Ireland clergy to thank William for preserving Ireland from popery, whilst recognising that the church's support for his rule 'may possibly be censured by those, who understand not the Grounds and Reasons of our continuance in this Kingdom, as Trimmers'.[35] On the day designated as a formal thanksgiving for William's accession the following November, King preached a sermon entitled *Europe's deliverance from France and slavery*, which cited no less than nineteen instances of evidence to persuade his listeners that their allegiance was now owed to the new monarch.[36]

Given the country's overwhelming Catholic majority, Irish Episcopalians – unlike their English and Scottish colleagues – could ill afford to scruple about disavowing former oaths sworn to James II. In 1692, however, one of the few non-juring Church of Ireland clergy produced by the Williamite Revolution, Charles Leslie, trenchantly rejected King's claims that James's attempts to replace Protestantism with popery in Ireland provided sufficient justification for the Church of Ireland to transfer allegiance. It was somewhat ironic, as Leslie pointed out, that allegiance to William was justified on what 'it was only alleged that King James intended to do in Ireland, what he did not do' compared to 'what King William actually did in Scotland; viz. To overthrow the Church then by Law Established'. Since it had been argued that Presbyterianism's re-establishment reflected the wishes of the majority of the Scots population, such reasoning would render it 'as just to set up Popery in Ireland, as Presbytery in Scotland'. As Leslie rued, 'Thus fell Episcopacy in Scotland! Two Months and eleven Days after King William and Queen Mary took upon them the Crown of that Kingdom.'[37]

III

If the re-establishment of Presbyterianism in Scotland in 1690 reflected popular ecclesiastical proclivities, it also signalled a continued Erastianism on the civil magistrate's part, since William did not permit repeal of the Assertory Act of 1669 until after the issue of church government had been resolved. The introduction of ecclesiastical pluralism into the later Stuart multiple monarchy also prompted an increased polarisation between Scots Presbyterians and Episcopalians from the 1690s onwards which ultimately militated against comprehension of nonconformists within the national church. The Westminster Confession of Faith, emphasising Christ's foundation of the church, was increasingly demanded by Presbyterians as satisfaction of doctrinal orthodoxy, with newly licensed preachers and staff members at Scotland's universities required to subscribe from 1690, and all ruling elders from 1700. As the Principal of Edinburgh University, Gilbert Rule, confirmed in 1690, the correct form of church government was 'not left indifferent to Men, (whether the Magistrate or the Church) to chuse, but is determined by Christ, and revealed in the New Testament'.[38]

A more inclusive settlement was, however, nevertheless promoted by the civil authorities. When the new king commented on the proposed draft Act for settling Scottish church government in 1690, for example, he clearly envisaged a national church that would not regard its external form as divinely sanctioned and would not confine its government exclusively to Presbyterian ministers. Indeed, William confirmed his wish 'that such as are of the Episcopall perswasion in Scotland have the same Indulgence that Dissenters have in England, provided they give security to live peaceably under the Government, and take the Oath of Allegeance'.[39] Crown attempts to influence ecclesiastical policy in a more inclusive direction soon, however, provoked tensions with Presbyterian ministers, particularly concerning the crown's contested capacity to summon, adjourn and dissolve the Kirk's General Assembly. In 1692, William presented confidential proposals to the Assembly, through his commissioner, Robert Kerr, earl of Lothian, to enable around 180 deprived Episcopalian clergy to be received into the church, having confirmed the ministers' willingness to subscribe to the Confession of Faith and to submit to Presbyterian Church government as established by law. Their earlier willingness to avail themselves of James VII and II's toleration in 1687 notwithstanding, the Presbyterian establishment nevertheless proved reluctant to pursue the proposals and prevaricated, before Lothian dissolved the Assembly, which, as one Episcopalian observed, came 'like a Thunder Bolt to the Brethren'.[40] Similar resentments were prompted by subsequent dissolutions of the Assembly in 1702 and 1703, by which time crown policy had changed, when an Act concerning the church passed in 1695 conferred royal protection on loyal Episcopalians whilst not insisting on their admission to the church.[41]

The inability of William's administration to comprehend moderate Episcopalians within the national church in Scotland was matched, across the Irish Sea, by its failure to maintain the relatively generous policy towards Catholics that had been assumed after the final Jacobite surrender at Limerick in October 1691. As the first article of the Treaty of Limerick indicated, Irish Catholics would henceforth 'enjoy such toleration in the exercise of their religion as were consistent with the laws of Ireland or as they had enjoyed in the reign of King Charles II'.[42] That same year, however, the English parliament passed legislation stipulating that all Irish office-holders and members of the Irish parliament should take new oaths of allegiance and supremacy and also subscribe a declaration against transubstantiation, thereby ensuring that the Irish parliament would henceforth become an exclusively Protestant preserve. Moreover, when the parliament convened in October 1692, the new Lord Lieutenant, Henry, Viscount Sydney complained, twelve days into its sitting, that its members had 'begun like a company of madmen' in their determination to ensure that Catholics could never again achieve the dominant political position threatened under James II.[43] Following Sydney's replacement as Lord Lieutenant in 1694 by the more overtly anti-Catholic Henry, Lord Capel, the Irish parliament passed further legislation disarming Catholics; penalising those who educated their children abroad; banishing Catholic bishops and regular clergy; forbidding Protestants from marrying Catholics; and preventing Catholics from acting as solicitors.

Unity against a common Catholic enemy did not, however, promote Protestant co-operation. In 1662, the Dublin parliament had self-consciously sought to attract Protestant immigration with an 'Act for encouraging Protestant strangers', whilst a clause had been inserted into the Irish Act of Uniformity exempting 'foreign or aliens of the foreign reformed churches' resident in Ireland from civil penalties imposed on other Protestant dissenters. Thirty years later, legislation again encouraged 'Protestant strangers', such as French Huguenots, to settle in Ireland, guaranteeing them a freedom of worship denied to Scots Presbyterians in Ulster. Indeed, from the mid 1690s, the Church of Ireland evidently regarded Protestant nonconformists as a more potent threat than the Catholic majority, primarily on account of the re-establishment of Presbyterianism in Scotland, together with the potential demographic threat posed by large number of Presbyterian emigrants fleeing Scotland's 'seven ill years' in the 1690s and arriving in Ulster. Whilst the *regium donum* paid to Presbyterian ministers was increased under William, the establishment of a 'General synod' of the Presbyterian Church in the 1690s occurred at a time when the Church of Ireland's convocation was not meeting. Moreover, the self-confidence of the Scots Presbyterian Church in Ulster had also been revived by the decision, in the 1670s, to commission its own institutional history, which was eventually achieved by Patrick Adair. Following the Williamite Revolution, the Church of Ireland's clergy could no longer press for punitive coercion on the grounds of political security, since Presbyterians had strongly supported William's accession and were conspicuously more allergic to the possibilities of Jacobite intrigue than were members of the established church. In Scotland, by contrast, Presbyterian ministers styled themselves guardians of the Revolution, correctly suspecting the majority of Episcopalian clergy of being actively or passively Jacobite.

Rather than seeking a formal toleration, as had been enacted in England in 1689, the Church of Ireland's clergy inclined towards comprehending dissenters within the national church. Having been promoted to the bishopric of Derry in 1690, William King addressed the large number of Presbyterian nonconformists in his diocese in 1694, emphasising the potential for convergence with the established church, since 'both own National and Provincial Churches', unlike other dissenting sects such as Congregationalists. Acknowledging that their disagreements primarily concerned the established church's use of the Book of Common Prayer, together with divergent views regarding the use of scripture in church, forms of worship, the role of music in religious services, and the frequency of communion, King insisted that it was only 'in these outwards acts that we are more immediately concerned as publick worshippers; for we cannot know the inward worship which Men pay to God in their minds, but as it appears to us by these outward acts'. Over such issues, 'all Men are fallible, and You may as well be mistaken, as you suppose We are'.[44] Trenchant rebuttals from Joseph Boyse and Robert Craghead, among others, nevertheless reiterated fundamental Presbyterian objections to the established church's use of the Book of Common Prayer, together with other aspects of ceremonial worship regarded as unacceptable, such as the sign of the cross in baptism, kneeling at communion, and the belief that children were regenerate by baptism.[45]

Notwithstanding the political support lent to William's rule by Presbyterian dissenters, the Church of Ireland's support for the imposition of a sacramental test evinced its endemic sense of insecurity. Since 1673, office holders in England had been obliged to qualify themselves by taking Anglican Communion, but no such parallel requirement existed in Ireland. Increasingly fearful of numerical eclipse by expanding Scots Presbyterian congregations, members of the established church resisted attempts to enact religious toleration for Protestant dissenters, as existed in England, without an accompanying sacramental test. As the bishop of Dromore, Tobias Pullen, argued in 1695, it was as unlikely that 'those who are so Turbulent in their own Countrey, shou'd be quiet in ours' as the hope 'that by their being transplanted into another Soil, and by a kind and indulgent Cultivation of them, we may gather Figs off this sharpest sort of Thistles'. Pullen further rejected Presbyterian complaints of uncharitable exclusion by pointing out that similar reasoning was deemed 'so good an Evidence of a Truly Christian Zeal, and so effectual an Instrument of publick Good in Scotland'.[46] Bishop Anthony Dopping of Meath likewise observed that the Kirk 'would allow no Toleration to the Church Party in Scotland, tho' they received several messages from His Majesty, in favour of their Persecuted Brethren', frankly acknowledging to Irish nonconformists that 'we are afraid of opening a Door to let the whole Party in'.[47]

More broadly, increased anxiety amongst Anglicans concerning 'the Church in danger' following the passing of the English Toleration Act in 1689 reverberated across the Irish Sea, confirming Toby Barnard's view of 'the essentially imitative character of the Church of Ireland'.[48] As in England, the providential character attributed to the Williamite victory prompted fears of divine vengeance if popular moral laxity, doctrinal error, and irreligious irreverence were not curbed. An alarming popular propensity to embrace heterodoxies, including deism, Socinianism, and even atheism, was confirmed when the notorious freethinker, John Toland, returned to his native Dublin in 1697, although he quickly left Ireland following a parliamentary order for his arrest, together with the public burning of his *Christianity not mysterious* (1696). Whilst parliamentary legislation enacted in 1695 enforced sabbatarianism and penalised profane cursing and swearing and the Church of Ireland's clergy called for national amendment and renewed pastoral activism, there were few Irish towns outside Dublin and Ulster with sufficient numbers of Protestant parochial administrators to effect real reform. Ironically, therefore, whilst Barnard has shown how Toland's short-lived Irish residence 'merely crystal-lized the anxieties of a church constantly exposed to lay ridicule, Presbyterian competition and Catholic enmity', it was also Ulster Presbyterian enthusiasm that endowed moral reform with an 'ineradicably non-conformist aura' which 'damned it in too many anglican minds'.[49] Preaching in Dublin in 1698, Peter Browne – later Provost of Trinity College and bishop of Cork – thus welcomed dissenting involvement in the reformation of manners, but feared that 'our separate Communions have been the immediate Natural Cause of all that Torrent of Profaneness and Irreligion, Immorality and Lewdness, which during the two late Reigns came in upon these Lands with an Irresist-ible violence'. As the established church found itself 'forc'd to fly to Temporal Laws for the Suppression of such Sinners', Browne exhorted conformist clergy to undergo strict self-scrutiny to 'defend us from the Imputation of a Solemn National Hypocrisie'.[50]

Parallel concerns to preserve Presbyterianism's providential re-establish-ment also prompted renewed determination to eradicate error by the Scottish authorities, which culminated in the controversial execution for blasphemy of a theology undergraduate, Thomas Aikenhead, in January 1697.[51] Concerns over immorality and irreligion were, however, often subsumed within sectarian divisions, as Presbyterians insisted that the defects of a debauched Restoration church had created the current crisis which justified the imposi-tion of rigorous discipline and the thorough purging of parishes and universi-ties. From 1690 onwards, the Scottish parliament repeatedly authorised civil authorities to indict individuals accused of scandalous behaviour, whilst the Privy Council issued a proclamation in 1698 confirming the main statutes passed against vice and insisting that they be read aloud, twice yearly, in all the country's churches.[52] Following a devastating fire in Edinburgh in 1701, the Presbyterian judge, Francis Grant, Lord Cullen, attributed the conflagration to divine wrath, and encouraged Scots to jettison any reluctance to be seen to 'be acting the Busie-body' and, instead, to act as zealous informers.[53] Although Cullen had previously published an account of the rise of the reformation of manners movement in England and Ireland to 'excite and encourage these of this Kingdom of Scotland, to imitate so laudable an example', its failure to do so reflected Presbyterian conviction that such initiatives were unnecessary distractions from the work of kirk sessions and renewed ecclesiastical reform.[54] Indeed, the surviving minutes of one Edinburgh society for the reformation of manners indicate that, rather than bridging divisions between conformists and nonconformists as in England, Episcopalian dissenters were not only excluded from membership, but the society actively campaigned against use of the Book of Common Prayer.

IV

By the early eighteenth century, the Book of Common Prayer's growing popularity among Scottish Episcopalians undermined hopes of religious comprehension, as its Presbyterian adversaries insisted that liturgical worship lacked scriptural warrant. Queen Anne's accession in 1702 further shifted the impetus towards toleration, since her hereditary claim proved acceptable to non-juring Episcopalians, who could now accept the sovereign authority required in any statutory toleration offering protection from perceived Presbyterian persecution. A draft Act unsuccessfully presented to the Scottish parliament in 1703 proposed a general indulgence of Episcopalian meetings and allowed ministers to enjoy their full stipends, but laid no obligation on such clergy to subscribe the Confession of Faith or to swear prescribed oaths of allegiance. In the accompanying pamphlet debate, opponents insisted that, since it was 'the Civil Interest of every Nation to have but one established National Church-Government, Disciplin and Worship', toleration would destabilise the state by allowing dissenters 'to Traffique and Practise for the Pretender at St Germains, according to their known Inclinations'.[55] James Ramsey likewise objected that toleration would 'seem to Revive and really Fortify' the Anglican Church's claims to ecclesiastical superintendence and would thereby 'Enslave this Nation to that of England', pointing out that toleration was only possible south of the border because the Anglican Church was protected by Test Acts and the Act of Settlement (1701).[56] In response, Episcopalians printed the General Assembly's rejection of the toleration proposed in 1703, juxtaposed with the grateful 'address of thanks' presented by Presbyterian nonconformists to James VII and II in 1687.[57] Deeming it 'strange to see into what different Shapes Men turn themselves' when in authority, the Episcopalian George Garden not only reminded Presbyterians of their earlier enthusiasm for toleration, but also doubted that there was more 'Vice and Immorality, Hatred and Lying, Back-biting, Strife and Envy' in countries with a history of toleration, such as the Netherlands.[58]

Meanwhile, the Church of Ireland's anxieties were unexpectedly assuaged in 1704 when a sacramental clause was suddenly inserted by ministers in Whitehall into a draft 'Act to prevent the further growth of Popery' submitted for approval by the Dublin parliament and primarily restricting Catholic land ownership. Since Catholics were already barred by earlier legislation from holding civil or military office, including membership of borough corporations, the additional sacramental clause was evidently directed towards Protestant nonconformists, especially in Ulster, where Scots Presbyterians dominated civic office holding. Although pressure soon mounted for the test's abolition, Jonathan Swift – who would become dean of St Patrick's Cathedral, Dublin in 1713 – acknowledged the established church's dependent position but insisted that 'we of this Kingdom believe the Church of Ireland to be the National Church'. Hence, although Swift was prepared to countenance toleration for Protestant nonconformists, he insisted that the sacramental test and penal laws be retained, for otherwise there would 'be as many Established Churches as there are Sects of Dissenters'. From bitter memories of his early ministry in the strongly nonconformist parish of Kilroot, Co. Antrim, Swift knew that Scots Presbyterians had 'a most formidable Notion of our Church, which they look upon at least three Degrees worse than Popery', having 'come over full Fraught with that Spirit which taught them to abolish Episcopacy at home'.[59] Equally stubborn was Swift's Antrim colleague, William Tisdall, who published a selective anthology of nonconformist pronouncements to prove 'that there ever was a perfect Harmony both in Principles & Practice amongst all the Dissenters of England, Scotland and Ireland', being all 'equally deep in the Plots, Associations, and Factions against the King ... in every Turn of Government since the Reformation'.[60]

In 1703, the established church's standing was further enhanced when Queen Anne authorised the meeting of the Irish houses of convocation, in parallel sessions with the Dublin parliament. Despite their original ambitions to promote pastoral effectiveness and implement clerical reform, convocation's proceedings were soon derailed by the importation of Anglican 'High' and 'Low' Church divisions, stimulated by the leader of the 'High Church' agitators in England and dean of Carlisle, Francis Atterbury, seeking support from his cousin, Bishop Thomas Lindsey of Killaloe, and others, who cited alleged Irish practices to support Atterbury's insistence that English bishops could not terminate sittings of convocation's lower house by adjournment. As initiatives towards practical reform were marginalised, convocation's main achievement was compiling *A representation of the present state of religion* (1711), which vigorously denounced heterodox theology, sceptical freethinking, assertive Presbyterianism, Quaker insubordination, moral dereliction, and the perennial threat of international popery.[61]

Confirmation of the extent to which English party politics had permeated Irish ecclesiastical affairs was also evident in the sobriquet of 'the Irish Sacheverell' being attached to one of Atterbury's Irish followers, Francis Higgins, in reference to the Anglican controversialist, Henry Sacheverell, whose notorious trial and impeachment prompted a High Church–Tory electoral landslide in

1710.[62] A prebendary of Christ Church, Higgins had earlier provoked contro-versy in 1707 by an Ash Wednesday sermon preached at the Chapel Royal, Whitehall, which attacked the English Toleration Act on the grounds that 'there is not one Word of Toleration in that Statute, tho' we are sensible of its Effects, and Consequences to that Purpose'. Higgins further denied that the Act 'in the least Repeals, or Weakens one Tittle [*sic*] of the Act of Uniformity, which God be praised is Yet in force'.[63]

In Scotland, sectarian divisions remained sufficiently sensitive that eccle-siastical issues were omitted from the remit devised for bilateral discussions concerning Anglo-Scottish union. Pressure from the Kirk's Commission of the General Assembly persuaded the Scottish parliament, however, to pass an Act for Securing the Protestant Religion and Presbyterian Church Govern-ment in November 1706, which allayed most Presbyterian opposition to union, despite residual concerns about the presence of twenty-six Anglican bishops in a British House of Lords. Moreover, although Presbyterians also feared that a united parliament, especially under an English Tory majority, might not only grant toleration to Scottish Episcopalians, but even jeopardise the Presbyte-rian establishment in Scotland, both Presbyterians and Episcopalians recog-nised that union would secure Protestantism, whereas opposition to union risked encouraging a French-sponsored pro-Catholic Jacobite restoration.[64]

The threat of just such an invasion in 1708, however, reinforced Presby-terian suspicions that Episcopalian dissent masked Jacobite attachments. Among those who appeared before the Edinburgh presbytery for conducting unlicensed liturgical worship was James Greenshields, who had left his native Scotland and served as the Church of Ireland minister in Tynan, Co. Armagh, before returning to Edinburgh in February 1709. Despite praying loyally for Queen Anne, Greenshields used the Book of Common Prayer during services for a congregation that included English staff at the Customs, Excise and Exchequer departments established in Scotland after the union. Following his imprisonment in the Edinburgh Tolbooth for disregarding a ban imposed on his ministry by the Edinburgh presbytery, Greenshields unsuccessfully appealed to the Court of Session, before appealing to the House of Lords at Westminster, where his petition was read on the same day in February 1710 as that of Sacheverell, subsequently earning for Greenshields the sobriquet of 'the Scots Sacheverell'.[65] In the pamphlet debate that accompanied the case, the Jacobite MP for Edinburghshire, George Lockhart, lobbied Tory peers to rule in favour of Greenshields, warning that since 'there has all along pass'd a close and intimate Correspondence' between Scots and English Presbyte-rians, the peers should consider 'what Addition of strength the Dissenters in England may hope to acquire to their Interest and Party', if the Kirk succeeded in eradicating Episcopalianism north of the border.[66] In March 1711, the House of Lords dramatically reversed the sentences of both the Edinburgh magistrates and the Court of Session and awarded costs against the magistrates, wholly undermining the Church of Scotland's attempts to suppress disestablished Episcopalians.

In making his case, Greenshields had argued that private use of the Anglican liturgy was not prohibited by laws prescribing uniformity of worship in the established Presbyterian Church, and nor was there legislation 'of Conformity, which obliges the Laity to be of their Communion'.[67] The House of Lords thereby accepted Greenshields's denial of the authority of the Edinburgh presbytery, or the established church more broadly, to ban his ministry. Following the judgment, Episcopalian confidence in Scotland predictably soared, with the heritors of Kilmuir Wester, for example, self-consciously mimicking the language of the 1689 Claim of Right in objecting that the imposition of a Presbyterian minister in their parish was 'a grievous encroachment upon our consciences, and against the inclinations of us and our people, which by our law is declared the foundation of Church government in Scotland'.[68] Although regarded by many Presbyterians as a major breach of the Union's provisions, a Toleration Act was passed in March 1712, followed by separate legislation restoring lay patronage of ministers.

To conclude, the vision of a single Episcopalian Church serving multiple Stuart nations, outlined by John Travers at the start of this chapter, was not wholly illusory. In the final, Tory-dominated years of Queen Anne's reign, Scots Episcopalians could plausibly hope that the Williamite settlement might be reversed. Anne's death, however, precipitously reversed recent advances, as latent Jacobite sympathies among ejected Episcopalians resurfaced during the failed 1715 Rebellion. Presbyterian retribution was swift and depositions by church courts ensured that a total of over 660 conformist clergy had been removed from 950 parishes between 1689 and the aftermath of the 1715 Rebellion.[69] Meanwhile, the Church of Ireland's vulnerabilities soon reappeared during the Whig ascendancy that accompanied the early years of George I's reign, as the Irish convocation was effectively abolished and an Irish Toleration Act was passed in 1719, modelled on the English Toleration Act of 1689. Despite being accompanied by an Indemnity Act which undermined the sacramental test's practical impact on certain office holders, the fact that the test remained on the Irish statute book until the 1780s confirmed that the eighteenth-century state's toleration of a diversity of Protestant religious beliefs did not confer an equality of civic identity.

NOTES

I am grateful to Will Ferguson, Mark Goldie and Ian Higgins for commenting on an earlier draft of this chapter.

1 John Travers, *A sermon preach'd at Christ-Church in Dublin, before his Grace, James, duke of Ormonde, Lord Lieutenant of Ireland; on Monday the fifth of November 1711* (Dublin, 1711), pp. 5, 6, 19–20.

2 A. Ford, J. McGuire and K. Milne, 'Preface', in A. Ford, J. McGuire and K. Milne (eds), *As by law established. The Church of Ireland since the Reformation* (Dublin: The Lilliput Press, 1995), p. vii.

3 J. McGuire, 'Policy and patronage: the appointment of bishops, 1660–61', in in A. Ford, J. McGuire and K. Milne (eds), *As by law established. The Church of Ireland since the Reformation* (Dublin: The Lilliput Press, 1995), p. 112.

4 *Records of the Parliament of Scotland to 1707* (hereafter '*RPS*'), K.M. Brown *et al.* (eds), (St Andrews, 2007–11), 1662/5/9. (Accessible online, via http://www.rps.ac.uk.)

5 O. Airy (ed.), *The Lauderdale papers*, 3 vols (Camden Society, n.s., 1884–85), I, 95.

6 Quoted by A. Ford, 'Dependent or independent? The Church of Ireland and its colonial context, 1536–1649', *The Seventeenth Century*, 10 (1995), 176.

7 Gilbert Burnet, 'A memorial of diverse grievances and abuses in this church', in H.C. Foxcroft (ed.), *Miscellany of the Scottish History Society. Volume II* (Edinburgh, 1904), p. 354.

8 [James Gordon], *The reformed bishop or XIX articles tendered by ... a well-wisher of the present government of the Church of Scotland* (1679), p. 161.

9 Airy (ed.), *Lauderdale Papers*, II, App. A, xv, vi, xxix, lxvi.

10 *Ibid.*, II, 152.

11 Jeremy Taylor, *Via intelligentiae: a sermom* [sic] *preached to the University of Dublin* (1662), p. 59.

12 Richard Tenison, *A sermon preached at the primary visitation of the most Reverend Father in God, Michael, Lord Arch-Bishop of Armagh* &c. (Dublin, 1679), pp. 5, 4, 7, 6.

13 Samuel Foley, *A sermon preached at the primary visitation of his Grace, Francis, Lord Archbishop of Dublin* (1683), pp. 32–3.

14 Quoted by S.J. Connolly, *Religion, law and power. The making of Protestant Ireland 1660–1760* (Oxford: Oxford University Press, 1992), p. 31.

15 Quoted by R. Mant, *History of the Church of Ireland, from the Reformation to the Revolution*, 2 vols (1840), II, 637. I owe this reference to Will Ferguson.

16 P. Kilroy, *Protestant dissent and controversy in Ireland 1660–1714* (Cork: Cork University Press, 1994), p. 228.

17 Quoted in *ibid.*, p. 231.

18 Quoted by R.L. Greaves, '"That's no good religion that disturbs government": the Church of Ireland and the nonconformist challenge, 1660–88', in A. Ford, J. McGuire and K. Milne (eds), *As by law established. The Church of Ireland since the Reformation* (Dublin: The Lilliput Press, 1995), p. 130.

19 *A true and exact copy of a treasonable and bloody paper, the fanatics new Covenant &c.* (Dublin, 1680).

20 W.N. Clarke (ed.), *A collection of letters, addressed by prelates and individuals of high rank in Scotland ... to Sancroft &c.* (Edinburgh, 1848), p. 5.

21 *Ibid.*, p. 42.

22 *Ibid.*, p. 86.

23 *Ibid.*, p. 96.

24 See J. Miller, 'The earl of Tyrconnell and James II's Irish policy, 1685–1688', *HJ*, 20 (1977), 803–23.

25 William King, *An answer to the considerations which obliged Peter Manby, late dean of London-derry in Ireland, as he pretends, to embrace what he calls, the Catholick religion* (Dublin, 1687), pp. 22–3, 34. For more on King, see P. O'Regan, *Archbishop William King of Dublin (1650–1729) and the constitution in church and state* (Dublin: Four Courts, 2000); C.J. Fauske (ed.), *Archbishop William King and the Anglican Irish context, 1688–1729* (Dublin: Four Courts Press, 2004).

26 Clarke (ed.), *Collection of letters*, p. 89.

27 *Ibid.*, pp. 102, 94.

28 D. Laing and A. Urquhart (eds), *Historical observes of memorable occurrents in church and state from October 1680 to April 1686 by Sir John Lauder of Fountainhall* (Edinburgh, 1840), p. 243.

29 T.N. Clarke, 'The Scottish Episcopalians 1688–1720' (PhD dissertation, University of Edinburgh, 1987), pp. 77, 8.

30 *RPS*, 1689/3/108.

31 [John Sage], *The case of the present afflicted clergy in Scotland truly represented &c.* (1690), sigs A2r, [A4v]; see A. Raffe, 'Episcopalian polemic, the London printing press and Anglo-Scottish divergence in the 1690s', *Journal of Scottish Historical Studies*, 26 (2006), 23–41.

32 For further discussion of 'latitudinarianism', see Nicholas Tyacke's chapter in this volume.

33 A. Raffe, 'Presbyterianism, secularization and Scottish politics after the Revolution of 1688–1690', *HJ*, 53 (2010), 327.

34 M. Goldie, 'The political thought of the Anglican Revolution', in R. Beddard (ed.), *The revolutions of 1688* (Oxford: Clarendon Press, 1991), p. 131.

35 *Speech of the Right Reverend Father in God, Anthony, Lord Bishop of Meath, when the clergy waited on His Majesty at His camp nigh Dublin, July 7. 1690* (1690), p. 1.

36 William King, *Europe's deliverance from France and slavery: a sermon preached on 16 November, 1690 &c.* (Dublin, 1691).

37 [Charles Leslie], *An answer to a book, entituled, The state of the Protestants in Ireland under the late King James's government &c.* (Dublin, 1692), sigs Civ, Div.

38 [Gilbert Rule], *A true representation of Presbyterian government &c.* (1690), p. 2.

39 William Melville (ed.), *Letters and state papers chiefly addressed to George, earl of Melville, Secretary of State for Scotland 1689–1691* (Edinburgh, 1843), p. 438 ('His Majesties Remarques upon the Act for settling Church Government in Scotland'). William thus

objected to Presbyterianism being described as 'the only Government of Christs Church in this Kingdom', and suggested that it should instead be termed 'the government of the Church in this Kingdom established by Law' (p. 437).

40 Quoted by Clarke, 'Scottish Episcopalians', p. 106.

41 RPS 1695/5/186.

42 Quoted by J. McGuire, 'Government attitudes to religious nonconformity in Ireland 1660–1719', in C.E.J. Caldicott, H. Gough and J.-P. Pittion (eds), *The Huguenots and Ireland. Anatomy of an emigration* (Dublin: Glendale Press, 1987), p. 269.

43 Quoted by Connolly, *Religion, law and power*, p. 75.

44 William King, *A discourse concerning the inventions of men in the worship of God* (Dublin, 1694), pp. 176, 4, 170.

45 See, for example, Joseph Boyse, *Remarks on a late discourse of William, Lord Bishop of Derry, concerning the inventions of men in the worship of God* (Dublin, 1694), and [Robert Craghead] *An answer to a late book intituled, A discourse concerning the inventions of men in the worship of God, by William, Lord bishop of Derry* (Edinburgh, 1694).

46 [Tobias Pullen], *An answer to a paper entituled The case of the Protestant dissenters of Ireland, in reference to a Bill of Indulgence, represented and argued* ([Dublin, 1695]), pp. 2–3.

47 [Anthony Dopping], *The case of the dissenters in Ireland consider'd, in reference to a sacramental test* (Dublin, 1695), pp. 3, 6.

48 T. Barnard, 'Reforming Irish manners: the religious societies in Dublin during the 1690s', *HJ*, 35 (1992), 805.

49 *Ibid.*, p. 838.

50 Peter Browne, *A sermon preached at St-Bride's Church, Dublin, April 17. 1698. Upon occasion of a resolution taken in this city, of putting the laws in execution against vice and immoralities* (Dublin, 1698), pp. 12–13, 36.

51 See M. Hunter '"Aikenhead the atheist": the context and consequences of articulate irreligion in the late seventeenth century', in M. Hunter and D. Wootton (eds), *Atheism from the Reformation to the Enlightenment* (Oxford: Clarendon Press, 1992), pp. 221–54.

52 A.J.N. Raffe, 'Religious controversy and Scottish society, c.1679–1714' (PhD dissertation, University of Edinburgh, 2007), p. 98.

53 Sir Francis Grant, *A vindication of informers of the breaches of the laws against prophaneness and immorality* &c. (Edinburgh, 1701), p. 12.

54 [Francis Grant], *A brief account of the nature, rise and progress, of the societies, for reformation of manners* &c. *in England and Ireland* &c. (Edinburgh, 1700), p. 5.

55 [Anon], *Draught of an Act for Toleration with a few short remarks thereupon* ([Edinburgh, 1703]), p. 2.

56 [James Ramsey], *A letter from a gentleman, to a Member of Parliament; concerning Toleration* &c. (2nd edn, [?Edinburgh], 1703), p. 7.

57 [*Act for a toleration of the Episcopal] Church in Scotland, which was thrown out by the Scotch Parliament, An. 1703* (1703).

58 [George Garden], *The case of the Episcopal clergy, and those of the Episcopal perswasion considered, as to the granting them a Toleration and Indulgence* ([Edinburgh], 1703), p. 17.

59 [Jonathan Swift], *A letter from a Member of the House of Commons in Ireland, to a Member*

of the House of Commons in England, concerning the Sacramental Test (1709), pp. 10–11, 13; the first edition appeared in 1708. For more on Swift, see C.J. Fauske, *Jonathan Swift and the Church of Ireland 1710–1724* (Dublin: Irish Academic Press, 2002); L.A. Landa, *Swift and the Church of Ireland* (Oxford: Oxford University Press, 1954).

60 [William Tisdall], *A sample of true-blew Presbyterian loyalty, in all changes and turns of government* &c. (Dublin, 1709).

61 *A representation of the present state of religion, with regard to infidelity, heresy, impiety and popery: drawn up and agreed by both Houses of Convocation in Ireland* (Dublin, 1711); for High Church activity in the Irish convocation, see D.W. Hayton, *Ruling Ireland, 1685–1742: politics, politicians and parties* (Woodbridge: Boydell, 2004), chapter 4.

62 For discussion of the Sacheverell affair, see Grant Tapsell's essay in this volume.

63 Francis Higgins, *A sermon preach'd at White-Hall; on Ash Wednesday, Feb. 26, 1706/7,* (1707), p. 9.

64 See J. Stephen, *Scottish Presbyterians and the Act of Union 1707* (Edinburgh: Edinburgh University Press, 2007).

65 Clarke, 'Scottish Episcopalians', p. 226.

66 George Lockhart, *The case of Mr. Greenshields, fully stated and discus'd in a letter from a commoner of North Britain, to an English peer* ([1711]), p. 4.

67 *James Greenshields, clerk, appel', the Lord Provost and magistrates of Edinburgh, resp., the appellant's case* ([1710], p. 1.

68 Quoted by Clarke, 'Scottish Episcopalians', p. 295.

69 *Ibid.*, p. 422.

Chapter 6

The later Stuart church and North America

Jeremy Gregory

The presence of the Church of England in North America offers an interesting case study of the later Stuart church, where some of the issues and problems encountered by the church in Old England were transplanted to British North America, but also where the radically different religious, political, and socio-cultural contexts across the Atlantic threw up new challenges for the church. This chapter will focus on two aspects of the church's North American experience which both complicated and extended its role as it had developed in the home country. First, the place of the church in North America was very dissimilar from its position in England. Even in those colonies where it was established, the church in America lacked the massive apparatus of bishops, dioceses, archdeaconries, and church courts which had been crucial to its functioning at home and which were restored there in the first couple of years after the Restoration.[1] Moreover, its position varied considerably in the different colonies, providing pragmatic alternatives to the models of establishment and uniformity familiar in England. In broad terms, mainland British North America can be regarded as being divided ecclesiastically into three 'regions' by 1714: the south, where the Church of England was increasingly established; the north-east, where Congregationalism was the effective establishment; and the middle colonies, which were, on the face of it, more tolerant and more pluralistic.[2] There was also a strong Anglican presence in several of the Caribbean Islands, most notably Barbados, Jamaica, and the Leeward Islands.[3] The church's status in the colonies during the late Stuart period thus mirrored its mixed situation in Britain as a whole, where its standing stretched from being established with the vast majority of the population being members (as in England), to established but only with a minority supporting it (as in Ireland), and dissenting (as in Scotland after 1690). The issues of establishment, dissent, and toleration – which so dominated political and religious life in Old England during the later Stuart period – were therefore made more complex in the New World, with the church finding itself in novel and unfamiliar situations.

Second, North America gave the Church of England in the fifty years after 1660 the possibility of operating on a far broader canvas and the prospect of bringing its brand of Protestantism to a far wider world than had been dreamt of in the first century of the Reformation. It has often been (rightly) claimed that the Church of England in the first part of the seventeenth century had been rather slow at conceiving of North America as either a mission field or an opportunity for enlarging the territories under its charge,[4] despite George Herbert's vision in 1633 of the shift westward of true religion from England to America, in which 'Religion stands on tiptoe in our land / Readie to pass to the *American* strand'.[5] However, more practically, the 1662 Book of Common Prayer included a new baptism service 'for those of riper years', added in part because it was hoped that it 'may be always useful for the baptizing of Natives in our Plantations and others converted to the Faith'. Moreover, the religious rhetoric in the charters issued for a number of colonies after 1660 stressed the ambition of converting the Amerindians to Christianity, and the church itself participated in this discourse and aspiration. The later Stuart period also saw the founding of two organisations which would have a tremendous impact on the church's activities in North America and elsewhere: the Society for the Propagation of Christian Knowledge (SPCK) in 1698 and, even more pertinently, the Society for the Propagation of the Gospel [in Foreign Parts] (SPG) in 1701.[6] This was established by royal charter, with its three-fold mission to the native Americans, negro slaves, and European settlers, and was instrumental in co-ordinating transatlantic Anglican activity by sending over and supporting missionaries, books,[7] catechists and schoolmasters to those colonies where the church was not established. Archbishop Tenison presided over its first meeting at Lambeth Palace, symbolising the high regard that the SPG (and the North American mission) was given at the top level of the early eighteenth-century church.[8] The SPG also held an annual fundraising sermon in London as a means of disseminating information about the church's colonial project to the metropolis. These developments and initiatives within the later Stuart church, firmly set in place by 1714, provided the framework for the church's global endeavour in the next two centuries and beyond.

In the years immediately after the Restoration, the most pressing problem for the fortunes of the church in America was the shortage of clergy. There were at that time only ten clergy ministering to the whole of Virginia (which had forty-five parishes and was the flagship Anglican colony), and a couple in Maryland, and apart from these there may have been no other Church of England clergy serving on the mainland.[9] A proposal made to Bishop Sheldon in 1661 to set up special 'Virginia fellowships' in Oxford and Cambridge, where after seven years the fellow would be expected to minister in Virginia for another seven years before deciding whether to stay in America or return to England,[10] came to nothing, although five clergy were sent to Jamaica, and Barbados' eleven churches were regarded as being supplied by an adequate number of clergy in 1664.[11] Matters had improved only slightly by 1679, when it was reckoned that outside the two southernmost colonies (where Virginia now had seventeen clergy and Maryland thirteen) there were only four Church of England clergy for the entire mainland continent.[12] Absence of clergy on the ground, as well as of the formal ecclesiastical hierarchy and institutions which had been re-established in Old England, meant that the church in America was heavily reliant on lay members for providing leadership. This dependence can be seen most obviously in Virginia, where the church was established early on, but where the laity, through the powers of the General Assembly (which framed legislation for the church as a whole) and vestries (which had oversight of individual churches, including the right to elect ministers annually) had much control over day-to-day activities.[13] Historians have traditionally viewed the 'laicisation' of the church in America in negative terms, confusing laicisation with secularisation, but in fact it can be seen more positively as members of the laity taking their religious duties seriously and not wanting to confine religious leadership to the clergy.[14] Throughout North America, the church was reliant on lay members in other ways, not only contributing to the support of the fabric, but also providing lay readers and, in areas such as New England where the church was on an unsure footing, providing spaces in private houses for meetings before a church could be built.[15] In addition, the church, even in those colonies where it was established, always had to negotiate its position with those in power, such as royal governors, and while there is evidence of co-operation between church and state, there were also occasions where clergy could accuse colonial rulers and leading planters of neglecting their duties of supporting the church and furthering its interests.[16]

The full range of the church's situation at the Restoration can be seen in the cases of Virginia, on the one hand, and the New England colonies, on the other. As the first British colonies to have been settled on the North American mainland in the early seventeenth century, they offered two contrasting positions for the church, in the early 1660s, which mirrored the differing and at times competing religious sensibilities of those who emigrated to the New World. In Virginia (founded in 1607), attempts had been made to replicate the religious order of the home country, albeit in a very much pared-down form.[17] After the Restoration, in 1661 Virginia quickly formulated a set of canons which listed the fundamental components of an established church[18] and which anticipated the English 1662 Act of Uniformity in a number of ways.[19] These canons decreed that a publicly funded church or chapel was to be built in every parish, and that clergy were to be provided with glebe lands and a house, as well as having a salary (with recourse to law for non-payment); they laid down regulations for the choice, rights, and responsibilities of vestries; they decreed that only clergy who had been episcopally ordained, and had the backing of the governor and vestry, could be inducted; they stipulated that services had to be performed according to the Book of Common Prayer; and required services on Sundays and certain holy days (including a fast day on 30 January for the martyrdom of Charles I), with a sermon every week and twice-yearly celebrations of the sacrament. The canons also decreed that only Church of England ministers could perform marriage ceremonies, and required vestries to deal with those found swearing, breaking the Sabbath, missing church, committing slander or backbiting, or the 'foule and abominable sins of drunkenness, fornication and adultery'; they stipulated that births, marriages, and burials be registered, and that land should be given for a school. Under a 1662 law, 'scismaticall persons' who did not have their children baptised were to be fined, and other laws barred Quakers from coming to live in the colony and made Quaker meetings unlawful.[20] Taken together, this legislation created a religious establishment for Virginia by requiring inhabitants to attend church, maintaining clergy, gate-keeping who could be a religious professional, prescribing the form and matter of services, giving civil roles to clergy, and inflicting penalties on non-Anglicans. It is also indicative of the ways in which post-Restoration Anglicanism, both at home and in the plantations, was able to absorb the Puritan programme of godliness and reformation of manners under its own auspices.[21] Moreover, the general revision of laws in 1662 underscored the crucial place of the parish vestry in Virginian local government, indicating the close connection between church and state.[22] In 1699 the Virginia General Assembly acknowledged the Toleration Act, but at the time there were very few nonconformists in the colony and the main principles of the Virginia establishment remained intact.[23] Everyone (whether Church of England or not) still had to contribute to the support of the clergy, and Anglican clergy presided over all marriage ceremonies, and these were factors which would become increasingly irksome to the growing numbers of dissenters after 1740.

In contrast to the position in Virginia, where the church both before and after the Civil War and Interregnum enjoyed the same legal security as its counterpart at home, further north in New England its opponents had created their own religious laboratories. Plymouth (1620), Massachusetts Bay (1630), Connecticut (1636), and New Haven (1639) had been founded by Calvinist groups who came to be regarded as 'dissenters' from the English establishment. The Massachusetts Bay settlers persecuted anyone within their jurisdiction (as they defined it) who challenged them. Even during the Interregnum, when the suspension of any sort of establishment in most of the Anglophone world permitted new religious groups such as the Quakers and Baptists to proselytise with success,[24] 'Puritan' New England's establishments survived.

However, as Carla Pestana has shown, the Restoration regime opposed both the intolerance and the established faith of most New England colonies, and worked, without much success, to replace diversity and dissent with a Church of England establishment.[25]

The New England establishment, particularly after 1660, was in an inherently uncomfortable situation in dealing with the metropolitan authorities, since Congregationalists were excluded from the established Church in England, while adherents of the Church of England in New England were the ones to be treated as dissenters. To avoid dealing with this problem head on, religious legislation in Massachusetts after 1692 (after the new charter was issued) did not refer by name to any denomination, and instead demanded that all towns outside Boston should maintain 'an able, learned and orthodox minister', elected by the vote of the male members of the church, approved by the congregation, and provided for by taxation.[26] Almost always this resulted in a Congregationalist establishment. The most notorious exemption to this was Swansea, where Baptists were the largest grouping from 1693, with the result that for a time Swansea had the only Baptist establishment anywhere on the globe.[27] Excluding or otherwise persecuting dissenters from their establishments became increasingly difficult after 1689. The new 1691 Massachusetts charter, for example, guaranteed a 'liberty of conscience ... to all Christians (except Papists)'.[28] Nevertheless, it is misleading to suggest, as some historians have done, that early eighteenth-century New England saw the development of a 'multiple religious establishment'.[29] In the later Stuart period and beyond in both Massachusetts and Connecticut all inhabitants were presumptively Congregationalists and thereby liable for the support of the church in their parish, and concessions were only grudgingly given to named dissenting groups. But non-named groups had no protection whatsoever. In New Hampshire, 'conscientious' dissenters were ostensibly let off paying ministerial taxes from 1692, as long as they 'constantly attend the publick worship of God on the Lord's day according to their own persuasion',[30] although this led to disputes over whether individuals were actually conscientious dissenters or just wanting to avoid paying taxes, and it would not be until the late 1720s that Anglicans in the various New England colonies were able to forgo paying for Congregational ministers and to support their own clergy instead.

In exploring the place of the colonial church in the later Stuart period, it is instructive to examine religious directives and statements about religion in the charters issued for various colonies after the Restoration. Whereas parliamentary legislation in the 1660s and 1670s tightened the definition of the Anglican establishment in England itself, *royal* charters for the colonies had the opposite effect. They were far more likely than statutes to indicate the personal sympathies and inclination of an individual monarch, and what is particularly noticeable is the way that a number of charters for the colonies issued by Charles II well before the 1689 Toleration Act built in some form of religious toleration, while at the same time advocating an establishment. In this the language of the charters echoed that used by the king in the Declaration of Breda in April 1660, where he declared 'a liberty to tender consciences ... that no man shall be disquieted or called in question for differences of opinion in matter of religion which do not disturb the peace of the kingdom',[31] and it is striking how far the Breda formulation became a template for the charters which were issued during his reign. The charter for Rhode Island and Providence Plantations issued in 1663 – within a year of the hard-line 1662 English Act of Uniformity – is noteworthy in giving royal mandate that 'no person within the sayd colony, at any tyme hereafter, shall be any wise molested, punished, disquieted or called in question for any differences of opinione in matters of religion, and do not actually disturb the civill peace of our sayd colony', although there is something of a crossing of fingers in the hope that 'by reason of the remote distances of those places [this] will (as we hope) bee no breach of the unite and uniformitee established in this nation'.[32]

While the Restoration parliament tended to see the re-establishment of the Church of England as crucial within England, Charles personally was rather more inclined to religious liberty[33] and, as he had more say over religious policy in the colonies, he could sanction some degree of religious freedom there. In the colonies, the absence of the kinds of constitutional and political constraints that made Charles anything but an absolute monarch at home allowed him (in effect, arbitrarily) to do such things as demanding William Berkeley, the High-Church Governor of Virginia, 'not to suffer any man to be molested, and disquieted in the exercise of religion'.[34] In a similar vein, the charter for Carolina issued in 1663 gave the colonial proprietors control over the religious complexion of the colony with 'such indulgences and dispensations and with such limitations as ... [they] shall think fit and reasonable',[35] and the 1665 charter went further in ordering that 'no person ... be molested ... for any differences in opinion or practice in matters of religious concernments who do not actually disturb the civil peace', allowing them to act according to their 'judgements and conscience', 'any law, statute or clause contained or to be contained, usage or custom of our realm of England, to the contrary thereof, in any-wise notwithstanding'.[36] The fortunes of the Church of England looked unprepossessing, since in practice there was no Anglican minister or church in the colony for the first decade. The 'Fundamental Constitutions of Carolina' (1669–70), written in part by John Locke but never fully put into operation, did grant public maintenance for the Church of England alone, 'which being the only true and orthodox, and the national religion of all the king's dominions is also of Carolina'. But they also recognised the Amerindians, who were deemed 'utterly strangers to Christianity, [but] whose idolatry, ignorance or mistake give us no right to expel them or use them ill', and the Constitutions also acknowledged the need to attract others to the colony who 'will unavoidably be of different opinions concerning matters of religion', and they hoped that 'Jews, heathens, and other dissenters from the purity of the Christian religion may not be scared and kept at a distance'.[37] The 'Constitutions' envisaged that bringing these kinds of people to the colony would be a way of 'acquainting themselves' with the truth of the Christian religion, and even allowed for any seven or more people 'agreeing in any religion' to worship together as long as they acknowledged there was a God who should be publicly worshipped in some external way, and provided they did not use abusive language against other religions.

Despite this lofty rhetoric, in fact the religious establishment in both Carolinas came to have the same features as the Virginian settlement, although it was by no means wholly implemented, particularly in North Carolina, where there were not enough Anglican clergy to sustain an establishment and where nonconformists were tolerated more readily. In the late seventeenth century almost 50 per cent of the colony's inhabitants were nonconformist (generally Presbyterians or Quakers), as were several of the governors, and they were keen to tempt dissenters to settle.[38] Yet rather than foster religious liberty, in 1704 the South Carolina assembly passed legislation (very similar to that adopted in Virginia in 1661) which made the Anglican church the sole establishment, demanding that the Book of Common Prayer be used, forbidding nonconformists from having a role in the government, stipulating that only marriages conducted by Anglican clergy were valid, and supporting clergy and church buildings from the public purse.[39] North Carolina, after debates about tax support and church power, adopted an Anglican establishment in 1715.[40] Dissenters in both Carolinas were treated far more leniently than they were in Virginia; nevertheless, in all three colonies in the early eighteenth century there was such a thing as establishment and dissent. A full picture of all legislation for colonial religious establishments can be traced in Nicholas Trott's *The Laws of the British Plantations in America, relating to the Church and the Clergy, Religion and Learning.*[41] Published in 1721, it illustrates graphically the ways in which the legislatures of the various colonies after 1685 effectively reversed the relatively liberal measures of the Restoration era, when an interventionist Crown had attempted to impose a degree of religious diversity in America.

The same consolidation of the position of the Church of England in the southern colonies after the mid 1680s was continued in the cases of Maryland and Georgia. Maryland became Anglican in 1691 (confirmed in 1702), after the Glorious Revolution. The proprietorship was taken away from the Catholic Calvert family, and an Act 'for the service of Almighty God and the Establishment of the Protestant Religion within this province' was passed by the colonial assembly, establishing the Church of England in ways reminiscent of the Virginia establishment.[42] It has been suggested that after this date Maryland became one of the most fiercely anti-Catholic colonies, and the exclusive position of the established church there was reinforced by further legislation passed between 1697 and 1707.[43] All inhabitants had to pay to maintain the church and Catholics, as in England, paid double taxes and were barred from political office, while Catholic services were forbidden.

Standing somewhat apart from the south and New England, the middle colonies provided an anti-establishment model of sorts. Both Anglicans and Congregationalists were under-represented here, partly because, in addition to the British settlers, including Scots and Scots-Irish, these colonies began to attract an increasing number of non-British immigrants, particularly from Germany, from the mid 1680s onwards.[44] But, in their day, the middle colonies were regarded with suspicion by the inhabitants of the other colonies, and they were not quite the unqualified bastions of religious liberty that we sometimes imagine. For example, there were religious tests for office holders, as well as laws against blasphemy, echoing the 1698 Blasphemy Act in England, which penalised those who denied the Trinity, believed in more gods than one, denied that Christianity was true, or denied the divine authority of scripture.[45] Presbyterians were strongly represented in the middle colonies, some from New England Congregational stock, and also Scots-Irish immigrants who were keen to attack the Church of England but demanded an establishment for themselves, citing Scottish precedent.[46] And while most of the colony of New York did not have a religious establishment, in metropolitan New York successive attempts to gain government support for the Church of England were relatively successful, in the main. After the Dutch ceded power to the English in 1664, the new government agreed to tolerate the Dutch Reformed Church, and gave religious freedoms to Protestant nonconformists. Nevertheless the authorities demanded that each parish should choose overseers who were to select a minister and to raise taxes as well as supporting the Dutch church, thereby in effect creating a binary establishment.[47] Then, during the governorship of the Anglican Benjamin Fletcher, the assembly passed the Ministry Act in 1693, which created parishes in metropolitan New York (New York, Richmond, Westchester, and Queens), and authorised the salaries of 'a good, sufficient Protestant minister'.[48] The governor took this to mean a Church of England cleric, although this was contested by other Protestant groups.

Having explored the legislative contexts in which the church operated in North America, the chapter will now consider the progress and initiatives made by the church in America during the later Stuart period. Although Archbishop Laud as early as 1634 had handed the responsibility of overseeing the interests of the Church of England in the colonies to the bishops of London, nothing significant was accomplished during the disruptions of the 1640s and 1650s or in the first decade of the Restoration, given the pressing problems at home. But in 1675, the Board of Trade took on a more proactive role vis-à-vis the colonies and in the same year the new bishop of London, Henry Compton, took a more active line as bishop for North America (as well as being a member of the Board of Trade himself).[49] Indeed, Compton can be credited with initiating a more determined religious policy for the colonies.[50]

Compton was also responsible for promoting the careers of two clergy who were important for the strengthening of the Anglican presence in British North America from the 1680s onwards: James Blair and Thomas Bray.[51] Blair was appointed rector of Henrico parish in Virginia from 1685, and from 1689 until his death in 1743 commissary in the colony, with delegated powers from the bishop and oversight over the clergy. He was minister of James City parish from 1694 to 1710, when he became the incumbent of Bruton parish in Williamsburg. Blair became strongly entrenched in Virginia society by marrying into a leading family, which helped to secure the interests of the church (and indeed he himself was to serve as acting governor of the colony in the early 1740s). Nevertheless, and indicative of the complex relationships that could exist between representatives of the church and representatives of the state, he fell out with three royal governors whom he considered to be neglecting the concerns of the church, and he was able to use his influence with Compton and the Board of Trade to remove Sir Edmund Andros in 1697, Francis Nicholson in 1705, and Alexander Spotswood in 1722.

As far as the functioning of the church was concerned, clergy in Virginia undertook their duties more diligently and were better educated as a consequence of Blair's oversight.[52] Virginia also had the advantage, unique to it, of Blair's creation of the College of William and Mary in 1693 (founded by royal charter), where (as in Oxford and Cambridge) faculty and students had to subscribe to the Thirty-nine Articles. The dream of founding a college in the colony can be traced back to at least 1618, when the Virginia Company had granted funds for the establishment of the University of Henrico, but the plan ended with the Good Friday Indian uprising of 1622. At the Restoration, the General Assembly had mooted founding a college to train clergy for the church in the colony, but nothing was done. For Blair, a college would be key to the training up candidates for orders, and it was he who secured the funds and the royal charter, with first Compton and then Tenison being made chancellor. The college buildings were destroyed by fire in 1705 and the college was effectively closed until 1716. So, although the college actually achieved rather little in the later Stuart period, it was at least instituted and would become a bastion of Anglican identity in the Georgian period.[53]

Another of Compton's protégés, Thomas Bray, was appointed commissary in the newly Anglican Maryland in 1695, although he did not arrive until 1700 because of some uncertainty over whether the church was actually established in the colony or not. Bray also published *An essay towards promoting all necessary and useful knowledge ... in all parts of His Majesties' dominions* (1697), which argued for the funding of libraries for the use of clergy in the colonies, and he was one of the principal instigators of the SPCK. He returned to England in early 1701 and presented Tenison with *A Memorial Representing the Present State of Religion on the Continent of North-America*. This was a plea for the provision of adequate numbers of missionaries to be sent to the colonies, and was written, according to Bray, 'in order to the Propagation of the true Christian Religion in those Parts, at a Crisis, when, as many Thousands are in a happy Disposition to embrace it, so Infidelity and Heresie seem to make their utmost Efforts to withdraw, and to fix these People at the greatest distance from it'.[54] Having surveyed the state of the church in the various colonies (and giving much more praise to the work of Governor Nicholson of Virginia than James Blair was wont to do), Bray concluded: 'nor do I think myself oblig'd to speak here of New-England, where Independency seems to be the Religion of the Country. My design is not to intermeddle, where Christianity under any Form has obtained possession; but to represent rather the deplorable State of the English colonies, where they have been in a manner abandoned to Atheism; or, which is much at one, to Quakerism, for want of a Clergy settled among them'.[55] Bray then outlined what he thought should be the person specification of those sent as missionaries, and suggested a scheme for funding them, including getting each bishop to recommend someone from his diocese, and to get the church dignitaries and the laity in the diocese to subscribe so that each diocese could send over at least one missionary. Bray's stress on the crucial role of missionaries would be highlighted in his move in 1701 to set up the SPG, which took on this role in a more organised way, and with royal backing.[56] Later, Gilbert Burnet would remember William III's support for the SPG, occurring as it did within a year of the king's death, as 'among the last of the publick Actions of a Life, that had been all imployed in defending and securing true Religion, both here and elsewhere'.[57]

The founding of the SPG marked a decisive development in the church's relations with, and presence in, North America. Concerned with those colonies where the church was not established, it provided clergy, bibles, books of common prayer, and tracts for the plantations, and it remains an important missionary force in the world today. By the end of the later Stuart period, the SPG was maintaining nearly thirty clergy in America, with support also from the colonial laity. Archbishop Tenison showed an especial interest in this early cohort of SPG-backed clergy, and, although the role of licensing clergy for the SPG mission officially fell to the bishop of London, even as late as 1710 the archbishop insisted on vetting their credentials himself and meeting them before departure.[58]

In the first anniversary sermon preached before the SPG in 1702, Richard Willis, the dean of Lincoln, noted that the Church of England had been rather slow in reaching out to America, in comparison to the Church of Rome: 'The little care that we have hitherto taken of the State of Religion in those Plantations continues a standing reproach upon our Church and Nation: and this is what is often objected to us by those of the Church of Rome; We have indeed many things to say against their ways of Managing these matters, and in defence of ourselves, but after all I am sorry that we can't give them the only full answer to the Objection, which is the denial of the matter of fact.'[59] The fact that Roman Catholic Church had beaten the Church of England to the missionary field by nearly two hundred years would be a recurring theme in these sermons, but clergy were quick to contrast the violent and persecutory methods of Rome with the educational and instructional (and more sincere) methods of the Anglican Church. Indeed in 1712 White Kennett, the dean of Peterborough dwelt on the atrocities of the Popish Church in the mission field. This sermon was a review of the various impediments to 'planting and propagating the Gospel of Christ' and included a long discussion of 'the exercising of Force and Cruelty to compel' the Indians to convert, 'instead of the persuading and convincing of them'.[60] The printed sermon contained a graphic instance of how Anglican discourse highlighted the violence associated with its rivals:

> The horrible ways of converting the Poor Indians by the Bigots of the Church of Rome, would draw Tears, and make hearts to bleed ... Men hunted down like Beasts, and devoured by the Dogs; Women and Children maimed, and hang'd, and burnt in one and the same way of execution. This Relation is given by a *Spanish* Bishop settled in those parts. When the *Spaniards* first landed in the Isles, there were above Five Hundred Souls; they cut the throats of a great part of these, and carried away the rest by Force; to make them work in the mines of Hispaniola – As for the Continent, 'tis certain, and what I myself know to be true, that the *Spaniards* have ruined Ten kingdoms there bigger than all *Spain*, by the commission of all sorts of Barbarity and unheard of Cruelties. They have driven away or killed all the Inhabitants, so that all these Kingdoms are desolate to this Day – We dare assert, without Fear of incurring the Reproach of exaggerating, That in the Space of the Fourty Years, in which the *Spaniards* exercised their intolerable Tyranny in this New World, they unjustly put to Death above Twelve Millions of People, counting Men, Women, and Children. And it may be affirm'd without Injury to Truth, upon a just Calculation, That during this Space of Time above Fifty Millions have died in these Countries – They valued them Worse than Beasts – They ripp'd up Women with Child, that Root and Branch may be destroy'd together. They laid Wagers one with another who should cleave a Man down with his Sword most dexterously at one Blow. Or who should run a Man through after the most artificial manner. They tore away Children out of their Mother's Arms, and dash'd out their Brains against the Rocks. Others they threw into the Rivers, diverting themselves with this brutish sport &c. They set up Gibbets, and hang'd up Thirteen of those poor Creatures in Honour to Jesus Christ and his Twelve Apostles, as they blasphemously express'd themselves; kindling a great Fire under those Gibbets, to burn those they had hang'd upon them &c.[61]

Just as there was an Anglican/Protestant pornography (with stories of young girls being seduced in the confessional by lecherous Catholic priests) in this period,[62] so there was a genre of Anglican/Protestant blood-and-guts that dwelt on the physical atrocities employed by the Catholic 'other'. The mindless and gratuitous violence and cruelty displayed in this extract was seen as a testimony to the unnatural and perverse nature of Popery. In contradistinction to the detail given to popish methods of conversion, White Kennett summed up Anglican methods much more succinctly: 'I would only observe to you, that the Soft and Salutary Methods of Conversion, taken by this Society, are of a more Christian Nature; are far from breathing out any Threatenings, or any Slaughter, any Conquest of Slavery of the People of the Land.'[63]

In his 1702 sermon Willis also discussed the best ways of propagating the Gospel overseas: 'The design is in the first place', he argued, 'to settle the State of religion as well as may be among our own people there, which by all accounts we have, very much want their Pious care, and then to proceed in the best methods they can towards the conversion of the Natives: both these are works that will require a great expence, the sending ministers thither and to enable them to do their duty the better when they are there, the breeding up of persons to understand the great variety of languages of those countries in order to be able to converse with the natives, and preach the Gospel to them: these and other things which cannot now be named will require large contributions'.[64] Following Willis, the majority of preachers argued that the conversion of the native Americans could only come after they had been civilised, and this would only come after the English settlers had been properly Christianised. However, Charles Trimnel, the bishop of Norwich, in February 1710 reasserted the significance of the conversion of the native Americans as the number one priority for the SPG.[65] In the April of that year, four Iroquois sachems (styled princes in Britain) arrived in London and were presented to the queen, as well as being entertained at Lambeth Palace.[66] The SPG was excited by the prospect of sending a missionary or missionaries to them, as well as an interpreter, and eventually William Andrews was sent over, although his report of May 1714 detailed how difficult his work amongst them was.[67]

In 1711 William Fleetwood, bishop of St Asaph, acknowledging the bequest to the SPG the previous year in the will of Christopher Codrington of two plantations in Barbados, together with three hundred black slaves, considered the church's position vis-à-vis slavery. He attacked those planters who did not want their slaves to be instructed in Christianity on the grounds that they feared that if their slaves became Christian they would have to be freed. Fleetwood noted that even if this were true it would not really be a problem, since there were no slaves in England but this had not led to the collapse of society. But Fleetwood confirmed that there was nothing in the Bible to condemn slavery (and that Christian freedom was an entirely spiritual matter), although he reminded his audience that Christians should treat slaves kindly and that true Christians should always be moderate.[68]

Indicative of the increased ambition of the church in the late seventeenth century is the fact that Anglicans had begun to have a presence even in Congregational New England, with King's chapel, Boston the first Church of England building erected in New England, built in October 1689 by a congregation which had been meeting since 1686 at the instigation of representatives of James II's government.[69] John Dunton, the Presbyterian London bookseller who was in Boston in May 1686 when the Anglican clergyman Robert Ratcliffe sailed into the harbour as part of the retinue of Edward Randolph, councillor in the new Dominion of New England (a political entity which overrode the original Massachusetts charter, and was thus detested by many New Englanders), noted the strangeness of the situation: 'on Lord's Days [he] read the Common Prayer in His Surplice, and preach'd in the To[w]n-House. Mr Ratcliffe was an Eminent Preacher, and his Sermons were useful and well dress'd; I was once or twice to hear him, and 'twas noise'd about that Dr Annesly's son-in law was turn'd Apostate. But I cou'd easily forgive 'em, in Regard, the Common Prayer, and the Surplice were Religious Novelties in New England'.[70] But two years later, Randolph informed Archbishop Sancroft that Ratcliffe was attracting opprobrium: 'some calling our minister Baal's priest and some of their ministers from the pulpit calling our prayers leeks, garlick and trash'.[71] Ratcliffe's congregation soon included Edmund Andros, a crony of James II and the loathed President of the Dominion, who was imprisoned during Boston's own version of the Glorious Revolution in April 1689.[72] The chapel was used, and financially supported, by naval officers, who, among other things, had pews installed in the new building in 1694 (where, up until then, seating had been on low wooden benches used in Congregational meetings) and received an altar and gifts of plate from William and Mary, as well as a library.[73] Although the SPG did not pay for the minister of King's Chapel (his income came from pew rents and subscriptions), it did contribute to the salaries of other minsters in New England. By 1714, four Anglican congregations with clergy (including the King's Chapel) could be found in Massachusetts and Rhode Island, which was notoriously tolerant in New England terms, and two other congregations were in negotiation with the SPG for a missionary, although it would not be until the 1720s that it penetrated Connecticut and New Hampshire.

The presence of the Church of England in the heartland of Puritan New England aroused alarm amongst leading Congregationalists. Increase Mather's voluminous publications included *A Brief Discourse concerning the Unlawfulness of the Common Prayer Worship* (1686), provoked by the use of the liturgy in Boston by Ratcliffe and his congregation, which made conventional 'Puritan' criticisms of the Prayer Book as being no better than the popish mass, likening the formulaic responses to 'tennis balls' tossed between the priest and the congregation, and decrying the hopeful prayers in the burial service, the use of the ring in marriage, making the sign of the cross at baptism, and kneeling when taking the sacrament.[74] His *A Testimony against several prophane and superstitious new customs now practised by some in New England* (published in London in 1687), which railed against the performance of stage-plays, putting up maypoles, drinking healths, playing cards, dice or the lottery, giving new-year presents, observing saints' days, Candlemass and Shrove Tuesday, watching cock fighting, and the keeping of Christmas, which, he was appalled to find, were now being talked about in New England, of all places (and where 'promiscuous dancing' had been practised the previous year),[75] urged New Englanders to stay away from these wicked pastimes.

To add to Mather's fears of an Anglican intrusion and attack on Puritan New England, some English settlers saw the potential of imposing Anglicanism on New England. Lewis Morris, an active Churchman, member of the SPG, and later governor of New Jersey, wrote to the English High-Churchman William Beveridge from Boston in 1702: 'If the Church can be settled in New England, it pulls up schism in America by the roots, that being the fountain that supplys with infectious streams the rest of America.'[76] Aggressive Anglicanism both in New England and in other parts of North America can also be seen in the extraordinary career of George Keith in the early years of the eighteenth century. A Quaker hothead and controversialist, Keith had been appointed Surveyor General of East Jersey in 1684. He published against the new generation of Quakers and also the New England Congregationalists. Having returned to England, he became increasingly critical of the Quakers and was taken on by the SPCK to preach in the colonies against Quakerism, and in February 1700 he officially conformed to the church, and was ordained deacon by the bishop of London three months later. He was ordained priest in 1702 and was sent to America by the newly formed SPG to assess the state of the church in the colonies, and fell out with leading New England Congregationalists (including Increase Mather and Samuel Willard, president of Harvard College) as well as Quakers, and so pleased the SPG that he was made a life member. He finally returned to England in 1704.[77]

There were also several developments within New England Congregational circles in the late seventeenth and early eighteenth centuries which made it more receptive to Anglicanism. A number of leading Congregationalists by that time had considered it important to participate in the early European Enlightenment and were taken with the publications of those who might be deemed 'moderate' Anglicans, making the works of Archbishop Tillotson, at least according to one historian, the most widely read books in North America by the early eighteenth century.[78] But alongside Increase Mather, Samuel Sewall, the redoubtable Puritan judge, was, from the mid 1680s to the late 1720s, on the look-out for Anglican encroachments in Boston, and his diary annually reported, with regret and dismay, the Christmas Day services at the King's Chapel (as well as Shrove Tuesday festivities and sports), and he noted with displeasure those Bostonians who declined to work on 25 December (pouring scorn on this as just a popish holyday) and, even more disturbingly for him, those who attended Christmas Day services, including, on occasion, some of his extended family.[79] On 25 December 1697 Sewall recorded: 'I took occasion to dehort mine from Christmas-keeping and charged them to forbear', but evidently without much success, as he went on to lament: 'most of ye Boys went to Church'.[80]

The arrival of Anglicanism in New England from the 1680s onwards can be seen as part of a wider Anglican renewal and revival throughout the colonies which lasted until 1714 and beyond. This can be witnessed particularly in the southern colonies and in the Caribbean Islands, where, as we have seen, the church was now on a sounder legal footing. Between 1680 and 1688 more than forty-five clergy were sent to North America (nine to Virginia, two to Maryland, twenty-one to the Leeward Islands, five to Jamaica, three to Barbados, and one to the West Indies).[81] These were the result of a number of schemes designed to encourage clergy to the colonies, including the setting up of a royal bounty for clergy to encourage them to go overseas with a payment of £20 for moving costs.[82] The revival also found tangible expression in the building of new churches and the refurbishment and improving of others, and the building of Christ Church, Philadelphia in 1696 indicated that the church was also beginning to make inroads in Pennsylvania, the one-time haven for Quakers, founded in 1681 by William Penn as a grant from Charles II.[83] Indeed three out of the four major cities in the colonies between 1695 and 1705 built Anglican churches which dominated their cities' skylines: New York, Philadelphia, and Boston.[84] In Virginia the number of Anglican churches increased from thirty-five in 1680 to sixty-one in 1724, paid for by mandatory church taxes and built in brick.[85] The Anglican strengths in the colony were highlighted in Robert Beverley's *History and Present State of Virginia* (1705).[86]

Further signs of increasing Anglican confidence can be seen in the renewal of interest in the scheme of procuring a bishop for the colonies. Without a bishop (or bishops) there could be no ordinations in America, and thus ordained clergy would have to be sent over from the old country or, and this would increasingly be the case after the 1720s, American-born clergy would have to travel to London to be ordained, risking two long sea journeys. There could also be no confirmations or consecrations, no effective form of line management and clerical discipline, and no synodical meetings. As far back as 1638 Archbishop Laud, concerned with the religious make-up of New England, and four years after he had established the Commission for New England (which, with its brief to establish church courts and to discipline those who were deemed refractory in religious matters, had aspired to impose his policy of Thorough on the northern colonies), attempted to send a bishop there,[87] but the outbreak of rebellion in Scotland ensured that he had more pressing matters to deal with nearer to home. Within a year of the Restoration, a request for a bishop came from Virginia, but this came to nothing, no doubt because the church was preoccupied with its own process of re-establishment in Old England.[88] There were, however, rumours (probably unfounded) among the Dutch in 1664 – then on the brink of war with England – that Charles II 'being inclined to reduce all his kingdom under one form of government in Church and State, hath taken care that Commissioners are ready to repair to New England to install bishops there as in Old England',[89] although this was counter to the Privy Council's instructions in April 1664 to Richard Nicolls to 'let them [the New Englanders] know that you have no orders from us ... to make the least attempt to encourage alteration in the way they profess their religion ... we could not imagine it probable that a confederate number of persons, who separated themselves from their own country and religion established, principally (if not only) that they might enjoy another way of worship ... could, in so short a time, be willing to return to that form of worship they had forsake'.[90] In 1671 Sir Charles Wheeler asked Charles II to send Francis Turner, the master of St John's, Cambridge and future bishop of Ely, to be made bishop of the Leeward Islands with an income of £400 p.a., and accompanied by eight fellows.[91] Wheeler's scheme envisaged that Turner only needed to be resident for a few years until Anglicanism had been fully established, after which he could return to England, but the proposal came to nothing, probably because Turner himself didn't see this as a wise career move. In 1672, Alexander Murray, who had accompanied Charles II in exile, was nominated bishop of Virginia, but this scheme also fell through, this time because of a failure to secure an endowment (which was intended to have been paid through customs duties).[92] Interestingly, the proposed diocese was to include all churches from Virginia northwards, including the Caribbean Islands, although the draft patent was careful to stress that 'the bishops of Virginia, shall in no manner enforce their Episcopal jurisdiction and authority [over] New England'.[93] Despite these failed efforts, the attempt to procure a bishop for North America continued to animate leading Church of England clergy and was reignited with the setting up of the SPG, who discussed the matter formally on several occasions. In its first report (1704) the Society enquired 'whether under the Act 2 Hen. VIII cap. xiii, the Bishops suffragan of Colchester, Dover, Nottingham and Hull might be disposed of for the service of the Church in foreign parts', and asked whether it would be possible to have bishops in foreign parts 'with no other jurisdiction but that of Commissary or the like'.[94] In 1705 Tenison (who was the first archbishop since Laud to have taken the situation of the church in America strategically, although Sancroft had been in correspondence with Boston Anglicans in the late 1680s) took the issue up with Queen Anne, who gave it her support. Some potential candidates for the post were mentioned, and it was rumoured that Jonathan Swift would be the first bishop of Virginia.[95] In 1711, the SPG bought a bishop's house in Burlington, New Jersey and a draft Bill was prepared for parliament in 1712, at the request of Edward Hyde, Lord Clarendon, a former governor of New York and New Jersey and a staunch defender of the church and now a leading politician in the House of Lords.[96] But the scheme was to all intents and purposes scotched by Anne's death in 1714, and although it continued to receive clerical backing – it was, for instance, frequently mentioned in the SPG's anniversary sermons – the idea would not have effective government support for the rest of the colonial period.[97] On his death in 1715, Tenison left £1,000 for the establishment of two bishops in America (one for the continent and one for the Caribbean Islands),[98] and the SPG established a bishopric fund, which received further bequests from later archbishops.[99]

By the end of the later Stuart period, the church had made some considerable advances in North America. Its legal position had been strengthened in a number of colonies and in the south it was now taken for granted that it was the established church (and this continued to be the case when the last colony, Georgia, was founded in the 1730s). By 1714 an impressive number of new churches had been built, clergy were increasingly better trained and monitored, an Anglican college had been created and, as far as the church was concerned, the chance of securing a bishop in the colonies seemed more than wishful thinking. The church had also consolidated its institutional presence in America with the creation of the SPG. Furthermore, startling-seeming Anglican successes had occurred in those colonies which had traditionally rejected the Church of England, revealed by its arrival in 'Puritan New England'. As the links between colonial and home administration strengthened even more in the decades after 1714, the church's establishment position in Old England meant that it would be increasingly powerful amongst significant sections of Hanoverian America. In the long run, of course, this close association would lead to problems, and even to the ousting of the church from parts of North America during the Revolution. But for now the prospects for the church looked bright and Churchmen could congratulate themselves on the progress that had been made in the colonies since the Restoration.

NOTES

1 I.M. Green, *The re-establishment of the Church of England, 1660–1663* (Oxford: Clarendon Press, 1978). See also C. Pestana, *Protestant empire. Religion and the making of the British Atlantic world* (Philadelphia: University of Pennsylvania Press, 2009).

2 J. Gregory, 'Establishment and dissent in British North America: organising religion in the new world', in S. Foster and E. Haefeli (eds), *The American Colonies in the British Empire, 1607–1776*, Companion VI to the *Oxford History of the British Empire* (Oxford: Oxford University Press, 2013). For a survey of the developing position of the church throughout the British colonies during the seventeenth and eighteenth centuries, see J.F. Woolverton, *Colonial Anglicanism in North America* (Detroit: Wayne State University Press, 1984). More recently see, J.B. Bell, *The imperial origins of the King's church in early America, 1607–1783* (Basingstoke: Palgrave Macmillan, 2004).

3 P.S. Haffenden, 'The Anglican Church in Restoration colonial policy', in J.M. Smith (ed.), *Seventeenth-century America: essays in colonial history* (Chapel Hill, NC: University of North Carolina Press, 1959), pp. 166–91.

4 H. Cnattingius, *Bishops and societies. A study of Anglican colonial missionary expansion, 1698–1850* (SPCK, 1952), pp. 1–12.

5 George Herbert, 'The church militant', in H. Wilcox (ed.), *The English poems of George Herbert* (Cambridge: Cambridge University Press, 2007), pp. 667–73.

6 Standard histories of the SPG are H.P. Thompson, *Into all lands: the history of the Society for the Propagation of the Gospel in Foreign Parts* (SPCK, 1951) and D. O'Connor et al., *Three centuries of mission. The United Society for the Propagation of the Gospel, 1701–2000* (Continuum International Publishing Group, 2000). See also R. Strong, *Anglicanism and the British Empire, c.1700–1850* (Oxford: Oxford University Press, 2006) and A. Porter, *Religion versus empire? Protestant missionaries and overseas expansion, 1700–1914* (Manchester: Manchester University Press, 2004), pp. 16–28. See J.K. Nelson, 'Anglican missions in America, 1701–1725. A study of the Society for the Propagation of the Gospel in Foreign Parts' (PhD dissertation, Northwestern University, 1962).

7 The SPG's export of suitable books for the New England mission needs to be seen as part of the broader book trade between Britain and the colonies: see H. Amory and D.D. Hall (eds), *A history of the book in America, volume 1: The colonial book in the Atlantic world* (Cambridge: Cambridge University Press, 2000).

8 E. Carpenter, *Thomas Tenison, his life and times* (SPCK, 1948), p. 344.

9 W.H. Seiler, 'The Anglican parish of Virginia', in J.M. Smith (ed.), *Seventeenth-century America: essays in colonial history* (Chapel Hill, NC: University of North Carolina Press, 1959), p. 129.

10 Haffenden, 'Anglican Church in Restoration policy' p. 180. The proposal was made in R.G., *Virginia's cure, or, An advisive narrative concerning Virginia discovering the true ground of that churches unhappiness, and the only true remedy: as it was presented to the Right Reverend Father in God Gilbert Lord Bishop of London, September 2, 1661: now publish'd to further the welfare of that and the like plantations* (1662), pp. 10–11.

11 Haffenden, 'Anglican Church in Restoration policy', p. 174, citing Minutes of Council for Foreign Plantations, no. 664, 18 Feb. 1664.

12 *Ibid.*, p. 181, citing David Humphreys, *An historical account of the Society for Propagating the Gospel in Foreign Parts ... to 1728* (1730), pp. 8–9.

13 R. Isaacs, *The transformation of Virginia, 1740–1790* (Chapel Hill, NC: University of North Carolina Press, 1982). See also Dell Upton, *Holy things and profane. Anglican parish churches in colonial Virginia* (New Haven and London: Yale University Press, 1986).

14 E.L. Bond (ed.), *Spreading the Gospel in colonial Virginia: sermons and devotional writings* (Lanham, MD: Lexington Books, 2004). See also L.F. Winner, *A cheerful and comfortable faith. Anglican religious practice in the elite households of eighteenth-century Virginia* (New Haven and London: Yale University Press, 2010).

15 On the church in New England, see J. Gregory, 'Refashioning Puritan New England: the Church of England in British North America, c.1680–c.1770', *TRHS*, 6th ser., 20 (2010), 85–112.

16 For example, J.H. Bennett Jr, 'The S.P.G. and Barbadian Politics, 1710–1720', *HMPEC*, 20 (1951), 190–206.

17 Similar arrangements were put in place in the first island colonies: Bermuda (settled in 1613), St Christopher (1622), Barbados (1627), Nevis (1628), Montserrat and Antigua (1632): Pestana, *Protestant Empire*, p. 68.

18 W.W. Hening, *The statutes at large, being a collection of all the laws in Virginia* (New York, 1823), II, 41–2.

19 For the Act of Uniformity, see J.P. Kenyon (ed.), *The Stuart constitution 1603–1688: documents and commentary* (Cambridge: Cambridge University Press, 2nd edn, 1986), pp. 378–82.

20 Hening, *Statutes at large*, II, 165–6; G.M. Brydon, *Virginia's mother church and the political conditions under which it grew*, 2 vols (Virginia History Society, 1947–52), I, 474–7.

21 Cf. J. Barry, 'Bristol as a "Reformation city", c.1640–1780', in N. Tyacke (ed.), *England's long Reformation, 1500–1800* (University College London Press, 1998), pp. 261–84; J. Gregory, *Restoration, reformation and reform: archbishops of Canterbury and their diocese, 1660–1800* (Oxford: Clarendon Press, 2000), pp. 241–2.

22 Hening, *Statutes at large*, II, 44–5.

23 *Ibid.*, III, 170–1.

24 C.G. Pestana, *Quakers and Baptists in colonial Massachusetts* (Cambridge: Cambridge University Press, 1991).

25 C. Pestana, *The English Atlantic in an age of revolution, 1640–1661* (Cambridge, MA: Harvard University Press, 2004), pp. 213–19.

26 S.M. Reed, *Church and state in Massachusetts, 1691–1740* (Urbana, IL: The University of Illinois, 1914).

27 L.W. Levy, *The establishment clause: religion and the first amendment* (New York: Macmillan, 1986; new edn 1993), p. 17.

28 Quoted in C.H. Moehlman, *The American constitutions and religion. Religious references in the charters of the thirteen colonies and the constitution of the forty-eight states. A source book on church and state in the United States* (Berne, Indiana, 1938), p. 23.

29 Levy, *Establishment clause*, chapters 2–3.

30 S.H. Cobb, *The rise of religious liberty in America. A history* (New York: Macmillan, 1902; repr. 1970), pp. 298–9.

31 The text of the Declaration of Breda is printed in Kenyon (ed.), *Stuart constitution*, pp. 331–2.

32 Quoted in Moehlman, *American constitutions*, p. 27.

33 Green, *Re-establishment*, pp. 3–36.

34 Quoted in Pestana, *English Atlantic*, p. 223.

35 J.W. Brinsfield, *Religion and politics in colonial South Carolina* (Easley, SC: Southern Historical Press, 1983).

36 Quoted in Moehlman, *American constitutions*, p. 29.

37 *Ibid.*, p. 30.

38 Brinsfield, *Religion and politics*, pp. 6–9. See also R.M. Weir, '"Shaftesbury's darling": British settlement in the Carolinas at the close of the seventeenth century', in N. Canny (ed.), *The Oxford History of the British Empire, vol. 1: Origins of Empire* (Oxford: Oxford University Press, 1998), pp. 375–97.

39 Brinsfield, *Religion and politics*, pp. 23–4.

40 J. Butler, *Awash in a sea of faith: Christianizing the American people* (Cambridge, MA: Harvard University Press, 1990), p. 103.

41 Nicholas Trott, *The laws of the British plantations in America: relating to the church and the clergy, religion and learning. Collected in one volume* (1721).

42 Cobb, *Religion*, 381–6.

43 N.W. Rightmyer, *Maryland's established church* (Baltimore, MD: Church Historical Society Diocese of Maryland, 1956), pp. 14–54.

44 S.L. Longenecker, *Piety and tolerance: Pennsylvania German religion, 1700–1850* (Metuchen, NJ: Scarecrow Press, 1994). See also, H. Lehman *et al.* (eds), *In search of peace and prosperity: New German settlements in eighteenth-century Europe and America* (University Park, PA: Pennsylvania State University Press, 2000), part IV; L.F. Bottinger, *The Germans in colonial times* (Philadelphia, 1901).

45 Levy, *Establishment clause*, p. 5.

46 N.C. Landsman, *From colonials to provincials: American thought and culture, 1680–1760* (New York: Twayne Publishers, 1997), p. 21 and his 'Nation, migration and the province in the first British Empire: Scotland and the Americas, 1600–1800', *AHR*, 104 (1999), 471–2. See also his *Scotland and its first American colony, 1683–1765* (Princeton, NJ: Princeton University Press, 1985), on New Jersey.

47 M. Kammen, *Colonial New York: a history* (New York: Scribner, 1975), pp. 220–1.

48 H. Hastings (ed.), *Ecclesiastical records of the state of New York*, 2 vols (1901), I, 570.

49 For a slightly later period, see I.K. Steele, *Politics of colonial policy: the Board of Trade in colonial administration, 1696–1720* (Oxford: Oxford University Press, 1968).

50 Investigated in detail in J.B. Bell, *The imperial origins of the King's church in early America, 1607–1783* (Basingstoke: Palgrave Macmillan, 2004), pp. 10–73. See also G. Yeo, 'A case without parallel: the bishops of London and the Anglican Church overseas, 1660–1748', *JEH*, 44 (1993), 450–75, and H.E. Kimball, 'The Anglican Church in British North America: ecclesiastical government before 1688', in S.C. McCulloch (ed.), *British humanitarianism: essays honouring Frank J. Klingberg* (Philadelphia: Church Historical Society, 1950), pp. 216–30, and J.H. Bennett, 'English bishops and imperial jurisdiction, 1660–1725', *HMPEC*, 32 (1963), 175–88.

51 For biographies of Blair and Bray, see *ODNB*.

52 J. Nelson, *A blessed company. Parishes, parsons and parishioners in Anglican Virginia, 1690–1776* (Chapel Hill, NC: University of North Carolina Press, 2004).

53 C. Dickon, *The College of William and Mary* (Mount Pleasant, SC, 2007).

54 Thomas Bray, *A memorial representing the present state of religion, on the continent of North America* (1701), p. 5.

55 *Ibid.*, p. 9.

56 See H. Thompson, *Thomas Bray* (SPCK, 1954), pp. 72–81.

57 Gilbert Burnet, *Of the propagation of the gospel in foreign parts. A sermon preach'd at St. Mary-le-Bow, Feb. 18. 1703/4. before the society incorporated for that purpose. Exhorting all persons in their stations, to assist so glorious a design* (1704), p. 24.

58 Carpenter, *Tenison*, pp. 352–3.

59 Richard Willis, *A sermon preach'd before the Society for the Propagation of the Gospel in Foreign Parts, at their first yearly meeting on Friday February the 20th 1701/2 at St. Mary-le-Bow* (1702), p. 21.

60 White Kennett, *The lets and impediments in planting and propagating the Gospel. A sermon preach'd before the Society for the Propagation of the Gospel in Foreign Parts, at their anniversary meeting, in the parish church of St Mary-le-Bow, 15 February 1711/12* (1712).

61 *Ibid.*, pp. 24–5.

62 See J. Gregory, 'Gender and the clerical profession in England, 1660–1850', *SCH*, 34 (1998), 251–3.

63 Kennett, *Lets and impediments*, p. 10.

64 Willis, *A sermon preach'd*, p. 17.

65 Charles Trimnel, *A sermon preached before the Society for Propagation of the Gospel in Foreign Parts, at the parish-church of St. Mary-le-Bow, on Friday the 17th of February, 1709/10* (1710).

66 E. Hinderaker, 'The "four Indian kings" and the imaginative construction of the first British Empire', *WMQ*, 53 (1996), 487–526.

67 Carpenter, *Tenison*, pp. 346–7.

68 William Fleetwood, *A sermon preached before the Society for the Propagation of the Gospel in Foreign Parts, at the parish church of St. Mary-le-Bow, on Friday the 16th of February, 1710/11* (1711), pp. 15–23. On Codrington's bequest, see S. Mandelbrote, 'The vision of Christopher Codrington', in S.J.D. Green and P. Horden (eds), *All Souls under the ancien regime. Politics, learning and the arts, c.1600–1850* (Oxford: Oxford University Press, 2007), pp. 132–74. For some of the issues raised in the subsequent decades by the church's ownership of slaves, see J.H. Bennett Jr, *Bondsmen and bishops: slavery and apprenticeship in the Codrington plantations of Barbados* (Berkeley: University of California Press, 1958).

69 H.W. Foote, *Annals of the King's Chapel. From the Puritan age of New England to the present day*, 2 vols (Boston, 1882), I, 41–89.

70 [John Dunton], *The life and errors of John Dunton late citizen of London; written by himself in solitude* (1705), p. 152.

71 Bodl. MS Tanner 30, f. 257: Randolph to Sancroft, 7 July 1688.

72 P. Haffenden, *New England in the English nation, 1689–1713* (Oxford: Oxford University Press, 1974).

73 Foote, *King's Chapel*, p. 116. The Library is now housed at the Boston Athenaeum.

74 Increase Mather, *A brief discourse concerning the unlawfulness of the Common Prayer worship* (Boston, 1686), pp. 2–8, 12, 14, 17, 19–20, 21.

75 Increase Mather, *A testimony against several prophane and superstitious new customs now practised by some in New England* (1687), sig. A2.

76 W.S. Perry III *Historical collections of the American colonial church* (Massachusetts, 1873), p. 72: Lewis Morris to Archdeacon Beveridge, 27 July 1702.

77 See George Keith, *A journal of travels from New Hampshire to Caratuck* (1706).

78 N. Fiering, 'The first American Enlightenment: Tillotson, Leverett, and philosophical enlightenment', *NEQ*, 54 (1981), 307–44, at p. 309, and J. Corrigan, *The prism of piety: Catholick Congregational clergy at the beginning of the Enlightenment* (New York: Oxford University Press, 1991). See also, B. Tucker, 'The reinvention of New England, 1691–1770', *NEQ*, 63 (1985), 315–40, and M.P. Winship, *Seers of God: Puritan providentialism in the Restoration and early Enlightenment* (Baltimore, MD: Johns Hopkins University Press, 1996).

79 M.H. Thomas (ed.), *The diary of Samuel Sewall, 1674–1729*, 2 vols (New York: Farrar, Straus and Giroux, 1973), I, 406 (4 Jan. 1699); II, 779 (25 Dec. 1714).

80 *Ibid.*, I, p. 385 (25 Dec. 1697).

81 Haffenden, 'Anglican Church in Restoration policy', p. 181.

82 *Ibid.* Sir Leoline Jenkins, secretary of state, bequeathed money for two fellowships at Jesus College, Oxford and the holders were to be ordained and serve either in the plantations or at sea. Nothing seems to have come of this plan.

83 E.B. Bronner, *William Penn's holy experiment: the founding of Pennsylvania, 1681–1701* (New York: Columbia University Press, 1962).

84 Butler, *Awash in a sea of faith*, p. 113.

85 *Ibid.*, p. 99.

86 Robert Beverley, *The history and present state of Virginia* (1705), pp. 226–30.

87 H. Trevor-Roper, *Archbishop Laud, 1573–1645*, 2nd edn (Macmillan, 1962), pp. 258–62.

88 R.G., *Virginia's cure*, p. 22; E.S. Baldwin, 'American jurisdiction of the bishop of London in colonial times', *American Antiquarian Society, Proceedings*, n.s., 12 (1899–1900), 201.

89 Baldwin, 'American jurisdiction', p. 202.

90 Haffenden, 'Anglican Church in Restoration policy', p. 177.

91 *Ibid.*, p. 182.

92 M.F. Goodwin, 'The Reverend Alexander Moray [Murray], MA, DD, the first bishop-designate of Virginia, 1672–3', *HMPEC*, 12 (1943), 59–68. See also, W. Gibson, 'A bishop for Virginia in 1672: a fragment from Bishop Ward's papers', *Archives*, 120 (2009), 36–41. For an overview of attempts to have a bishop in the colonies, see F.L. Hawks, 'Efforts to obtain the episcopate before the Revolution', *Protestant Episcopal Society Collections* (New York, 1851), I, 136–57.

93 Quoted in H.W. Foote, *Annals of the King's Chapel. From the Puritan age of New England to the present day*, 2 vols (1896), II, 229–30.

94 Quoted in Carpenter, *Thomas Tenison*, p. 351.

95 *Ibid.*

96 *Ibid.*, p. 352. Hyde, as Lord Cornbury, had been a controversial figure in New York and New Jersey politics, and was accused of transvestism by his political opponents. P. Bonomi, *The Lord Cornbury scandal: the politics of reputation in British America* (Chapel Hill, NC: University of North Carolina Press, 1998), p. 161 quotes a contemporary charge that he cross-dressed 'on all the great Holy Days and even in an hour or two after going to the Communion'.

97 For fear of inflaming the political scene in the colonies, see S. Taylor, 'Whigs, bishops and America: the politics of church reform in mid-eighteenth-century England', *HJ*, 36 (1993), 331–56. See also P.M. Doll, *Revolution, religion and national identity: imperial Anglicanism in British North America, 1745–1795* (Madison, NJ: Farleigh Dickinson University Press, 2000).

98 Carpenter, *Thomas Tenison*, p. 350.

99 For example, Archbishop Secker left money to the fund in 1768: LPL, Secker Papers 7, fols 367–73.

Chapter 7

The Church of England and the churches of Europe, 1660–1714

Tony Claydon

S tandard histories of the Anglican Church between 1660 and 1714 combine the story of its relations with dissenting rivals and its record of defence against Catholicism with accounts of internal tensions between church 'parties'. These narratives cover the important ecclesiastical developments of the period, but they concentrate on events within a narrow English frame-work. This chapter will consider a wider European context: it will retell the story of Anglicanism in terms of debates about its place in a spectrum of foreign churches. When recast in this way, the tale allows us to extend Anthony Milton's brilliant analysis of the pre-Civil War clergy, and it may get us closer to the true concerns of people in the late Stuart age.[1]

Every major issue faced by clerics in the half century after Charles II's return had an important Continental aspect. Most obviously, the Catholic threat to the church was seen as part of an aggressive Counter-Reformation which appeared to be advancing across Europe. Over the seventeenth century as a whole, the Protestant portion of Europe's population dropped from about a half to about a quarter, and the decades after 1660 were key. In these years, the Huguenots of France found their liberties undermined, a process which culminated in the 1685 outlawing of French Protestantism with the revocation of the Edict of Nantes. Meanwhile, Louis XIV's state expanded along its eastern border and began to suppress the Reformed faith in such captured territo-ries as Orange and Strasbourg. In 1672, French forces occupied much of the Protestant Netherlands; whilst from 1689 to 1697 and again from 1702 from 1713, Louis fought long wars against the English, Dutch, and Germans which many feared would destroy the European Reformation. In these struggles, Protestants were so badly outnumbered that they were forced to ally with the Habsburgs of Spain and Austria, but (as the English sometime commented) these dynasties themselves had not always been kind to the Reformed cause.[2] Meanwhile Louis encouraged anti-Protestant policies in Savoy, and a series of

173

German princely dynasties converted to the Catholic faith. It was this pattern which ensured that Anglicans could not see calls for toleration by Charles II and James II as generous extensions of a private liberty. For Churchmen were vividly conscious of what was happening across the Channel. Foreign affairs were widely reported in a press which was deeply interested in Europe, and which was remarkably free during the exclusion-era lapse of censorship and after pre-publication control of the press ceased in 1695. The fate of foreign Protestantism was also obvious from the streams of French and German refugees who arrived in London throughout the period. Being so aware of what was happening abroad, Anglicans came to the darkest conclusions about Stuart toleration. For them, indulgence of Catholicism must be a first step to bringing the country back to the pope and to snuffing out Protestants' rights to worship. This led most clerics to be critical of the court before 1688, and the majority to be staunch opponents of James's cause once he was exiled at the Revolution.[3]

At the same time, the church's disputes with dissent had foreign contexts. Taking up the arguments of their Puritan forebears, nonconformists argued that the establishment failed to match the pattern of the best Reformed churches abroad. Calls for less ceremony, and objections to government by bishops, were encouraged by comparisons with Protestant churches in France, the Netherlands, Switzerland, and the Rhineland which had moved much further from the patterns of medieval Catholicism than had the English. Similarly, dissenting calls for greater understanding were made with reference to what was happening on the Continent. With France and Savoy persecuting their Protestants, it was easy to accuse Anglicans of matching that cruelty as they disciplined Englishmen who departed from their rules.[4] Europe also provided models of a more forgiving relationship between official churches and religious minorities. For example, in the United Provinces of the Nether-lands, a dominant Calvinist communion extended degrees of liberty to other kinds of Protestant (and even to Catholics and Jews) and was held up as an example of the spiritual, political, and economic benefits that such flexibility might bring. This happened particularly in the 1660s and 1670s, when Dutch military prowess humiliated England, and in the 1690s, when William of Orange's control of England encouraged direct comparisons between the two countries.[5] Certain German cities, and parts of eastern Europe, also showed how different kinds of Christian might live peacefully together. After the exhausting religious battles of the Thirty Years' War (1618–48), great swathes of the Continent sought ways to minimise religious tensions. Finally, the need for Europe to unite against Louis produced a diverse wartime alliance of Catholics, Lutherans, and Calvinists for fourteen years after 1689. This also questioned whether common causes might not override disagreements of faith. Again, the press (including the emerging genre of travel guides) spread knowledge of conditions beyond England and provided plenty of foreign instances for use in domestic debate.[6]

But it was not only the church's disputes with others which were fuelled by evidence from abroad. So were her internal battles. As we shall see, clerics of different stripes saw affinities with different foreign communions. Whilst initially agreeing that dissenters were wrong to depart from the national church, they used different arguments to show this, and these arguments suggested rather different things about who were the true Christians overseas. As these contradictions became clearer, Anglicans fell out about exactly why they were policing nonconformity. In time, debates led to dispute about whether this was a good idea. As we shall come to argue, therefore, Europe played an important role in the rupture of the church into competing 'High' and 'Low' parties. This was the division which would structure ecclesiastical politics in the post-revolutionary world.

All this demonstrates why Europe mattered to Churchmen. Yet to understand the Continental dimension fully, we have to make a modest detour. We need to consider Anglicans' thinking about their own legitimacy, since this fundamentally affected their sense of their place in the range of European Christianity. The church had long had a problem with its legitimacy. From the time of its Tudor foundation, the establishment's Roman Catholic rivals had asked how it could claim to be a true church. It had, they suggested, defied papal authority, and was based on nothing but royal whim and parliamentary diktat.[7] English clerics had formulated answers to these charges – but their weakness had been to devise too many. Essentially, writers had come up with three broad legitimations, and advanced them in parallel. They did this despite the differences between their apologias, especially when it came to identifying the true church beyond England's shores.

The first and most direct apology for Anglicanism was Erastian. Far from flinching when accused of being a royal or parliamentary church, many English clerics embraced the role of lay authority. They argued that Christ had given power over all earthly affairs to secular rulers, and that this included ecclesiastical structures, staffing, and forms of worship. Put this bluntly, the view did not sound particularly spiritual. Yet it could be presented as a vital part of Christ's message of peace. Errors over minor issues such as the exact form of church government, or about precise ceremony, were never going to endanger people's souls, but disputes over these things could disrupt Christian communities. Given this, it was more important to suppress division than to try to fathom God's will in trivial areas – and lay authority, charged with ensuring peace in temporal affairs, should impose the necessary uniformity. Consequently, it was entirely right that the English state had shaped a monopolistic church. In late Stuart times, this line of argument might weaken in the face of the 'non-Anglican' rulers such as James II and William III, but it would survive in sporadic enthusiasm for the royal supremacy (not least under Anne), and more explicitly in arguments for dissenters to obey the legally established communion, such as that put stridently by Edward Stillingfleet in his 1680 sermon *The mischief of separation.*[8]

The second defence of Anglicanism was episcopal. Building on scholarship that suggested bishops were an original feature of Christianity, many clerics came to feel this form of government was the only valid structure for a church, and also that bishops represented an unbroken link to Christ. Many argued that Jesus had given his apostles an episcopal authority which they had then transferred to their successors. Developing a case for peace similar to that used by Erastians, this polemic also stressed that episcopal rule must be absolute if it were to bring order. A bishop should not be challenged in his diocese, either by the people worshipping there or by anyone outside – and this included the bishops of other dioceses. Taken together, this case provided a defence of the Church of England. The establishment had had a right to defy the pope (the bishop of Rome's claim to supremacy over other dioceses was illegitimate interference in their affairs); and its bishops – who had unbroken succession from Christ through the medieval episcopacy – had had every right to reform worship. In the late Stuart period, this set of ideas was prominent in Anglican insistence that all clergy must be ordained by bishops as the living embodiments of Christ's mission, and in the writings of particular episcopal enthusiasts such as Herbert Thorndike in the 1660s, Henry Dodwell and William Sherlock in the exclusion era, or Charles Leslie under Queen Anne.[9]

The final apologia for the establishment was Protestant. In this vision, the Church of England was legitimate because it had participated in the great renewal of the sixteenth century. After the Middle Ages, in which the church had been subjected to an anti-Christian papal power and had been corrupted into false doctrine by the greed of its clerics, the English establishment had heroically regained its original purity. It might not have purged all of its medieval heritage, but it had removed the harmful parts of this legacy, and so could claim to have played a full part in the European Reformation. Following Martin Luther, it had replaced lavish ceremony and superstition with a simple, scripture-based worship; it had rejected the pope's supremacy and the invented theology of the Roman Church; and it had restricted clerical power to its proper functions of pastoral guidance. This had all brought it close to the patterns of the very first Christians, and this legitimated its current structures. In the late Stuart period, this strand of thought was manifested in the continuing anti-popery of Anglicanism (including its post-1689 cheerleading for wars against Louis XIV); in continued pride in the church's inheritance from Tudor reformers (especially the prayer-book, still heavily based on Cranmer's liturgy and scriptural translations); and in the debts to the first generation of European Protestants, acknowledged in such works as Gilbert

Burnet's monumental *History of the Reformation* (1679–81), or his stirring preface to his *Discourse of the pastoral care* (1692).[10]

This rapid dash through Anglican apologetic will have puzzled some. There were obvious differences of emphasis – even downright contradictions – between the strands of thought, and one might wonder how one institution could have sponsored them all. A partial explanation is that the legitimations were rarely spelt out with full logic. Instead, they remained broad modes of discussion, tendencies of thought with very vague edges, to be drawn upon promiscuously according to the rhetorical demands of the moment. Many clerics felt the pull of all three justifications of their status, and could express each at different times. This gave Anglicans some polemic flexibility. For example, they could stress the doctrinal purity of Protestantism to counter Catholics, and then insist on the Erastian commands of the English state when enforcing the Act of Uniformity. Yet, however rarely most Churchmen were conscious of the problem, there were damaging divergences between their strands of discourse. This was especially true in the pressing issue of where the establishment should sit in the range of European churches – those churches which, as we have shown, were busy challenging, persecuting, and accommodating one another in the later seventeenth century, and whose features, plights, and behaviour were drawn upon in domestic English debate. The diversity of Anglican thought meant that the church was unable to give a clear answer to a question vital to its political stance: what did it think was the true church beyond England?

A moment's reflection will reveal the problem. If the Church of England was justified by Erastianism, then the church elsewhere was the communion endorsed by the local ruler. But that varied from place to place. Could the rigid Calvinism of Geneva really be the true church there just because the city magistrates said it was, whilst only a few miles away, in Louis XIV's territories, the true church was that royal brand of Catholicism which cheered the king's campaigns against Protestant Europe? Of course there was the alternative that Anglicanism was justified on episcopal grounds. This would mean that a foreign church governed by bishops was the true one in its locality. However, this usually comforted Catholics rather than Protestants, given that many Reformed Christians on the Continent had abolished episcopacy. It also cut straight across Erastian arguments in places like Switzerland or the Netherlands where the state had supported the removal of bishops. The third option, the Protestant identity of the English church, had similar internal difficulties, and again clashed with other visions. In many parts of Europe, Calvinist and Lutheran Protestants were rivals. A Protestant understanding of Anglicanism helped little in deciding which were the true Christians here, since the Church of England was so different from both rival groups. A conception of the Reformation broad enough to bracket the English with either the Lutherans or the Calvinists tended to include the other faction as well. Worse, the Protestant conception of the English church contradicted its other apologia. In the Netherlands, for example, Erastianism would identify the Calvinist Church as Christ's true communion. But episcopacy would plump for the Dutch followers of the pope, whilst a broad Protestant sympathy might give the local Lutherans substantial claims.

Since all three legitimations of the Church of England remained current in the late Stuart period and, since their logic created incoherent havoc in Anglicans' understanding of their place in the wider world, it is tempting to draw a veil over the complexity. It would be a relief just to remark that Churchmen were muddled about the foreign faithful, and that it was fortunate they rarely thought through their arguments. Yet we cannot simply ignore the international dimension of religious politics. As we shall see, many ecclesiastical disputes after 1660 brought out exactly the difficulties we have surveyed. Indeed, many debates were essentially about the identity of the true church abroad. Mercifully, though, there was a pattern of change which allows us to tell a relatively clear story. One kind of Anglican identity gained ground at the expense of the others, and the tensions this created drove the key disputes about England and European Christianity.

In the years after Charles II's restoration, the episcopal understanding of the English church advanced markedly. Partly this resulted from the kind of cleric who led ecclesiastical re-establishment in 1660. Although some historians have quibbled at the label, many would agree that the most influential positions in the restored church were taken by 'Laudians'.[11] Men who had supported Archbishop William Laud in the 1630s certainly figured prominently in the pro-Anglican press: especially in the person of Peter Heylin. As any student of the early Stuart period knows, 'Laudians' championed bishops' power as much as they promoted greater ceremony, and their influence in the later seventeenth century ensured a firm clerical insistence on episcopacy as a mark of a true church.[12] Quite apart from any 'Laudian' predominance, the experience of the 1640s and 1650s pushed Anglicans towards an episcopal identity. Erastianism had let the church down once Charles I's state was replaced by that of the regicides. Under Cromwell the lay ruler had proscribed rather than decreeing Anglican worship. Protestant identity, meanwhile, had been soured by the arguments that the rebels of the Civil War had used against the church. Calling for reform, parliamentary forces had denounced features of the old establishment such as episcopacy and liturgical worship as remnants of corrupt popery, and had demanded that the church adhere more closely to the purest Protestant models abroad. Seeing two of their traditional identities turning against them, supporters of the old-style establishment became more attracted to their remaining argument. In the 1640s and 1650s, episcopacy had proved the church's most secure rhetoric.

This polemical shift changed the perceived place of the English church in the spectrum of European faiths. Anthony Milton has explored how pre-war 'Laudians' softened the old hostility to Rome. They had denied that the pope was the Antichrist and had suggested that Catholicism was more of an error than a soul-destroying heresy. Laud's allies also distanced themselves from Protestant churches abroad – particularly questioning if there they could have true communions without bishops. The greater stress on episcopacy after 1660 continued these tendencies. If bishops were essential to Anglicanism, and to any true church, apologists might come to look more kindly on Roman establishments (which had retained an ecclesiastical hierarchy), but would view non-episcopal Protestant churches (such as those in Switzerland, the Netherlands, France, and the Rhineland) much more harshly. They might even look askance at Protestants who had bishop-like offices in their churches but could not boast a continuous line of succession from the apostles. This was the case with the north German and Scandinavian Lutherans, who had refounded at least quasi-episcopal office after a break, and so had had to use ordinary clerics to ordain their first bishops.

In the late Stuart era, such trends were increasingly apparent. As John Spurr has shown, the steady rehabilitation of Rome continued after 1660.[13] Fewer and fewer clerics took the time to prove it was formally anti-Christian, more and more viewed its doctrines as mistaken rather than sinful. At the same time, affinity with European Protestant churches weakened. Some writers, such as Heylyn, denounced them stridently. In an extraordinary series of works published soon after the Restoration, he blamed the Civil War on a Puritan poison which had flowed into England from Geneva via the Netherlands, and France.[14] Elsewhere the validity of overseas ministry was increasingly questioned. A vivid example came in 1662, with consequences for the whole late Stuart period. In that year, the Act of Uniformity stated that any minister of a foreign non-episcopal church had to be ordained by an English bishop before he could take a pastoral role in England. This denied the authenticity of the original Continental ordination of these people, and so went further than the early Stuart church in rejecting of the truth of the churches themselves. This had not happened even under Laud. Before the Civil War, a minister who had been ordained without a bishop in France or the Netherlands would have been accepted as a Church of England cleric on arrival without a second, episcopal ordination.

It is worth pausing here to stress that the triumph of episcopacy was not absolute. Some Anglicans actively opposed it, and many others retained their traditional muddle of identities, as they felt the pull of episcopal argument. For instance, even as the church cast doubt on the validity of European Protestantism, it led protests against attacks on that movement. This was to be the meat of its fast-day sermons during William and Anne's Continental wars.[15]

The church also made huge efforts to comfort Reformed Christians who fled Catholic intolerance or conquest. It was active in raising funds for the displaced Huguenots in the 1680s, and for the persecuted Waldensians of the Alpine valleys in the 1690s.[16] Similarly, Erastian and Protestant arguments were still used alongside episcopacy in the old blunderbuss fashion – even to support the episcopal principle. So, nonconformists were told to obey the local Anglican bishop because he was the successor of Christ, but also because parliament ordered this, and because the English church was so admired by all the Protestants of Europe. The continued attachment to a Reformation identity was also seen in efforts to soften any erosion of brotherhood with the Reformed abroad caused by stronger attachment to episcopacy. For instance, many Anglicans explained that some foreign churches had lost their bishops through no fault of their own. There was a world of difference, a man such as Gilbert Burnet would say, between a wilful and sustained abolition of the episcopal office, and the situation in those Continental communions which had had to rebel against popish bishops at the Reformation and had subsequently been unable to restore a clerical hierarchy in conditions of dislocation or persecution.[17] Similarly, some writers tried to contain the logic of their discourse within the British Isles. They said they were only insisting on episcopacy in the Stuart realms, claiming too little knowledge of elsewhere to know if their arguments travelled. In the case of the polemicist Robert Conold, this led to the disarming admission that his prose was unlikely to be read in Holland or Switzerland, and so wouldn't cause offence overseas.[18] Despite all this, however, there was a palpable swing in understanding of the European position of the church between 1660 and 1714. If it had not abandoned its old Reformed identity, it had assumed a place more equidistant from Catholic and Protestant churches. For Anglicans there was still much wrong with Rome, but it was becoming less clear that the errors of popery were worse than those of foreign Protestants.

The first consequence of this shift was to sharpen, and perhaps to define, the tension between the church and nonconformity. Of course this schism can be explained in domestic terms. English Puritans objected to the ceremonies reimposed in 1662, and could not consent to a settlement which questioned their ministerial work in the 1640s and 1650s. Conformists, meanwhile, were driven to intolerance because they thought that indulgence of religious foibles had caused the Civil War. Yet, examining the rhetorical battle between church and dissent, and the cases of real individuals caught in the crossfire, it is clear that the dispute was a clash of European identities.

Let us take one rather sad example. In 1660 the Somerset Presbyterian John Humfrey briefly rejoined the church, accepting episcopal ordination from his local bishop. In a published explanation, he said that he had done this because he did not want to cause needless rents in English Protestantism, and because his new institution as a minister was really just confirmation of his old status by incoming ecclesiastical governors. Soon, however, he was driven to reverse his decision by a barrage of Puritan objection.[19] Pamphlet attacks repeated standard Presbyterian objections to bishops, but also stressed that a church which insisted on episcopal ordination had cut itself off from foreign Protestants. The doctrine was a scandal to the Reformed Christians abroad, they said; it cast reflections on and subverted their churches; it was a step to Rome; it might even provoke foreign Protestant princes to take action against England.[20] As Humfrey himself claimed as he announced his change of mind, high notions of episcopacy had blackened the reputation of the English in Europe and cut them off from the Reformed churches there. It had also disrupted what Humfrey had admired as the easy flow of ministers across the Channel. People from France, the Netherlands, or Germany would not join a church which denied their own communion was valid because it lacked bishops.[21] Thus Humfrey's charitable accommodation with the established church was destroyed, but the Anglicans' pinched view of his European brethren had been the issue.

The fault line revealed in the Humfrey story remained central to the dissenting schism in the next half century. In fact, nonconformists went out of their way to stress the divide, because it provided them with a powerful rhetorical weapon. When popery was rampaging across Europe, it was tempting to align Anglican enemies with this terrifying force. So dissenters charged established clerics with recognising Catholicism as the true church in most of the Continent, because that was where their support for bishops (and indeed their Erastianism) led them. Richard Baxter, the nonconformists' chief propagandist, was particularly adept at the trick. During the exclusion crisis he lambasted Stillingfleet's argument for state churches because it legitimated popery in France, Italy, and Spain – but he was even more vigorous against Dodwell and Sherlock's episcopalianism.[22] This, he said, meant that those who lived under popish bishops in Mediterranean lands must submit to their commands, whilst the Reformed Christians of Germany, the Netherlands, and Switzerland had no valid churches.[23] Most damagingly, perhaps, Baxter and others pointed to the case of France. Which, they challenged their Anglican rivals, was the true church there? Given that Churchmen themselves refused to respond to a question which would reveal their ideological muddle, the dissenting writers answered for their enemies. There was, they said, a choice. Anglicans could remain true to their Protestant roots and identify the Huguenots as God's faithful. But the Huguenots objected to the French state church because of its bishops, doctrine, and ceremony. As these were broadly the grounds on which English dissenters rejected England's establishment, Anglicans who supported the Huguenots should not be condemning domestic nonconformity. On the other hand, England's church could follow their episcopal arguments and recognise France's Catholics as their brethren. This, however, tore off the mask. As dissenters had long hinted, the established church was in league with popery. Its prosecution of Protestants at home simply mirrored the cruelty of its allies abroad.[24]

Nonconformist attacks demonstrate the power of the European dimension in disputes between denominations. This style of polemic lasted well beyond the Revolution of 1689 and Baxter's death in 1691. For example, fear that the official church had drifted towards Rome fired much of Daniel Defoe's political writing under Queen Anne, and it was a standard part of the Whig party's case when it defended dissent in the last Stuart decades.[25] However, this rhetoric also had a profound impact within the Anglican Church itself. As the episcopal version of the establishment's identity grew in strength, and as dissenters pointed out the consequences of this, some Churchmen grew uneasy and began to protest about what was happening. The traditional balancing of discourses became harder, the more nonconformist critique forced clerics to think about the true church abroad. In response, some began to transform one of the old languages. This proved so controversial that it ultimately fed – perhaps even created – the fully formed battles between 'High' and 'Low' Church parties which marked the period after 1689.

The transformed polemic was the church's Protestantism, including its declared fraternity with Reformed Christians abroad. Under the Tudors and early Stuarts, this conception of the national establishment had been used to prove its credentials. The official communion was legally the only one in England, and this was justified because it was a Reformed church conforming to both ancient Christian truths and the best models abroad. In the immediate aftermath of 1660, Protestant identity continued to act this way, except that the battle with nonconformity gave it a sharper edge. This led to a neglected irony. Anglicans deployed Protestantism, and their solidarity with foreign Protestant people, against domestic Protestant enemies. The phenomenon emerged as early as 1660. Then, a group of newly restored bishops replied to Baxter that compromise with his brand of religion was impossible because European Protestants admired the traditional forms of the Anglican Church. Faithful folk abroad had praised the English establishment through the decades, and they would be horrified at any changes to suit discontented Puritans.[26] Such rhetoric was given canonical form in 1662 in Jean Durel's *View of government and publick worship of God*. Often quoted or plagiarised in the years to 1714, this work claimed that the leading thinkers of the Reformed Continent had always approved of the English church, and then convened a sort of fantasy ecclesiastical council in which such luminaries as Luther, Calvin, Zwingli, Melancthon, and Bucer were quoted defending features of the English establishment to which nonconformists were objecting.[27] In the light of these comments, Durel claimed, England's dissenters would receive cold comfort if they fled abroad.

Far from finding churches more purely Protestant overseas, and so more to their liking, they would in fact discover that they were 'a sect by themselves'.[28]

This style of argument survived into the later Stuart decades – for example, we will see it used in the 'comprehension' debates of 1689, and it was deployed by Francis Atterbury when condemning what he thought were heresies emerging amongst a pro-dissenting wing of the church in the late 1690s.[29] Yet concern that the church was turning its back on Protestant brethren abroad, and that its increasingly episcopal style of argument might confirm allegations of popery, appears to have stimulated a new style of discourse around 1680. During the exclusion crisis, some began to suggest that there was a different way to read foreign Reformed approval of Anglicanism. Instead of simply citing it as proof of the establishment's legitimacy, clerics such as Samuel Bolde and Daniel Whitby stressed that people who differed from Anglican practice could nevertheless recognise the soundness of the English communion. They also pointed out that English acceptance of their praise suggested that Anglicans themselves did not insist on absolute conformity to their models in all faithful Christians. This all implied that the European Reformation was a flexible entity, which could stomach variety within its ranks. Crucially, this meant that the Church of England should tolerate English Protestant dissenters. If Anglicans were happy to accept plaudits from non-episcopal Protestants in Holland, France, or Switzerland – the argument went – they should be happy to live alongside such people in England. Thus Bolde echoed Baxter in decrying the high English Episcopalianism which unchurched men such as the France's Huguenots, and suggested that sympathy for Protestants overseas should extend to the English dissenters.[30] Similarly, Whitby complained about the growing alienation between many Anglicans and the Reformed churches abroad. He then cited examples of different brands of Protestants burying their differences in many parts of Europe in order to defend themselves against Catholicism, and recommended this as the correct path for English Churchmen and nonconformists.[31] A tolerationist strand of Anglican thought was therefore born out of thinking about the international Reformation. The entity was reconceived as a complex mesh of mutually sympathetic communions, rather than as an alliance of national churches, each enjoying a monopoly within their territories.

Bolde and Whitby's position was pioneering, and proved highly controversial in the early 1680s. Both men were ridiculed by the Tory press, and hauled before their bishops' courts for punishment. Soon, however, their radical reimagining of England's place in the European Reformation became far more mainstream. Circumstances soon showed the attractiveness of conceiving Anglicanism not as the sole and rightful representative of Protestantism in the Stuart lands but, rather, as part of a complex international movement with overlapping strands which had to be tolerant within each particular nation.

Once James II was on the throne, and was trying to emancipate the Roman Church, Anglicans began to look for whatever allies they could find, and this included their erstwhile enemies the dissenters. The need to win over nonconformists was particularly pressing, since the king was himself trying to woo them with promises of religious indulgence and political support. At the same time, Churchmen came to realise that their best hope of relief came from William III, prince of Orange – a man who was both the leader of the Netherlands and husband of James's heir, Princess Mary. Since William belonged to the Dutch Reformed Church (Presbyterian, unceremonial, and rigidly Calvinist), and since he was cool towards the official brand of English Protestantism, Anglicans were keen to play down hostility to the more thoroughgoing versions of Reformed Christianity. Moreover, William was building a very wide alliance against Louis XIV (he had been convinced that the French monarch was a threat to all other European nations since the invasion of the Netherlands in 1672). As this alliance came to include various brands of both Lutherans and Calvinists, William was becoming a symbol of broad Protestant unity, and this provided another reason for liberal thinking as Churchmen looked towards him for deliverance – and once he became their king in 1689.

All of this provided fertile ground for Bolde and Whitby's vision of international Protestantism. It was used widely in the propaganda William directed at England to build support and to urge unity between English Protestants in the anti-French cause, but it also gained wide currency among English clerics themselves. Particularly over the winter of 1688–89, Churchmen argued for united support for the invading Dutch from both Anglicans and dissenters by appealing to a broad European Protestantism.[32] The preceding summer, this international vision had been prominent in the closest the church came to an official olive branch to nonconformity. In July the archbishop of Canterbury, William Sancroft, was opposing James's Declaration of Indulgence because he feared it was a ruse to help the conversion of England to Catholicism. Keen to avoid alienating dissenters, however, he sent instructions to the clergy to treat their rivals kindly and to explain that the church wanted a real religious settlement which would avoid the popish dangers of the king's initiative. Sketching the thinking behind this accommodation, Sancroft stressed the international dimension. He portrayed the whole Continental Reformation in danger and in need of 'godly love' between its parts, whilst asking his colleagues to join other denominations in 'an Universal Blessed Union of all Reformed Churches, both at Home and Abroad, against the Common Enemy'.[33] There was a subtle but significant shift here. By talking of Reformed churches in the plural and numbering some of these at home, Sancroft was tacitly acknowledging that there was more than one valid communion in England. Yet the vision which allowed this was European. The Reformation was a great alliance of different, and sometimes overlapping, churches across the Continent.

Sancroft's initiative yielded few long-term results. It may have helped to secure English Protestant unity during the 1688–89 Revolution, but many Churchmen rapidly became wary of any deeper reconciliation with dissent. In a process which saw the emergence of well-delineated church parties, some Anglicans ('Low' Churchmen) pressed on for a generous settlement with dissenters, whilst others (the 'High' church party) recoiled. High Churchmen began to fear that their institution was being fatally weakened under William and thought that any further concession to nonconformity would compound these reverses. The High Church was disgusted that the new Presbyterian king had gone beyond his initial promise merely to destroy James's Catholic advisers and took the throne itself. The party was also wary of the Toleration Act secured by William's pressure in 1689. Again, it was fearful of royal calls for an end to the Test Acts, horrified by William's acceptance of a Presbyterian settlement in Scotland, and disappointed at his removal of clergy who would not swear allegiance to his new regime. With this shift back to intransigence by some clerics, outright party battle could begin. By the autumn of 1689, organised groups were campaigning against each other in the press, and in elections to a convocation to meet in the winter. One side – the Low Churchmen – advocated a scheme of 'comprehension', urging compromise on points of liturgy and episcopal ordination to bring moderate dissenters back into the church.[34] Their rivals – the High Churchmen – opposed, saying that nonconformists deserved no consideration. All this is well known, but we need to concentrate in the large part played by Europe in this polarisation.

Low Church polemicists stressed their new vision of an international Reformation. As they argued for comprehension, Low Churchmen reversed Jean Durel's old sense of what foreign Protestants wanted. In their rhetoric, Reformed Christians overseas no longer chorused their admiration for the established church or demanded that dissenters end their schism from it. Instead, they begged the English to lead the Continental cause against Catholicism and urged Anglicans to make concessions to nonconformity so that the leading Protestant nation could be united. So, Thomas Tenison's *Discourse concerning the ecclesiastical commission*, which can be seen as the manifesto of comprehension, said 'the Eyes of the World are upon us' and that 'all the *Reformed Churches* are in expectation of something to be done which may make for Peace and Union'.[35] Other pamphleteers had Continentals asking the church to show flexibility so that it could become 'the *Centre of Protestant Unity*', or 'the greatest bulwark of the Protestant Religion in *Europe*'; whilst Gilbert Burnet used the debate to launch a central theme of his late career.[36] In a preached intervention, he suggested that it was internal quarrel which had reversed the progress of the European Reformation in the seventeenth century. William's accession to the English throne offered a chance to roll back the forces of popery – but this opportunity would be wasted if Protestants went on bickering.[37]

Opposing comprehension, High Churchmen rejected this vision of the flexible international Reformation. Rather than presenting Anglicanism as merely one version of Protestantism, which should respect all the others, they insisted that the church was unique. Its forms, they claimed, were closer to true, primitive Christianity than its rivals, so it was monstrous to suggest that they should be changed. Curiously, some of this rhetoric revivified Jean Durel's polemic. Facing pro-comprehensionists who cited international Protestant opinion in favour of their scheme, their opponents went on insisting that most Reformed Christians abroad revered the Church of England in its exact current form.[38] This should again warn us against ideological tidiness in ecclesiastical discourse: the High Church could cherish a notion of the European Reformation when it suited. Some argument, however, pulled Anglicanism much closer to Episcopal churches abroad, even if these were not Protestant. Several pamphleteers insisted that Anglicans could not make the concessions that dissenters might want because they could not break with the norms of a universal church. This mystical body was far broader than the European Reformation. When William Beveridge opposed change by saying that the English establishment had 'the most illustrious Image and Resemblence to the Catholick [communion]', he of course meant a universal, rather than the specifically papal, church – but his choice of the word 'Catholic' implied that the Rome-led institution had strong claims to belong, even if it faults meant that it was not so perfect a member.[39] Henry Maurice opposed comprehension because the Church of England already had 'the common badge of Christianity' and conformed to 'the practice of the Universal Church', again implying something broader than simple Protestantism; whilst William Jane feared that alterations would take England too far from 'Apostolick Churches'.[40] This was easy to read as another alliance with international episcopacy: Churchmen had stressed that bishops were their proudest inheritance from the days of the apostles.

To an extent, therefore, the debate over comprehension was a debate over the new, flexible vision of the international Reformation. If this was England's correct European context, then efforts should be made to reach out to other Protestants – at home as much as abroad. If, however, England actually fitted into a different conception of the international church, comprehension was less pressing, or might even be harmful. Confirmation of the centrality of Europe came with the meeting of convocation in November 1689. This assembly, effectively a clerical parliament, had been called to consider proposals for comprehension. It never got to discuss these, however, as it fell into argument about its opening address to William. A Low Church group, dominating the upper house of bishops, originally wanted to thank the monarch for his zeal for 'the protestant religion in general, and the church of England in particular'. This, however, was unacceptable to the High Church majority in the lower house of the convocation, because it made the English establishment sound like a run-of-the-mill member of a wider and diverse Reformation. When they suggested that the address thank William only for protection of the English church, the Low Churchmen objected in turn. They protested that this would raise questions about England's commitment to the wider Protestant movement and 'would be liable to strange constructions both at home and abroad'. From here, various versions of the address were batted between the houses – debates turning on such minutiae as whether to set Anglicanism in the context of a Protestant 'religion' (which might be flexible in structure) or a series of Protestant 'churches' (which might be interpreted as monopolistic each in their own country) – but by the time a final version was settled, the king had lost patience and dissolved the assembly.[41] Such rhetorical slogging sounds absurd, but it does reveal a key dispute at the birth of church parties. While Low Churchmen insisted that Anglicanism was part of a diverse and international Protestant movement, High Churchmen resisted such logic.

This remained largely the pattern through to 1714. These post-Revolutionary years are often described as a series of battles between two church parties. In the late 1690s, for instance, High Churchmen campaigned for a recall of convocation (a body on which the king had given up after the debacle of 1689). They hoped that this would prevent further accommodation with dissent and stop a perceived drift to doctrinal laxness. The Low Church, by contrast, opposed any meeting of convocation because they feared it would lead to a witch hunt against them. In the next decade, the factions clashed over 'occasional conformity' and claims that the church was 'in danger' from external and internal enemies. While High Churchmen wanted legislation to ban occasional conformity (the practice by which dissenters qualified for public office by infrequent participation in Anglican communion) and worked for a parliamentary resolution declaring that the establishment was indeed in peril, Low Churchmen opposed these campaigns as uncharitable scaremongering. Soon, the parties were also dividing over the union with Scotland. The 'low' group supported the creation of a fully unified Britain, whilst their rivals were terrified that it would strengthen Presbyterian influence in England. In 1709 the groups split again over refugees from the German Palatinate. Low Churchmen welcomed these victims of Louis's war, whilst High Churchmen worried that more non-Anglicans were arriving in the country. By 1710, the factions were embroiled in the trail of Henry Sacheverell. As Low Churchmen supported the government's claim that Sacheverell had disparaged the Toleration Act (which they had come to see as an unofficial part of the English constitution) and had accused law-abiding dissenters of treason, the High Church defended the turbulent preacher. To add to all these ecclesiastical disputes, high and low factions tended to align on other issues with the Tory and Whig parties, respectively. This meant that most High Churchmen wanted an early end to the war with France after 1710 (even if this meant giving up the original war aim of ejecting Louis's relatives from the throne of Spain), and some were cool on the Hanoverian succession. Low Churchmen, meanwhile, supported Whig demands that war continue till France was crushed, and Whig insistence that the Protestant House of Hanover succeed when Queen Anne died. These arguments kept up constant struggle among clerics but, as this summary already hints, Continental issues played a huge part in the debates.

On each issue, Low Churchmen defended a diverse, flexible, and international Reformation which, they said, should ignore internal differences. It was therefore right to welcome closer relations with Protestant Scots, and right to accept Germans fleeing French aggression, even if neither group were Anglicans. Sympathy for English dissent – evident in all Low Church campaigns – was similarly expressed as part of a broad Protestant solidarity. So, Gilbert Burnet's speeches on occasional conformity stressed that banning this practice would alienate European Protestant churches because their members, like English nonconformists, sometimes took Anglican communion.[42] In the same vein, anti-Sacheverell pamphlets accused the preacher of failed charity to Protestants abroad. His hell-fire support for the English church seemed to send such men 'to the Devil' and would condemn not only local dissenters 'but almost all other Reform'd Churches, as the Dutch, North British, Swiss etc.'[43] Again, low clerics perceived strange European loyalties in the 'church in danger' agitation. The party that imagined the establishment was in peril seemed to think its best refuge was a closer understanding with the Catholic Church, rather than uniting with Reformed Christians overseas.[44] As for the war and the Hanoverian succession, most Low Churchmen used the political rhetorics centred on the 'balance of power' and English constitutionalism which dominated discussion of these issues, but defence of a broad Reformation also lay behind their attitudes. Securing a German Lutheran dynasty in London would of course prove the tolerant flexibility of the international Protestant movement, whilst advocates for continuing conflict with Louis (especially the duke of Marlborough's chaplain, Francis Hare) could still breathe a spirit of Protestant crusade, and imply that those who wanted an early peace wanted to surrender to Catholics.[45]

And High Churchmen did use language which gave grounds for suspicion. In advancing their causes, they demonstrated deep hostility to foreign Protestants, whom they often presented as infiltrating anti-Episcopalian principles into England. So, as we saw, Scots and Palatines were rejected as near-heretics, and when the establishment was undermined, the leading sappers were always thought to come from abroad. Thus the chief pamphlet in the 'church in danger' controversy, *The memorial of the Church of England*, thought emissaries from Geneva had been attacking the establishment for decades.[46] Similarly, Sacheverell accused Dutch and Huguenot agents of backing dissenting subversion; whilst leading agitators against occasional conformity acknowledged that they were breaking bonds of respect between Europe's Protestants, but said they did not care.[47] For these high-flyers, most of the Reformed churches abroad had no episcopacy, so were not entitled to sympathy.[48] Meanwhile, any willingness among High Churchmen to see the exiled Stuarts back after Anne's death implied a relaxed attitude to Catholicism, given that the family refused to renounce its Rome-looking faith (and indeed some men of this faction, such as Francis Atterbury, would eventually turn to Jacobite plotting); whilst calling for peace with France suggested détente with an active persecutor of foreign Protestants. It is true that one version of the peace argument seemed to be rooted in concern for the international Reformation. It suggested that France had been so weakened by the war that the main dangers to European Protestantism were now England's Habsburg allies, and that war must end soon so that they did not gain too much. However, this rhetoric was developed principally by Defoe. He was a writer of Low Church sympathies, but one paid by the Tory ministry after 1710 to develop arguments to sell to moderate opinion.[49]

Taking this pattern as a whole, we might wonder why the church did not split asunder on its disputed European identity. This is a good question. The answer may lie in that old muddle of principles which had long prevented absolute ideological polarisation. Even as the parties argued in the terms just laid out, their members retained some sympathies with their rivals' understanding of themselves. Not only did High Churchmen still cite foreign Protestant approval of Anglican forms but – till at least 1710 – they supported William and Anne's wars as a defence of a European Reformation which they still clearly wanted to survive (indeed Sacheverell used his enthusiasm for the battle during his trial defence).[50] Low Churchmen, meanwhile, retained a longing for an international Episcopal Church, if only it could be purged of its popery. Gilbert Burnet and William Wake, for example, seized on instances of Catholic reform or challenges to the pope's power within the Roman Church as possible signs of a new Reformation. This, they clearly hoped, might allow the English to rejoin a universal, and bishop-led ecclesia.[51] If this is what glued the church together in the last Stuart period, Europe was key to its unity as well as its division.

Surveying the arguments of this chapter, we can stage our retelling of English church history after 1660. We can relate the tale as a struggle between understandings of the communion's place in the spectrum of European Christianities – and the narrative runs as follows. Until the monarchical restoration, Anglicans had held a number of international identities in balance. Yet, once Charles II returned, this equilibrium was disturbed. First, the events of the Civil War gave the episcopal principle an advantage over other identities in the church's mix. Second, the spread of Catholicism across the Continent rendered this Episcopalianism unsettling because it bracketed the English establishment with an aggressive popery. Third, the new nonconformist movement used that unease against the church – particularly exploiting the terrifying events in France. Fourth, elements in the church became disturbed by the dissenters' accusations, and by the distancing from foreign Protestantism that support for bishops entailed. Fifth, those disturbed elements used the cohabitation of different kinds of Protestant in some parts of Europe, in the face of Louis XIV's threat, to fashion a new vision of the international Reformation. This no longer demanded that Anglicanism enjoy a monopoly in England. Once this final step had been made, the way was clear for church parties to form, and the pattern of post-Revolutionary ecclesiastical politics was set – though lingering discursive confusion perhaps preserved some sympathy between the sides.

This is neat, but perhaps we should end with a warning. It is an exaggeration to lay all at the door of the Continent. There were plenty of solely domestic causes of the developments we have surveyed – and many are covered in other contributions to this volume. Yet, at the same time it is important not to underestimate how much rhetorical energy Churchmen put into constructing the faithful abroad. Virtually all the disputes of the day had this dimension. Recognising this, we find the debates enriched, and ourselves closer to the true worldview of the late Stuart church. Perhaps, also, we dispel two myths about the whole early modern period. First, the English were not the insular and xenophobic folk of much commentary.[52] Clerics, and indeed a much wider public, were keenly aware of what was going on in Europe, and were fascinated because they saw struggles there as part of their own domestic disputes. Second, Protestant Anglicanism was only a highly problematic foundation for English national feeling. Far from uniting the Stuarts' subjects against foreign 'others' – as some historians have argued – official English religion created allegiances which spanned a Continent.[53] Whether these were to a league of Erastian establishments, to international Reformation, or to the universal Episcopal Church (or, confusingly, to all three at once), they meant that God's people were never limited to the English people. Faith and nationality inhabited rather different mental spheres.

NOTES

1 A. Milton, *Catholic and reformed: Roman and Protestant churches in English Protestant thought, 1600–1640* (Cambridge: Cambridge University Press, 1994).

2 For example, see Defoe's *Review* for late Oct. and early Nov. 1711.

3 About three hundred non-juring clergy refused to swear allegiance to William: but this was less than 5 per cent of the total clerical workforce, and most objected to the Revolution on grounds of personal conscience – not out of Catholic sympathy.

4 See below for this rhetorical move.

5 For example, William Temple, *Observations upon the United Provinces* (1673) – with later editions in 1676, 1680, 1690 and 1693; [William Carr], *An accurate description of the United Netherlands* (1691).

6 For travel guides, see T. Claydon, *Europe and the making of England, 1600–1760* (Cambridge: Cambridge University Press, 2007), chapter 1.

7 Such accusations remained live – note the 1673 Paris reprint of translation of Nicolas Saunder's classic sixteenth-century attack *De origine ac progressu schismatic anglicani liber.*

8 Edward Stillingfleet, *The mischief of separation* (1680). For the royal supremacy, see Jacqueline Rose's contribution to this volume.

9 For example, Herbert Thorndike, *Just weights and measures* (1660); Henry Dodwell, *The separation of churches from episcopal government* (1679); [William Sherlock], *A continuation and vindication of the defence of Dr Stillingfleet* (1682); Charles Leslie, *The true notion of the Catholic Church* (1703).

10 For the church's broad support for the wars, see T. Claydon, *William III and the godly revolution* (Cambridge: Cambridge University Press, 1996), chapter 4; for pride in the prayer-book see one of the period's best-selling works: William Beveridge, *A sermon concerning the excellency and usefulness of the Common Prayer* (1681).

11 The most authoritative guide to the Restoration church uses the term with only modest caveat: J. Spurr, *The Restoration Church of England, 1646–1689* (New Haven and London: Yale University Press, 1991), p. 35.

12 N. Tyacke, 'Archbishop Laud', in K. Fincham (ed.), *The early Stuart Church, 1603–1642* (Basingstoke: Macmillan, 1993), pp. 57–8.

13 Spurr, *Restoration Church*, pp. 121–2.

14 Most vehemently stated in Peter Heylyn, *Aerius redivivus* (1670), preface.

15 For my latest insistence on this, see T. Claydon, 'Protestantism, universal monarchy and Christendom', in E. Mijers and D. Onnekink (eds), *Redefining William III* (Aldershot: Ashgate, 2007), pp. 125–42.

16 For examples of the charity see, *An account of the disposal of the money* (1688); William Wake, *The case of the exiled Vaudois* (1699).

17 For example, Gilbert Burnet, *A modest survey of the most considerable things* (1676), pp. 26–8.

18 Robert Conold, *The notion of schism stated* (2nd edn, 1677), p. 104.

19 John Humfrey, *The question of re-ordination* (1661).

20 [Zachary Crofton], *A serious view of presbyters re-ordination* (1661); I.R., *A peaceable enquiry into that novel controversy* (1661); R.A., *A letter to a friend* (1661).

21 John Humfrey, *A second discourse about ordination* (1662).

22 Richard Baxter, *Richard Baxter's answer to Dr Edward Stillingfleet* (1680).

23 Richard Baxter, *An answer to Mr Dodwell and Dr Sherlock* (1682).

24 For example, *ibid.*; also [Vincent Alsop], *The mischief of impositions*; [John Humfrey and Stephen Lobb], *A reply to the defence of Dr Stillingfleet* (1681).

25 For an example, see below, n. 44.

26 Matthew Sylvester (ed.), *Reliquiae Baxterianae* (1696), pp. 242–7.

27 For works repeating Durel's points see Thomas Long, *Calvinus redivivus* (1673) and his 1689 works in n. 38; John Norris, *A discourse concerning the pretended religious* (1685).

28 Jean Durel, *A view of the government and public worship of god* (1662), p. 313.

29 [Francis Atterbury], *A letter to a convocation man* (1696), pp. 3–6.

30 Samuel Bolde, *A sermon against persecution* (1682); Samuel Bolde, *A plea for moderation* (1682).

31 [Daniel Whitby], *The Protestant reconciler* (1683); [Daniel Whitby], *The Protestant reconciler: part two* (1683).

32 Claydon, *Europe*, pp. 317–18.

33 William Sancroft, *The articles recommended by the archbishop* (1688).

34 For the dating of church parties to this point, see J. Spurr, 'Latitudinarianism and the Restoration church', *HJ*, 31 (1988), 61–82.

35 [Thomas Tenison], *A discourse concerning the ecclesiastical commission* (1689), p. 24.

36 N.N., *A letter to a member of the parliament* (1689), p. 6; *The interest of religion in England* [1689?], p. 7.

37 Gilbert Burnet, *An exhortation to peace and union* (1689).

38 See particularly Thomas Long's writings, for example, *The case of persecution* (1689); *The healing attempt examined* (1689).

39 William Beveridge, *A sermon preached before convocation* (1689), preface.

40 [Henry Maurice], *Remarks from the country* (1689), p. 12; [William Jane], *Letter to a friend* (1689), p. 2.

41 The debates have been overlooked, but can be followed in [Long], *Vox cleri* (1690).

42 Gilbert Burnet, *The bishop of Salisbury's speech to the House of Lords* (1704).

43 *An answer to Dr Sacheverell's sermon* (1710), p. 10; William Bisset, *Remarks on Dr Sacheverell's sermon* [1709?], p. 4.

44 A view expressed by Daniel Defoe in his *Review* 2: 65 (2 Aug. 1705).

45 See Claydon, *Europe*, pp. 198–9; for an example of Hare in flow: Francis Hare, *The charge of God to Joshua* (1709).

46 *The memorial of the Church of England* (1705), p. 20.

47 [Henry Sacheverell], *The rights of the Church of England* (1705), pp. 6–7.

48 For example, [Samuel Grascombe], *The mask of moderation pulled off* (1704); or Tory contributions to the parliamentary debate over occasional conformity: William Cobbett, *Cobbett's parliamentary history, 1066–1803*, 36 vols (1806–20), VI, 76.

49 See Claydon, *Europe*, pp. 201–7.

50 Claydon, *Europe*, pp. 340–1; *The tryal of Dr Henry Sacheverell* (1710), pp. 345–6.

51 Claydon, *Europe*, pp. 343–4.

52 For example, P. Langford, *Englishness identified* (Oxford: Oxford University Press, 2000), pp. 199–225.

53 For the classic statement of this view, see L. Colley, *Britons: forging the nation, 1707–1837* (New Haven and London: Yale University Press, 1992).

Part IV

Rivals

Chapter 8

Dissent and the Restoration Church of England

George Southcombe

Peter and *John* they Rebels were also,
By that same Argument which use you do.
To Magistrates they did refuse to bend,
Wherein they knew they should the Lord offend.
In civil things they always did submit,
And Preached also, it was a thing most fit,
In things which unto man doth appertain,
But Christ o're Conscience ought alone to reign.
Ev'n so those Martyrs bare an upright mind
Unto their Prince, and ever were inclin'd
In all just things obedient for to be:
Yet did stand up for Christ his Soveraignty[1]

And I will place within them as a guide
My umpire conscience, whom if they will hear,
Light after light well used they shall attain,
And to the end persisting, safe arrive.[2]

Patrick Collinson dated the end of the birth pangs of Protestant England to the Restoration. In 'formalising the division of English Protestantism', the Restoration regime 'built into the succeeding centuries of English history a pluralistic diversity which English Protestantism had neither expected nor desired'.[3] It is an attractive argument, and the metaphor of 'birthpangs', already under considerable strain, looks palpably ridiculous if it is extended past 1660. And yet, while the legal category of nonconformity was formalised in the Restoration, the debates concerning the relationship of Protestant dissent to the Church of England continued. The Restoration church and dissent might thus continue to be conceptualised, in terms used by Collinson of the earlier church and Puritanism, as two halves 'of a stressful relationship', defining and shaping each other.[4] What follows is an attempt to probe the nature of this relationship.

Throughout it will be necessary to reconfigure some of the ways in which Restoration nonconformity has been understood. First published in 1984, Christopher Hill's *The Experience of Defeat: Milton and Some Contemporaries* is a morose book. It functions primarily as a lament for the passing of that world turned upside down which he had so brilliantly recreated.[5] He asks finally 'But what of the saints?' and answers: 'After two decades of prophecy whose message still survives for us, they were defeated and silenced. Milton was almost alone in continuing to exercise his talent as poet and prophet.'[6] Saints, of course, is a somewhat amorphous category, and in fact Hill was careful to distinguish the different experiences of various groups and his work is subtler than is often suggested. Nonetheless, the concept of defeat – and its corollaries in the supposed withdrawal and increasing quietude of nonconformist groups – has cast a long shadow over the history of Restoration dissent.[7] Hill's work, as his subtitle reveals, had been conceived of as a study which spanned the boundaries between literature and history, and it is noticeable how far the history of Restoration nonconformity has been advanced by those engaged in studies of literary culture. Neil Keeble's magisterial study of 1987, *The Literary Culture of Nonconformity*, in some respects differs from, but in others sustains, the general account provided by Hill. Political quietism and withdrawal are seen as elements of nonconformity, and the literature of nonconformity is defined as having a distinctive aesthetic: 'Hence, as its experiential basis preserved nonconformist writing from the escapist flights of romance, so its supernatural faith preserved it from sardonic preoccupation with political machinations and social *mores*.'[8] As Keeble has emphasised recently, quietism 'was not a counsel of despair or defeatism', and the implicit distinction here between experiencing defeat and acting in a defeated way is an important one.[9] However, in what follows I want to sharpen this distinction further, and question how far withdrawal and quietism serve as useful analytical terms in defining Restoration dissent. In their relationships with the Church of England, dissenters came to rely on a vigorous, often polemical, print culture that represented and conceptualised the church in robust terms as a persecuting authority. This lack of passivity and the media through which it was expressed are thus a significant part of the story, a key component of what made the relationship 'stressful'.

In analysing the points of contact and contention between the church and dissent there are three broad areas of investigation: the legacies of the Civil War and Interregnum; the ways in which dissenters related to and conceptualised political and ecclesiastical authority; and the positive relationships that might develop between Churchmen and dissenters and their limitations.

I

The foundations of Restoration religion were primarily laid in the 1640s and 1650s. Those years of religious experimentation traumatised the Church of England but, in the face of the abolition of bishops, compulsory church attendance, and the prayer-book, saw it respond with remarkable tenacity in a context where it was not, paradoxically, the national church.[10] As the proscribed church showed its instincts for survival, a torrent of radical religious ideas poured out of Revolutionary England. Liberty of conscience had always been a nebulous term, and the failure of successive regimes to define it, along with the army's sense that it was central to the Good Old Cause for which they had fought and thus had to be defended, meant that a startling array of religious voices were heard.[11] This disgusted many who, in an earlier context, had been the central proponents of radicalisation. Presbyterians who had preached in the parliamentarian cause, and called for the dismantling of the government and liturgy of the Church of England, in the 1640s were appalled by the regicide, and some started plotting on behalf of the exiled Charles.[12] However, despite their public protestations against regicide, many Presbyterians served energetically within the Interregnum church.[13]

Some of the more *outré* religious individuals shone briefly like bright stars before burning out at the Restoration, but a number of the religious groups that had either come into being or gathered strength in the Interregnum – the Particular and General Baptists, the Quakers, and the Congregationalists – survived it. And the Presbyterians were, after 1662, to form the largest group of nonconformists. The experiences of the 1640s and 1650s profoundly affected all of these groups and, what is more, they affected the discourses which their enemies used against them. Far from being a homogenous group, dissenters were multifarious and often engaged in polemical conflict with each other. Presbyterians sought to retain a distance from groups like the Quakers, with whom they shared little but the legal status of nonconformity. And yet to their enemies they were inextricably linked: whatever the Presbyterians pretended, it was their actions which had produced both the regicide and the explosion of sectarianism, and their compromises with the Interregnum regimes were not quickly forgotten. In the midst of the exclusion crisis, the bitterly anti-nonconformist writer Roger L'Estrange was able to ventriloquise a Presbyterian speaking of his licentious sectarian offspring: 'Oh! of *themselves*, they're e'en a *Vip'rous Brood*; / *Begot* in *Discord*, and *brought up* with *Blood*. / 'Twas *We* that gave 'um *Life, Credit*, and *Name*: / Till the *Ungrateful Brats* devour'd their *Dam*.'[14]

The 1640s and 1650s thus shaped the ways in which dissenters were perceived, and yet they were not simply the passive victims of this process. Radical works that were composed in the 1650s continued to be published into the 1660s. Keeping alive the potential that had opened up in the Civil War for female voices to be heard, Katherine Sutton's millenarian hymns were printed in 1663 as part of an autobiographical account, with a preface by the Particular Baptist Hanserd Knollys.[15] Songs that in their original context would have formed part of millenarian criticism of the Protectorate of Oliver Cromwell found a new context in the years of the early Restoration. The Quaker John Perrot, who was ultimately schismatic within the movement, published his *A Sea of the Seed's Sufferings* in 1661, which had been composed in the late 1650s, when he had taken part in an ambitious mission to convert the pope and the sultan. His poems, blending accounts of his harrowing experiences during this mission with biblical allusion and spiritual meditation, were a forceful reminder of how far religious boundaries had been pushed. Through Perrot's verse, God's voice lambasted maintained clergy:

> *Arts* painted *Image* with *Apology*,
> Is but the *Wash-pot* of *Theology*,
> Which tracks out *Hirelings* in their *subtil traces*,
> And spreads with Dung *Baals Diviners* faces;
> Whilst *Light reveals*, a *shovel* is their tongue,
> Which in the *Bride-groom's room* heaps *noisome dung*
> So *dung* for *dung*, repaid's their *equal way*,
> Till their *work's* up, and wrath *cuts down* their stay.[16]

Others reinvigorated the discourses of the Civil War in less abstract ways. The Welsh Fifth Monarchist Vavasor Powell, entering into the debates about the Restoration church settlement of 1660–61, produced a pamphlet against the prayer-book and episcopacy that went through four editions in those years. In it he ruthlessly pillaged the work of the Presbyterian ministers who, under the acronym Smectymnuus, had launched a sustained attack on church government and the liturgy in 1641. And he pointedly asked his readers to consider '*Whether the imposing of the* Scottish Liturgy *(which in some things was better, though in some others worse than the English) was not the beginning, and first Cause of the late grievous Wars; and if so, whether men should not be more cautious to do the like for the future?*'[17]

As the Restoration began, the ghosts of earlier times were proving hard to lay, and were even being explicitly summoned within dissenting circles. Such summonings were dangerous, and served to remind Churchmen of the years of their proscription. The 1640s and 1650s had raised a series of questions about the nature of political and ecclesiastical authority and provided some brutal answers. The Restored church sought to reassert the old answers, but it was resisted both from within the dissenting communities and, at points, by its own Supreme Governor.

II

Throughout history the faithful had suffered for Christ, and in 1661 Vavasor Powell was in little doubt that they were entering a new period of persecution: 'the floods are but beginning to rise ... the furnace yet, is but making hot'.[18] His words, written from prison, were prescient. The return of the King had been followed quickly in the localities by the harassment of Quakers, Baptists, and radical sectaries through the courts, but this was just the beginning.[19] From 1661 to 1665 the Cavalier Parliament passed a series of Acts which defined the parameters of conformity and provided new means to police those boundaries.[20] The parameters were drawn considerably more narrowly than might have been expected in 1660 and, most significantly, the Act of Uniformity in 1662 contained stipulations which meant that many Presbyterian ministers, who had played a key role in the Restoration, and who expected to find themselves accommodated within the Church of England, were ejected from it.[21] While nonconformists remained heterogeneous – Baptists and Quakers continued their disputes, and Presbyterians inhabited a different theological and ecclesiological world from the groups with which they now shared the label of dissent – legislation meant that they would, to varying degrees, share an experience of persecution.[22]

The broad contours of persecution in the late seventeenth century are clear and may be mapped in relation both to the legislation which provided the basis for the repression of dissent and to the various attempts, legislative and otherwise, to ease this repression. The Acts of 1661–65 were passed by the Cavalier Parliament and both clarified the legal definition of dissent and restricted the movement and actions of dissenters. While they are inappropriately named the Clarendon Code, it was following Clarendon's fall in 1667 that schemes for toleration and comprehension were once again debated, in both the corridors of power and out of doors. Nonetheless, a second Conventicle Act was passed in 1670, which again rendered nonconformist meetings illegal and escalated the unpleasant trade of informers. Acting through prerogative rather than legislative means in March 1672, Charles II issued a Declaration of Indulgence. This attempt to impose toleration by the word of the King, however, was short lived. In 1673 the Declaration was revoked and a Test Act – requiring office holders to be communicating members of the Church of England – was passed by parliament (a hoped-for Bill for the ease of Protestant dissenters did not make it into the statute book before parliament was prorogued). The heady days of the exclusion crisis witnessed again the opening up of debates about toleration and comprehension, and attempts were made to enact legislation on these issues, but they were ultimately curtailed. The period after was marked by the intensive harrying of dissent, and the years of 1681 to 1686 remained burned into dissenting memories as a time of brutal persecution.

The Catholic James II, driven primarily by concern for his co-religionists, did establish a broad toleration, working, as his brother had attempted, through the prerogative and a Declaration of Indulgence (1687; reissued 1688). But it was only following the Revolution of 1688–89 that toleration of nonconformist worship was encoded in legislation, in an Act of 1689. The civil restrictions of the Test and Corporation Acts were not lifted. Toleration, when it came, was therefore limited, and the period following it was not free either of persecution or of further attempts to reimpose restrictions on dissent. In the furore surrounding the Sacheverell trial in 1710, for example, popular violence exploded against dissenters.[23] The next year the practice of occasional conformity (whereby a dissenter would take communion with sufficient regularity to hold office) was clamped down upon by parliament, and in 1714, at the end of our period, the Schism Act sought to restrict dissenting educational initiatives. It was not till 1719 that these latter two Acts were repealed.[24] Such a summary, of course, hides much of the diversity of local response, and the fact that enforcement of the law was heavily dependent on the willingness of those in the localities to act against their neighbours. Even in the period 1681–86 there was considerable variation in the imposition of laws against dissent.[25] But there is also no doubt that, taken as a whole, this was a period in which many men and women suffered terrible privation for their consciences. Some groups suffered more than others. Later Quakers were to record for posterity how widespread persecution had been, and how much the earlier generation of Friends had endured, but even Presbyterians could point to those who were imprisoned for their cause.[26] The means by which the laws were enforced encouraged so-minded individuals to act against nonconformists in the most malicious of ways. In 1664 in Berkshire one such man, in his zeal to suppress Quakers, stabbed them with 'a Staff that had a Goad or some sharp Prick at the end of it', making them 'very sore and black'.[27] Most infamously, a malevolent gang of informers, led by the self-serving John Hilton, prowled the streets of London from 1682 to 1686. While it is difficult to find clear, unproblematic evidence of the collusion of specific Anglican clergy with the gang, it is striking that when Archbishop Sancroft was tackled about them by the Quaker George Whitehead he replied that 'there must be some crooked timber used in building a ship'.[28] Attitudes like that could only bolster the enemies of dissent, and harden the sense of nonconformists that, for all its complexities, they lived in a persecutory age.

Responses to this persecution, and the legislation which legitimated it, provide a means of understanding how nonconformists conceived of authority. The Presbyterian poet Robert Wild, who had produced robust verses, larded with scatological humour, throughout the early years of the Restoration, wrote his *The Loyal Nonconformist* in response to the Five Mile Act. Passed in October 1665, this Act sought once and for all to sever both the ties which still bound many ministers to their old congregations and, in the context of London, the new ties which had developed as a result of nonconformist pastoral activity during the plague.[29] The failure of a nonconformist minister to swear the Act's 'Oxford Oath' – which required its takers to renounce resistance and not to 'endeavour any Alteration of Government either in Church or State' – precluded him from coming within five miles of 'any Corporation sending Members to Parliament', or place where he had acted as a minister or preached to a nonconformist meeting since the Act of Oblivion (1660). Informers, who could receive a third of any fine, helped to enforce the Act.[30] *The Loyal Nonconformist* responded to the new strictures placed on the consciences of nonconformist ministers by the Five Mile Act, and it was read widely: one of Baron Wharton's correspondents opined in May 1666 that it was 'little lesse than impossible' that the peer had not already seen this poem.[31] Wild critiqued the attempt to coerce the conscience, but also laid bare many of the tensions that remained for Presbyterians in their relationship with ecclesiastical and political authorities: tensions encapsulated in his subtitle: *An Account of What he Dare Swear, and What Not.*

A paradox at the heart of Restoration Presbyterianism is expressed in Wild's title. Presbyterian loyalism was conjoined uneasily with enforced nonconformity. Swearing not to 'endeavour Alteration / Of Monarchy, or of that Royal Name, / Which God hath chosen to comand this Nation' was easy enough, but swearing complete obedience was something else:

> What he commands, if *Conscience* say not nay,
> (For *Conscience* is a greater King than he)
> For *Conscience-sake*, not *Fear*, I will obey;
> And if not *Active*, *Paßive* I will be.

Conscience did not legitimate active resistance, but it did justify passive noncompliance with policies that offended it, and provided the strength stoically to endure the consequences.

Monarchy may have been ordained by God but, for Wild, episcopacy was but *jure humano*, and therefore to swear against its alteration was unnecessary, erected it to a wholly unwarranted status, and precluded the possibility of further reformation. This was significant because most Restoration Presbyterians, including Wild, were not interested in calling for the complete abolition of episcopacy.[32] Rather, following James Ussher's ideas for a reduced episcopacy, Presbyterians sought a decrease in the size of dioceses, and the appointment of suffragan bishops to aid in the running of them:

> And yet Church Government I do allow,
> And am contented Bishops be the men;
> And that I speak in earnest, here I vow
> Where we have one, I wish we might have ten.

These were ideas that for a time from 1660 to 1662 appeared to be gaining support and which, if implemented, would have formed part of the comprehensive church settlement desired by Presbyterians.[33] Wild helped to keep the ideas alive, but he also directly criticised the Church of England, which had failed to encompass them, and its mechanisms of persecution:

> I dare not swear that Courts Ecclesiastick
> > Do in their Laws make just and gentle Votes;
> But I'l be sworn that *Burton*, *Pryn* and *Bastwick*
> > Were once *Ear witnesses* of harsher Notes.

The Puritans Henry Burton, William Prynne and John Bastwick had all, famously, had their ears lopped for sedition under the Laudian regime of the 1630s – a regime which Wild sought to link to the church of his own day.[34]

This public representation of the church as persecutor, and the refusal to bow to its authority, was a leitmotif of dissenting literature and shared across the nonconformist groups. Writing from prison in c.1662, the Lincolnshire General Baptist Thomas Grantham personified this church in the character of the inconstant and arbitrary Cathedral, whose defence of the punitive actions taken against his detractors ('I punish such indeed as go amiss, / That I might them reduce from Heresie, / Or others keep in Christian purity') is met with a forthright: 'That thou'rt a Persecutor is too plain'.[35] Grantham's sometime adversary, the Quaker John Whitehead, co-authored a work addressed directly to the bishops which proffered them some clear 'advice' about how to solve their image problem, while at the same time hardening the characterisation of them as persecutors and linking this to potent biblical archetypes: 'for until you have sound Doctrine, and the example of a good Conversation, with Christian love and charity, to draw us to a conformity, ye may despair of hope to drive us by force and cruelty; for the more of that ye do exercise upon us, the more shall we be confirmed; and it will also manifest your Church not to be the Lambs Wife, but rather a Daughter of that mother of Harlots, that hath drank the blood of the Saints and Martyrs of Jesus'.[36]

The coruscating wit of Andrew Marvell, MP for Hull until his death in 1678, added another dimension to the figure of the persecuting Churchman. While his own precise religious identity remains elusive, Marvell produced swingeing attacks on those who sought to legitimate the crushing of dissent.[37] His widely read *The Rehearsal Transpros'd* took aim at the intolerant cleric Samuel Parker:

> He saith, the Nonconformists should communicate with him till they have clear evidence that it is evil. This is a civil way indeed of gaining the question, to perswade men that are unsatisfied, to be satisfied till they be dissatisfied. He threatens, he rails, he jeers them, if it were possible, out of all their Consciences and Honesty; and finding that will not do, he calls out the Magistrate, tells him, these men are not

fit to live, there can be no security of Government while they are in being: Bring out the Pillories, Whipping-posts, Gallies, Rods, and Axes, (which are *Ratio ultima Cleri*, a Clergy-mans last Argument, ay and his first too:) and pull in pieces all the Trading Corporations those Nests of Faction and Sedition.[38]

The persecution of dissent was thus met with a series of public and pointed denunciations of intolerance. Such denunciations were based on a different conception of the ecclesiastical and political authority from that held by men like Parker. Dissenting profession of these principles therefore formed part of a paradox, in that it both aided nonconformists' survival and fuelled the fears of their opponents.

Of course, their opponents really wanted to be able to say that they were rabid republicans. But this was not always made easy by the actions of the Supreme Governor of the Church of England. Marvell wrote of Parker's hopes for the role the king would play: 'It were a worthy Spectacle, were it not? to see his Majesty like the Governor in Synesius, busied in his Cabinet among those Engines whose very names are so hard that it is some torture to name them; the *Podostrabae*, the *Dactylethrae*, the *Otagrae*, the *Rhinolabides*, the *Cheilostrophia*, devising, as they say there are particular Diseases, so a peculiar Rack for every Limb and Member of a Christians body.' But, Marvell sighed, 'God be prais'd his Majesty is far of another temper.'[39] Indeed, in 1672 Charles II was of another temper. In March he had proclaimed his Declaration of Indulgence, and many nonconformist ministers took out licenses under it.[40] The fact that Marvell's vitriolic prose hit the booksellers was due in no small part to the earl of Anglesey's passing on a message to the Surveyor of the Press in no uncertain terms: 'Look you M^r L'Estrange there is a Book come out, (the Rehearsall Transpros'd) I presume you have seen it.) I have spoken to his Ma:^{ty} about it, and the King says he will not have it supprest, for Parker has done him, wrong, and this man has done him Right.'[41] However, significantly, the Declaration of Indulgence did not necessarily produce a reduction in the polemic aimed against the church, and neither did dissenting acceptance of it point to an accommodation with the absolute authority of the king.

Robert Wild, who was one of around 1,500 licensed under the Declaration, wrote of how the newly tolerated dissenters would relate to the Church of England in terms which did little to suggest any softening of his attitudes.[42] Giving a particular emphasis to the fable of the belly, he wrote: 'We'l be the *Feet* the *Back* and *Hands*, and they / Shall be the *Belly*, and devour the *Prey*, / The Tythe-pigg shall be theirs; we'l turn the spit, / We'l bear the *Cross*, they only *sign* with it.'[43] For the Presbyterians, the Declaration raised peculiar problems, as acceptance could be taken as a signal that they had given up hope of being comprehended within the church. But many dissenters had qualms about the way the Declaration had been imposed by the king's will, and retained an underlying sense that it was really intended for Roman Catholics rather than for them.[44] Such fears were replicated *a fortiori* (and with good reason) when the Catholic James II produced his Declaration in 1687. While there was support for James from dissenters, particularly from Quakers who had not accepted the terms of Charles's Indulgence, and some Baptists, much of the co-operation was again tactical. One anonymous poet took aim against those Anglicans who now sought to offer the dissenters 'friendly' advice and encourage them to reject the Indulgence, but he or she also was also under no illusions that anything but a Catholic future was intended and that that would be just as oppressive as the Anglican past: "Tis but conforming t'other step and then / Jure Divino, whipp and spur again.'[45]

The nonconformist response to persecution was therefore principled, visible, and powerful. The character of the persecutory Churchman was solidified and vilified in nonconformist literature. But underlying this vilification was a conceptualisation of authority which differed from that which had been encoded in the Restoration church settlement. As Gary S. De Krey has demonstrated in his careful reconstruction of cases for conscience from 1667 to 1672, even among those who did not challenge in principle the prince's authority in ecclesiastical affairs, there were those who nonetheless 'may be regarded as radical both because of the challenges they offered to the institutions of the restoration and because of their repudiation of the political assumptions upon which the restoration rested'.[46] Even when the monarch seemed to offer the best hope for the dissenting future, acceptance was not predicated on any fundamental alteration in this perspective. As such, the fears of those Churchmen who held a very different understanding of political and ecclesiastical authority were not paranoia.[47] Neither were such Churchmen able to comfort themselves with the thought that nonconformists, even if they wanted to say egregious things, were not particularly audible in their attacks on the church. The direct, sometimes *ad hominem*, attacks on Churchmen were in some ways more damaging than the principles which supported them. They fed a public thirst for satire, and seemed to clarify a simple distinction between the church and dissent which, while it hid the complexities in that relationship, crystallised the issues, and did so in a way that could make reconciliation, co-operation, or even communication difficult.

III

But just as the binary opposition set up between the church and dissent in some nonconformist culture is important to understand, so are the complexities which could be submerged beneath it. Some such complexities continue to point to conflict, but also reveal that such conflict could occur over shared discourses. In particular, both Churchmen and dissenters sought legitimation through history.[48] This in itself created oddities, in that many dissenters found themselves using authorities produced by sixteenth- and early seven-teenth-century Churchmen in their polemical writings. Thomas Grantham, while engaged, as we have seen, in lambasting the church, still in the space of two pages referenced Andrew Willet's *Synopsis Papismi* (first published 1592), John Marbeck's *A Booke of Notes and Common Places* (1581) and Daniel Featley's 1623 disputation with the Jesuits John Percy (alias Fisher) and John Sweet.[49] One area in which, unsurprisingly, given their on-going experience of persecution, dissenters became major producers and users of historical work was martyrology. The Church of England's answer to the question 'where was your Church before Luther' was appropriated by nonconformists.[50] In 1667 the Quaker leader George Fox produced with Ellis Hookes the histor-ical collection *The Arraignment of Popery*, which detailed persecutions from ancient to recent times.[51] It was republished in 1669, 1675 and 1679. As the title suggests, one further element of previous historical controversial writing which the dissenters were able to embrace was the attack on the Church of Rome. Indeed, the events of the Irish rebellion of 1641 and the massacre of Waldensians in Piedmont in 1655 had provided further martyrs to be placed within the schema most famously established in the sixteenth century by John Foxe. The Particular Baptist Benjamin Keach wrote in sickening detail of the events of 1655 ('Some with sharp spears thrust through their privy parts, / Whilst some others stabbed were unto their hearts. / Some babes they cut in pieces, some they roasted / And some upon the tops of spears they toasted') before pointing his readers to Samuel Morland's recent history of events and moving on to enumerate the deaths in Ireland ('Two hundred thousand Protestants or more, / Were Massacred by this vile bloody Whore').[52] As for the early Puritans, anti-popery could form the basis of some accommodation with the church, although it is also clear that anti-popery could form a 'safe' language with which the persecutory tendencies of Restoration Anglicanism could be critiqued.

The tensions inherent in the use of history by dissenters were nowhere clearer than for the Presbyterians. In many ways the most historically minded of all the dissenting groups, Presbyterians were nonetheless caught in a bind by their position. Still desirous of a national church, and believing that their heritage was to be found within the Church of England, they were in an unenvi-able situation. Samuel Clark's tireless production of godly lives and martyrolo-gies legitimated the Presbyterian position and located it firmly within Christian history in general, and English history in particular. However, the greatest attempt to write a comprehensive history of Puritanism remained stillborn. Roger Morrice's antiquarian collections for this history have bequeathed to modern scholars a rich resource (without them, for example, we would not have that phrase which epitomises Puritan attitudes to the church: it was 'but halfly-reformed'), but it was a history he was unable to write. As Mark Goldie has demonstrated, he was caught in a historiographical schizophrenia, writing for 'separatists who did not believe in separation', and thus unsure whether he was producing a history 'of insiders or outsiders'.[53] The Presbyterians' use of history is a peculiar part of the 'stressful relationship' which they shared with the church, and reveals much about how unresolved and contested the identities of both remained. But, as has been suggested, history created points of contact and contention between the church and dissent in general. Questions continually arose over the right use of history, and much of the basis for that history was shared. It is important, however, that this shared basis did not ineluctably lead to either co-operation between or toleration for competing religious groups. As often as not, the turn to history highlighted irresolvable difference. It is finally necessary, therefore, to examine in closer detail the more positive interrelations between Churchmen and dissenters that could occur, and the limitations to them.

On occasion, dissenters were certainly indebted to the support provided by Anglicans. In 1682, when John Whitehead was imprisoned, accused, quite typically, of being a Jesuit, he presented a certificate from Swine in Yorkshire asserting his 'good Credit' and peaceable living with 'his Neighbours'. It was signed by parishioners, two churchwardens, and the vicar.[54] The production of such certificates by Quakers' neighbours was not rare.[55] Similarly, when Thomas Grantham came to be falsely accused of sheep-stealing at various points from the late 1670s to the 1690s – accusations which were fuelled by animus borne against him as a Baptist – he too was able to call on the testimony of neighbours within the Church of England. Indeed, in 1691, even though he had moved from the place of the initial accusation in Lincolnshire to Norwich, when the slander reared its head again, his old neighbours wrote on his behalf, and he published their letters in a pamphlet, emphasising their Anglicanism.[56] Such examples of good neighbourliness are suggestive of the ways in which dissenters could be viewed within local society. But they do not necessarily point to any greater accommodation between the church and dissent. At the same time as producing the testimony of the local vicar, Whitehead could still write a dire warning to 'the *Watch-men* of the *Church of England*' to 'beware lest they strike hands with the *Papists*, to help to root us from being a Posterity in the Earth, lest they also be swallowed up of their Helpers'.[57] The idea of the church as a persecutory body could coexist with the knowledge of individual Anglicans (including clergymen) who sought to protect their Quaker neighbours.

The limitations to more positive relationships between the Churchmen and dissenters may be brought more sharply into focus through the analysis of a remarkable cache of letters between Thomas Grantham and the Church of England clergyman John Connould, produced from April to September 1691. Connould had first written to Grantham when it became apparent that the Baptist had 'bid open defiance to ye Church of England' in a meeting place 'but a little way from' his 'Parish Church'.[58] Their correspondence revolved around two questions which Connould raised in his first letter: from what authority or calling could Grantham claim his right to gather a church? What justification existed for infant baptism?[59] In many ways, while it demonstrates the intense interaction between a Churchman and a dissenter which could occur, it serves to highlight the parameters within which those interactions could take place. Grantham claimed that he loved and honoured 'ye Church of England w[i]th respect to her Excellent Articles of Faith, as now qualified by Law' (that is, the provisos in the Toleration Act which exempted dissenting ministers from swearing to certain articles), but he still retained his reasons for separating from her.[60] Grantham had previously, it transpired, approached other clergymen in his attempts to forge relationships within the church. William Lloyd, at the time of their meeting bishop of St Asaph, had, according to Grantham, had with him 'a very Christian Conference at London w[hi] ch ended with much friendship.'[61] Thomas Barlow, bishop of Lincoln 'had (through his gentleness) much friendly conference w[i]th him in his study at Bagden' and 'did not dispise' to refer to Grantham's community as 'his Brethren'.[62] And yet, Lloyd, following the Rye House Plot in 1683, spat the venom he had previously secreted for Catholics at nonconformists, and while he did play a part in drafting the failed Comprehension Bill of 1689, in the 1690s he remained conscious of the difficulties which the Toleration Act had created for the church.[63] Barlow was horrified by toleration, claiming that it was '"against the express law of God, of nature, and all" to grant freedom to those who had "ruin'd church and state, and murder'd their kinge"'.[64] Dialogues between Churchmen and dissenters were possible, but the religious identities of both ultimately remained firm. Connould and Grantham, while at times respectful, could also charge their words with rhetorical gunpowder. Connould wrote of how those like Grantham 'put' their 'sycle into other mens Labours, make disturbances, & schisms in churches already planted, and rightly constituted; poysoning mens minds w[i]th dangerous opinions, & damnable Heresies'.[65] Grantham polemically associated Connould with popery; Connould raised the spectre of Munster, the home of extreme Anabaptist social radicalism in the early sixteenth century.[66] These letters are witness to the ways in which academic and open debate between Churchmen and dissenters, in which there was a broad level of agreement on a number of issues, could easily slide back into the polemical mode which precluded a priori the possibility of compromise. The slide into polemic was also not simply the product of intemperance and tactical blunders, but reflected immutable cores of religious identity within the participants. But the letters illuminate not only limitations to, but the basis for, more positive relationships between Churchmen and dissenters.

After Grantham's death in January 1692 Connould conducted Grantham's funeral service, proclaiming that 'this day is a very great man fallen in Israel'. To protect his corpse from desecration, Connould had him buried near the south porch of St Stephen's Church.[67] These events are suggestive of a very different kind of relationship from that recorded in the above outbursts. The letters provide some key to understanding it. This lies in the use of a language which, because of its quotidian nature, can seem merely conventional, but which was in fact potent: the language of *caritas*, Christ's injunction that we love our neighbours as ourselves. In the letters they spoke of the charity they had towards one another. Even following a letter which was angry in tone, Connould could write: 'I have no more at present but to tell you (that altho' you have given me just cause to express my selfe more warmly, in my two last letters than heretofore) I am yet in charity with you.'[68]

Charity was at the heart of the thinking of some clerics even during 1681–85. In 1682 Bishop John Fell of Oxford requested information about nonconformity in the parishes of his diocese. Some of his correspondents were scathing. 'To mention' Hugh Boham of Harpsden wrote with mock-sorrow, 'the Inquisition in Spayne, or our owne Bedlam in England ... would be abhorrent to a true christian temper, if any milde method may prevayle; which ought to be heartily wisht, but hardly to be expected.' Alexander Charnelhouse of Salford mocked: 'These are they that have such tender stomacks, that cannot endure milk, but can very well digest iron, consciences so tender that a ceremony is deadly offensive, but rebellion is not.' But even at this point, when the Tory reaction was gathering force, there were those among the church who wrote in a very different way. Nathaniel Collier of Duns Tews had confronted the three 'Anabaptists' living in his parish and had found that 'what I have done already has very much abated their Prejudice, and changed them into a more charitable opinion of our Church, Conformity and Conformists, which is well worth my pains though nothing else be effected.' John Bayly of Fringford put the case in biblical terms: 'I doubt not but there are many Fatherly Abrahams amongst us who would condescend a little in the smallest matters for the sake of saveing Unity, and I hope there are not few Lots amongst them who by charitable condescentions would be won to hearken to Councells of Necessary Union.'[69] *Caritas*, the Christian language of good neighbourliness, was not a universal panacea, and it was not a discourse which precluded unevenness in the relations which might be formed: for both Connould and Fell's correspondents, the use of *caritas* was in part a way of maintaining a dialogue with, at the same time as asserting power over, dissent. Nonetheless, Christ's words provided a powerful bond and a maxim that circumscribed action. As such, they could form the basis for beneficial relationships, even co-operation, between the church and dissent.

For those who believed that William of Orange's invasion was literally a providential deliverance from Catholic tyranny, the new king's reign was ripe with possibilities. In particular, the licentiousness and immorality which appeared to have infected the polity from the court down during the reigns of Charles and James could come under a renewed attack. Central to attempts to invigorate this moral campaign were the Societies for Reformation of Manners that proliferated from the 1690s into the eighteenth century. By the 1700s they had spread throughout rural and urban centres, and retained a strong position in London, where they had originated. These societies, unlike the contemporaneous Society for Promoting Christian Knowledge and the Society for the Propagation of the Gospel in Foreign Parts, which only included members of the Church of England, functioned through the co-operation of Anglicans and dissenters.[70] The dissenter John Howe laid out the rationale for such an endeavour in a sermon of 1698:

> An Agreement in Substantial Godliness and Christianity, in humility, meekness, self-denial, in singleness of heart, benignity, charity, entire love to sincere Christians, as such, in universal love to Mankind, and in a design of doing all the good we can in the world, notwithstanding such go under different denominations, and do differ in so Minute Things, is the most valuable Agreement that can be among Christians.[71]

The societies' mechanisms for imposing moral reform, ironically, contained the seeds of developments which would mean that this had become much more difficult by 1800. However, in their terms, they enjoyed some initial success. From 1700 to 1710 in excess of 1,000 of those who had committed sexual offences were prosecuted in London as a result of the societies' actions. These figures grew from 1715 to 1725, with some years seeing almost 2,000 convictions. As Faramerz Dabhoiwala has suggested on the basis of these figures, 'Probably not since the reign of Elizabeth had sexual discipline been enforced on such a scale.'[72] In addition, the publication of an annual *Black Roll* or *Black List* from 1694 to 1707, which contained the details of those who had been convicted during the year, served both further to humiliate the guilty and as a caution to others (although the circulation of reformist intentions in this medium was presumably aided by the titillation it provided).[73] But, despite the achievements of the societies in these years, they also attracted criticism and detraction.

For some Churchmen, they represented a dangerous alliance. Thomas Caryl, vicar of St Mary's Nottingham, thought a Society nearby had good intentions but was unsure about the effects it would have: 'especially when I consider in what danger those churchmen (whom I believe to be the minority) among 'em will be in, of being first work'd into an indifferency and afterwards quite drawn off from the Establishment'.[74] William Nicolson, archdeacon of Carlisle, was later a supporter of the societies, but in 1700 he predicted 'the ruin which such Societies (if not discountenanced) must speedily bring on the Established Church', and one of his correspondents opined: 'As to joining with the Dissenters in this specious matter, I must always look upon them as the real cause why our Church discipline is not powerful enough at present to correct the vices they now complain of. It is they that have taught the people to slight the Ecclesiastical censures.'[75] The way in which the societies used paid informers was always going to recall painful memories for some of when dissenters were the primary prey of such men.[76] And a number of dissenters retained an unease about the workings of the societies. Daniel Defoe, who was educated at Charles Morton's dissenting academy, wrote of '*Societies* ill Manners to suppress' and how 'With *Jehu*'s Zeal they furiously reform, / And raise false Clouds, which end without a Storm; / But with a loose to Vice securely see / The Subject punish'd, and themselves go free', before proclaiming 'For shame your *Reformation-Clubs* give o'er, / And jest with Men, and jest with Heaven no more'.[77] Any attempt to reform the manners of others could lead to the charge of hypocrisy.[78]

There is one final element of the critique of the Societies for Reformation of Manners which should be emphasised. As Craig Rose has noted, John Howe, quoted above, had served as Oliver Cromwell's household chaplain, and the spectre of the Civil War and Interregnum could easily be seen within the societies. William Nicolson explicitly saw the roots of the societies as lying in the associations that had blossomed in this period, particularly referring to the Worcestershire Association of Richard Baxter.[79] Indeed, for Nicolson the societies were coloured in the most damning fashion by the way in which they resonated with the past: 'Holy Leagues, and National Covenants (to which ours will grow up in time) have occasioned so much bloodshed in this and the neighbouring kingdoms that I tremble at the prospect: especially since I see with what haste we are approaching to our own destruction.'[80] Into the eighteenth century, relationships between the church and dissent could still be refracted through the lens provided by the Civil War. Some Anglicans could still discern the political and religious radical lurking beneath the exterior of the reforming dissenter.

In a work of 1719 which may have been written by Daniel Defoe, the character of a Turkish spy is used to satirise Christian Europe. He comments on the divergences within Christianity: 'There are divers Sects of these People, who have broken off from the great Mufty [the pope] ... and though I look upon these to be ... the better Sort by far, as to their Morality, and as to their Principles; yet they differ again one from another, and separate even in Charity and Affection, as much as the *Ottomans* and *Persians* do, about the Successors to our Great Prophet *Mahomet*; Nay, they have likewise proceeded to Persecution, and even to Blood.'[81] As it was in the macrocosm of Christendom, so it had been in later Stuart England. Following the return of Charles II in 1660, those who had rejected Rome nonetheless persecuted one another. But, as has been suggested, the relationship between the church and dissent was not simply one of persecutor and persecuted. Certainly persecution and dissenting resistance to it did much to harden identities, confirm opinions, and limit the opportunities for compromise. But in many ways, the relationship remained fundamentally dialogic, bound up with the questions of defining the true nature of the English Reformation and the future for Protestant England. The relationship was never an easy one, yet it profoundly shaped both the church and dissent. That so much of the dialogue was carried out in such heated terms might suggest that Protestant England emerged straight from its birth pangs into its adolescence.

NOTES

I am very grateful to the British Academy for funding my years as a Postdoctoral Fellow at Somerville College, Oxford, in the course of which this chapter was researched and written, and to Clive Holmes and Grant Tapsell for their comments on a draft.

1　Benjamin Keach, *War with the devil* (1673), p. 166.

2　John Milton, *Paradise lost*, ed. A. Fowler, 2nd edn (London and New York: Longman, 1998), III, 179 (lines 194–7).

3　P. Collinson, *The birthpangs of Protestant England: religious and cultural change in the sixteenth and seventeenth centuries* (Basingstoke: Macmillan Press, 1988), p. 155.

4　Collinson, *Birthpangs*, p. 143.

5　C. Hill, *The experience of defeat: Milton and some contemporaries* (Faber and Faber, 1984); cf. Hill, *The world turned upside down: radical ideas during the English Revolution* (Temple Smith, 1972).

6　Hill, *Experience of defeat*, p. 328.

7　Further critiques of Hill's position may be found in G.S. De Krey, 'Rethinking the Restoration: dissenting cases for conscience, 1667–1672', *HJ*, 38 (1995), 53–83; B. Adams, 'The experience of defeat revisited: suffering, identity and the politics of obedience among Hertford Quakers, 1655–1665', in C. Durston and J. Maltby (eds), *Religion in revolutionary England* (Manchester: Manchester University Press, 2006), pp. 249–67.

8　N.H. Keeble, *The literary culture of nonconformity in later seventeenth-century England* (Leicester: Leicester University Press, 1987), p. 284.

9　N.H. Keeble, *The Restoration: England in the 1660s* (Oxford: Blackwell, 2002), p. 145.

10　K. Fincham and S. Taylor, 'Vital statistics: episcopal ordination and ordinands in England, 1646–60', *EHR*, 126 (2011), 319–44; J. Maltby, 'Suffering and surviving: the civil wars, the Commonwealth and the formation of "Anglicanism", 1642–60', in C. Durston and J. Maltby (eds), *Religion in revolutionary England* (Manchester: Manchester University Press, 2006), pp. 158–80; J. Morrill, 'The Church in England, 1642–9', in J. Morrill (ed.), *Reactions to the English Civil War 1642–1649* (Macmillan, 1982), pp. 89–114. See also the introduction to this volume.

11 Hill, *The world turned upside down*; S. Mortimer, *Reason and religion in the English Revolution: the challenge of Socinianism* (Cambridge: Cambridge University Press, 2010); B. Worden, 'Toleration and the Cromwellian Protectorate', *SCH*, 21 (1984), 199–233. For the argument that radical theological speculation was not simply the preserve of the sects, and was indulged in by some clergy of the proscribed church, see A. Milton, 'Anglicanism and royalism in the 1640s', in J. Adamson (ed.), *The English Civil War: conflict and contexts* (Basingstoke: Palgrave Macmillan, 2009), pp. 61–81.

12 A. Hughes, *Gangraena and the struggle for the English Revolution* (Oxford: Oxford University Press, 2004); E. Vernon, 'The quarrel of the Covenant: the London Presbyterians and the regicide', in J. Peacey (ed.), *The regicides and the execution of Charles I* (Basingstoke: Palgrave Macmillan, 2001), pp. 202–24; B. Worden, *The Rump Parliament, 1648–1653* (Cambridge: Cambridge University Press, 1974), pp. 243–8.

13 A. Hughes, '"The public profession of these nations": the national Church in Interregnum England', in C. Durston and J. Maltby (eds), *Religion in revolutionary England* (Manchester: Manchester University Press, 2006), pp. 93–114; E. Vernon, 'A ministry of the gospel: the Presbyterians during the English Revolution', in *ibid.*, pp. 115–36.

14 *The committee; or popery in masquerade* (1680). For more on L'Estrange's anti-nonconformist views, see A. Dunan-Page and B. Lynch (eds), *Roger L'Estrange and the making of Restoration culture* (Aldershot: Ashgate, 2008), especially the essay by N. von Maltzahn on L'Estrange and Milton.

15 K. Thomas, 'Women and the Civil War sects', *P&P*, 13 (1958), 42–62; Katherine Sutton, *A Christian womans experiences* (Rotterdam, 1663), pp. 13–14, 43.

16 John Perrot, *A sea of the seed's sufferings* (1661), p. 12.

17 Vavasor Powell, *Common-Prayer-Book no divine service* (1661), sig. A2v. Smectymnuun material was itself republished at this stage, see e.g., *Smectymnuus redivivus* (1660).

18 Vavasor Powell, [Hebrew: *Tsofer bepah*] *or the bird in the cage* (1661), part 1, p. 16.

19 See e.g. C. Holmes, *Seventeenth-century Lincolnshire* (Lincoln: History of Lincolnshire Committee for the Society for Lincolnshire History and Archaeology, 1980), pp. 218–22.

20 P. Seaward, *The Cavalier Parliament and the reconstruction of the old regime, 1661–1667* (Cambridge: Cambridge University Press, 1989), chapter 7.

21 G.R. Abernathy Jr, 'The English Presbyterians and the Stuart Restoration, 1648–1663', *Transactions of the American Philosophical Society*, n.s., 55:2 (1955). Of the 2,029 ejected in England and Wales from 1660–62 the vast majority were Presbyterians. Only 194 were Congregationalists and a mere 19 were Baptists. See Keeble, *Literary culture of nonconformity*, pp. 31–2.

22 T.L. Underwood, *Primitivism, radicalism, and the lamb's war: the Baptist–Quaker conflict in seventeenth-century England* (Oxford: Oxford University Press, 1997). My doctoral thesis was particularly concerned with the heterogeneity of dissent: G. Southcombe, 'The responses of nonconformists to the Restoration in England' (DPhil dissertation, University of Oxford, 2005).

23 See the chapter by Grant Tapsell in this volume.

24 N. Tyacke, 'The "rise of Puritanism" and the legalizing of dissent', in O.P. Grell, J.I. Israel and N. Tyacke (eds), *From persecution to toleration: the Glorious Revolution and religion in England* (Oxford: Clarendon Press, 1991), pp. 17–49; G.S. De Krey, 'The first Restoration crisis: conscience and coercion in London, 1667–73', *Albion*, 25 (1993), 565–80; H. Horwitz, 'Protestant reconciliation in the exclusion crisis', *JEH*, 15 (1964),

201–17; J. Spurr, 'The Church of England, comprehension and the Toleration Act of 1689', *EHR*, 104 (1989), 927–46. Relevant legislation, and the declarations of indulgence, are usefully collected in A. Browning (ed.), *English historical documents, 1660–1714* (New York: Oxford University Press, 1953), part IV, section A.

25 G. Tapsell, *The personal rule of Charles II, 1681–85* (Woodbridge: Boydell, 2007), chapter 3.

26 Joseph Besse, *A collection of the sufferings of the people called Quakers*, 2 vols (1753); e.g. N.H. Keeble, 'Richard Baxter', *ODNB*, Sharon Achinstein, 'Edmund Calamy', *ODNB*.

27 Quoted in M. Knights, *The devil in disguise: deception, delusion, and fanaticism in the early Enlightenment* (Oxford: Oxford University Press, 2011), p. 71.

28 M. Goldie, 'The Hilton gang and the purge of London in the 1680s', in H. Nenner (ed.), *Politics and the political imagination in later Stuart Britain: essays presented to Lois Green Schwoerer* (Rochester, NY: University of Rochester Press, 1997), pp. 43–73, at p. 43.

29 De Krey, 'The first Restoration crisis', 567.

30 'Charles II, 1665: An Act for restraining Non-Conformists from inhabiting in Corporations', *SR*, V, 575 (URL: http://www.british-history.ac.uk/report.aspx?compid=47375); Keeble, *Restoration*, p. 121. The 'Oxford Oath' was so named because parliament was sitting in Oxford, due to the plague in London. For a related discussion concerning oaths and conscience see J. Spurr, '"The strongest bond of conscience": oaths and the limits of tolerance in early modern England', in H.E. Braun and E. Vallance (eds), *Contexts of conscience in early modern Europe, 1500–1700* (Basingstoke: Palgrave Macmillan, 2004), pp. 151–65, 219–22.

31 Bodl. MS Rawlinson Letters 53, fol. 233, 'G.T. to Philip, Baron Wharton'; Robert Wild, *The loyal nonconformist* (1666).

32 Although Wild did allow himself to indulge the fantasy of the king's abolishing the episcopate: see Wild, *Loyal nonconformist*.

33 M. Goldie (gen. ed.), *The entring book of Roger Morrice, 1677–1691*, 7 vols (Woodbridge: Boydell, 2007–9), I, 231–4.

34 D. Cressy, *Travesties and transgressions in Tudor and Stuart England: tales of discord and dissension* (Oxford: Oxford University Press, 2000), chapter 13.

35 Thomas Grantham, *The prisoner against the prelate* (1662), p. 49.

36 John Whitehead and Martin Mason, *An expostulation with the bishops in England* ([1662]), p. 6. The phrase 'sound Doctrine, and the example of a good Conversation' echoes article 36 of the Instrument of Government, demonstrating once again the ways in which interregnal discourses were kept alive in the Restoration. See S.R. Gardiner (ed.), *The constitutional documents of the Puritan Revolution 1625–1660* (Oxford: Clarendon Press, pbk edn, 1979), p. 416.

37 For the elusiveness of Marvell's religious identity cf. W. Lamont, 'The religion of Andrew Marvell: locating the "bloody horse"', in C. Condren and A.D. Cousins (eds), *The political identity of Andrew Marvell* (Aldershot: Scolar Press, 1990), pp. 135–56; and N. von Maltzahn, 'Milton, Marvell and toleration', in S. Achinstein and E. Sauer (eds), *Milton and toleration* (Oxford: Oxford University Press, 2007), pp. 86–104.

38 Andrew Marvell, *The rehearsal transpros'd*, in Andrew Marvell, *The complete prose works of Andrew Marvell*, ed. M. Dzelzainis *et al.*, 2 vols (New Haven and London: Yale University Press, 2003), I, 146–7.

39 Marvell, *Rehearsal transpros'd*, I, 108–9.

40 F. Bate, *The Declaration of Indulgence, 1672: a study in the rise of organised dissent* (University Press of Liverpool, 1908).

41 Dzelzainis *et al.* (eds), *Complete prose works of Andrew Marvell*, I, 23–4.

42 Bate, *Declaration of Indulgence*, p. 98.

43 Robert Wild, *Dr Wild's humble thanks* (1672).

44 Goldie (gen. ed.), *Entring book of Roger Morrice*, I, 236–7; J. Spurr, *The Restoration Church of England, 1646–1689* (New Haven and London: Yale University Press, 1991), pp. 61–2; Richard Baxter, *Reliquiæ Baxterianæ*, ed. Matthew Sylvester (1696), part III, 98–101.

45 Bodl. MS Don. e. 23, fol. 66r. See further G. Southcombe, '"A prophet and a poet both!": nonconformist culture and the literary afterlives of Robert Wild', *HLQ*, 73 (2010), 249–62.

46 De Krey, 'Rethinking the Restoration', pp. 74–5.

47 M. Goldie, 'The theory of religious intolerance in Restoration England', in O.P. Grell, J.I. Israel and N. Tyacke (eds), *From persecution to toleration: the Glorious Revolution and religion in England* (Oxford: Clarendon Press, 1991), pp. 331–68.

48 J. Spurr, '"A special kindness for dead bishops": the church, history, and testimony in seventeenth-century Protestantism', *HLQ*, 68 (2005), 313–34; A. Starkie, 'Contested histories of the English church: Gilbert Burnet and Jeremy Collier', *ibid.*, 335–51; J.A.I. Champion, *The pillars of priestcraft shaken: the Church of England and its enemies, 1660–1730* (Cambridge: Cambridge University Press, 1992); Tony Claydon, *Europe and the making of England, 1660–1760* (Cambridge: Cambridge University Press, 2007), chapter 2.

49 Grantham, *Prisoner against the prelate*, pp. 17–18.

50 This is for many reasons not surprising. But it is worth noting that dissenting use of martyrology ran alongside the rejection of the Foxeian scheme among some Churchmen that developed in the early seventeenth century: see A. Milton, 'The Church of England, Rome, and the true church: the demise of a Jacobean consensus', in K. Fincham (ed.), *The early Stuart Church, 1603–1642* (Basingstoke: Macmillan, 1993), pp. 187–210.

51 George Fox and Ellis Hookes, *The arraignment of popery* (1667).

52 Keach, *War with the devil*, pp. 165–6; Samuel Morland, *The history of the evangelical churches of the valleys of Piemont* (1658). The figure of 200,000 dead in Ireland, while completely inaccurate, was commonplace.

53 Goldie (gen. ed.), *Entring book of Roger Morrice*, I, chapter 7 at p. 276.

54 John Whitehead, *The written gospel-labours* (1704), pp. 249–50.

55 S. Dixon, 'Quakers and the London parish 1670–1720', *The London Journal*, 32 (2007), 236. On neighbourly relations with Quakers more broadly see also J. Miller, '"A suffering people": English Quakers and their neighbours c.1650–c.1700', *P&P*, 188 (2005), 71–103.

56 Thomas Grantham, *The slanderer rebuked* ([1691]). See also the very full account provided in C. Bass, *Thomas Grantham (1633–1692) and General Baptist theology* (Oxford: Centre for Baptist History and Heritage, forthcoming 2012), pp. 35–7.

57 John Whitehead, *A general epistle* ([1682]), p. 3.

58 YUB MS Osborn c. 228, fol. 108. In the nineteenth century Adam Taylor commented on this correspondence and reprinted a few extracts. However, whilst he drew attention to some of the material discussed below, his analysis differed from the one offered here: *The history of the English General Baptists*, 2 vols (1818), I, 308–13.

59 YUB MS Osborn c. 228, fol. 1.

60 *Ibid.*, fol. 2.

61 *Ibid.*, fol. 33.

62 *Ibid.*, fol. 178. 'Bagden' refers to Buckden, the location of the bishop of Lincoln's palace.

63 M. Mullett, 'William Lloyd', *ODNB*; A.T. Hart, *William Lloyd 1627–1717: bishop, politician, author and prophet* (SPCK, 1952), pp. 47–8, 134–5 and *passim*; Tapsell, *Personal rule*, pp. 86–7.

64 J. Spurr, 'Thomas Barlow', *ODNB*.

65 YUB MS Osborn c. 228, fol. 73.

66 See e.g. *ibid.*, fols 127, 155.

67 Bass, *Thomas Grantham*, p. 37; C.B. Jewson, *The Baptists in Norfolk* (Carey Kingsgate Press, 1957), p. 36. Grantham had commented himself on attacks made on Baptist corpses: Thomas Grantham, *Christianismus primitivus* (1678), part III, 56.

68 YUB MS Osborn c. 228, fol. 59.

69 M. Clapinson (ed.), *Bishop Fell and nonconformity: visitation documents from the Oxford diocese, 1682–83* (Oxfordshire Record Society, 52, 1980), pp. 20, 28, 15, 17. For a similar invocation of Spain's infamous persecutory body to Boham's, see the words of the Recorder at the trial of the Quakers William Penn and William Mead in 1670: Samuel Starling, *An answer to the seditious and scandalous pamphlet* ([1670]), p. 29.

70 C. Rose, 'Providence, Protestant union and godly reformation in the 1690s', *TRHS*, sixth series, 3 (1993), 151–69; F. Dabhoiwala, 'Sex and societies for moral reform, 1688–1800', *JBS*, 46 (2007), 290–319; T. Isaacs, 'The Anglican hierarchy and the reformation of manners 1688–1738', *JEH*, 33 (1982), 391–411; T.C. Curtis and W.A. Speck, 'The Societies for the Reformation of Manners a case study in the theory and practice of moral reform', *Literature and History*, 3 (1976), 45–64.

71 Quoted in Rose, 'Providence, Protestant union and godly reformation', 168.

72 Dabhoiwala, 'Sex and societies for moral reform', 301.

73 Dabhoiwala, 'Sex and societies for moral reform', 299–300.

74 Quoted in J. Spurr, 'The church, the societies and the moral revolution of 1688', in J. Walsh, C. Haydon and S. Taylor (eds), *The Church of England c.1689–c.1833: from toleration to Tractarianism* (Cambridge: Cambridge University Press, 1993), p. 131.

75 John Nichols (ed.), *Letters on various subjects, literary, political, and ecclesiastical, to and from William Nicolson, D.D.*, 2 vols (1809), I, 153, 165. Nicolson's later support is noted in Isaacs, 'Anglican hierarchy and the reformation of manners', 399, 403.

76 On the ways in which the use of informers ultimately limited the success of the Societies see Dabhoiwala, 'Sex and societies for moral reform', pp. 311–12.

77 Daniel Defoe, *Reformation of manners, a satyr* (1702), pp. 60–1.

78 Defoe himself was a member of the Edinburgh Society for Reformation of Manners in

1707, and apparently of English Societies. He 'withdrew from active participation in the work of the Edinburgh Society because he could no longer support its policies.' See C.E. Burch, 'Defoe and the Edinburgh Society for the Reformation of Manners', *Review of English Studies*, 16 (1940), 306–12 at p. 308.

79 Rose, 'Providence, Protestant union and godly reformation', 168–9; C. Rose, *England in the 1690s: revolution, religion and war* (Oxford: Blackwell, 1999), pp. 208–9.

80 *Letters on various subjects*, I, 153–4.

81 Daniel Defoe, *A continuation of letters written by a Turkish spy* (1718), pp. 20–1. The question of Defoe's authorship is raised in G. Sill, 'The source of Robinson Crusoe's "sudden Joys"', *Notes and Queries*, 45 (1998), 67–8.

Chapter 9

The church and the Catholic community
1660–1714

Gabriel Glickman

In 1689, in the wake of the Revolution that toppled a Catholic king from the throne of the three kingdoms, an anonymous treatise was circulated among the clergymen of the English College at Douai. 'Lost or stolen from the Ld Archbishop of Canterbury', it advertised, 'a Cassock and Cloak made up of the Church of England', a garment 'finely dyed with the Doctrine of Non-resistance ... that shined like Religion, [was] lived quite through with Self-Interest, bound up with the oaths of Allegiance and Supremacy, and buttoned up with the Test.'[1] This piece of satire characterised the polemical reflexes among Catholic Jacobites who diagnosed the Revolution as the start of a new crisis in the relationship between England's recusant minority and their compatriots. It was not new to find Catholic commentators anathematising 'fanatical' Protestant tendencies in the realm; more novel was the extent to which they fixed their gaze upon the Anglican High Church. The document circulated at Douai spoke for a strain of thought common within the English recusant community, which identified the Revolution as a calamity with implications just as serious for the Anglican flock. The casting-out of its own Supreme Governor was an act so perverse that it could only end with the immolation of that 'false deceitful Jezebel', the Church of England.[2]

The rhetorical assault upon the Church of England by the Catholic Jacobites was the culmination point of four years of public controversy between the two communities, after Anglican apologists had issued their clarion call against James II's Declarations of Indulgence, the imposition of Catholics and dissenters onto public institutions and the planned overthrow of the Test Act. However, the trajectory taking English Catholics towards the bitter indictments delivered in 1689 was longer and larger. The depth of disenchantment with the Anglican leadership can be explained by the fact that for over two decades recusant authors had identified a new affinity with the Restoration church as an essential stepping-stone in the campaign for greater accommodation within the life of their realm. Recusant authors had endeavoured to construct a scholarly and ideological relationship with sympathetic elements within the established church, exploiting the political divisions in English Protestantism, cultivating the 'catholic' over the Reformed strand of theological opinion, even opening up the grander prospect of Christian reunion. This chapter will suggest that the self-representation of English Catholics after 1660, together with many of the internal debates within the community, was shaped by patterns of correspondence or confrontation with the established church. A closer study of the relationship offers insights into the varieties of debate not just between but *within* each congregation, at a time when affairs of the spiritual estate came into collision with the instability of domestic politics, and English ecclesiastical policy appeared far from fixed.

The recent renewal of scholarly interest in the 1688 Revolution has served a reminder of how the fear of popery supplied a gripping leitmotif in public affairs after the Restoration.[3] However, while many works focusing on the public meaning of Catholicism in Restoration politics have concentrated overwhelmingly on *anti-Catholicism*, most studies of English recusancy have accentuated the internal dynamics of the community over its connection with the wider Protestant nation. This chapter will look at the practical relationship forged between recusants and Anglicans in the parishes, and then turn to the public exchanges between the two communities, reviewing the rhetorical stratagems called upon by Catholics variously to court or critique the church by law established, and charting the shifts and reverses within the Protestant response. I will argue that the clash between 1685 and 1688 arose from causes wider than simply the policies of James II: an ideological divergence created as much by an alteration in the tone of Anglican polemic, and the sidelining of that strand within the Restoration church that had placed itself within the 'catholic' tradition, in favour of a more broadly Protestant ecclesiastical vision. The experience of the reign of James II left bitter memories stored within the imagination of each community. However, as the last section of the chapter will argue, the same flickers of spiritual and intellectual attraction between recusants and Anglicans could be seen enduring into the eighteenth century: the sign that not every Englishman perceived an inevitable equivalence between the Catholic religion and the 'popish' dystopia.

I

Across the spectrum of English society, the Church of England was forced to confront an active community of Catholic dissenters, represented in disproportionate numbers among the gentry and aristocracy. The 60,000 individuals uncovered by the Compton Census of 1674 were dispersed through certain regional enclaves dominated by the estates of wealthy Catholic magnates, whose education in the clerical seminaries at Lisbon, Douai, Paris and St Omer had opened up recusant England to the pressures of the Counter-Reformation.[4] Here, Catholicism could make for a robust and even confrontational figure in the religious landscape. In West Lancashire, the manorial chapel at Little Crosby attracted a regular seventy-five communicants to vespers, while the village itself could boast, according to its wealthiest landowner, William Blundell 'not a beggar', 'not an alehouse', 'not a Protestant in it'.[5] In the neighbouring district, a gentry-sponsored 'riding mission' shaped a commitment scarcely less tenacious among the weavers and reed-makers of Preston and Walton-le-Dale: the local Anglican parson complained of Catholic ceremonies brazenly conducted at the market cross.[6] Reporting on 'the dangerous Growth of Popery in these your Majesty's Dominions' in 1671, a committee of the House of Lords cited quotidian examples of Catholic indiscretion: rooms allocated for mass in the taverns of Oxford, schools proliferating along the Welsh borders, 'Horsemen, Coaches, and lighted Torches' congregating for public interments with religious rites in Winchester, and a Benedictine convent operating in the heart of the city of Westminster.[7] Yet many within the church itself appeared tentative as to how to respond. Appealing to Archbishop Sheldon, the bishop of Chester declared his anxiety that 'To make pecuniary mulcts upon them is base, To proceed by Church-censures is vaine, to leave them unobserved, is to multiply them, I can but wayt for my direction.'[8]

As the hints behind such reports suggested, the heroic caricature of separation and refusal represented no true summation of the recusant world: the preservation of the faith owed as much to the hidden cohorts of church-papists, conservative conformists and silent sympathisers, as the public persuasions of those who defied the magistrate. Anglican parsons voiced regular anguish about inner convictions concealed beneath the outward form of church attendance and, at a provincial level, the official notifications of Catholic numbers offered some grounds to support these fears. Religious convictions among the farming families of the East Riding district of Bubwith and Howden fluctuated according to the clerical provision made available by the local recusant houses of Langdale and Vavasour.[9] The porous reality of the divide between Catholicism and conformity was especially pronounced among the political elites. During the years of Interregnum, notables of the old Caroline regime had placed their offspring inside the English colleges and convents in Spain and the Low Countries – Jerome Weston, the nominally Protestant second earl of Portland had conferred patronage upon the Augustinian nuns at Bruges – while émigrés such as Sir Henry Bennet and the earl of Bristol returned from the Continent with religious identities highly ambiguous.[10] Sir Solomon Swale exploited the legal loopholes to remain sitting in the Commons after the passing of the Test Act in 1673, while in the House of Lords, members of the Howard family weaved in and out of recusant status, depending on the pressures of the day.[11] Protective loyalties towards papist neighbours were often most pronounced among Tory Anglican gentry families with recusant ancestry or marital connections, such as the Oglethorpes in the West Riding, the Pakingtons in Warwickshire, and the Bradshaighs in West Lancashire.[12] It was those individuals who formed the outer shell of English Catholicism that often played the salient role in its preservation. In 1667 Bishop Hall professed doubts as to whether the 1,500 recusants presented at the Lancaster Assizes would face judicial action – 'it may be imprudence, to undertake a prosecution of them to no issue'. The fact that only £157 could be collected through penal fines between 1660 and 1672 betokened the currents of feeling in England that proved resistant to a major anti-popish inquisition.[13]

The closely interwoven lives of the different congregations tested the resolve of the Anglican priesthood. Legal requirements pushed them together, when Catholic marriages had to be formalised by Anglican chaplains: the Blundells paid the local parsons a token half-guinea to put their names to a ceremony that had been previously undertaken inside the household chapel.[14] Commercial opportunities could soften the edges of the religious divide: the mines on the Gascoigne family estate provided the stone to keep York Minster in good repair.[15] The main cause of interaction, however, arose from the continuous claim of property rights levied by English landowners over local parish structures: the provision of schools and almshouses, the nomination of churchwardens, and even the appointment of clergymen.[16] In Sussex, the Carylls controlled their parish by the writ of the bishop of Chichester; in Stoke-by-Nayland, recusant authority was symbolised when the bodies of successive Mannock squires were entombed beneath eye-catching church monuments.[17] Catholic landowners had to operate within a public space, and it was in their interests to conform to the local panoply of shared values and expectations. Nicholas Blundell upbraided Jesuit missioners for their failure to extend Christian friendship to local Protestant clergymen, while it was a common dictum within the Tempest family at Broughton Hall that any discussion among Catholics and Protestants 'not resolved to eavil' would see theological conflicts reduced to 'the splitting of a hair'.[18]

However, it is too rosy a picture to see the Catholic involvement with their parish churches as purely an expression of paternalism and nostalgia. In 1671, the House of Lords attributed the plethora of 'scandalous and unfit Ministers' in the church to the high quantity of 'Advowsons and Presentations to Livings ... disposed of by Popish Recusants or by others intrusted by them', in Stonyhurst, Sir Nicholas Shireburne had certainly advanced his interest by intruding a Protestant kinsman into one of the parish livings.[19] 'The Churches in past tymes were ours', claimed a set of verses inside the papers of the Dicconson family, 'That little which antiquity assures / Falles upon the Romish Church, not yours'.[20] Sir Robert Throckmorton decreed that the reliquaries preserved at Harvington Hall would be conferred back upon the parish church on the day that England returned to its older faith.[21] In polishing ancestral tombs and recasting the armorial engravings as 'marks of honour derived from so many Ages and Generations', the actions of the squires could be seen in a less comforting light: placing a territorial claim over the institutions of a land where public opportunities did not match the ambition stored within their estates.[22] Moreover, both communities remained participants in a larger contest that left private religion closely intertwined with public, temporal ramifications. When pamphlets, newsbooks, and rumours poured into the provinces, religious communities were forced to mediate between the ideal of communal harmony and the pressures stirred by the Popish Plot furore, the rise and fall of a Catholic agenda under James II, and, after 1689, the whispers of Jacobite plots hatched in recusant mansions. The participation of the local parson in an armed search of the Throckmortons' Coughton Court estate in December 1688, the suspicion of Sir Francis Mannock that Suffolk clergymen had been involved in attempts to prosecute Catholic labourers on his estate in 1708, and the allegation that Anglican authorities had fomented mob attacks on a Preston chapel after the 1715 Jacobite rebellion showed the limits of local impulses towards conciliation.[23]

II

The relationship between Catholics and the Restoration church developed against a background of rising recusant confidence and visibility. From the Inns of Court, to the boards of merchant companies, to the colonial bases at New York and Tangier, Catholic aspiration could be seen entering into the apparatus of the state.[24] In Maryland, the plantation settled upon the proprietorship of Lord Baltimore, Catholics enjoyed executive office.[25] In the counties, a number of dynasties that had previously sheltered within the carapace of church-papistry – Scropes, Shireburnes, Bedingfields – moved towards a more open recusant identity.[26] If Catholic activity in England did not amount to the orchestrated plot of Protestant nightmares, it was built upon the conviction that experiences shared between 1641 and 1660 had earned Catholics the right to claim moral parity with their Anglican compatriots. Sir Nicholas Shireburne believed that concrete evidence of 'Loyal Fidelity to King Charles 1st of Ever Blessed Memory during the long war carried on by the Usurping Powers' served as sufficient evidence to wipe out the aspersion that loyalty to Rome placed limitations on the temporal allegiances of his co-religionists; Sir Francis Throckmorton made the same point in 1662 when he commissioned the monument in Christ Church, Oxford to an uncle, Sir John Smith, who had lost his life redeeming the king's standard at Edgehill.[27] Exiled clergymen anticipated that the domestic mission would be shaped by contact with other faiths. Alexander Dunbar surmised from Paris that 'who deals with protestants in this countrie will com off with shame & discredit to ther profession, if ... they be not well versed in Controversie & other learning'.[28]

The Catholic campaign for civil accommodation was centred on the lobbying and pamphleteering exertions of a network of priests and laymen present in the entourage of Henrietta Maria – and later Catherine of Braganza – at Somerset House.[29] Ushered onto the London print market and circulated in manuscript through recusant mansions, their argument was pitched to meet the sensibilities of an Anglican audience and aspired self-consciously towards friendship across the confessional divide. John Caryll, the scholar and playwright, wished his reflections to be received by 'all Protestants in general, but more especially to those who pretend a good blood in their veins, & have any value for their ancestry'.[30] The construction of an appeal for liberty of conscience was built upon old Elizabethan and Jacobean foundations, harking back to the rhetoric of 'Catholic loyalty' developed by Anthony Copley, Thomas Preston, and Leander Jones.[31] Yet for over a decade after the Restoration, Catholic apologetic went significantly further, steered by a striking number of former Anglican converts, who had seemingly retained much of their old political theology. The Benedictine monk Hugh Cressy, whose spiritual route had taken him from the Great Tew circle of Viscount Falkland in 1641 into the Order of St Benedict, desired to engage the minds of those English Protestants 'whose tenents are least discrepant with the Church of Rome': and 'lessen ye number of differences between Christians'.[32] James Maurus Corker yearned for an end to the 'endless and frivolous conferences ... Partiality and Prejudice' that had disfigured European religious debate.[33] They dispensed praise upon features of the Anglican confession, and claimed to glimpse shades of Christian truth stored within the language and liturgy of the Church of England. Cressy commended the King James Bible as far more 'exact and elegant' than 'the rudeness of the Translations ... made at Rhemes and Doway, in use now among Catholicks'.[34] The Franciscan John Vincent Canes believed that the Church of England had risen through its learning and spirituality to become a model of 'order', 'decency', and 'peace': the 'choisest flower' in the Protestant world.[35]

The search for amity obliged Catholics to promote a view of their own religion that de-emphasised doctrinal differences with the English church. Catholic historians placed the Christian institutions of the medieval kingdom at arm's length from the court of Rome: to the monk Philip Ellis, the ecclesiastical law-giving offices performed by the Saxon kings had created a uniquely 'English Church, comprehended within the limits of that nation and confined to the nature thereof' – its monarchical ideology was affirmed by its thirty royal saints.[36] The theological armouring was provided by the precedents of the French Gallican church: a counterblast, for Cressy, towards 'the clergy among us' who 'have been hitherto ... zealously addicted to the Spaniards and by their example exalted the Power and Jurisdiction of the court of Rome'.[37] The anti-papal example of Henri IV, the 1626 condemnation of doctrines of papal infallibility by the University of Paris, and the Four Gallican Articles of 1682 infused a political theology into English Catholic polemic that elevated kings and bishops above the pontiff in temporal and even many ecclesiastical affairs. Catholic authors extracted their case from the most irenic elements within the Gallican tradition – Hugh Cressy revived the thoughts of Etienne Pasquier and Francois Veron, who had sought grounds for the toleration or comprehension of the Huguenot community, while John Gother turned to the rigorist, Jansenist theology of the Dominican Noel Alexandre, a critic of Louis XIV.[38] Placing translations of French texts at the forefront of the Catholic literary campaign under James II, the convert monk Henry Joseph Johnston affirmed that 'Catholicks do not take the Church of Rome as it is the Suburbican Dioecese to be the Catholick Church, but all the Christian Churches in Communion with the Bishop of Rome'. His vision of an England bound by Catholic doctrines, but governed by royal 'Nursing Fathers', cleaved close to the ideas of the Restoration High Church.[39]

Catholic authors believed therefore that a wide expanse of common ground could be uncovered, once their own communion had been cleansed of distorting associations with the papalist and republican doctrines of Persons and Mariana. For over sixty years, it was a particular motif in the polemic of the 'secular clergy' that the greater commonality existed between their own brethren and the Church of England – the Jesuits, to Richard Smith, John Sergeant, and Charles Dodd, were the Catholic equivalents of the Puritans, dissenters, and 'fanatics' who resisted the authority of Canterbury.[40] However, compatibility did not connote equal spiritual worth. Vincent Canes believed that the Anglican tradition represented a broken corpus, wrecked amid the civil and religious storms that had cast the kingdom into the maelstrom of competing sects, who 'run themselves restlessly into endless schisms, denying one thing after another, still from less to more, till at length all Christianity be cancelled'. The holy life could never be compassed in any nation that had sliced itself apart from an 'ancient apostolicall tradition', 'so mixt and intangled in the very nerves and sinews of the laws' of Christian kingdoms. Canes observed that defenders of the Church of England were forced, in their battles with dissenters, to grope towards 'those very principles' its founders had hitherto branded 'popish' – 'the difference betwixt clergy and laity, the efficacy of Episcopal ordination, the authority of a visible Church'.[41] For John Caryll, Anglican dependence upon the older faith – 'from her doth ye Church of England immediately derive her Xianity, a lawfull ordination, ye scriptures, and consequently the very essence and being of a Religion' exposed the English Reformation as a needless historic error.[42]

Catholics urged potential converts that a crossing of the confessional threshold should represent not the disavowal but the logical completion of Anglican religious intuitions. The duchess of York professed that she had been beckoned into the Catholic fold by readings of Peter Heylyn: at the centre of her own conversion narrative stood a claim to have been assured by two Anglican bishops that the Church of Rome was a legitimate – in some of its doctrines, superior – counterpart to that of Canterbury.[43] The greatest indication of Catholic confidence was evinced in the willingness of its scholarly advocates to raise hopes not simply for legal toleration, but for institutional reconciliation between the churches. In his Oxfordshire manor, John Belson amassed papers affirming the 'desirability of means to reconcile the C of E with Church of Rome'; at the University of Paris, Henry Holden believed that his minimalist conception of papal authority and rigorist approach towards saint-worship and reliquary devotion 'laid open a way for an Union between the Church of England and the Roman'.[44] Others were prepared to stretch Tridentine doctrines to breaking point. The Franciscan Christopher Davenport retained a conviction first voiced at the court of Charles I, that the doctrines of the Thirty-nine Articles could be interpreted in a form compatible with Catholic ortho-doxy.[45] In 1669, Hugh Cressy told Lord Treasurer Thomas Clifford that such 'speciall points' on which concessions could legitimately be sought included a vernacular liturgy, the continuation of clerical marriage, and a system of 'communion in both kinds' with separate altars raised in every church for separate Anglican or Catholic rites.[46] On the strength of these arguments, he was convinced, it would be possible to widen the space of Christendom and so call back the disciples of Hooker, Andrewes, Laud, and Heylyn.

III

The willingness of Cressy, Davenport, and their coevals to re-imagine the post-Tridentine ecclesiastical order, positing even English bibles and married clergymen as examples of legitimate 'indulgences' within their church, made their writings, for Anglicans, infuriatingly difficult to oppose. 'They are visibly weary (all but the Jesuits) of insisting upon the Pope's Infallibility', the earl of Clarendon commented in 1674: 'you scarce meet with an argument from it in any Book that is Printed, nor can you engage them in it upon discourse'.[47] Within a decade of the Restoration, there were murmurs of Protestant concern that such arguments were beginning to find an audience. To George Morley, bishop of Winchester, the 'Cavaleers of the Church of Rome vainly vaunt of how many and how great Proselites they have made, and of how many consid-erable persons of both sexes they have gained from our Church unto theirs'.[48] The more invidious possibility, suggested by Gilbert Burnet, was that 'popery' had been allowed to grow because some within the Anglican communion themselves harboured suppressed anxieties about the Reformation.[49] While the main cluster of clerical conversions was largely confined to pockets of High Church Oxford, the official stance of the Restoration episcopate was softening sufficiently for Archbishop Sheldon himself to deny that Rome pointed towards an anti-Christian false church. Archbishop Bramhall of Armagh was prepared to grant the Catholic corpus the possession of a 'metaphysical being'; its 'errors' lying 'rather in superstructures, than in fundamentals'.[50]

The currents of exchange between the churches could be traced through shared ecclesiological principles in the writings of Richard Hooker, Archbishop Bancroft, and the Gallican jurists. Later, a crop of Tory pamphlets observed similarities between 'the Liberties of the *Gallican* Church' and 'the Prelacy and Prerogatives of the Church and Monarchy of *England*', while John Dryden's Catholic conversion was prefigured by his discovery of Gallican texts and arguments.[51] The poet laureate believed that promotion of the royalist, anti-papal precedent from Paris could separate the 'true Episcopal Man' within the Church of England from the more irredeemably Protestant 'Latitude Man'.[52] Theology, as well as ecclesiology, appeared to press the parallels when the tradition embellished by William Laud and Peter Heylyn had aimed to reposition English Christian institutions within an 'universal congregation' composed of national episcopal churches: peeling back Lutheran or Calvinist affinities and accentuating continuities with medieval Christianity, the idea allowed them to claim spiritual kinship with the Catholic world.[53] Elements within the two churches even drew upon the same pool of devotional literature: the High Churchmen Henry Dodwell and John Norris produced the first English translations of the spiritual works of St François de Sales and Nicholas Malebranche, while English Catholic editions of the medieval mystical writings informed the Scottish spiritual writers George Garden and James Cunningham.[54] Recusants and Anglicans were, as the monk Henry Johnston saw it, laying claim to the same intellectual territory of 'Unity, Sanctity, Universality and Antiquity'.[55]

Visions of spiritual concord moved from the imagination of the Somerset House chaplains onto the threshold of international diplomacy on 22 May 1670, when Charles II acceded to the secret 'Catholic' clauses stored within the Anglo-French Treaty of Dover, permitting Thomas Clifford to draw up plans to present before the pontiff the possibility of a distinctive Anglican rite created within the Catholic Church, justified by Gallican precedents.[56] It was a moment, in the words of Cressy, with the potential to 'almost intirely change the face of all the affaires of Europe'; yet it was a moment that collapsed swiftly and brutally. Within two years, the new French alliance and the ensuing war on the Dutch had unleashed a wave of anti-popish agitation in English politics, culminating in 1673 with the shattering blow posed by the passing of the Test Act. If recusants had believed that the endurance of 'Catholic' tendencies within the Church of England was producing a collective shift in the direction of

Rome, the ensuing round of pamphlet exchanges left them disabused. Anglicans, as Bishop Morley contended, might place themselves within a universal 'catholick' church, but they contested the notion that this entity was confined to the 'Roman Catholic' corpus, and that its membership entailed 'submitting to the dictates of ye Pope and Popish Councells, particularly to that of Trent ... many of them nothing of kinne to the Canon of Scripture'.[57] As the earl of Clarendon saw it, the communion of Canterbury was already authentically 'Catholic' in 'all the substantial and extensive points', and separated only by such minor degrees of distance from the Gallican church, which also 'holds a Council to be above the Pope', as could satisfy all true Christians. Defenders of the church restated a conservative interpretation of Anglican identity that nonetheless constructed firm doctrinal walls against Rome. For Clarendon, the Reformation represented simply such jurisdictional 'alterations' as 'by the laws of the Kingdom they could lawfully do ... agreeable to the manners of the Nation'. There was no compelling reason why renewed obeisance to Rome would lift Anglican institutions into a greater state of spiritual completion.[58]

The shifting of English sensibilities after the outbreak of the third Dutch War (1672–74) proved the dangers attendant on Catholic interventions in state affairs – the closer they advanced towards the public sphere, the greater the backlash they risked engendering in Protestant opinion. The recusant response to the Test Act fluctuated from the forlorn jeremiads of Henry Neville Payne's play *The Siege of Constantinople* – invoking the rising Turkish threat to lament the collapse of Christian unity in Europe – to the vitriolic anonymous lament for *The Banished Priests*, which perceived a betrayal of Catholic sacrifices in the Civil Wars: 'Did we contend for you with blood and treasure / That you should plague and banish us at pleasure?'[59] Such authors were at one in identifying the passage of the legislation as an irreversible moment in the relationship between their own communion and the established church. While the Church of England still shed a scattering of high-profile communicants into the Roman fold after 1673, the new infrastructure of legal barriers was conceived expressly to close down the routes for Catholic activism within the public domain. At court, the earl of Danby insisted that ecclesiastical authorities had to be seen to be taking up the cudgels against Catholicism in order to head off the destabilising political potential of 'anti-popery'; duly pressured, the bishops rebalanced their pulpit fulminations, to pitch the claims of the church just as vehemently towards Catholics as Protestant nonconformists.[60] Moreover, the emergent conflict over English foreign policy showed that, regardless of the theological subtleties upheld by the bishops, Anglican lay opinion was as decidedly hostile to Rome as to dissent: a sentiment that needed only the catalyst of a rise in French power to lodge itself upon the legislative agenda in Westminster.[61] Across the counties, the reactivating of penal measures against recusants brought the most visible indication of a kingdom intent on reasserting its Protestant identity. Within a year, the intellectual architects of the Treaty of Dover – Hugh Cressy and Thomas Clifford – had died, defeated and exhausted.

IV

In the political and religious environment created by the Test Act, utopian schemes of religious reunion were markedly less apparent in recusant thought, though vestiges of the hope endured into the following century among superiors of the English College, Douai, where Edward Dicconson believed that since 'often ye Parsons do preach to ye people that Rome is better than Geneva', there remained tendencies which 'if artfully improved' could turn towards 'the reunion of yt great Church' with Rome.[62] Catholic authors of the 1670s still aimed to exploit 'Cavalier' impulses in English politics, and still pressed for an alliance with Anglican opinion against dissenters, 'republicans', and 'fanaticks', but the amity they sought possessed a more narrowly political character, accentuating the demonstration of civic virtues over inquiries into the truth of Catholic doctrine. In reaction to the tumults of the Popish Plot and exclusion crisis, Catholic leaders undertook the defence of their community by locating themselves within a wider loyalist culture that de-emphasised their confessional identity, to desire simply, as the monk Philip Ellis put it, that 'nothing should be restored but our Reputation, and to be thought by our fellow Countrymen, neither Pernicious nor Useless members of our Country'.[63] John Caryll's poem *Naboth's Vineyard* captured the suffering recusant as the law-abiding man of property, 'his neighbour's safeguard and their peace', harried by mobs and plotters who coveted their estates.[64] Reporting on the currents of opinion in London, George Throckmorton urged his family to repudiate any vaulting ambitions for religious change and embrace the appellation 'Tory' as the means to 'give credit' to their 'obedience to the Crown'.[65] The writings of Roger L'Estrange and John Dryden had, he said, 'layd open the Villainy and Ignorance of the Whiggish scribblers and swearers', and begun to expose the 'fiction' of the plot as 'a machine contrived by the Presbyterians' to 'fix the supream power in the People ... til they destroyd our monarchy'. In tying their claims of conspiracy to an attempt to break the line of royal succession and reduce the powers of the bishops, the Whig party had, he believed, delivered a gift into the hands of those authors who argued that, since 1641, the enemies of the recusant community were also the adversaries of the crown and the established church.

There was certainly sufficient material within the nascent culture of Tory Anglican campaigning that proved welcoming to English Catholics. Roger L'Estrange, who called upon friendships with the Blundells and the Carylls to gather news and information from the counties, agreed that if the essential component of 'popery' was a belief that kings could be deposed in the name of religion, it was Whigs and dissenters who bore more of a resemblance to the radical Jesuits of the previous century and had proved the real 'papists in masquerade'.[66] George Throckmorton was especially enamoured of Dryden's play *The Duke of Guise*, which drew parallels between the confessionalised Whigs and the mob-raising republicans of the Catholic League in sixteenth-century France.[67] If Tory literature offered few signs of a religious affinity for the English Catholic community, it appeared nonetheless to extend the hope that loyal subjects of the house of Stuart could be united upon a common civic platform. L'Estrange and Fabian Phillips both asserted that 'Disagreements in Religion' should never be put before the 'interests of state', had declared that the magistrates should not trouble themselves with 'meer religion', but judge confessional communities on the grounds of their capacity for public peace, and, above all, insisted that the personal Catholic allegiances of the duke of York carried no repercussions for his right to the Crown.[68] By 1682, Anglican gentlemen appeared to be heeding such advice, speaking out in defence of their recusant neighbours, while county juries began to return verdicts of 'not guilty' on individuals accused of being privy to the plot.[69] The Anglican confession, in its politicised coloration, appeared to be centred on loyalty to the throne, and reactions to the Monmouth rebellion (1685) seemed to affirm this truth, when sermons obligingly placed the bonds between king and people before confessional loyalties to a rebel Protestant prince.[70]

V

The experience of the civil conflicts between 1678 and 1683 gave recusants the rhetorical tools with which to approach their compatriots two years later, when providence and political virtue appeared to have conferred their reward in the coronation of a Catholic king. The Jesuit Edward Scarisbrick chose the thirty-seventh anniversary of the 1649 regicide to offer a public sermon *Upon the Subject of Government and Obedience*, suffused with features of Anglican political theology, remembering 'a day for sackcloth and ashes ... weeping eyes and bleeding hearts', that served reminders of the perils of such 'false maxims' that had torn a king from his throne.[71] Catholic expectations at the opportunity created by James II did not inevitably connote support for the direction of the new king's policies: between 1685 and 1688, as even some Whig commentators acknowledged, many representatives of the old recusant families professed disquiet at the pace and ambition of the royal plan for Catholic advancement.[72] Nor, however, did private anxiety necessarily translate into outright opposition. From the lords Powis and Belassis on the Privy Council, to the new entrants into the county shrievalty and the commissions of the peace, the majority of Catholics who were offered the chance *did* opt to take up public office.[73] Moreover, whatever their qualms over dispensing with the Test Act, a much wider level of Catholic support was declared for the new Declaration of Indulgence (1687): the means, according to John Belson, to render 'all jars apt to rise upon differences in Religion cut up by ye roots, & things settled upon a lasting basis of quiet and security for ever'. Belson retained his affinity with Tory Anglican notables: lobbying the court against the dismissal of the second earl of Clarendon and the Scottish Lord Advocate Sir George Mackenzie. Yet, to these friends, he declared bewilderment at signs of Anglican opposition even to the extension of legal religious freedoms. The faith placed by the established church in its own penal protection represented an affront, Belson argued, not merely to the temporal 'common good', but to the 'law of God' and the 'charity' required of a Christian institution.[74]

There was, in some counties, scope for compromise. The Yorkshire Tory Sir John Reresby could concede to the tolerationist core of the king's policies when 'most men were now convinced that liberty of conscience was a thing of advantage to the nation, if it might be settled with due regard to the rights and privileges of the Church of England'.[75] Within the ecclesiastical hierarchy in 1685, it was still possible to find Erastian voices willing to tie their church to the temporal duty of passive obedience – the 1707 'Collection' of material on the life of James II by the monks Henry Johnston and Ralph Weldon was pointedly prefaced with a published sermon by Bishop Turner on the imperative of submission before the 'imperial crown'.[76] Yet, with the increasingly isolated exception of Samuel Parker, this tendency dwindled to a muted minimum in the face of the legal controversies engendered by the king's policies, and recusants were confronted with a stark picture of the limits of the Tory alliance created in 1678.[77] During the reign of James II, 228 Anglican literary attacks upon popery were launched, compared to just three published dissenting works, laying down a theological assault upon the doctrines of the Catholic Church that, for Gilbert Burnet, moved 'far beyond anything that had before that time appeared in our language'.[78] The church's battle was framed in a polemical form for lay readership, with much of the energy provided by a network of younger London clergymen. Burnet identified John Tillotson, Edward Stillingfleet, Thomas Tenison, and Edward Gee alongside the Tories William Sherlock and Francis Atterbury; John Belson believed that the same names represented the moving spirit threatening to make a wider body of the kingdom 'disaffected to his M[ajes]ty'.[79] For Burnet, their labours served not merely to salvage the privileges of the Church of England but rescued English Protestanism itself in a time of peril: 'Popery itself was never so well understood by the Nation, as it came to be upon this occasion.'[80]

The political turn within Church of England literature was accompanied by a theological shift in emphasis, and a tilt towards those aspects of Anglican thought that placed the clearest degree of difference between Anglicans' own communion and that of Rome. The London divines engaged in point-by-point refutations of Catholic apologetic, launching instantaneous replies to the works issued by the newly converted John Dryden, and subjecting John Gother's outline of *A Papist Represented and Misrepresented* to fourteen barbed responses.[81] They slanted the debate away from the ground preferred by Catholics – questions of church origins and antiquity, apostolic succession and, in Dryden's words, 'the rule for determining controversies' – into a more broadly Protestant line of attack.[82] Concentrating, in Stillingfleet's words, not on 'a Succession of Persons, but of Doctrine', they reframed the clash between the churches on a series of point-by-point interrogations of Tridentine teachings, so as to level claims against Catholic casuistry, innovation, and superstition as an affront to the biblically based 'Practice of Virtue, and a good Life' that was 'the great design and concernment of the Christian Religion'.[83] The declared aim was to pinpoint the fallibilities of the irenic 'New Popery': at best, the preserve of a small and unrepresentative faction within the French clergy and, at worst, 'the Instrument to divide our Clergy and to fill them with suspicions of one another'.[84] For Burnet, the pamphlet controversy 'gave occasion to inquire into the true opinions of that Church, not as some artful writers had disguised them, but as they were laid down ... in all those countries where Popery prevails without any intermixture with hereticks'.[85] To Abednego Seller, a convert could be seduced into a false conception of the Catholic religion, but 'who knows how much further he must go, when he is under the new Oaths of Obedience to that Church, who ... binds all her followers to an Implicit Faith to believe whatever she shall reveal?'[86] While John Gother insisted that his opponents probed only 'the sinks, Jakes and Dunghills' of the Catholic faith, Anglican clergymen were beating the drum against Popery with a vigour rarely glimpsed inside the church of Gilbert Sheldon, re-entering the rhetorical universe of John Foxe with incessant reminders of persecuting tendencies in the Gallican church so beloved of recusant opinion, and a heightened concern for the sufferings of fellow Protestants in Europe.[87] The legacy of this campaign for the identity of the Church of England was affirmed in 1738, when the pamphlets were lovingly assembled in a three-volume collection by Bishop Edmund Gibson.[88]

Stung by the intensity of these attacks, Catholic commentators retreated from their Tory alliance. By 1687, John Dryden's call for concord between the Catholic 'hind' and the Anglican 'panther' against the dissenting 'wolves' ran contrary not merely to the direction of royal policy, but to the grain of political and religious literature produced in defence of the court.[89] Most of the preachers commissioned by the court of James II chose simply to ignore the Church of England: while the Vicars Apostolic urged their flock to 'prevent and suppress all irregular motions' and 'edify' critics 'by your good example', their vision centred on a Catholic institution rising independently and providentially within the kingdom.[90] Few authors matched the zeal of John Everard, who believed that the chance 'to rescue the Virgin Spouse of Christ, the Roman Catholick Church from the jaws of the Dragon' would serve as an inevitable '*Winding-sheet for the Schism of England*'.[91] But at court, the convert earl of Perth concluded, in correspondence with Bishop Bossuet of Meaux, that Tory Anglican conceptions of political and religious uniformity could only be provided for inside a Catholic state.[92] Even decidedly moderate Catholic notables co-operated with the dissenting interest in overturning the borough corporations, blending their justifications with the civic argument for toleration articulated by Royal Society authors such as William Petty and Sir Peter Pett.[93] Pamphlets printed by the court reminded Protestant nonconformists that Anglicans had never offered them the warmth now extended by the king: the church 'esteems her Dissenters, and, as such, she (when in power) constantly ... labours to destroy them'.[94] A treatise received by the Scarisbrick family in Lancashire argued that against the 'Mallice' of the established church, liberty of conscience represented 'the onely thing left' as a means for James II 'to build his Glory or Safety for the Future'.[95] It was, perhaps, no coincidence that the Catholic barrister Robert Brent, one of the architects of the alliance with Nonconformists, had been a landholder in the Catholic colony Maryland, where official toleration prevented the growth of *any* clerical power. If the Catholic laymen who entered into the corporations with Quakers, Baptists, and Independents upheld any ideological vision, it was certainly closer to the experience of Lord Baltimore's domain than the older clerical dream of Catholic and Anglican differences collapsing into the fold of a single national church.[96]

Reactions to the royal toleration policy drove Catholics and Anglicans into an ideological divergence that was sealed in the response to the Revolution. Pinning particular blame upon the established church, Jacobites scattered vitriol upon 'England's Pharisees', adopting a language often strikingly similar to the rhythms of dissenting polemic. For Sir John Lytcott, the Church of England was composed not of priests but of 'magicians', and 'slaves' to a Machiavellian 'reason of state'.[97] For the convert-poet Jane Barker, the events of 1688–89 unmasked a church gripped by idolatrous worship of the penal laws that brought its temporal dominion, centred on craven submission to 'the monster Test'. Where Catholics had fought without hope of reward for Charles I – 'none such fools as we in forty-one' – their compatriots conditioned their loyalties upon material ambition: 'you till a soil in which you treasure find'. For, Barker, the Revolution mocked High Church claims to stand apart from other Protestant congregations: like the radical Calvinists of the Civil War, Anglicans had placed congregational affinities before allegiance to the throne, and the recurring tragedy of English civil suffering arose because 'her chief religion in Rebellion lies ... Though different sects themselves the true Church call / Yet still Rebellion comprehends them all'.[98] For the Irish Jacobite courtier Thomas Sheridan, the outcome carried far graver consequences for Anglicans than for their Presbyterian counterparts, since the English church had based its claims so emphatically upon the relationship with its monarchical Supreme Governor. In subverting their own founding principle, they had made their church an unsustainable living contradiction, and proved that 'the King of England's interest is so interwoven and blended with the Catholic religion that they cannot possibly be separated or divided'.[99] For Lytcott, Barker, and Sheridan, political defeat was tempered by a fleeting intellectual consolation. If they had lost their king, Catholics had won assurance that only their own 'ancient mother church' could stand above such a descent into worldly corruption.

VI

Through the reign of William III, a more assertively anti-popish identity was consolidated within the Church of England. After the non-juring schism cut adrift the leading lights of the High Church persuasion, the occupancy of the bishops' bench by appointment of William and Mary mirrored to a striking degree the roll-call of the most prolific anti-Catholic pamphleteers to emerge during the reign of James II. The Whig-inclined church of John Tillotson, Thomas Tenison, Gilbert Burnet, and Edward Stillingfleet realigned the Anglican corpus within a more broadly Protestant identity, heightening its concerns with Calvinist and Lutheran congregations abroad, and mobilising the nation behind a conception of the 1688 Revolution centred on the providential trial of the war against France.[100] John Dryden believed that the pressure for 'a persecution' of Catholics stemmed not from William III, but from the archbishop of Canterbury; the recusant lawyer Nathaniel Pigott likewise saw the charge for stronger penal laws being led by the ecclesiastical ranks in the House of Lords.[101] From London to the American plantations, Anglican moral campaigns were certainly informed by a vivid consciousness of the battle against 'popery'.[102] The Society for the Propagation of the Gospel offered material support for clergymen confronting, as Burnet put it, the 'many insolencies committed both by the laity and priests of that religion' in recusant county strongholds.[103] London sermons thundered against 'Popish Tyranny ... Papal Invasion ... Papal Persecution ... Papal Superstition', and apostates from the Catholic Church were cultivated, nurtured, and encouraged to declare their spiritual trajectory in pamphlets and treatises.[104] A 1704 remonstrance from Lambeth Palace to the Privy Council exhorted the state to investigate the 'Rights of Preservation, Donation of Churches, Benefices or Schools': identified as the essential privileges that inspired 'the great boldness and presumption of ye Romish Priests and Papists' across England.[105]

The turn within the political and theological culture of the Church of England was not uncontested. Some Catholics gleaned potential reserves of sympathy in the creation of a large, disaffected party, embodied within the non-juring congregation and, through the reign of Queen Anne, increasingly salient in the lower house of convocation, where fulminations were unleashed against Whig bishops, indulgence shown towards dissenters, and the drift towards an 'Erastian' or 'Latitudinarian' vision of the church.[106] When he drafted his plan to strip recusant squires of their rights over local churches, Archbishop Tenison warned of obstruction from parsons prepared to conceal the Catholic influence over their parish.[107] In 1714, Jesuit missioners read ideological fellow feeling into Jonathan Swift's *Examiner*, as a guard against the 'persecution' raised by 'the Low Church'.[108] The Lancashire lawyer Roger Kenyon believed that a vindictive state would be equally liable to target those of his own High Tory persuasion, who were represented glued to the Jacobite interest 'as clay at the feet of Nebuchadnezzar's image'.[109] Within a generation of the Revolution, such anxieties had fostered a rich scholarly commerce, when High Church, non-juring, and recusant antiquarians worked together in studies of the medieval past that were charged with contemporary political and confessional concerns. Thomas Hearne, Richard Rawlinson, and Nathaniel Johnston boasted a string of Catholic contacts with whom manuscripts were exchanged, treatises annotated, and lamentations shared upon successive interventions by the civil power in the independence and integrity of the English church.[110] While recusant historians – Robert Manning, Benet Weldon, John Stevens – embedded into their works the Gallican idea of distance from the papacy, their counterparts cherished the pre-Reformation church no less for its freedom from the English state.[111] The scholarly monk John Anselm Mannock filled his commonplace notes with the writings of High Church historians and commented approvingly that 'a spiritual supremacy is still claimed by their clergy, an entire independence of their prince as to matters spiritual'.[112] Setting the Anglican Church within the afterglow of English Christian history, Thomas Hearne was indeed willing to see 'popery' as a description of the '*Errors* of the Church of Rome' but not an appellation to account for the entirety of that congregation.[113] Gilbert Burnet was sufficiently alarmed by such affinities to warn that 'the secret poison of those principles has given too many of the Clergy a bias towards Popery, with an aversion towards the Reformation, which has brought them under much contempt'.[114]

However, for many other Catholics, memories of the reign of James II prevented reversion to the straightforward anti-Whig alliances of the past. In a waspish response to the trial and acquittal of Henry Sacheverell in 1710, the Benedictine James Maurus Corker mocked Tory clergymen at once for their intolerance and their hypocrisy: in fulminating against the dissenters they accused of threatening 'the Queen's white neck', they had refused to accept that the same injunctions towards obedience 'impeach the Legitimacy of the Late Revolution'. For Corker, 'Varnishes and Flourishes of Rhetorick and Sophistry' could not conceal the fact that High Churchmen followed temporal self-interest. At best, 'you mistrust the ... Integrity of your Cause, in not being able to support it otherwise than by obloquy, virulency and Oppression of your Neighbours'.[115] Indeed, some of the most acute divisions within post-Revolution Catholic life were underlain by conflicting attitudes towards the Church of England. In the retinue of the exiled Stuarts, Robert Brent, John Caryll, and the earl of Melfort turned not to High Churchmen but to the networks of dissenters who had supported the fallen king's toleration policy, in their attempts to create a bastion of English Jacobite support. Tory Jacobites expressed bewilderment as to the eagerness of the Catholics to court 'republicans' from the circle of William Penn who would reduce a restored Stuart to the status of 'a doge of Venice'.[116] Conversely, a small but pronounced recusant anti-Jacobite tendency urged repudiation of the Stuart cause precisely *because*, by 1714, it was perceived to have become a vehicle for a doctrinaire Tory Anglicanism that would offer nothing to Catholics were it to be successful, and ruin them in its failure. 'Is not their whole cry *The Church! The Church!*', demanded the polemical scholar Charles Dodd, 'And which Church, I pray, but their own, which they truly pretend to be in Danger.'[117] Heaven, he insisted, 'had no wardrobe of laurels' to crown such 'politick notions'.[118] Adding his voice after the failure of the 1715 rebellion, Bishop John Stonor urged co-religionists to release themselves from 'the fetters of an erroneous conscience', imposed by association with the 'High flyers' of the Church of England and seek a secular accommodation with the Whig state, alongside other 'Lawfull Dissenters'.[119]

The fear articulated by Dodd, Stonor, and the small scattering of recusant Hanoverians was that Catholicism, by a Jacobite association, would become a front purely for 'juro divino', branded with partisan politics in the eyes of their compatriots. Through the reign of William and Anne, while a Bourbon–Jacobite peril overshadowed national politics, interest in the English Catholic inheritance was indeed confined to the meditations of dissentient voices within the established church. Yet the Anglican Church held within it a capacious body of thought. After 1715, with the house of Stuart wounded by a failed rebellion and geo-political shifts pushing the kingdoms of George I into a new alliance with France, some of its members began to look beyond the parameters of the Protestant world. Without suspending his hostility to the papal power itself, Archbishop William Wake yearned for a 'new Reformation' that could 'unite with us ... a large part of the Churches of the Roman Catholic communion', and extended his ideas in discreet consultation with a Benedictine monk, Gilbert Knowles. Wake's search to expand church horizons won an audience for one Paris theologian, Pierre Courayer, at the court of George I and encouraged another, Louis Ellies-Dupin, to raise again the possibility of reunion between Anglicans and the French Gallican institutions.[120] As Catholics had anchored hopes of fraternity upon the distinction between the Anglican High Church and Low Church, so Wake's sympathisers believed that they could disentangle the papalist and cismontane traditions, and were intrigued by the emergence of an avant-garde Jansenist tendency within the Gallican church itself. Travelling through the kingdom of Louis XV in 1725, the Whig magnate Sir John Percival estimated that two-thirds of the French clergy could be linked to such a party.[121] He was delighted to find men who believed 'that the Roman and Protestant Divines had both gone too far in imputing matters of Belief to their adversarys' and 'think most of our disputes are about words', rather than doctrine.[122] One Paris monk he discovered already to be a correspondent of the bishop of Oxford. Wake's interest did not dislodge the penal structures of the British state, nor drive out anti-popery within his church, but, like his Restoration predecessors, the archbishop had shone a light upon the competing instincts within the theology of the Church of England. If the dream of Christian Reunion opened up mainly paths not taken, its appeal remained no less beguiling.

VII

Despite the preferences of many of its members, the English recusant community stood within the glare of the national public sphere. The relationship between Catholics and their compatriots represented a touchtone for the shifts and reverses created by struggles over foreign policy, the safety of the constitution and the composition of the royal court, underlain by fluctuating ideas of the linkage between an individual's private religion and their stance in temporal affairs. Yet a scholarly narrative overwhelmingly devoted to the fears and animosities injected into religious discourse offers an incomplete picture of the relationship between the different congregations. For all the force of the legal structures, penal prohibitions, and political tempers that pushed Catholics and Anglicans apart, the preservation of social or scholarly associations enabled laymen and clergy of both denominations to look outside the confessional fold. The resultant pattern of engagements revealed much about the cultural and intellectual character of each congregation.

Few Catholics believed that the Church of England could simply be eclipsed or demolished, but their view of the Anglican corpus was intertwined with a variety of different images of their own community, and of the larger realm of which they were a part. For some – those Catholics who cultivated nonconformist alliances under James II, or styled themselves 'lawfull Dissenters' for George I – the route to elevation lay in a non-confessional, tolerationist relationship with the English state. Yet others looked to unlock the hidden sympathies within the established church, and saw the divisions engendered through the Reformation as needless theological misconstructions, when the church remained, in its essential instincts, Catholic. To this end, the pursuit of conversions, the promotion of a Gallican ideology, and the hopes expressed for Christian Reunion undermined the idea that 'loyalist' Catholicism was a quietist phenomenon, with few aspirations to change the character of English life. Recusant ambitions grew because of their ability to convince a sufficient number of Anglicans that Catholicism did not inevitably mean 'popery', and to attract audiences ranging from Restoration bishops, Tories and non-jurors to the Whig episcopate after 1689. That so many Anglicans were unable to suppress fascination with the Catholic religion, whether encountered through cismontane traditions on the Continent or in recoveries of the English medieval past, stood testament to the competing identities stored within a 'Catholic and Reformed' established church. Against the moments of denunciation, coercion, and interrogation, the preservation of these fragile links between the congregations served at least to lower the walls that kept their worlds apart.

NOTES

This chapter was researched and written whilst I held a British Academy Postdoctoral Fellowship at Hertford College, Oxford, and I am grateful to both the Academy and Hertford for their support.

1 AAW, Main Series, 36/10.

2 BL Add. MS 21621, fols 43–4, Jane Barker, 'A collection of poems referring to the times', 1700.

3 T. Harris, *Revolution: the great crisis of the British monarchy 1685–1720* (Allen Lane, 2006); S. Pincus, *1688: the first modern revolution* (New Haven and London: Yale University Press, 2009).

4 A.C.F. Beales, *Education under penalty: English Catholic education from the Reformation to the fall of James II* (Athlone Press, 1963).

5 M. Blundell (ed.), *Cavalier: the letters of William Blundell to his friends* (Longmans Green and Co, 1933), pp. 27, 251.

6 *Lords Journal*, XVIII (1705–9), p. 154; F. Coupe, *Walton-le-Dale: a history of the village* (Preston: Guardian Press, 1954); C. Haydon 'Samuel Peploe and Catholicism in Preston, 1714', *Recusant History*, 20 (1990–91), 76–80.

7 *Lords Journal*, XII (1666–75), pp. 449–51.

8 Bodl. MS Add. C 305, fol. 68, George Hall, bishop of Chester to Gilbert Sheldon, n.d. I owe this reference to Grant Tapsell.

9 J. Raine (ed.), *Depositions from the castle of York: relating to offences committed in the northern counties in the seventeenth century* (Surtees Soc., 40, Durham, 1861), pp. 119–21; 'Catholic registers of Holme-on-Spalding Moor' (CRS, IV, 1901), pp. 272–3.

10 V. Barbour, *Henry Bennet, earl of Arlington, secretary of state to Charles II* (Washington,

DC and London: Oxford University Press, 1914). For Bristol as a spokesman for the Catholic interest, see Bodl. MS Clarendon 80, fols 223–4. For the Westons, see the Queen Mary, University of London database 'Who were the Nuns?' http://www.history.qmul.ac.uk/wwtn/index.html.

11 A. Browning (ed.), *Memoirs of Sir John Reresby: the complete text and a selection of his letters* (Glasgow: Jackson, 1936), p. 125; *Letters of Philip, Cardinal Howard, 1646–1694* (CRS, London, 1925) p. 13; J.M. Robinson, *The dukes of Norfolk* (Oxford: Oxford University Press, 1982), pp. 100, 121, 133, 145.

12 Blundell (ed.), *Cavalier*, p. 210; Warwickshire RO Throckmorton MSS, CR 1998/Box 65/ Folder 2/2, Nathaniel Pigott to Sir Robert Throckmorton, 1 July 1711; *Douai College diaries* (CRS, X, 1911), p. 265.

13 Bodl. MS Add. C 305, fol. 58, George Hall to Gilbert Sheldon, 5 Apr. 1667; J.H.C. Aveling, *The handle and the axe: the Catholic recusants in England from Reformation to emancipation* (Blond and Briggs, 1976), p. 195

14 F. Tyrer and J.J. Bagley (eds), *The great diurnall of Nicholas Blundell of Little Crosby, Lancashire* 3 vols (Lancashire and Cheshire Record Society, 110, 112, 114, Manchester, 1968–72), I, 37.

15 J.H.C. Aveling, *Northern Catholics: the Catholic recusants of the North Riding of Yorkshire 1558 –1790* (Chapman, 1966), pp. 140, 190.

16 Lancashire RO Shireburne MSS, DDST 100/5 77/8; 77/9, accounts for building almshouses, n.d.; Warwickshire RO Throckmorton MSS, CR 1998/CD/Folder 55/6, Henry Bell to Sir Robert Throckmorton, 4 May 1692.

17 Suffolk RO, Mannock MSS, F/15, will of Sir Francis Mannock, 1728; BL Add. MS 28250, fol.73, Henry King, bishop of Chichester to John Caryll, n.d.

18 Tyrer and Bagley (eds), *Diurnall*, II, 286–7; Broughton Hall, private collection, Stephen Tempest, 'Religio Laici'.

19 Lancashire RO Shireburne MSS, 101/26, Sylvester Shireburne to Sir Nicholas Shireburne, 20 August 1695; *Lords Journal*, XII, 449.

20 Lancashire RO Scarisbrick MSS 78/1, Dicconson family papers, 'Poetry'.

21 Warwickshire RO Throckmorton MSS, CR 1998/ LCB/ 62, Buckland and Coughton Library papers.

22 Lancashire RO Shireburn MSS, DDSt 97/14, Sir Nicholas Shireburne to the earl of Bindon, 21 Dec. 1708.

23 C.A. Lowe, 'Politics and religion in Warwickshire during the reign of James II, 1685–1688' (PhD dissertation, University of Warwick, 1992), pp. 172–3; *Catholicon, or the Christian philosopher*, 5 vols (1815–18), III (1816), 131–3; Suffolk RO Mannock MSS, E17, 'The case brought by Sir Francis Mannock, Bt vs Sir John Williams, JP', 1713.

24 G. Glickman, *The English Catholic community 1688–1745: politics, culture and ideology* (Woodbridge: Boydell, 2009), p. 31.

25 J. Krugler, *English and Catholic: the Lords Baltimore in the seventeenth century* (Baltimore, MD: John Hopkins University Press, 2004).

26 *Bedingfield papers* (CRS, 7, 1909), pp. 9–22; Broughton Hall, Yorkshire, will of Dame Mary Scrope of Cockerington; Lancashire RO Shireburne MSS, DDSt 101/12, Shireburne pedigree.

27 E.A.B. Barnard, *A seventeenth-century country gentleman* (Cambridge: Heffer, 1944), p. 44; Lancashire RO Shireburne MSS, DDSt, 101/26, Sir Nicholas Shireburne, notes on the family pedigree, Feb. 1662; Warwickshire RO Throckmorton MSS, CR 1998/CD/Drawer 3/8, p. 5.

28 Scottish Catholic Archives, Blairs Letters 1/43/12, A. Winster [Dunbar] to William Leslie, 4 Mar. 1675.

29 Anthony a Wood, *Athenae Oxoniensis* 4 vols (1817), I, 45, 48.

30 BL Add. MS 28252, fol. 146, John Caryll, 'Not guilty, or the plea of Catholicks in England'.

31 K.L. Campbell, *The intellectual struggle of English papists in the seventeenth century: the Catholic dilemma* (New York: Edwin Mellen Press, 1986), pp. 39–75.

32 BL Add. MS 65138, fols 132–6, Hugh Cressy, 'Instructions for the envoye to his H.', 1669; Hugh Cressy, *Exomologesis, or, a faithfull narration of the occasions and motives of the conversion into Catholique unity of Hugh-Paulin de Cressy* (Paris, 1647), preface, p. 8.

33 James Maurus Corker, *A rational account given by a young gentleman to his uncle of the motives and reasons why he is become a Roman Catholick* (1684), pp. 2–3.

34 BL Add. MS 65139, fols 8–9, Cressy, 'Reunion'.

35 John Vincent Canes, *Fiat Lux, or a general conduct to a right understanding and charity in the combustions and broils about religion here in England* (1662), pp. 189–90.

36 Douai Abbey, Ralph Benet Weldon, 'Memorials', 6 vols, IV, 9–10.

37 BL Add. MS 65139, fol. 8, Cressy, 'Reunion'.

38 *Ibid.*, fol. 19, Cressy, 'Concerning the present disturbances in England about Religion'; Cressy, *Exomologesis*, pp. 81–2; William Wake, *A continuation of the present state of the controversy between the Church of England and the Church of Rome* (1688), p. 43.

39 Henry Joseph Johnston, *A vindication of the Bishop of Condom's exposition of the doctrine of the Catholic Church* (1686), preface.

40 RC [Charles Dodd], *History of the English College at Doway, from its first foundation in 1568, to the present time* (1713), pp. 16–17; Berkshire RO, Reading, Belson MSS, F/1/4/MS/20, John Sergeant, 'Upon the late Declaration from the Propaganda', n.d.; A.F. Allison, 'Richard Smith's Gallican backers and Jesuit opponents', *Recusant History*, 18 (1987), 329–401.

41 Canes, *Fiat lux*, pp. 194, 237.

42 Berkshire RO, Reading, Belson MSS, F/1/4/MS/11, [John Caryll], 'A discours concerning ye punishment of Roman Catholics in England occasioned by ye heats of ye year 1666 by J.C. Esq'.

43 Bodl. MS Clarendon 87, fols 62–3, 'The motives and reasons wch induced the Duchess of Yorke to embrace the Catholique religion, written by her own hand', 20 Aug. 1670.

44 Berkshire RO, Reading, Belson MSS, F/1/4/MS/66, 'On the desirability of means to reconcile the C of E with Church of Rome', 1660; Henry Holden, *The analysis of divine faith*, trans. William Graunt (1658), 'To the reader'.

45 J.B. Dockery, *Christopher Davenport: friar and diplomat* (Burns and Oates, 1960), pp. 36–40.

46 BL Add. MS 65139, fols 8–9, Cressy, 'Reunion'.

47 [Edward Hyde] *Animadversions upon a book intitutled Fanaticism fanatically imputed to the Catholick Church honour* (1674), p. 224.

48 Bodl. MS Clarendon 87, fol. 76, George Morley, bishop of Winchester, to the duchess of York, 24 Jan. 1670/1.

49 M.J. Routh (ed.), *Bishop Burnet's history of his own time*, 6 vols, 2nd edn (Oxford: Oxford University Press, 1833), II, 369.

50 J. Spurr, *The Restoration Church of England 1646–1689* (New Haven and London: Yale University Press, 1991), pp. 121–2.

51 J.H.M. Salmon, 'Catholic resistance theory and the royalist response', in J.H. Burns with M. Goldie (eds), *The Cambridge history of political thought, 1450–1700* (Cambridge: Cambridge University Press, 1991), pp. 219–53, at 231–6; *A second dialogue between the pope and a phanatick, concerning affairs in England* (1675), p. 21.

52 John Dryden, *A defence of the papers written by the late king ... and duchess of York* (1686), p. 25; Louis Maimbourg, *History of the league*, trans John Dryden (1684).

53 T. Claydon, *Europe and the making of England 1660–1760* (Cambridge: Cambridge University Press, 2007), pp. 90–3, 98–101.

54 Henry Dodwell, *An introduction to a devout life ... fitted for the use of Protestants* (Dublin, 1673); BL Add. MS 28252, fol. 56, John Caryll, 'A caracter of Father Malebranche's search for truth from Mr Norris's book, entitled spiritual counsels or the father's advice to his children'; T.A. Birrell, 'English Catholic mystics in non-Catholic circles', *Downside Review*, 94 (1976), 58–78.

55 Johnston, *Vindication*, p. 104.

56 BL Add. MS 65138, fol. 77, 'A project of a secret treaty between the king of Great Brittain and the most Christian king'.

57 Bodl. MS Clarendon 87, fol. 76, George Morley, bishop of Winchester to duchess of York, 24 Jan. 1670/1.

58 Clarendon, *Animadversions*, p. 260.

59 *The banished priests* (1674), p. 2; B. Orr, *Empire on the English stage 1660–1714* (Cambridge: Cambridge University Press, 2002), p. 82.

60 Spurr, *Restoration Church*, pp. 67–8, 72.

61 S.C.A. Pincus, 'From butterboxes to wooden shoes: the shift in English popular sentiment from anti-Dutch to anti-French in the 1670s', *HJ*, 38 (1996), 333–61.

62 AAW, Epistolae Variorum, V/93, Edward Dicconson to Lawrence Mayes, 5 May 1715.

63 Douai Abbey, Weldon, 'Memorials', IV, 10; V, 311–12.

64 [John Caryll] *Naboth's vineyard or the innocent traytor* (1679).

65 Warwickshire RO Throckmorton MSS, LCB 17, George Throckmorton to Sir Robert Throckmorton, 20 Apr. 1682; same to the same, 31 Aug. 1682.

66 BL Add. MS 28237, fol. 6, Roger L'Estrange to John Caryll, 12 Sept. 1700; Blundell (ed.), *Cavalier*, p. 102; Roger L'Estrange, *The character of a papist in masquerade* (1679); G. Kemp, 'L'Estrange and the publishing sphere', in J. McElligott (ed.), *Fear, exclusion and revolution: Roger Morrice and Britain in the 1680s* (Aldershot: Ashgate, 2006), pp. 67–90.

67 Warwickshire RO Throckmorton MSS, LCB 17, George Throckmorton to Sir Robert Throckmorton, 2 Apr. 1683.

68 L'Estrange, *Character of a papist*, pp. 17–18; Fabian Philipps, *Ursa major & minor, or, a sober and impartial enquiry into those pretended fears and jealousies of popery and arbitrary power* (1681), pp. 15, 30–3.

69 J. Kenyon *The popish plot* (William Heinemann, 1972), pp. 227–8; P.J. Harth, *Pen for a party: Dryden's Tory propaganda in its contexts* (Princeton, NJ: Princeton University Press, 1993), pp. 36–9, 107, 150–4, 194.

70 Harris, *Revolution*, pp. 85–7.

71 Edward Scarisbrick, *Catholic loyalty upon the subject of government and obedience* (1686), pp. 3–4.

72 Routh (ed.), *Burnet's history*, II, 353.

73 W.E. Buckley (ed.), *Memoirs of Thomas, Earl of Ailesbury ... 2 vols* (Roxburgh Club, Westminster: Nichols and Sons, 1890), I, 157, 165–6.

74 Berkshire RO, Reading, Belson MSS, F/1/4/C1/17, John Belson to Sir George Mackenzie, Sept. 1686; Belson MSS. F/1/4/C1/13; same to the same, 2 Nov. 1686.

75 Browning (ed.), *Reresby memoirs*, p. 393.

76 BL Add. MS 10118, pp. 19–24, Weldon, 'A collection of sundry things yt may contribute to ye history of Great Brittain's late glorious monarch'.

77 W.A. Speck, *Reluctant revolutionaries: Englishmen and the Revolution of 1688* (Oxford: Oxford University Press, 1988), pp. 179–82.

78 Routh (ed.), *Burnet's history*, II, 366; Harris, *Revolution*, p. 199.

79 Routh (ed.), *Burnet's history*, II, 367; Berkshire RO, Reading, Belson MSS, F/1/4/C1/14, John Belson to the earl of Melfort, 2 Sept.1686; Spurr, *Restoration Church*, pp. 90–1.

80 Routh (ed.), *Burnet's history*, II, 367–8.

81 Edward Gee, *The catalogue of all discourses published against popery* (1689).

82 John Dryden, *A defence of the papers written by the late king ... and duchess of York, against the answer made to them* (1686), pp. 25–6.

83 Edward Stillingfleet, *A vindication of the answer to some later papers concerning the unity and authority of the Catholick Church* (1687), pp. 54–7, 71–6; William Wake, *Present state of the controversy*, p. 43.

84 Stillingfleet, *Vindication*, p. 104.

85 Routh (ed.), *Burnet's history*, II, 366.

86 Abednego Seller, *Remarks upon the reflections of the author of popery misrepresented, &c. on his answerer, particularly as to the deposing doctrine* (1686), p. 26.

87 John Gother, *A papist represented and misrepresented, or, a two-fold character* (1686), p. 146.

88 Edmund Gibson, *A preservative against popery*, 3 vols (1738).

89 John Dryden, *The hind and the panther* (1687).

90 *Pastoral letter from the four Catholic bishops to the lay Catholics of England* (1688).

91 [John Everard] *A winding-sheet for the schism of England* (1687), 'To the King's most excellent Majesty'.

92 S. Rosa, 'Bossuet, James II and the crisis of Catholic universalism', in *Eighteenth-Century Thought*, 1 (2003), 52–61.

93 William Petty, 'Of reconciling the English and Irish and reforming both nations' (1686), in Marquis of Lansdowne (ed.), *The Petty papers*, 2 vols (1967 edn, New York: A.M. Kelley), I, 59–63; Peter Pett, *The happy future state of England* (1688).

94 *An answer to a letter to a dissenter, upon occasion of his majesties late gracious Declaration of Indulgence* (1687); *Remarks upon a pamphlet stiled A Letter to a dissenter, in another letter to the same dissenter* (1687); *Animadversions on a later paper, entitled A Letter to a dissenter* (1687).

95 Lancashire RO Scarisbrick MSS, 78/2, 'Political papers'.

96 Bodl. MS Rawlinson A183, fol. 32, Charles Smith, Lord Carrington to Robert Brent, 18 May 1688; M. Goldie, 'James II and the dissenters' revenge', *Historical Research*, 66 (1993), 94–121; LPL, Fulham Papers 183–4, 'Memorial representing the present case of the church in Maryland', 1698; J.J. Hennesey, *American Catholics: a history of the Roman Catholic community in the United States* (New York: Oxford University Press, 1981), p. 48.

97 BL Add. MS 10118, p. 225, Weldon, 'Collection'.

98 BL Add. MS 21621, fols 28, 44–5, Jane Barker, 'A collection of poems referring to the times', 1700.

99 Windsor Castle, Stuart Papers, Miscellaneous Volumes, VII, p. 175, Thomas Sheridan, 'Political reflexions'.

100 Pincus, *1688*, pp. 415–21; Claydon, *Europe*, pp. 159–70.

101 Warwickshire RO Throckmorton MSS, CR 1998/Box 65/Folder 2/10, Nathaniel Pigott to Sir Robert Throckmorton, 22 Nov. 1705.

102 LPL, Fulham Papers 98–9, 'Proclamation against papists', Annapolis, 29 Mar. 1698.

103 Routh (ed.), *Burnet's history*, IV, 141.

104 Charles Trimnell, *Sermon preach'd before the House of Lords ... on Tuesday, February 17th 1708* (1708); E. Duffy, '"Over the wall": converts from popery in eighteenth-century England', *Downside Review*, 94 (1976), 1–25.

105 LPL MS 930/83, 'Order of council concerning papists'.

106 G.V. Bennett, *The Tory crisis in church and state 1688–1730: the career of Francis Atterbury, bishop of Rochester* (Oxford: Oxford University Press, 1975); A. Starkie, 'Contested histories of the English church: Gilbert Burnet and Jeremy Collier', in P. Kewes (ed.), *The uses of history in early modern England* (San Marino, CA: University of California Press, Huntington Library, 2006), *pp. 329–45*.

107 LPL MS 930/83, 'Order of council concerning papists'.

108 Archives of the English Province of the Society of Jesus, Farm Street, Notes and Fragments, II/94, William Kennet to Richard Plowden, Mar. 1714.

109 HMC, *Kenyon*, p. 370, Roger Kenyon, draft parliamentary speech, 1694.

110 *Reliquiae Hearnianae: the remains of Thomas Hearne, M.A. of Edmund Hall, being extracts from his ms. diaries* (Oxford: Philip Bliss, 1857), p. 212; Birmingham Diocesan Archives, Z5/2/35/1, Dodd MSS, Charles Dodd, 'Observations on the first volume of the Ecclesiastical History of Great Britain by Mr Jeremy Collier. 1708'; T. Harmsen, *Antiquarianism in the Augustan age: Thomas Hearne 1678–1735* (Oxford: Peter Lang AG, 2001), pp. 231, 267.

111 G. Glickman, 'Gothic history and Catholic Enlightenment in the works of Charles Dodd (1686–1742)', *HJ*, 54 (2011), 347–69, at pp. 364–5.

112 Downside Abbey, Mannock Miscellany, p. 461.

113 Hearne quoted in Robert Manning, *England's conversion and reformation compared. Or, the young gentleman directed in the choice of his religion* (1725), p. 205.

114 Routh (ed.), *Burnet's history*, III, 418–19.

115 James Maurus Corker, *Queries to Dr Sacheverell from North Britain* (1710), pp. 3, 5–6.

116 Glickman, *English Catholic community*, pp. 105–9.

117 P.R. [Charles Dodd], *A Roman Catholick system of allegiance in favour of the present establishment* (1716), p. 83.

118 *Catholick system*, pp. 4, 34.

119 AAW Epistolae Variorum VI/47, John Talbot Stonor to Lawrence Mayes, 13 May 1717.

120 L. Adams (ed.), *William Wake's Gallican correspondence and related documents, 1716–1731*, 5 vols (New York: Peter Lang, 1988–91), I, 92, 98; N. Sykes, *William Wake*, 2 vols (Cambridge: Cambridge University Press, 1957), I, 261–75.

121 BL Add. MS 47031, fols 1–4, Sir John Percival to Daniel Dering, 11 Sept. 1725.

122 BL Add. MS 47031, fols 23–4, John Percival to Mr Newman, 22 Sept. 1725.

Index